NEW ESSAYS ON CANADIAN THEATRE
VOLUME FOUR

THEATRES OF AFFECT

NEW ESSAYS ON CANADIAN THEATRE
VOLUME FOUR

THEATRES OF AFFECT
EDITED BY ERIN HURLEY

To Jill, my
dear friend,
Because Theatre — + feeling —
matter.

Love, as ever,

E.

PLAYWRIGHTS CANADA PRESS
TORONTO

Cover photo of Magalie Lépine-Blondeau and Céline Bonnier by Yves Renaud, provided courtesy of Théâtre du Nouveau Monde.
Cover design by Leon Aureus.
Screen shots on pages 77, 82, 90, and 91 © and provided courtesy of Haukur Björgvinsson, from video of the students of the TPER 398F Emo Lab, Concordia University, winter 2013.
Photos on pages 112 and 116 © Angel Mae Wells and reprinted with the permission of Kyla Wazana Tompkins.
Photos on pages 176 and 189 © Jeremy Minmagh and provided courtesy of Theatre Replacement.
Photos on pages 199 and 207 © and provided courtesy of Caleb Johnston.
Photo on page 266 © and provided courtesy of Shannon Scott.
Art on pages 269 and 272 © and provided courtesy of Helene Vosters.

Library and Archives Canada Cataloguing in Publication
Theatres of affect / edited by Erin Hurley.

(New essays on Canadian theatre ; volume four)
Includes bibliographical references and index.
ISBN 978-1-77091-216-8 (pbk.)

    1. Theater--Canada--History and criticism. I. Hurley, Erin, editor of compilation II. Series: New essays on Canadian theatre ; v. 4

PN2301.T63 2014   792.0971   C2013-908493-2

We acknowledge the financial support of the Canada Council for the Arts, the Ontario Arts Council (OAC)—an agency of the Government of Ontario, which last year funded 1,681 individual artists and 1,125 organizations in 216 communities across Ontario for a total of $52.8 million—the Ontario Media Development Corporation, and the Government of Canada through the Canada Book Fund for our publishing activities.

For Beatrice,
bringer of joy,
with love.

CONTENTS

EMPATHY

GENERAL EDITOR'S PREFACE

RIC KNOWLES

New Essays on Canadian Theatre (NECT) is a book series designed to complement and replace the series Critical Perspectives on Canadian Theatre in English (CPCTE), which published its last three of twenty-one volumes in 2011. CPCTE was primarily a reprint series, with each volume designed to represent the critical history since the 1970s of a particular topic within the broader field of Canadian theatre studies. Most volumes, however, also included essays specially commissioned to fill gaps in the coverage of their respective topics and to bring the books up to the moment. These new essays, some of them scholarly prize winners, were often among the volumes' most powerful, approaching the field and the discipline from important new perspectives, regularly from those of minoritized and other under-represented communities.

NECT consists entirely of newly commissioned essays, and the volumes themselves are designed to fill what I perceive to be gaps in the critical record, often, once again, taking new approaches, often, again, from minoritized and under-represented perspectives, and always introducing topics that have never before received book-length coverage. NECT volume topics may range as broadly as did those of CPCTE, from the work of an individual playwright to that of a whole community, however defined, and they are designed at once to follow, lead, and instantiate new and emerging developments in the field. Volume editors and their contributors are scholars, artists, and artist-scholars who are doing some of the most exciting and innovative work in Canadian theatre and Canadian theatre studies.

Like those published in CPCTE but more systematically, NECT volumes complement the catalogues of Canada's major drama publishers: each volume serves as a companion piece either to an already existing anthology or to one published contemporaneously with it, often by the editors of the NECT volumes themselves. As a package, NECT and their companion volumes serve as ideal introductions to a field, or indeed as ready-made reading lists for Canadian theatre courses in these topic areas.

But generating new materials and entirely new fields of study takes time, and while CPCTE published at the heady pace of three volumes per year, the production of NECT is more leisurely with, initially at least, only one volume launched each spring, beginning in 2011. The first of these was *Asian Canadian Theatre*, edited by Nina Lee Aquino and myself and designed to ride the tide of a flurry of activity in the first decade of the twenty-first century among Asian Canadian theatre artists. It complements Nina Lee Aquino's two-volume anthology *Love + Relasianships*, published by Playwrights Canada Press in 2009. The second, *New Canadian Realisms,* edited by Roberta Barker and Kim Solga, dealt with a wholesale revisioning of realism in Canada, and was published alongside the companion anthology *New Canadian Realisms: Eight Plays*, also edited by Barker and Solga. And the third, *Latina/o Canadian Theatre and Performance*, together with its companion anthology *Fronteras Vivientes: Eight Latina/o Canadian Plays*, both edited by Natalie Alvarez, launched an exciting and vibrant new sub-field within the disciplines of Canadian Theatre Studies and Latina/o Studies more broadly. It is enormously satisfying that each of these volumes has been recognized by awards for their editors, contributors, or both; a sign, I believe, of the tremendous health of a field of study that is still young.

The current volume, Erin Hurley's *Theatres of Affect*, also has its companion anthology, *Once More, With Feeling: Five Affecting Plays*, and together they virtually introduce to Canadian theatre scholarship and teaching the rich approach to theatre study that is involved in taking feelings seriously. Future volumes include Richie Wilcox's collection of essays on the egregiously understudied work of Daniel MacIvor, complementing MacIvor's award-winning anthology *I Still Love You* and his many other published plays, and a projected new collection on Indigenous theatre edited by Yvette Nolan and myself, accompanying Playwrights Canada's two-volume anthology *Staging Coyote's Dream*.

It has been exciting for me to see the development of Canadian theatre criticism since its inception as an academic discipline in the mid 1970s, when the first academic courses on the subject were offered and the first journals were founded, together with the then Association for Canadian Theatre History (now the Canadian Association for Theatre Research)—the first and only scholarly association to specialize in Canadian theatre. It was also very satisfying to serve as founder and general editor for the CPCTE series that tracked that development and made some of its key writings widely available and key critical histories and genealogies visible. In embarking on this still young series, I am equally excited by the opportunity to contribute to the further development of the field by opening up new areas of study, introducing fresh new voices, and making innovative new work readily available to scholars, teachers, students, and the interested general public.

ACKNOWLEDGEMENTS

The contributors to these pages, and those who participated in the Affect/ Theatre/Canada working groups at the 2011 and 2012 conferences of the Canadian Association for Theatre Research, have made the process of sleuthing out, developing, and finally editing research on affect and theatre in Canada a rewarding journey. I thank them all for their inspiring company along the way as well as for their concrete suggestions, comments, ideas, writings, and conversations.

Jen Harvie recognized before I did my tendency to feeling and nurtured the same in her invitation to write expressly on the subject for her book series. Sara Warner has been a valued fellow traveller across these emotional and theatrical territories; always clarifying, always historicizing, Sara's thinking on affect, its "turn," and its investments orients my own. Ric Knowles offered me this wonderful opportunity and has supported my efforts to bring it to completion throughout. I am grateful for his patience and guidance. Let me also express my sincere thanks to Annie Gibson and Blake Sproule at Playwrights Canada Press.

I would work with you all again in a heartbeat.

INTRODUCTION: THEATRE MATTERS

ERIN HURLEY

One conviction has motivated this collection on affect in Canadian theatre: that theatre matters. That is to say, it is consequential; it makes an impression. Let me walk through some of theatre's "matterings" using the example of Annabel Soutar's *Seeds*, a cornerstone play of Porte Parole, the Montreal-based documentary-theatre company. I choose this documentary-theatre piece for its attention to "life" as the fundamental "matter" of theatre—both as a key contemporary issue in its narrative and as an affective quality in its staging. In what follows, I will suggest that theatre matters because of its "life," which is to say, its affecting address and force that affirm the audience's own liveliness.

Theatre matters, makes an impression, through its statements, its meanings, its ideological underpinnings, and its public displays, of course. Porte Parole aims to be consequential by fostering a dialogic arena in which their pieces on current and pressing issues are performed. *Seeds*, for instance, opens with a Q & A session with the audience by posing the question, "What is life?" For Porte Parole, theatre matters precisely for its powers of publicity, of making public and putting into active circulation matters of concern that might leave their mark on their audiences. Their website articulates this belief: "Porte Parole: Where spectators become engaged citizens through the power of theatre" ("Home"). Theatre matters, then, for its impact, but also for its "matters," that is to say its topics and its topicality.

It matters too for its affective force, an aspect on which the production of *Seeds* also capitalizes. While the overall aesthetic treatment of the hot topic is fairly cool (lab coats and screens feature here), *Seeds* is structured as a series of probing intersubjective encounters between "Annabel Soutar" and her interview subjects. These one-on-one dramas between "Soutar" and her subjects—some of them quite charged, as when she confronts the spokesperson for Monsanto, the producer and patent-holder of genetically modified agricultural seeds—are then framed out with direct-address segments ranging from dry and technical legal testimony to fiery speech-making. She meets the Schmeisers, the "real-life" farmers who were sued by Monsanto for illegally growing the multinational's patented, herbicide-resistant canola seeds. On stage in this documentary piece, she visits their cozy Saskatchewan farm home where afghans cover easy chairs and the soup is always hot. In the 2013 Centaur Theatre production directed by Chris Abraham and starring Eric Peterson as Percy Schmeiser, Schmeiser's climactic speech on farmer's rights is delivered just downstage from his "home," which sits upstage right. It is also on this side of the stage that the symbol of "life" in the play emerges, when a scientist retrieves an egg from a chicken in the upstage right corner. The "life" of the play transpires for the most part in this affectively warmer, stage-right arena. In contrast, the stage-left area tends to feature scientific and legalistic discourse, compelling in its own right, but not as affectively convincing as Percy Schmeiser's folksy righteousness nor as fortifying as Louise Schmeiser's cooking.

As it happens, "Soutar" is pregnant during her trip to the Prairies and has temporarily absented herself from her life in Montreal, where her husband and young daughter await her return. These personal conditions intensify the stakes of her encounters, due to the time limitations of pregnancy and by focusing again on the basic issue—in the lawsuit and in her belly—of "life." What are the personal, social, and health consequences of genetic material's recombination and transfer in plants and in people? When does it become publicly traded—or privately owned—property? Who are life's proper stewards? And what are its fundamental properties—Roundup resistance or developing according to its own genetic plan?

Seeds offers some provisional answers to these questions. Near the play's beginning, "Soutar" ventures that "[s]cientifically, life is defined by its capacity to reproduce," for instance (*Seeds*). Let me propose that the production's generic properties and modes of address highlight another aspect of "life"—a responsive, expressive sensorium. In its slightly melodramatic first-act tale of good farmers and bad corporations (which is then quite thoroughly complicated in the play's second half); its touches of humour (often thanks to Mariah Unger's multi-character performances) and pathos (courtesy of Peterson); and its kinetic staging with multiple diagonal crosses, changing video feeds projected onto upstage screens, and moving properties, *Seeds* works on the sensate body, activating its sensorium. This is a crucial aspect of what theatre scholars and artists understand as this performance form's "liveness." It is not simply that theatrical performance is a live art that takes place in the present (a supposition that intermedial performance forms and scholars such as Philip Auslander and Rebecca Schneider have challenged). It is also that in its address to the audience's sensorium through what Nicholas Ridout qualifies as its "vibratory dimensions," theatrical performance can activate that which allows one to assert and to register one's being in the world ("Welcome" 227). In short, the affect-producing machine of theatre lets us know that we are (by letting us feel that we are here).

PUBLIC FEELINGS

With this brief example, I'd like to suggest that as much as theatre is a project in thinking and discussing publicly, it is also what some (predominantly literary) theorists might call a "Public Feeling Project." Ann Cvetkovich in her book, *Depression: A Public Feeling*, describes her collaborative engagements with fellow scholars under this rubric of "Public Feelings." She writes that their "open-ended and speculative inquiry that fans out in multiple directions" places at its centre the description and analysis of "sensation and feeling as the register of historical experience" (5, 11). Sensation and feeling tell them where and when they are. Consistent with the feminist theory and activism that precede and sustain this particular bend in the "affective turn" (Clough and Halley), the Public Feelings Project moves what are often understood as personal or intimate terrains of feeling into public forums to test the political and social resonance of the personal and to sense the ideological contours of lived experience. In "Whose Awkward Moments?" Kirsty Johnston writes against the privatization (and minoritization) of the sexual feelings and activities of persons with disabilities by examining three recent productions that staged intimate details of disabled sexualities—*The Book of Judith*, *Time to Put My Socks On*, and *The Glass Box* (the last of which is anthologized in the companion volume *Once More, With Feeling*). But she also uses disability theory to illuminate a blind spot of affect theory around shame. Following disability theorist Tobin Siebers, she writes, "If shame is a primary human affect, then it is important to account for how shame is felt by the full spectrum of human experience, including those bodies whose interests in and capacities for 'covering themselves,' and navigating public and private spaces are diverse."

Both Johnston's article and Kim Solga's "Meet Me at the Border: Theatre Replacement's *BIOBOXES*" enter a conversation begun by Christine Kim on the stakes of bringing the intimate stories of disabled, racialized, and otherwise minoritized bodies into the public sphere. The necessity of this work lies not only in its revelation of different affective registers of being here and now as more or less shameful, awkward, joyful, etc., but also in its revelation of how the here and now produce non-normative affective registers as, precisely, different and relegate them to the (properly/only) intimate. How might moving such felt lives into public spaces alter those spaces' contours in ways that make them more accommodating? As Sara Ahmed maintains in her monograph *Queer Phenomenology*, spaces, like people, have dispositions; they are oriented to accommodate some bodies—that then experience that space as a good fit—and not others (51–63). Such "others," whose extension in that space is somehow curtailed by, say, non-universal design architectural elements, have the experience of discomfiture, of being out of place. Solga too takes up the question of "awkwardness" in her reading of *BIOBOXES*, mining that minor affect for its political productivity in relation to Canadian interculturalism. She finds in *BIOBOXES* and in her own interactions with it the potential for what she calls "intercultural affect," an unsettling, "thoughtfully contestatory . . . persistently demanding *as well as* pleasurably inviting" relational space that cultivates an exchange of affecting and being affected.

But not all attempts to recalibrate the emotional temperature of the public sphere through the introduction of affective difference are successful. Two of the contributors dissect what we might understand as failed public-feeling projects. In "Complicated Feelings: *Tecumseh* as Literary Land Claim," Heather Davis-Fisch reads Charles Mair's Canadian classic, *Tecumseh*, as the remains of a failed transmutation of private feeling into public act. The mixed feelings Mair held toward Indigenous peoples and rights produced an ideologically incoherent play-script. Written during the 1885 Northwest Rebellion of the Saskatchewan Métis against the government of Canada, *Tecumseh*, in Mair's words, "depicts dramatically the time and scenes in which the great Indian so nobly played his part" in the War of 1812, seventy years earlier (Mair, Preface 4). In Davis-Fisch's reading, Mair's poetic drama, in its historical remove, its generic features of melodrama and "Indian tragedy," and its rhetorical strategies offers a feeling of closure to a painfully open social and political problem.

For second-wave women's liberation movements, emotional closure is not on the table. Rather, Sara Warner argues, it is the emotional baggage of second-wave feminist cultural production for third-wave and contemporary feminists that can simplify in our memory what was a rather more complex moment of intensely personal politics. She investigates the dynamics of memory and forgetting, influenced by how we feel about the past with repercussions for the historical record, through the non-release of Canada's first experimental feminist film by an all-female crew, *Jill Johnston: October 1975*. She at once takes out of the vault an important artifact from a lesbian-feminist archive of feeling (see also Cvetkovich, *An Archive*; and Cowan) and takes the measure of the intense feelings of attachment and of disidentification with remnants of this epoch.

Consistent with their indebtedness to feminist and queer theory and activism, members of the Public Feelings Project have often focused on everyday feelings and experiences, understanding them as a manifestation of social life (the personal is political, as second-wave feminists would say) and as a barometer of change or movement that is not yet consciously elaborated or historically manifest. For instance, Lauren Berlant in *Cruel Optimism* dwells on an experience of the present that she calls "the impasse": that is, "[A] stretch of time in which one moves around with a sense that the world is at once intensely present and enigmatic" (4). The enigma arises from the fact that the experience of the present has not yet coalesced into something else, "such as an orchestrated collective event or an epoch on which we can look back" (Berlant, *Cruel* 4). Despite it being not yet known or fully graspable, it is nonetheless there—active and pressing. In this way, everyday experience—like the impasse that Cvetkovich experienced as depression—is both complexly linked up with broader social forces (such as minoritization—see her chapter on racism and depression, *Depression* 115–53) and is a register of life's textures. For Cvetkovich, feelings of depression may open onto community formation; her "depression journals" document her own small but life-expanding social network of sustaining friendships and queer mourning rituals during her extended moments of impasse.

But not all "everyday" feelings are perceived as everyday or as community-forming when they enter the public sphere. Indeed, as Sunita Nigam argues about instances of blackface performance in Quebec media, some people's feeling responses are perceived as community-breaking. In "Feeling in Public: Blackface as Theatre of Action in Contemporary Quebec," she registers the "national" as an everyday structure of feeling, a tacit affective disposition, and one that the emotional repertoires of some Quebecers of colour exceed. When the latter's feelings "go public" in response to a televised blackface performance by a white comedian, they are read as "dramatic" (not everyday) and as not-Québécois. Introducing the idea of a "feeling-action"—the public disclosure of an affective tendency or rhythm that may or may not find its proper place in the public sphere—Nigam unpacks the fraught histories of racialization in Quebec, and returns us to the risky politics of making private feelings public.

AFFECT, EMOTION, AND FEELING IN CANADIAN THEATRE

Theatre and performance studies have long and proud histories of wrestling with emotional subtleties and complexities, and of parsing their relatively enigmatic or relatively formulaic formations.[1] *Theatres of Affect* reflects this history and ongoing project of discerning theatre's emotional effects and lures—from lighting colour washes to dramatic asides, from character types to soundscapes—in its attention to theatre practice. A number of authors in these pages speak to the specifically theatrical mechanisms of emotional provocation, differentiation, and management. Ursula Neuerburg-Denzer elaborates on actor training in her "Emotion Lab" at Concordia University, which builds on the classical Indian emotion schemes of rasa adapted by Richard Schechner. Importantly, and consistent with the teachings of Bharata Muni's *Natyashastra*, she insists on the distinction between lived emotion and performed emotion; it is the latter for which theatre has an extensive, discipline-specific vocabulary developed in practice and theory since Bharata and Aristotle. Dissecting the multiple sources of this tool of actor training—from Bharata to Artaud to Pavlov—Neuerburg-Denzer also helpfully produces a critical taxonomy of feeling derived from the neuroscientific models of Antonio Damasio. Here, "affect" names an immediate response to a stimulus; that response, to invoke Berlant above, has not yet coalesced into an "event." "Emotion" then describes the "events" of affect—that is, the visible and invisible bodily changes (e.g., blushing, increased or decreased heart rate) that arise and that may be conditioned and managed; unsurprisingly, emotions are central to actor training. And feeling is the conscious registration of emotions, where the event of emotion is given shape and meaning through narrative.

In his reflections on his own creative practices as writer, director, and actor trainer, David Fancy contributes the first of five "Artist Statements" in

---

1   For exemplary scholarship on theories of emotion and of aesthetic formations, see Roach, *The Player's Passion*, and Meisel, respectively; for an overview of theatre's engagements with feeling, see Hurley and Warner.

the volume, in which the authors approach the question of feeling primarily (though not exclusively) through their own embodied practices. These stylistically varied contributions tend toward the personal and meditative in tone as a means of communicating something of the lived experience of sensation, movement, and feeling. For his part, Fancy proposes a set of "relays" between theory and practice as a generative mode for working with affect in performance and in writing. Here, however, "affect" designates force, intensity, or the capacity to move and be moved, drawing out for readers another mode for thinking feeling in the Humanities, a monist philosophical tradition stretching from the seventeenth-century Dutch philosopher Benedict de Spinoza through twentieth-century French philosopher Gilles Deleuze to contemporary political theorist and communications scholar Brian Massumi, to name only its best-known proponents. In the deeply relational force of moving and being moved—or affecting and being affected—affect, in this tradition, harbours transformative potential for the subject. In "Becoming Imperceptible In the Studio," Fancy writes of his experiments as a playwright and director in such affective transformations, which he understands as usefully intervening in both the dominant Canadian actor training model—Stanislavsky's system and methods derived from it (see Migliarisi)—and in the notion of the human subject as a coherent organism that undergirds and is reinforced by that tradition. F.P. Favel's artist statement, "Monsieur Artaud and I: Peyote Has a Lasso," likewise articulates something of his creative process, tutored by the affective performance experiments of Artaud and by Jerzy Grotowski's requirements of the actor's "total act," his/her complete way of life as a theatre practitioner. Bringing these lines of influence together with his Cree worldview and traditions that carry their own vocabularies and techniques of emotional expression, Favel shares his journey to "find the true art within [him] out of the ruins of [his] culture."

Theatre's facility with feeling, its history of provoking, displaying, and managing emotion, also makes its refined vocabulary and practised techniques a resource for other domains. In her chapter, Natalie Alvarez takes us behind the scenes of Canadian military immersive training, revealing a world where "theatre" means "war" and high-repetition training in simulated environments according to detailed scripts prepares soldiers to manage potentially intrusive affects when being "peacewarriors" in Afghanistan. She unwinds the vying objectives of the training, crystallized in the name "peacewarrior," that is taking place in simulated Afghan villages reconstructed in Alberta. She further dissects how a wider cultural logic of "premediation"—the means by which "the experience of a traumatic future" is prevented in advance "by generating and maintaining a low level of anxiety as a kind of affective prophylactic"—is installed in soldiers' bodies and behaviours. Her chilling account of the efficacy of rehearsal for military training finds its artistic response in performance artist Helene Voster's account of her 2010–11 performance piece, *Impact Afghanistan War*, in which she fell 100 times a day for a year to recognize Afghan deaths. If Canada's "peacewarriors" in Afghanistan are trained in a way that lessens the affective impact of their actions, Voster's performance asks Canadian citizens to feel the impact of Canada's involvement in Afghanistan. She performs "being affected"—the force of another body on her own—as a means of affecting others.

AFFECTIVE ENGAGEMENTS

Dylan Robinson's and Julie Burelle's contributions caution against the theatre's emotional lures. In "Feeling Reconciliation, Remaining Settled," Stó:lō music scholar Robinson warns of performance's promise of affecting the audience. Pinpointing the emotional display of tears, he unpacks the differential "meanings" of this same act for different criers—one group moved and empathetic, the other angry and resentful. Instead of assuming "positive transformation" of the audience or a "utopian performative" in which a group shares in a sense of a better, more just world, he asks readers to consider that these tears may, rather, register the experience of schism between settler and First Nations "we's." The tears shed by some audience members in response signal their *feeling* reconciliation, a feeling generated in his two case studies of "inclusionary musical performance" (wherein First Nations people are "present" but not agential). Among the risks of musical structures of resolution and closure—those non-representational musical faculties that engender a felt

sense of closure—is precisely the efficacy of its emotional labour in convincing listeners that reconciliation has happened. Like Solga, Robinson advocates
instead for empathetic unsettling that would awaken non-Indigenous audiences to the great amount of political and social labour to be undertaken to
transform First Nations realities, their discomfiting experiences of non-fit. In
"Staging Empathy's Limit-Point: First Nations Theatre and the Challenges of
Self-Representation on the Settler Stage," Burelle considers the 2010 adaptation
of a Mayan court drama by Quebec First Nations theatre Ondinnok. Where
Robinson's focus is on the non-representational aspects of musical performance that trigger comforting (for some) affective response, Burelle tackles
the emotional and political stakes of representing trauma and dispossession
of Amerindian peoples. Working through a set of critical studies on empathy
that worry over its universalizing tendencies, Burelle advocates what she calls
a "desire-based dramaturgical approach" in Ondinnok's production that exacts
a more complex and responsive act of witnessing on the part of the audience.

In Nicole Nolette's contribution, the affective expressions of French and
English Canadian acting traditions mix on the stage of Winnipeg's Théâtre Vice
Versa Theatre. This bilingual theatre traverses the bridge uniting the divided
city/ies of Winnipeg/Saint-Boniface. While spotlighting the many ways in which
TVVT productively scrambles emotional geographies to create a more mixed environment via their linguistic and theatrical crossings, Nolette also pinpoints the
precarities and asymmetries of TVVT's hopeful project. A close reading of one
actress's performance in a single role in French and in English spotlights the limits
of this particularly Canadian utopic vision. Hope and bridges are likewise at issue
in Julie Salverson's artist statement; here, however, hope is excavated from disaster
via the bridge of her witnessing. In "The Secrets of Others," Salverson meditates
on what draws her to emotionally difficult projects—about the Holocaust, about
Hiroshima—interleaving these with memories of her "atomic childhood."

Community-based and/or socially engaged practices come to the fore
in these pages for their focus on connecting to and often mobilizing their
audiences. Cultural geographers Caleb Johnston and Geraldine Pratt extend their previous scholarship on their testimonial drama, *Nanay* [Nanny],
devised with the Philippine Women Centre of British Columbia, about

temporary domestic work of (largely) Filipina caregivers under Canada's Live-In Caregiver Program. It is significant that they chose theatre for this purpose: "We have turned to theatre to put disparate experiences of care and need into public dialogue; we have looked to harness the affective impact of theatre to put issues into greater visibility, to greater public effect." But their theatrical experiences with *Nanay* in Canada, Europe, and, as of this year, the Philippines have also brought to the fore "the understanding that there is a geography to the circulation of affects and that different affects travel differently in different contexts, with different political effects." These differential affective landscapes are further explored in Patrick Alcedo's discussion of the making of his documentary film, *A Piece of Paradise*, in which he details the dance-based traditions of veneration of the infant Jesus by Toronto's Filipino diaspora as part of the Aklan festival. In "Emotional and Religious Landscapes," Alcedo relates the stories of four women in the community, all of whom work in the personal or domestic-care industry in the Greater Toronto Area. They come together in the mutual tending of the festival's Santo Niño statue; enfolded into their kin-work, he becomes another "child" for which they care.

And so we come full circle in this introduction, back to the matter of life and its registration in the work and narrative and apparatus of the theatre. Theatre is an intensely relational space where what is ostended on stage appears *for* an audience (see Bauman). It is that disposition of the onstage presence and the audience presence—a disposition where they tend toward each other, even orient themselves to the other's place—that makes the experiences it offers potentially so *impressive*, and so very disappointing when they fail. For in addition to being orientating (audiences arrange themselves in relation to it) and intensely intersubjective (as Jill Dolan would say; see *Utopia* 471), theatre is a realm that tends to fuel desires of all kinds—and, of course, relies on the desires of audiences for its continued existence. It traffics in vicarious experience (that is, the taking of someone else's experience for one's own pleasure/excitation/etc.), and that is built scenically on what Adolphe Appia called "borrowed life" (Beacham 6). This makes of it a key realm for thinking through how feelings, desires, tendencies shape its spaces, undergird its dynamics, inform its conditions of possibility, and track its lively presence—both in its matters and its mattering.

AFFECTIVE TRAINING AND EMOTION MANAGEMENT (OR, ACTING)

AFFECT MANAGEMENT AND MILITARISM IN ALBERTA'S MOCK AFGHAN VILLAGES: TRAINING THE "STRATEGIC CORPORAL"[1]

NATALIE ALVAREZ

THE MASCAL

A foot patrol of soldiers enters the Afghan village in a relaxed posture. They smile at the villagers but their hands remain on their weapons, eyes scanning the scene continuously with a gaze that conveys caution. How you enter the village is key, a sergeant major tells me, "Always look like you could flip the switch one way or another. You can't look like you are slacking off. It's usually your eyes that are always moving . . . you aren't taking your hand off your pistol, but you are showing respect."[2] Suddenly, a loud blast. Grey clouds of smoke billow out from a car parked at the end of the village. The soldiers move into place, establishing a defensive perimeter around the scene, guns at their shoulders. A bloodied body becomes visible through the plumes of smoke; arms and legs have been amputated from the blast. The body is clothed in an Afghan National Police (ANP) uniform—a local national. The soldiers begin shouting, "Man down! Man down!" Local villagers, men and women, rush

1   Research for this essay was supported by the Social Sciences and Humanities Research Council of Canada.

2   These remarks are taken from an interview I conducted with a staff sergeant on 2 May 2011, following a scenario debrief. I have refrained from referencing the proper names of staff sergeants I interviewed in the field for security purposes. Where I do refer to proper names in the essay, the quotations are taken from formal interviews with military personnel at CFB Wainwright, which I conducted outside of field exercises.

to the scene wailing and shouting. They know the man that was hit. In a desperate frenzy they try to get to the body by pushing past the soldiers' safety cordon. The soldiers yell, "Stay back!" in Pashto, but the villagers don't listen. ANP, working with the Canadian Forces, start firing warning shots recklessly at the ground, in the air, attempting to scare back the villagers. The women scream and cower. A man from the village, a relation of the ANP officer killed in the blast, runs through the village and rushes toward the soldiers, screaming the ANP officer's name, "Kamal! Kamal!" emotionally distraught. He is tackled and held down by the soldiers. He tries to resist, wailing and shouting "Kamal!" at the top of his lungs. Three ANP officers restrain him and remove him from the scene.

My hands shake as I try to take notes. I try to conceal a rush of emotions, conscious of my present company: I stand on top of a shipping container that has been turned into a viewing tower for the military VIPs who have gathered to watch this afternoon's spectacle. I look to my right at two commanding officers and overhear fragments of their conversation: ". . . the traffic can be a bit of a nightmare getting there, but it's a great property right on the lake. I try to get there with the kids as much as I can over the summer . . . ." As "warriors," they have been through years of intensive military training designed principally to curtail affect in conflict situations much like these, and the grim realities they have seen first-hand in theatre—which is to say, the theatre of war[3]—no doubt foreground the fiction of this scene, which they view with an ease and critical distance.

---

3   In the context of this paper, which analyzes the immersive simulation through the lens of performance, references to "theatre" are, of course, references to "theatre of war," which shares disciplinary terminologies and methodologies with performance. As James Thompson, Jenny Hughes, and Michael Balfour maintain in their introduction to *Performance in Place of War*, "The connections between performance and war can be found . . . in the very terminology governing war zones. The 'theatres of war' are places where the destruction and obliteration of human lives are planned, often rehearsed, and finally enacted" (2). This paper concerns itself with the military's rehearsals for war and the implications of its (performative) methodologies. For an incisive overview of our discipline's unsettling terminological connections with the military and militarization, see also Diana Taylor's "Afterword: War Play." The phrases "theatre of war" and "theatre of

A man breaks free from the throng of villagers gathered at the scene of the blast and gets through the soldiers' safety cordon. He walks in an unsteady, almost drunken manner toward a soldier who stands alone in a relaxed posture. The soldier seems to have slipped out of the scene into spectator mode, bedazzled or, perhaps, impressed by the spectacle. The villager is now about six feet from the soldier. He reaches emphatically into his vest, as though trying to give the soldier one last opportunity to take notice and do something. Suddenly, another loud blast. The villager has detonated. The soldier is covered in a white powder signalling that he has been hit by the suicide bomb and is dead. He drops to the ground to screams and cries of horror from the villagers and shouts of "Man down! Man down!" from his fellow soldiers who rush to his aid. A commanding officer looks down from the viewing platform at the downed soldier who failed to notice the suicide bomber's approach and shakes his head: "We need poker players in the CF [Canadian Forces]—they're the best at reading faces." The deputy commander at his side expresses his pleasure that one of the soldiers in training got hit—a good lesson to learn here in the safety of a simulation, rather than out there, in theatre.

This simulated "mass casualty" event (or MASCAL, as it's referred to in military acronym speak) took place five days into the ten-day, force-on-force "Maple Guardian" training program offered at the Canadian Manoeuvre Training Centre (CMTC), a $500 million, state-of-the-art, full-immersion war-games facility created in 2004 at CFB Wainwright in rural eastern Alberta, which initiated large-scale exercises in 2006. The CMTC's formation occurred at a critical juncture in the Afghan mission. In the early stages of Canada's involvement in Afghanistan, the description of the mission remained more or less consistent with Canada's mythic legacy as a peacekeeping nation. In 2003, Canada, under the leadership of Canadian Brigadier-General Peter J. Devlin, had taken command of the Kabul Multinational Brigade in 2003—an international force of peacekeepers operating under the International Security

---

operations," Taylor notes, "have been used since the Napoleonic Wars by thinkers such as Carlo von Clausewitz and Henri de Jomini to refer to the entire bellicose enterprise and to discrete areas of engagement, respectively" (1888).

Assistance Force (ISAF). Between 2003 and 2005, Canadian soldiers were stationed in Kabul, an area of relative peace where they were deployed to maintain and consolidate peace in conjunction with other NATO forces. But in the summer of 2005, the nature of the Canadian mission shifted significantly (Coulon and Liégeois 43). The Canadian government decided to transfer its forces to the violent region of Kandahar in order to engage in force-on-force combat against insurgents. The authorities of National Defence in Canada described this move as "a more robust peace support role" (qtd. in Coulon and Liégeois 43). After 2005, Canada's mission shifted from peacekeeping to *peace enforcement*, leaving in its wake the tenets of classical peacekeeping instantiated in the 1950s under Lester B. Pearson, such as "gaining the parties' consent; the use of force only in cases of self-defense; and impartiality" (iv). The peace-loving, easygoing "peacekeepers of the sixties and seventies," as Jocelyn Coulon and Michel Liégeois point out, were supplanted by the "peacewarrior," authorized to engage in force-on-force combat in circumstances that required it (iv).[4] Since then, the principles of peacekeeping have been subsumed under the principles of a counter-insurgency mission (COIN), articulated in the broad tenets of SHAPE, SECURE, and DEVELOP—engage with key tribal leaders, separate insurgents from the population, maintain security for governance and development, and support development and stability—tenets that further obscure the punitive militarism involved in stamping out an insurgency.

The live immersive training environment at CMTC, designed to produce the next wave of front-line peacewarriors, simulates "real world" theatre

---

4   This shift in mission identity was obscured by government rhetoric: in 2007, the Strategic Counsel advised the Harper government to avoid "negative" expressions and focus on words like "peacekeeping," "reconstruction," and "stability," in its statements on the war (Coulon and Liégeois 46); "war," in fact, was rarely invoked to describe Canada's involvement in Afghanistan. Such rhetorical strategies reveal how affect and, in turn, public opinion, are regulated in order to galvanize support for the war effort. As Judith Butler queries in *Frames of War*, we must ask how the "continuation of war or, indeed, the escalation of war" is possible "without first preparing and structuring the public understanding of what war is" (xv).

conditions in Afghanistan in order to enable soldiers in training to become "completely absorbed in the exercise" ("CMTC") and put their prior training to the test in this intensive, final phase of exercises before deployment to Afghanistan. In this simulated environment, soldiers are trained to engage in a seemingly irreconcilable paradox of punitive yet culturally sensitive militarism—a paradox that is doubled in the notion of a "peacewarrior" who enforces peace through the use of robust force. Scenarios are designed to stress-inoculate soldiers, enabling them to face threats with an optimum level of cognitive and muscular autopilot while remaining sensitive to the Rules of Engagement (ROE) that govern the soldier and his or her relations with local nationals in this counter-insurgency mission. The MASCAL event just described is an illustrative test assessing how the soldier will negotiate these conflicting directions of required action: a direct insurgent attack triggers a reflexive and conditioned response in the soldier whose muscle memory draws on a repertoire of rehearsed tactical action, but in this condition, they must react with a sensitivity and openness to the immediate encounter of grieving villagers who complicate the soldier's ability to operate in a state of procedural autopilot and follow "mission process."

My study of this immersive simulation of war focuses on these kinds of affective collisions, in part as an inquiry of resistance against what James Der Derian has called the "Military-Industrial-Media-Entertainment" complex (786) that has produced increasingly *virtual* engagements in war through advancements in image technology. In Derian's formulation, "virtuous wars promote a vision of bloodless, humanitarian, hygienic wars" (772), which leave the casualties conveniently out of frame and out of view, obscuring the embodied engagements and bloody aftermaths in the war against terrorism. A study of affect in the arena of military training, where tensions and conflicts between civilians, civilian-insurgents, and military are staged, allows us to contend with the "stickiness" and messiness of these encounters between live bodies sharing real time and space. Affect, as Melissa Gregg and Gregory J. Seigworth contend, "marks a body's *belonging* to a world of encounters" (2); it is "persistent proof of a body's never less than ongoing immersion in and among the world's obstinacies and rhythms, its refusals as much as its invitations" (1). What this study reveals, in part, is that the modulation of affect in military training is historically contingent and inextricably tied to shifting geopolitical forces, which in turn impacts the kinds of bodies that perform in theatres (of war). The specific focus of this study lies in how affect management in military training invests in *virtual* engagements beyond those produced by the "Military-Industrial-Media-Entertainment" complex: immersive training such as CMTC's Maple Guardian exercise—which immerses soldiers in the "sights, sounds, and sensations of battle" (Archibald et al. 5)—aims to optimize the potential of the *virtual body* in order to produce an efficient peacewarrior, as I will explain shortly. What I query here are the implications of this large-scale rehearsal's broader objectives, which attempt to neutralize affective response in order to prepare a better peacewarrior by making the unfamiliar familiar and all possible futures apprehensible. How, I want to ask, does a privileging of "affect management" in military training potentially work against the intercultural relations and ethical engagements required of the peacewarrior in a counter-insurgency mission? And how are these vying objectives negotiated in the crucible of asymmetric warfare and the so-called "three-block war"?

Military analysts invoke a range of terms, such as "asymmetric warfare" and the "three-block war," to describe what they perceive as the changing nature of conflict in the twenty-first century, typified by the kinds of tactical strategies soldiers are currently encountering in Afghanistan. Asymmetric refers to the non-traditional and unpredictable actions undertaken *within* warfare by non-state and weaker parties against the conventional capabilities of major military-economic and technologically advanced state powers; such unconventional tactics are aimed at undermining the fundamental asymmetry *of* warfare and the power discrepancies between state and non-state powers.[5] These asymmetries *within* and *of* warfare unfold within the particular context of the so-called "three-block war," a type of irregular, urban warfare in which

---

5   For this explication of asymmetrical warfare and the "three-block war," I am indebted to military personnel at the Stanford Training Area (STANTA) in Thetford, Norfolk, England, for a 2009 "Information Note" they generously shared titled "Understanding Hybrid Conflict: Hybrid Adversaries and Hybrid Threats."

the distinctions between combatant and non-combatant, innocent civilian and insurgent are blurred and the entry-level soldier is confronted, as General Charles C. Krulak puts it, by the "entire spectrum of tactical challenges in the span of a few hours and within the space of three contiguous city blocks" (Krulak). In this particular theatre of the three-block war, individual soldiers at the lowest ranks may find themselves engaging in high-intensity, counter-guerilla warfare in one block, humanitarian aid and trust-building with local nationals in the next block, and arbitration between warring factions in the third. This continuum of activity in the "three-block war" informed the reconfiguration of Canada's "peacekeeping" mission after 2005, when Canadian forces ramped up their engagements in Kandahar; then minister of national defence, Bill Graham, described the demands on Canadian forces in this way: "[I]n order to be efficient in robust peacekeeping operations today, it is obvious that our troops must at once be warriors, diplomats, and humanitarian workers" (qtd. in Coulon and Liégeois 43). The complexity of different modes of engagement and moment-to-moment decision-making falls on the shoulders of individual riflemen who must "make well-reasoned and *independent* decisions under extreme stress"—decisions that, according to Krulak, are not only "subject to the harsh scrutiny of both the media and the court of public opinion," but also carry immense political and strategic weight. They hold the power to influence not only the "immediate tactical situation," but the larger operational, strategic, and geopolitical situation as well. In this respect, the individual soldier is—and must think and act as—the "Strategic Corporal," since s/he represents the face of a country's foreign policy on the global stage (Krulak).[6] The large-scale *mise en scène* of Afghan villages at CMTC, where improvisations unfold twenty-four hours a day across

---

6   This notion of the "Strategic Corporal" figured as a central theme of the After Action Review (AAR) or debrief with troops I witnessed for the MASCAL event at CMTC described at the outset, led by a Sergeant Major. The Sergeant Major praised the troops for not getting sucked into the reckless behaviour of the ANP who were firing warning shots in all directions to scare back villagers, which would have escalated matters, but he also insisted that their job was to exercise more control over the situation and the ANP's chain of command.

a ten-day period, are designed to replicate the conditions of the "three-block war" and its "entire spectrum of challenges" in order to foster the kind of stratified thinking required of the "Strategic Corporal."

CMTC: CREATING THE MAELSTROM OF WAR

Four mock Afghan villages have been mapped onto the arid Alberta prairie in reduced but nevertheless analogous geographic proximity to their locations in Afghanistan and have become home to a population of actors largely drawn from the Afghan diaspora in Edmonton. Allied Container Systems (ACS), a private company contracted by the Canadian Military to provide the realistic *mise en scène* required for the live training environment, posted ads through its cultural liaison, Mohammed Ahmadi, at Afghan community centres in Edmonton in an effort to recruit, as the ad stated, Afghans "interested in assisting with Canada's peacekeeping mission in Afghanistan" (Ahmadi). Role-players create a "pattern of life" in these mock Afghan villages from the innocuous to the suspicious, training soldiers' powers of observation and discernment as they try to build "an intelligence picture" of possible insurgent activity in each village.[7] But because Afghan role-players are not permitted to handle even simulated weapons in the exercise, for security reasons, insurgents are played by Individual Augmentees (IAs), Canadian military personnel with experience in theatre in Afghanistan who have been hired by the CMTC to

---

7   Simulations of Afghan villages such as those at CMTC can be seen as the by-product of the "cultural turn" in military strategy—precipitated by the wars in Iraq and Afghanistan— which has conscripted the social sciences, particularly anthropology, in order to develop a more robust Cultural Intelligence (CQ) of local populations. Military strategists contend that a more intimate knowledge of the local culture can be used as a "force multiplier" (Spencer and Balasevicius 41). This use of "strategic culture" sparked a controversy in the discipline—and a formal statement by the American Anthropological Association—after cultural anthropologist Montgomery McFate launched the Human Terrain System program with the US Army in 2007. For an overview of McFate's views and how anthropology has served historically as the handmaiden of war, see McFate's "Anthropology and Counterinsurgency: The Strange Story of Their Curious Relationship."

create a population of insurgents infiltrating each village. They serve as key members of the Contemporary Operating Environment Forces (COEFOR), a faction of the Maple Guardian exercise headed by Major Blouin, whose express purpose is to replicate a spectrum of tactical threats characteristic of irregular and asymmetrical warfare, ranging from "belligerents and small factions to a more robust and formidable force" (*CMTC Brochure*). ACS works in tandem with COEFOR to create the "real world" theatre conditions as authentically as possible for its Principle Training Audience,[8] which has a constant audience of its own: Observer Controller Trainers (or OCTs) observe the actions and comportment of the soldiers in training and offer counsel and feedback based on their own, first-hand experience as veterans of Afghanistan, which take the form of scenario debriefings, "hotwashes," or After Action Reviews (AARs). ACS field directors, in consultation with OCTs, the cultural liaison, and the Afghan role-players, assess soldiers' levels of cultural awareness. The soldiers' intercultural performances are reviewed, evaluated, and rendered into a series of graphs, called Village/Scenario Reports, that are presented each day at the afternoon Commander Update Brief—a performance review process that introduces yet another field to the far-reaching stratifications of performance efficiencies Jon McKenzie surveys in his *Perform Or Else*, namely, "cultural awareness performance."

The ten-day, force-on-force training of the Maple Guardian exercise is loosely guided by a script of multiple narrative threads operating at the micro- to the macro-level, from intelligence "injects" in which a vital piece of intelligence is planted on a detainee in the hopes that it will be discovered by a soldier to set up the next stage of the narrative, to large-scale attacks such as the MASCAL event described at the outset. The storylines, designed by lead planner Major Bauer and the colonels at CMTC, are based on current combat trends in theatre as well as field reports the planners receive from OCTs and

---

8   To the theatre and performance studies scholar, this terminology is undoubtedly curious if not confusing: soldiers in training are referred to as the "Principal Training Audience" (or PTA), even though they are hardly an audience to the scenarios of war that unfold in the simulation, but active participants who generate the narrative threads that unravel based on their responses, comportment, and levels of engagement.

platoon commanders after key scenarios; the summary of outcomes and the OCT assessments of soldier comportment and action will inform how the lead planners will shape the direction of the unfolding narrative and the nature of future "injects." The narrative strategizing takes place at CMTC headquarters or "The Crystal Palace" as ACS staff affectionately call it. The Crystal Palace houses Exercise Control (EXCON), "the electronic nerve-centre of CMTC," where control staff and contractor analysts monitor each soldier's and vehicle's movements through the EXCON GPS system. The Weapon Effects Simulation (WES) works in conjunction with this GPS system to show where soldiers and vehicles are on the ground at every moment in a network of patched-in vests and sensors that signal when a soldier or vehicle has been hit by simulated fire, simulated IED, etc., and the degree of the injury or damage—a hit, a near miss, or a kill ("CMTC").

While the exercise as a whole is loosely scripted, the reactions of the soldiers-in-training to the staged events are, of course, not, which pushes the exercise as a whole into the realm of "large-scale, live improvisational theatre," as ACS Managing Field Director Jesse Hendrikse puts it. In his invocation of live improvisational theatre, Hendrikse nods to Keith Johnstone, a pioneer of improvisational theatre who developed the widely used "Impro System" of theatrical performance training—a chilling reminder of how the performance paradigm has been taken up in the instrumentalist rationality of the military-industrial complex as it attempts to devise new training methodologies nimble enough to prepare its soldiers to take on this new frontier of irregular and asymmetrical warfare.[9] The script remains flexible and responsive to the soldiers' actions and modes of engagement. Chief planner Major Bauer meets with Hendrikse and ACS Operations Manager Gavin Biedler on a daily basis to "blue sky" the next twenty-four hours of events. Hendrikse and Biedler work with film-industry professionals in makeup and moulage to create wounds, body parts, and corpses so lifelike I dizzied

---

9   Diana Taylor shares this concern in her afterword to a special *PMLA* issue on war where she states: "I am troubled by the largely unexamined ways in which the tools of my field contribute to waging war" (1888).

at the sight of a body bag Biedler opened to reveal a dummy that had been done up as a fatality in a helicopter crash for a scenario that was to be staged later that afternoon. As a testament to the sophistication of the makeup and moulage team's creations, medics in training reportedly get sick at the sight of their work. As Captain Anderson tells me, the shockingly realistic makeup and moulage effects are designed to prepare soldiers for the sights they will witness first-hand in theatre: "[T]he challenge," he says, "is to go through mission process, communicating with the boss throughout, asking for air over-watch . . . a hundred other things you need to think about while you're under stress and seeing a bucket of body parts with blood after a suicide bombing" (J. Anderson). The exposure to all manner of graphic injury, blood, and destruction in rehearsal is another form of stress inoculation; by exposing the soldier to all possible forms of injury and fatalities, they will be more likely to maintain their composure, and the Rules of Engagement, in theatre when they witness these events first-hand. As former film-industry professionals themselves, Hendrikse and Biedler bring their own skill set in special effects and work with Major Bauer in realizing what is essentially an ongoing storyboarding process oriented toward the exercise's ultimate objective: to create the maelstrom of war and give the soldiers in training their worst possible day in theatre.

MANAGING AFFECT

The aim of subjecting soldiers to their worst possible day in theatre is held in the balance alongside a recognition that morale must be kept high in this prelude to "real war" in Afghanistan in order to send troops off to theatre with a confident sense of "Team Canada." At the same time, trainers must ensure that the exercise itself does not induce battle fatigue prior to deployment. But the exigencies of force-on-force combat and its physiological and psychological demands on the body require that soldiers experience intense, high-repetition training in order to, as combat psychologist Lt. Col. David

Grossman puts it, sounding as though he were citing Stanislavsky, "turn the skills that he needs to perform into 'muscle memory'" (33).

Indeed, the contemporary science that informed Stanislavsky's culminating life's work on his method of physical actions produced a vocabulary of actor training that would not seem altogether foreign to Lt. Col. Grossman. This convergence in vocabulary points to eerie intersections between theories of actor training and Lt. Col. Grossman's field of so-called "Warrior Science," which studies the psychological and physiological behaviour of soldiers in the crucible of the battlefield in order to advance current military training methodologies. Stanislavsky's method of physical actions relied on the doctrine of reflex conditioning, most notoriously developed by turn-of-the-century Russian physiologist Ivan Pavlov. Through rehearsal and repetition, the actor's work, for Stanislavsky, becomes an accretion of actions, a physical score that "automatically stirs the actor to physical action" (*Building* 62) and ultimately liberates the mind from a debilitating consciousness of the task; the actor's work on stage becomes a "conscious . . . construction automized into his muscles and nerves," which saves the actor from the "psychophysical paralysis" that often occurs with stage fright (Roach, *Player's Passion* 213, 207). In Lt. Col. Grossman's "Warrior Science," this form of reflex conditioning through high-intensity repetition in training allows the soldier to act on muscle memory in the thick of combat while maintaining a "freedom of mind," which not only mitigates "psychophysical paralysis" in combat but also functions as a form of stress inoculation.

In the field of "Warrior Science," psychologists such as Grossman and Bruce K. Siddle have conducted studies linking hormonal or fear-induced heart-rate increases, resulting from sympathetic nervous-system arousal, to task performance. Exercises are designed to train soldiers to perform tasks in what is called the "Condition Yellow" zone of arousal, where the soldier's heart rate sits between eighty and one hundred bpm: a stage of "basic alertness and readiness, a place where you are psychologically prepared for combat" (Grossman 31). But for force-on-force combat, the soldier is at an optimal survival and combat performance level in "Condition Red," wherein bpm sits anywhere between 115 and 145. Complex motor skills and visual and cognitive reaction time are all at their peak at this level; however, this level of engagement is not sustainable—fine-motor skills begin to deteriorate rapidly. The purpose of an onslaught of high-intensity training and repetition, then, is to provide soldiers with an opportunity to rehearse so that they can perform intricate tasks—such as magazine changes, misfeed drills, weapon handling, and handcuffing—without conscious thought, despite operating in Condition Red. The more intensely the soldier is trained, the more expertly s/he will be able to execute tasks without losing cognitive or visual reaction time or complex motor skills, even when bpm surges to the dangerous levels of Condition Gray or Condition Black—anywhere between 145 and 220 bpm. The more the soldier rehearses, the more apt s/he is to " 'push the envelope' of Condition Red, enabling extraordinary performance at accelerated heart rate levels," until the soldier is effectively stress inoculated (34–35); each task becomes a matter of muscle memory, enabling the soldier to function on "autopilot" at an "expert level in Condition Gray" (35). To paraphrase one soldier, who returned from a tour in Afghanistan in 2009 when some of his friends in theatre did not, this mode of autopilot is often referred to as going "in the black," a state of being in which the soldier "isn't really all there" and prior conditioning takes over.[10]

In effect, what sustained, repetitious, and intense training seems to afford is a containment of affective response, to the degree that it is possible to contain affect; in its most basic definitions, affect is largely understood as something that happens to us, that impinges upon us, something with which we are overcome, implying a profound kind of passivity. Affect itself is active, as Freud contended in his *Project for a Scientific Psychology* (1895); it acts on the body subtending both unconscious and conscious thought. But the subject herself remains constituted by it, a vehicle for its activity. Live, immersive training in an environment that mimics "real world" theatre conditions is designed to undermine affective response by subjecting the soldier

---

10   For these insights, I am indebted to an email exchange, conducted in July of 2013, with a Canadian veteran of Afghanistan who requested that his remarks remain anonymous.

to a whole spectrum of possible threats and deadly force encounters with the aim of making the possible future familiar, taking the surprise out of the event "when the real situation arises" (Grossman 36).

The motives behind said aims are critical in the context of war: reducing cognitive engagement in favour of increasing autopilot is not only a means of stress-inoculating soldiers, which in turn serves as a preventative measure against post-traumatic stress disorder,[11] it is also a way of inducing soldiers to kill. According to Grossman, during WWII, only fifteen to twenty percent of soldiers fired their weapons at an exposed enemy soldier. Twenty years later, in Vietnam, that rate increased to ninety-five percent (78). While there are, of course, a number of other contingencies that might have contributed to this increase in weapon fire, such as a change in weaponry and battle environment, Grossman attributes this increase to more "realistic training" with more lifelike and, in the case of live-simulation exercises like Maple Guardian, "live" targets, which allows the act of killing to be turned into a "conditioned reflex" (81). Unless operating on autopilot, soldiers are otherwise unlikely to kill. Turning to police psychologist Alexis Artwohl's research on perceptual distortions in combat, Grossman asserts that "74 percent of the officers involved in a deadly force encounter acted on automatic pilot. In other words, actions of three out of four officers in combat were done without conscious thought" (74).

Putting aside, for a moment, the unsettling notion of a soldier acting without conscious thought in a combat situation, the rationale behind these training regimes points to how the body's "incipient potential" can be harnessed to service the punitive militarism that is often required of the peace-warrior operating in counter-insurgency warfare. Training the body to operate in a condition of autopilot on the ground—or "in the black"—demonstrates the degree to which, in Brian Massumi's thinking, the body is "as immediately virtual as it is actual" (*Parables* 30). Turning to one of Spinoza's definitions

---

11   Just as this article goes to press, a wave of suicides among Canadian soldiers is making news headlines and raising serious questions and concerns about the efficacy of these training methods in PTSD prevention.

of affect as an "affectation [in other words an impingement upon] the body, *and at the same time the idea of the affection*" (Massumi's emphasis), Massumi describes the virtual body as one that is in a state of "passional suspension in which it exists more outside of itself, more in the abstracted action of the impinging thing and the abstracted context of that action, than within itself" (31). The body is, here, conditioned to draw on traces of "past actions, including a trace of their contexts" that are conserved "in the brain and in the flesh but out of mind and out of body" (30). As oft-reported accounts of soldiers who, operating on autopilot without conscious thought, have no rec-ollection of the moment they drew their guns to shoot (Grossman 74), the virtual body draws on "pastnesses" of actions that open "directly onto a future, but with no present to speak of." The body's virtuality, its "pressing crowd of incipiencies and tendencies" exists in the "realm of *potential*" and it is in po-tential "where futurity combines, unmediated, with pastness" (Massumi 30).

This future-past potential of the virtual body captures the particular tem-porality of the live, immersive simulation, which is prospective in its vision and future-oriented; it positions itself as a kind of rehearsal for the future while drawing on a past repertoire of behaviours that are trained to be auto-matically "restored," to invoke Richard Schechner.[12] But as Tracy Davis points out in her discussion of "performative time," Schechner's model of restored behaviour is "serial, with repetition predicated upon a temporal order of the behaved and *then* the twice-behaved behaviour" ("Performative" 152). The temporality of the simulation and that of the virtual body is significantly more complex, operating more accurately in the modalities of performative time. According to Davis, performative time "explains the capability not just to show or describe a speculated-upon future as the real world, but also to bring that future into the present, or the past, as a claimed observable ef-fect. The future is citable and thus becomes an imperative. The present must

---

12   I am alluding here to Schechner's notion of "restored behaviour" or "twice-behaved behaviour" in *Between Theater and Anthropology*: "Restored behavior is living behavior treated as a film director treats a strip of film. These strips of behavior can be rearranged or reconstructed . . . The performers get in touch with, recover, remember, or even invent these strips of behavior and then rebehave according to these strips" (35–36).

account for it" (151). By making the possible future familiar through the rehearsals of a repertoire of tactical action in the spirit of preparedness, the immersive simulation in military training contexts harnesses what Maurice Merleau-Ponty says of the experience of time: that "all prospection is anticipatory retrospection" (414). Preparedness relies on the past—whether it be, in this case, combat trends in theatre or repertoires of tactical action—in order to form ideas about the future "by analogy," as Merleau-Ponty proposes, and to bring it into being (414). The prospective vision of preparedness in the immersive simulation is retrospective, pointing to the complicated status of the "present" not only with respect to the affective negotiations of the virtual body in Massumi's formulation, but with respect to the conditions of the simulation itself. Affect, in its "relational aspects" between bodies and its "stickiness," as Rebecca Schneider emphasizes in her discussion of historical re-enactments, challenges us to think beyond the "modern Western conventions of temporal linearity" (35), pointing instead to a "cross-temporal mobility" in which the past is never quite past and the "negotiated future" is never quite in front of us; rather, these temporal dimensions coexist in "a kind of viscous, affective surround" (37). In the "anticipatory retrospection" of the simulation's prospective vision, affect and emotion play key roles, modulated for a state of heightened readiness and preparedness that is so crucial to the performance of war.

In a sense, the performative time that undergirds the immersive simulation's forward-looking vision, which makes the future a "claimed observable effect," as Davis argues, can be seen as an embodied form of processual "premediation" that affectively prepares the participant for all possible futures. In his *Premediation: Affect and Mediality After 9/11*, Richard Grusin invokes "premediation" as the means by which "the experience of a traumatic future" is prevented in advance "by generating and maintaining a low level of anxiety as a kind of affective prophylactic" (46). Spurred by the "tremendous media shock" the US experienced witnessing the collapse of the World Trade Towers "live" and in "real time," premediation engages in a proleptic modulation of affect in order to prepare the public for future uncertainties and to mitigate the experience of *im*mediate danger and disaster (35). Unlike prediction, premediation is not about "getting the future right," but rather about imagining all possible futures, which always already exist as "not quite fully formed potentialities or possibilities," not only as "they might become but also as they have already been in the past" (8). This mode of prophylactic preparedness characterizes a shift, in Grusin's view, post-9/11:

> [P]remediation took a fundamental American form in the years following 9/11, as the United States sought to try to make sure that the American public never again experienced live a large-scale catastrophic event that had not already been premediated. In some sense the event of 9/11 can be seen to have marked an end to the technocultural desire for immediacy fueled by the dot.com and virtual reality hysteria of the nineties, and to have replaced it with a desire for a nation (or indeed a world) in which the immediacy of the catastrophe, the immediacy of disaster, could not happen again—because it would always already be premediated. (12)

Grusin points to the formal conventions of cable news networks to demonstrate how premediation operates in ways that are indistinguishable from how events will be *re*mediated in news coverage after they strike: in the coverage prior to the war in Iraq, for example, the use of maps, commentary from retired generals, split-screen debates between "experts" and pundits, video clips, etc., all participated in the conventions of premediation before the war began, "prompting an affective orientation toward the war that prepared the media public to accept it as a *fait accompli* when it actually happened" (46–47).

The immersive simulation provides an arena for the rehearsal of all possible futures in order to anaesthetize its participants from future shock, surprise, and trauma by shoring up the past and future as an arsenal against unpredictable immediacy. The proliferation of large-scale rehearsal sites in military training post-9/11 can be seen, on the one hand, as a response to the particular challenges of what military analysts identify as an asymmetric, three-block war. But when placed in the context of the shift Grusin tracks post-9/11, the

advancement of immersive simulations as a site of training and preparedness is clearly in stride with this broader cultural formation and turns on the
logic of premediation.[13] What immersive simulation training makes legible
is how this logic gets folded into bodies and bodily behaviours. The Maple
Guardian immersive training can be seen as a site that provides the conditions
for soldiers to maintain "a low level of anxiety" in order to be combat ready
and prepared for all possible, imaginable futures, analogous to the Condition
Yellow state of "alertness and readiness" (Grossman 31).

The maintenance of a low-grade anxiety and Condition Yellow points
to one of the more innocuous challenges of theatre, to which many soldiers
I interviewed alluded, and, in some senses, this mode of engagement lies
on the flip side of the virtual body's potential in the face of high-intensity,
deadly force-on-force combat. This more innocuous challenge in theatre is
the tactical maintenance of a state of Condition Yellow—alert but not overly
aroused—during long durations of engagement when there is no immediate threat but when that threat always remains a looming possibility. In
an interview, one of the COEFOR augmentees relayed that he would keep
a round yellow sticker on the face of his watch or on the dashboard of his
military vehicle as a reminder to stay alert during long convoy operations
in Afghanistan. On tour, there are vast stretches of time in which nothing is
effectively happening, but soldiers must nevertheless maintain a Condition
Yellow of 360-degree awareness. In my observations of the ten-day Maple
Guardian simulation at CFB Wainwright, I queried the extent to which the
"give-them-their-worst-day-possible" approach to training would prepare

---

13   Tracy Davis's groundbreaking book *Stages of Emergency* analyzes rehearsals for civilians in Cold War civil defence exercises, pointing to a longer genealogy of rehearsals
for war, which can be seen as various forms of premediation. Davis begins and concludes
her book with references to the continuation of the practices she examines in the context of the War on Terror. Rehearsals in the form of large-scale field exercises designed
to prepare soldiers for combat (what I call "immersive simulations" here) have a longer
genealogy dating back to the creation of war games and the enactment of "sham fights" in
the eighteenth century. For a brief history of military field exercises see Peter Harrington's
"Portraying Maneuvers and Mock Battles."

soldiers for this more innocuous challenge of sustaining alertness during long periods of inactivity.

MANAGING AFFECT WITH FICTION

If we return to the soldier who slipped into spectator mode during the MASCAL spectacle described at the outset and who failed to notice the suicide bomber's approach, a question arises as to whether the sustained exposure to a whole host of possible future threats exposes a different kind of "(un)thinking" from that of the virtual body and, in Lauren Berlant's words, "all kinds of neutralizing affect management" ("Thinking" 6). She writes:

> Under the pressure of an intensified, elongated present moment where affective, experiential and empirical knowledge norms seem in disarray there develop states of sociopathic disavowal and ordinary compartmentalization . . . Being overwhelmed by knowledge and life produces all kinds of neutralizing affect management—coasting, skimming, browsing, distraction, apathy, coolness, counter-absorption, assessments of scale, picking one's fights, and so on. (5–6)

To what extent does the large-scale spectacle of live immersive training encourage a kind of "neutralizing affect management," particularly when the "fiction" of the exercise is always already available as grounds to "check out" of the exercise and operate at one remove with a level of "coolness" and "counter-absorption," as I witnessed on many occasions, when soldiers simply did not commit to the scene, much like our dazed soldier in the moments before the suicide bomber approached. To what degree, I want to ask, does the simulation as a fictional event encourage this kind of "zoning out"? When all possible futures are premediated the result is, arguably, a levelling effect in which all possible threats are of equal scale, equal magnitude, producing, in turn, a "neutralizing affect management" of disavowal.

For some of the Afghan role-players, this recourse to the fiction is a way to contain the trauma that these scenarios continuously re-inflict. For one of the Afghan–Canadian role-players I interviewed, Afia,[14] everything from the sounds of jets overhead to the bomb blasts and body parts are daily hauntings of the scenes of bloodshed she witnessed in war-torn Afghanistan: "It automatically takes you back. As soon as I hear the sounds of the bomb or the jets going, I'm just going back home. You see the blood and body parts. It immediately takes you back. I have to say, 'No, this isn't real. It's fake.'" At one point, Afia found herself bringing the fake blood to her lips in the hopes that the taste would dispel the illusion (Afia). While for the soldier, the fiction of the scenario allows for disengagement and "checking out," for the Afghan role-player, the fiction is kept in play as a distantiating frame in order to manage a traumatogenic affective response.

For other Afghan role-players, the fiction of the scenario is a way of containing and negotiating the intercultural encounter. Sabir, a former associate dean of the faculty of fine arts at Kabul University, who now works for ACS playing the role of the village *malik* or leader, is confident that his contributions to the cultural education of soldiers are making an impact when he reflects on the significant change he observed in the comportment of a young platoon commander within a twenty-four-hour period. One of the key "cultural intelligence" training scenarios in the Maple Guardian exercise is a Key Leaders Engagement (KLE) in the form of a *shura* (from the Arabic), in which Afghan village elders meet with the platoon commander, or officer commanding, to discuss local issues in the aim of making critical decisions through deliberation and consultation. At the first KLE of the Maple Guardian exercise, Sabir was struck by the platoon commander's evident discomfort and his inability to engage with him in-role as the village *malik*. The platoon commander entered the meeting place in the town of Nakhonay where the KLE was staged and did not remove his helmet, weapon, or body armour. He did not sit with the village elders but rather kneeled, showing the sole of

---

14   I have changed the names of the Afghan role-players cited in this section in order to protect their identity.

his shoe in the process (a cultural affront), and avoided making eye contact at any point with the *malik*. Instead, the platoon commander kept his focus on the translator during the course of the conversation, one of the basic misuses of a translator and a demonstration of disrespect to the interlocutor. Rather than feeling affronted by the platoon commander's evident disrespect for local cultural practices or feeling "othered" by the platoon commander's evident discomfort and inability to look him in the eye, Sabir observed the scene from a distance, invoking the split sign of the Brechtian stage figure, separating himself from the village *malik* he was playing: "I don't think, 'Look how he's treating me as an Afghan,' I think, 'Look how he's treating this village *malik*'" (Sabir).

The platoon commander initiated the *shura* with questions about possible insurgent activity in the village and local problems that the *malik* might want ISAF forces to address. Sabir, in role, gently guided the platoon commander away from the immediately instrumentalist direction of his questions to the kinds of intercultural relations that first need to be established: "It's not about you getting the information you need," Sabir recounts, "it's about building a relationship. First we become friends, then we'll talk about local issues" (Sabir). Between Sabir's gentle prompts and the ACS field director's Village/Scenario Reports, the platoon commander returned to the KLE the next day with a notably altered mode of engagement, entering respectfully with his right hand over his chest in greeting, removing his gear, and engaging directly with the *malik*, making a point of sustaining eye contact. These subtle but significant accretions of cultural awareness, from Sabir's point of view, ultimately save lives back home, which justifies, for him, his continued participation in ACS's program.

But as the substance of the daily briefing between commanders at CMTC revealed,[15] what is prioritized in the training outcomes is the tactical, not the intercultural. It's as though an immersion into the multi-million-dollar realism

---

15   In the Commander Update Briefs I attended each day of the ten-day Maple Guardian training, the Village Scenario Reports occupied less than roughly three minutes of a thirty- to forty-five-minute meeting. The commanders never queried the reported data, unless there was a significant drop in progress.

of the environment—with its sights, sounds, and smells—and the possibility of contact with Afghan actors, does its own teaching in and of itself. The weight of the emphasis placed on the tactical reflects the widespread opinion among military personnel I interviewed that "tactical skills are what save lives," as one sergeant put it, a COEFOR operative in-role as the chief of the ANP—a point of view that diverged significantly from the number of Afghan role-players I interviewed. Afghan role-players emphasized the importance of the cultural-intelligence aspects of the exercise in light of countless incidents they had witnessed in their own villages in Afghanistan where breaches of cultural respect and affronts to the basic dignity of Afghans either led to widespread, retributive violence, or resulted in increased recruitment for the insurgency.[16]

------

16   Exactly whose lives might be saved through an emphasis on cultural intelligence training versus an emphasis on the tactical is worth addressing more fully. The invocation of "lives" by both the Canadian soldier and the Afghan role-players I reference here is intended to connote the lives of both Afghans and Canadian Forces (and ISAF more generally). Its instrumentalist use in counter-insurgency aside, supporters of the "cultural turn" in military strategy argue—in keeping with the views of the Afghan role-players I interviewed—that cultural intelligence training is a means of preventing the cultural affronts that might lead to a vicious cycle of "retributive violence" by both Afghans and ISAF forces. It is also the means by which soldiers become familiar with Afghan cultural practices before deployment, thereby reducing the violence that results from basic misunderstandings. For an overview of the benefits of cultural intelligence training for both Afghans and ISAF soldiers, see Lieutenant-Commander Sylvain Therriault and Master Warrant Officer Ron Wulf's "Cultural Awareness or If The Shoe Does Not Fit . . ." But from the point of view of many soldiers I interviewed, an emphasis on tactical skills is what allows them to engage not only in effective force-on-force combat with insurgents but, within a counter-insurgency mission, to serve as a protective force not merely for their own personnel but also for Afghans. Many soldiers view themselves as an elite fighting force insufficiently trained for the "armed social work" of counter-insurgency (or COIN), and position themselves in villages as a protective force, since providing security is one of the key tenets of COIN doctrine (as I outlined briefly earlier). But, of course, some Afghans feel that the very presence of ISAF as an occupying force has incited more violence and caused more casualties. The ideological warfare within villages (which also figures into the narrative threads at CMTC) turns on who can better offer protection for Afghans—local insurgents or ISAF forces. In short, it goes without saying that lives on both sides of the cultural "divide" are

From the point of view of the Afghans, cultural intelligence training saves lives as much as the skills required, say, to establish an effective safety cordon to secure an area. Taking a step back from these conflicting perspectives and investments at work in the simulation, I am left to contend with the polarized demands placed on its soldiers in training: conditioned in training methods designed to manage and regulate affect in response to force-on-force combat, the soldier must also maintain a sensitivity to the affective exchanges between him/herself and civilians, an instrumentalist sensitivity aimed at establishing the relations of trust necessary to "get the intelligence"—the lynchpin of an effective counter-insurgency mission.

CONCLUSION: ASYMMETRIES OF AFFECT; ASYMMETRIES OF WAR

Both the soldiers' conditioning in the standards of military repertoire and the Afghan role-players' efforts to contain the trauma of recursive memory point to the ways in which the body, in Massumi's view, "doesn't just absorb pulses or discrete stimulations; it infolds *contexts*, it infolds volitions and cognitions that are nothing if not situated" (his emphasis, *Parables* 30). In the particular context of the intercultural theatre of the live, immersive simulation, we must query the aims and consequences of affect management for the soldier who is expected to engage in that seemingly irreconcilable paradox of punitive, yet culturally sensitive, militarism. What are the consequences of scenarios designed to regulate and, in some senses, undermine affect for the modern theatres of "asymmetrical warfare" and the "three-block war"? How to reconcile the purpose of the simulation, its raison d'être of making the unfamiliar familiar and the future apprehensible with the very nature of hybrid or asymmetrical warfare, which is by definition never static or predictive but constantly evolving and shifting? And what are the potential

---

at stake in these debates concerning the "cultural turn" in military strategy. Though the number of lives it both costs and saves is, of course, radically asymmetrical.

risks of rehearsals that attempt to make unfamiliar cultural "others" familiar in scenarios governed by what Derek Gregory has called a "hermeneutics of suspicion" (15) in which an enemy indistinguishable from an innocent civilian needs to be extinguished?

"Asymmetrical" captures not only the discrepancies of power between NATO forces and the Afghan insurgency; in the questions I propose here, it also speaks to one's relations with the other in the broader context of globalization, which has produced asymmetries of power that allow NATO forces to make Afghans "familiar" in multi-million-dollar mock Afghan villages on their own terms, for the instrumentalist purposes of a counter-insurgency mission. But asymmetry also captures the dynamic of affect itself—something that takes you by surprise, something to which you are subjected and that you cannot appropriate—a dynamic that also echoes, if we follow Emmanuel Levinas, an ethical mode of engagement with "the other."[17] While affect management allows the peacewarrior to respond efficiently to the demands of the modern battlespace, it arguably stands in the way of the asymmetrical relation required for the ethical encounter, one that reverses the broader asymmetry of war and one that is so vitally necessary to the work of the always Strategic Corporal.

---

17   I refer here to the idea of asymmetry as a foundational principle of Levinas's philosophy of ethics that rejects a reciprocal relation with "the Other." The "Other" summons one, he argues, to a sense of obligation and responsibility. In his chapter "The Asymmetry of the Interpersonal" in *Totality and Infinity*, for example, Levinas maintains that "[the] Other who dominates me in his transcendence is thus the stranger, the widow, and the orphan, to whom I am obligated" (215). This asymmetrical and non-reciprocal relation with the Other is defined as a state of being *for* the other and one that is held responsible for this other: "Subjectivity," he writes in *Otherwise Than Being*, "is being hostage"—it is an act of radical subjection to the other (127).

FEELING IN PUBLIC: BLACKFACE AS THEATRE OF ACTION IN CONTEMPORARY QUEBEC

SUNITA NIGAM

It is more likely that the "who," which appears so clearly and unmistakably to others, remains hidden from the person himself, like the *daimon* in Greek religion which accompanies each man throughout his life, always looking over his shoulder from behind and thus visible to only those he encounters.

—Hannah Arendt, *The Human Condition*

When Mario Jean, the host of Quebec's 2013 annual comedy awards show, appeared in blackface as an imitation of the well-known Senegalese Québécois comedian Boucar Diouf, he was not in command of his own disclosure. In the previously filmed musical opening of *Le Gala Les Olivier*, Jean sings about "*la grande famille de l'humour*" [the large comedy family], which is the theme of the show. During the song, Jean impersonates a succession of Québécois comedians, all of whom are white men, including André Sauvé and François Massicotte, until he finally appears wearing black face paint, short dreadlocks, and a flashily coloured shirt, reciting Diouf's catchphrase, "*Comme mon grand-père disait toujours, nous sommes tous partie d'la famille de l'humour*" [As my grandfather always said, we are all part of the comedy family]. This impersonation is the climax of the filmed opening sequence, after which Jean and his "wife," both of whom are white, enter the stage along with a procession of children, one of whom is a black boy, and two others who are people of colour.

The use of black face paint in this major media event unleashed a series of frustrated and shocked responses, many from black Québécois and
people of colour in the rest of Canada, on Twitter and Facebook, as well as
in *The Huffington Post* and several Montreal newspapers. The intensity of the
response had not to do with the event's singularity, but rather with the fact
that it was only the latest episode in a spate of performances of blackface in
Quebec over the past three years, many of which have been heavily mediatized
and denounced.[1] Five days after the awards show, Nydia Dauphin wrote an
article in *The Huffington Post* entitled "Why the Hell Are Quebec Comedians
Wearing Blackface?" Judith Lussier of the Montreal newspaper *Métro* quickly
fired back with a piece called "Les Québécois, tous des racistes," in which she
claimed never to have heard of blackface, and charged Dauphin with "Quebec-
bashing." The next few weeks were animated by an increasingly gridlocked
and hostile bilingual debate about blackface in Quebec so intense it has been
called a "media war" (Mercier Voyer). One side insisted on the violent history
of this popular performance form and shared feelings of anger about what
its use in contemporary Quebec says about its regard for black history and
Quebec's black citizens. The other side emphasized Jean's impersonation of
Diouf as a gesture of inclusion and insisted on the history of blackface and that
of racialized slavery to which it is connected as "American" phenomena (that

---

1 In his introduction to *Burnt Cork: Traditions and Legacies of Blackface Minstrelsy* (2012),
Stephen Johnson notes a contemporary resurgence of blackface, providing numerous examples from the United States and, to a lesser extent, Canada. The spate of blackface in
Quebec is then itself part of a transnational phenomenon. But Johnson asks the compelling question, "Did 'blackface' ever go away?" (2). Even though he agrees that blackface
"seemed largely to disappear from television, film, and other popular mass media from
at least the 1960s" (ibid), Johnson argues that "the blackface minstrel tradition has never
left us, not since the early nineteenth century" (ibid). As the essays in Johnson's collection
show, blackface briefly took on different forms that were not mass-mediatized and were
therefore less visible. Johnson contends that the Internet and YouTube have, however, increased availability of recordings of and information about instances of blackface. This
new digital mediascape has led to what seems like a resurgence of blackface.

is, ones anchored in the United States), not Quebec ones.[2] As Stephen Johnson notes in the introduction to the essay collection *Burnt Cork: Traditions and Legacies of Blackface Minstrelsy*, "[T]he intentions of blackface performance have always been flexible and its reception widely divergent" (4). The polarized reactions to Jean's act in Quebec are part of a much larger history of the performance and reception of blackface and blackface minstrelsy.

This essay offers an account of the embattled situation that arose out of *Le Gala Les Olivier* by bringing the heterogeneous and emotionally charged responses to the blackface incident into dialogue with Hannah Arendt's account of action and with local histories of blackface performance and national identity in Quebec. In her 1958 book *The Human Condition*, Arendt proposes that action (by which she means political action) is a form of public appearance that inevitably reveals more than is intended and that exceeds the individual actor. I suggest that Arendt's theories of action and publicity offer a compelling mode for reading the disclosure and circulation of feelings in public first as differentially risky, and second as disclosures of a tacit national affect. By positioning some of Quebec historiography's organizing tropes in relation to black histories, I reveal the stage upon which certain forms of "feeling-actions"—I mean by this the public disclosure of an agent that reveals a certain affective tendency or rhythm—have been made more- or less-easily possible, and more or less risky, within Québécois popular culture and politics. In the discussions that transpired after the comedy gala, certain

---

2   The idea that blackface is an American phenomenon, and not a Quebec one, is untrue. Blackface came from Europe (France and, less directly, England and Ireland, are here particularly important when considering the case of Quebec and Québécois theatre history), and the performance of blackface minstrelsy, though invented in the United States, was also exported back to Europe (see Rae Beth Gordon's *Dances with Darwin, 1875–1910: Vernacular Modernity in France* for examples of the use of blackface in French theatre) and various countries in Africa and Asia, where blackface minstrelsy developed in more local ways. For a brief general history of the routes of blackface (and scholarship on these routes), see Harvey Young's section on blackface in *Theatre & Race*. As the healthy body of scholarship on blackface shows, blackface is part of global performance practice, and elicits such strong reactions because it remains embedded in different ways in all of our cultures.

emotional disclosures were implicitly coded as national while others were coded as non-national or otherwise excessive and unassimilable.

APPEARANCE, ACTION, FEELING

For Hannah Arendt, action is the freedom to begin something new. "To act," Arendt writes, "in its most general sense, means to take initiative, to begin" (177). In Arendt's account, action is about the appearance of the actor to others within the public sphere. The public sphere is in turn a sort of commons of appearance, where individuals gather to become public, to debate, to act.[3] Nancy Fraser notes, Arendt is often understood as the "avatar of a performative, agonistic public space" (167). Indeed, for Arendt, the public sphere figures as a sort of political theatre, in which the structure of action is one of performer-spectators.[4]

Quite discernibly, the performance of Mario Jean at the comedy gala (which was televised by Radio-Canada, Quebec's version of the CBC, and which had over one million viewers upon its live airing) and the public and personal media scandal it catalyzed came to constitute this sort of performative and agonistic commons of appearance, involving multiple actors and

---

3   Rather than thinking of appearance (or disclosure) as a metaphysics of presence, in which an action somehow delivers an author without mediation, I suggest it is more useful to think of appearance as the evidence or trace of an actor.

4   Arendt's theory of action depends upon a gendered separation between the public, male sphere in which political action is possible and the private, female sphere in which individuals engage in repetitive forms of labour necessary to meet biological necessities. My focus on action within a public sphere in Quebec might seem to reify this separation; however, because so much of what is debated about within the public sphere has to do with the organization of conditions of labour (in the Arendtian sense), and because acting within a public sphere is only possible if one's biological needs have already been met, this separation seems to be a false one. What is more, because the specific ways in which the labour of survival is carried out can involve all sorts of public appearances and alliances full of promise and risk, what Arendt calls labour must also be understood as a space of action.

spectators. Jean's performance created what I call a "theatre of action," a series of meaningful if painful exchanges about a public matter of concern in which actors appear. Importantly, Arendtian action cannot be reduced to the intention of individual actors. While the actor, for Arendt, remains accountable for initiating the action, action "can almost never be achieved as a wilful purpose" (179). The actor is not the author of the action:

> Although everybody started his life story by inserting himself into the human world through action and speech, nobody is the author or producer of his own life story. In other words, the stories, the results of action and speech, reveal an agent, but the agent is not an author or producer. Somebody began it and is its subject in the twofold sense of the word, namely its actor and sufferer, but nobody is the author. (184)[5]

In relieving the action's agent of sole production of the action, Arendt proposes a shared authorship of and responsibility for the action, or a form of distributed agency. The action—in this case, that of blacking up on television—emerges out of the enabling constraints of a particular context involving a network of actors and spectators. Arendt's theory of action, then, helps to unlock the contemporary theatre of action considered in this chapter by relieving it from one term that was particularly important in the popular debate: intention.

---

5   Some readers may have noticed that this seems uncannily like an early version of Roland Barthes's 1968 essay "La mort de l'auteur" ["The Death of the Author"] in which he seeks to detach readerly practice from appeals to authorial intention and biography. For Barthes, texts derive their meaning from their existence within historically contingent semiotic systems. Judith Butler's concept of performativity also situates speech and gestures within semiotic systems, in which iterated performances construct a sense of the world at the same time as they are dependent on their social contexts for meaning. As Butler writes in *Excitable Speech*: "The one who acts (who is not the same as the sovereign subject) acts precisely to the extent that he or she is constituted as an actor and, hence, operating within a linguistic field of enabling constraints from the outset" (15–16). What Arendt had proposed in 1952 was that political action itself has no true author; it also depends on synchronic as well as diachronic semiotic systems for meaning.

Arendt proposes that the meaning of the action is itself distributed amongst the actor and the members of the public—actor and spectators. As Paul Yachnin reminds us in his reading of responses to the play within *Hamlet* in "Performing Publicity," spectators will judge actions in ways conditioned by heterogeneous histories. Indeed, "their responses to theatrical influence are conditioned by their individual history and identity, so that their reactions are to some degree self-disclosing" (207). People's responses to Mario Jean's action (already understood in Arendtian terms as more than simply "his") are likewise keyed to history and identity and so disclose more than an individual. The meaning of an action in Arendt's account is also distributed temporally. Spectators contribute to the meaning of these actions by interpreting them, remembering them, and re-narrating them within the public sphere over time. Actions, then, both on the part of actors and spectators, disclose a broader terrain of social negotiation and judgment. Moreover, because one can never predict how exactly one will be disclosed to others when one acts, action is all about risk.[6] It requires the courage and will to take a gamble, to give oneself over to a jury of spectators. Apparently unbeknownst to Mario Jean himself, his appearance in black face paint at the 2013 comedy gala was a form of risky public disclosure—not only of the composite "actor/agent" but also of the varied spectators to his appearance. He did not appear alone. Because it reveals the social network in which actions take place and through which they come to mean, Arendt's concept of action serves as a useful tool for unpacking the fiery debates and rampant feelings that so often surround irruptions of blackface in public spheres around the world. The example of the most recent scandal of blackface in contemporary Quebec shows how dramatically local

---

6   For all of Arendt's attention to action as risky, her work does not offer a satisfactory account of the unequal distribution of risk, or, for that matter, free speech according to the different material conditions from which one acts. In "Bodies in Alliance and the Politics of the Street," Judith Butler revises Arendt, considering the role that the body and other material conditions play in the space of appearance: "action is always supported, and [is] invariably bodily, even in its virtual forms. The material supports for action are not only part of action, but they are also what is being fought about, especially in those cases when the political struggle is about food, employment, mobility, and access to institutions."

culture informs—though does not wholly determine—the feelings, meanings, and judgments attached to blackface. To read blackface in terms of Arendtian action is to say that the authorship of blackface is distributed.

If the example of Mario Jean's blacking up is clearly a public action, feeling may be less immediately grasped as a form of action and publicity. Much in line with Jürgen Habermas's later definition of the public sphere as a sphere of "rational-critical debate," Arendt does not herself work directly with concepts of affect, feeling, or emotion. But what explains the conversion of certain actions, and not others, into public focal points if not the ways in which those actions function, for certain historically specific reasons, as lightning rods for affective intensities? The actions that surface into lively discussion, incentivizing further actions in the public sphere, are what might be described, to use Sara Ahmed's language of the stickiness of emotions, as "sticky performances," which interpellate subjects via the transference of affective intensity.[7] Jean's impersonation of Diouf, like so many formulations of blackface, was one such sticky performance. So, too, were many of the media responses to it. Take, for instance, the op-ed piece that set the media ball rolling and became a sticky performance: Nydia Dauphin's "Why the Hell Are Quebec Comedians Wearing Blackface?" published five days after the comedy gala on 16 May 2013. Dauphin opens her article:

> Quebec comedians have a strange affliction. It sporadically resurfaces time and again and it's proven almost impossible to cure. No one really understands where the resistance to its cure (that being education) comes from. Some have come to suspect that it is self-inflicted; that somehow, they do not want to be cured, that they enjoy wafting in the stench of their ignorance.
>
> The affliction in question is the Quebec comedy scene's sick obsession with blackface. Last Sunday it exposed itself yet again.

---

7   For a nuanced analysis of the stickiness of emotions, histories, bodies, and objects, see Ahmed's chapter on fear in a post-9/11 age in *The Cultural Politics of Emotion* (62–81).

Dauphin uses the language of psychoanalysis (ignorance about one's repressed fixations, the resurfacing of perverse repressions, the possibility of a form of talking cure—education), to diagnose Quebec comedians with what essentially amounts to a blackface fetish. Dauphin's provocative languages and rhetorical strategies are inflected by the fact that Jean's performance resonates with a recent spate of blackface in Quebec enumerated in Dauphin's post, the most famous action of which involved a group of over twenty École des Hautes Études commerciales de Montréal (HEC) students during frosh week in 2011.[8] Dauphin argues that, considering the history of blackface as a derogatory form, it is entirely unacceptable to see it used on a publicly funded television show. Finally, the piece becomes autobiographical as Dauphin shares her frustrations and exhaustions with being a black Québécoise raised in Montreal, including employment inequity for people of colour, scant education about black history in Quebec high schools, racial profiling, and seeing the topic of racism in Quebec become taboo to such an extent that "very little space is allotted for people other than francophone Quebecers to denounce discrimination." Part of the information communicated by Dauphin's cultural diagnosis is mood. Although

---

8   The students paraded around the city dressed in blackface and body paint as well as clothing representing Jamaica's yellow and green flag. They held stuffed monkeys and chanted "Ya mon" and "Smoke more weed." Participants later claimed it was intended as a tribute to Jamaican athlete Usain Bolt. Although black McGill law student Anthony Morgan, who had encountered and filmed the spectacle, had approached the Quebec media and the HEC with the information first, it was only after he uploaded the video to YouTube and the story was picked up by *The Montreal Gazette* and then CNN, thereby gaining a transnational public, that the Quebec media covered the story and HEC administrators issued an official apology for the students' stunt. Another public debate about blackface arose directly out of the comedy scene during the 2008 edition of Quebec's annual New Year's Eve show, *Bye Bye*, in which an actor appeared in blackface as an imitation of Barack Obama. In one of the skits, jokes were made about how it would be easier to aim for and shoot a black man in the White House. Radio-Canada received several complaints about the skit being racist. Though the producers of the show, Véronique Cloutier and Louis Morissette, issued an official apology at a press conference at the Hyatt Regency Hotel on 9 January 2009 for their lampoon of Barack Obama (see B. Kelly), *Bye Bye* continues to use black face paint to impersonate black people.

her response—and indeed, those angry, mocking, or vitriolic reactions to her diagnosis of the blackface situation in Quebec—involved a certain amount of rational-critical debate, its force derives from the ways in which it disclosed or registered more visceral reactions. I'd like to submit the public reactions to Jean's performance as "feeling-actions." By this I mean public disclosures of an actor that cannot be reduced to a rational-critical argument (what actions ever can entirely?) and that also reveal a certain affective tendency or rhythm, even as this tendency or rhythm is mediated by language. This insistence on feeling as a mode of action has something in common with J.L. Austin's positing of language as a type of doing. *How to Do Things with Words* becomes how to do things with feelings, or, more precisely, how to do things with feeling-words. Feeling-actions are especially sticky due to their nodal intensity within a historically contingent public economy of feeling. For Dauphin, like Jean, did not appear alone. She was joined by a series of commentators on the blackface action whose disclosures revealed other aspects of that public economy of feeling.

The first of these was penned by Judith Lussier in *Métro*, where she criticizes Dauphin for accusing all Quebecers of being backwards and argues that Dauphin is "Quebec-bashing." Lussier's piece became famous, in the remainder of the debate, for beginning with the statement, "I had never heard of blackface before stumbling upon this post appearing in *Huffington Post Canada*." She continues, "[A]fter doing a little research, I gathered that it was, in general, a stereotypical caricature of a black person. A phenomenon that has its roots in the segregationist history of the United States and that has almost no resonance in Quebec." For Lussier, blackface is a bad thing, but it is an "American" thing, and Jean's appearance in black face paint at the comedy gala was not blackface, which has "almost no resonance" in Quebec as a cultural form. This narrative, in almost the exact same structure (minus confessions of never having heard of blackface), was repeated by commentators from the (white) francophone press for the rest of the week-long debate, including Patrick Lagacé (*La Presse*), Lise Ravary (*Le Journal de Montréal*), and Sophie Durocher (*Le Journal de Montréal*). The consensus amongst every public commentator from the white francophone press was that Mario Jean's performance was *not* blackface. It did not present a generalized stereotypical image of black people; it was an imitation of the well-loved black comedian Boucar Diouf. And it was intended as a gesture of inclusion, not mockery.[9] In her work on the popular reception of representations of race amongst different groups in Quebec (white francophone Montreal publics on the one hand, and both racialized and white anglophone Montreal publics on the other), Karen Fricker has argued that "the gap between these reactions demonstrates a lack of comprehension and common discourse between Quebec's different communities regarding the appropriate ways to represent the other in a cultural context" (84–85). The Mario Jean incident is another example of the lack of what Fricker calls "a common discourse" about representations of race in Quebec.[10] This lack of common discourse amongst different interpretive communities generates what Dominic Hardy, writing about graphic satire in Quebec, calls an "ironic force . . . in which the national is nearly always engaged by positing one or the other of these two dominant reading communities [the francophone and the anglophone] as its principal 'audience,' while the second is tacitly acknowledged" (21). The double nation-making address requires a secondary reading community—and, I would add, feeling community—that is coded as non-national even as a national interpretive community is being primarily addressed.

BLACKFACE QUEBEC

The conflicting readings of Jean's performance reveal how drastically different judgments of blackface can be produced by individuals conditioned by divergent histories. This leads us to consider the slippery question of what

---

9   The idea that blackface and integration are sometimes (complicated) allies rather than foes has been explored by Eric Lott, as well as by W.T. Lhamon Jr. in "Turning around Jim Crow," in which Lhamon shows that Jim Crow was initially an integrationist and abolitionist figure.

10   More recently, disparities amongst these same groups in reaction to Quebec's controversial ban on religious clothing (except for Christian crosses) in hospitals, schools, and courthouses suggest a social outlook that extends beyond issues of representation in cultural productions.

exactly blackface is at all. What are its contexts and trajectories for meaning in Quebec? And does "intention" matter as much as many of the commentators on the Jean incident believe? As may be familiar to many of the readers here, blackface, also known as "blacking up," names the application of black makeup (sometimes in a mix of different shades or in combination with red lips) to the faces of performers. Blackface was historically used in the portrayal of black characters on stage. Some scholars trace the roots of blackface back to English masques in the sixteenth century, while others contend that it originated in the sixteenth-century Italian theatrical form *commedia dell'arte*. But scholars generally agree that blackface came from Europe, where it was practised in many different nations, before becoming foundational to the American performance genre of blackface minstrelsy (see Young 37). Blackface minstrelsy is one particular use of blackface, which originated in American circuses and became a hugely profitable entertainment business, eventually becoming part of vaudeville shows. It was the most popular performance form of the nineteenth century. Blackface minstrels were initially white men (and sometimes women), but there were also black blackface performers. Aside from following a specific structure, including the use of song and dance as well as the performance of a stump speech (an early comic monologue form), blackface minstrelsy relied heavily on the clownish performance of "black gestural charisma" (Lhamon 19) as well as on the supposed channelling of authentic blackness and southern plantation slave culture, paradoxically through the use of artificially black face paint and "exaggerated gestures, malapropisms, derogatory accents, and cartoonish dress [including curly wigs]" (Cole, "American" 233). Ralph Ellison famously observed that blackface was foundational to America's national iconography ("Change the Joke and Slip the Yoke"), while David Roediger has argued that blackface performances were a critical cultural form for the emergence of a white working-class consciousness in the United States between 1800 and 1865.

However, if blackface minstrelsy began as the first truly American performance form, it was also exported back to Europe, and various countries in Africa; Asia; and North, Central, and South America, where blackface or blackface minstrelsy developed in more indigenous ways. This signals what

Harvey Young calls the "global history of blackface minstrelsy" (47). And indeed, scholars working on blackface have done a great deal to unfasten blackface from its exclusive location within American national iconography, opening it up for consideration as a transnational sign.[11] For example, Catherine Cole's work on performances of blackface in Ghana demonstrates that it is not generally viewed as racist there but rather as part of a clowning tradition. Bobby Vaughn and Ben Vinson's article on the black Mexican comic-book character, Memín Penguin, also exemplifies "a careful and precise excavation of local meanings," which "hold[s] in abeyance the politically overdetermined, Americocentric baggage of blackface" (Cole and Davis 226). A similarly careful and precise excavation of local meanings is called for in the Mario Jean case.

Blackface minstrelsy was also popular in Canada, including in Quebec and Montreal, the latter of which was a lively hub of burlesque, vaudeville, and minstrel performances from the late-nineteenth century into the early twentieth century. In fact, in this era, the venues of and touring routes between Montreal and cities in the United States, including New York, Philadelphia, and Baltimore, were controlled by a trust of theatrical managers and booking agents called the Theatrical Syndicate. This means that these cities saw

---

11   The 2008 issue of *E-misférica*, *Race and Its Others*, reflects on performances of racial impersonation as constitutive of racial formations in the Americas. The issue as a whole—which includes essays on the use of blackface as an anticolonial practice in Cuba that nevertheless secured racial hierarchies and on blackface's complicated use by white supporters of the Afro-Peruvian revival—gives a strong sense of the complexly international yet local histories of blackface and sibling genres of racial impersonation (Lane and Godoy-Anativia). The essays in the issue join the work of scholars such as Eric Lott, Catherine Cole, Jill Lane, David Roediger, and Michael Rogin, to name only a few, who have helped to produce a sizable body of work on the incredibly complicated ways in which blackface has functioned in dually positive and negative manners in different contexts at different moments around the globe. For example, in the United States context, Eric Lott has shown that blackface was not always or only a mockery of black bodies but could also function as the performance of nostalgia for a simpler, less alienated, pre-industrial moment associated with black bodies, or instead the performance of racial desire or sympathy for black slaves (see *Love and Theft*).

the same shows, forming a transurban as well as transnational public.[12] In Montreal in the late-nineteenth and early twentieth centuries, minstrel performances could be taken in at the Theatre Royal (Yorston, "Memories" 27), Canada's first permanent theatre, or instead at Nordheimer Hall or Mechanics' Hall, the latter of which drew in large crowds when featuring the New York Minstrel Troupe, the Christy Minstrels, or the Toronto minstrel Cool Burgess (Graham 295). In the 1930s Montrealers could also listen to minstrel shows made for radio on the local station CKAC, where a minstrel program might have been sandwiched, for example, between the Friday evening anglophone feature and the francophone educational program *L'Heure provincial* (Yorston, "Radio"). If they tuned into New York's WEAF, Montrealers might have heard the famous radio sitcom *Amos 'n' Andy*, whose two white creators, Freeman Gosden and Charles Correll, impersonated the voices of black Harlemites. Blackface minstrelsy, and the ideas and feelings about race that it negotiated, was indeed very much a part of cultural life in Quebec in this period. In "Historical Ironies of Henri Julien (1852–1908): Researching Identity and Graphic Satire Across Languages in Québec," Dominic Hardy examines the marriage of political caricatures and the theatre in an 1899 series by French Canadian artist and cartoonist Henri Julien.[13] The series, called "The Songs of the By-Town Coons," which appeared biweekly between January and April in the conservative newspaper *The Montreal Daily Star* (10), depicted Canada's first French Canadian prime minister Wilfrid Laurier and his cabinet as members of a blackface minstrel troupe dancing and playing music as a satire of Liberal policies. Hardy argues that Julien found ways of using representational codes as a manner of creating an alliance between the denigration of blacks and that of French Canadians by English Canada, thereby "articulat[ing] a resistance" (10) to his commission from anglophone-run *The Montreal Daily*

---

12   While much of the history of blacking up in Quebec in this era remains to be written, one of the first images (from the Bibliothèque et Archives nationales du Québec) in Chantal Hébert's important book on burlesque in Quebec is a picture of performer Paddy Shaw, who went by the stage name Swifty in blackface (*Le burlesque au Québec* 23).

13   Henri Julien is the namesake of a street on Montreal's Plateau-Mont-Royal.

Star. Even as Hardy is attentive to the particular role blackface minstrelsy played in the negotiation of French Canadian racial identity at the end of the nineteenth century, he maintains that "the By-Town Coons belong firmly in discussions of the representations of blackness and accounts of minstrelsy in North America and Europe" (22). Indeed, Hardy reads representations of blackface in Quebec as "an important staging ground for the international movement of style and ideas" (22). While it is generally agreed that the wearing of blackface is a "seizure and possession of the black body for the other's use and enjoyment" (Hartman 32), the case of Quebec, where the historic English-French divide as well as the history of French Canadian oppression and racial ambiguity triangulates black and white binaries,[14] offers a unique and as yet uncharted context for considering the transnational performances and permutations of the form.

Instances of blackface in Quebec occur in the midst of a cultural traffic jam between mostly anglophone black history in North America and French Canadian history. In large part because of the civil-rights movement, during which black people became more powerful actors in the public sphere, blackface mostly disappeared from American and Canadian mass media by the 1960s. But the 1960s in Quebec looked quite different. It is not that Quebec did not have its own history of racialized slavery of both Indigenous groups and black people (see Marcel Trudel and Micheline D'Allaire; Frank Mackey; and Brett Rushforth) or racist cultural forms—it clearly did. But if the 1960s and 1970s in Quebec saw a collectivization of its black communities, especially in Montreal, at both the level of politics and cultural productions,[15] these communities did not compare in numbers to those in the United States,

---

14   And where the contemporary political climate is marked by a push toward religious and racial secularization and assimilation.

15   These include the 1968 Congress of Black Writers at McGill University; the explosive black protest that took place at Concordia (then Sir George Williams University) in 1969; the creation of the Black Theatre Workshop in 1970; and the Negro Community Centre, which was founded in 1928 but was an important resource for black community in the 1960s. Also, see David Austin's *Fear of a Black Nation*, which excavates a fleeting moment in the late sixties when Montreal became a hotbed for Black Power and the Caribbean left.

and so did not ultimately collectivize with the same force and publicity with which they were able to do across the border to the south. The language divide in Quebec and the fact that, at this point, most black Montrealers spoke mostly or exclusively English (predominantly because a large percentage of them were relatively recent immigrants from the Caribbean), also jammed traffic between black imperatives and French Canadian concerns. It was of course the latter of the two socially, economically, and racially[16] oppressed communities (whose salaries in Montreal were, at that point, about two-thirds of those of English Canadians), that *did* enjoy great enough numbers to properly collectivize and transform the social and political landscape of 1960s Quebec. Through civic politics, journalism, and artistic creations, they were able to invest the public sphere with a strong sense of cultural memory and history that Quebec's French Canadians—now called Québécois—could claim as their own.

One could argue that it was beginning in the 1960s and through the Quiet Revolution that French Canadians became white themselves. If, for Irish and Jewish immigrants to the United States (see Roediger) as well as the Irish in relation to the English in Europe,[17] "becoming white" was a complex political and symbolic process, this was also the case for French Canadians, who were still told by Anglo Canadians in the 1960s to "speak white."[18] José Esteban Muñoz has made the case that national affect in the United States forms the basis of standard models of citizenship.[19] In "Feeling Brown: Ethnicity and

---

16   Austin thoughtfully explores the relationship between a colonized, racialized Quebec in the 1960s and metaphors of blackness.

17   The nineteenth-century English writer Charles Kingsley wrote in a travelogue documenting his visit to Ireland, "I am haunted by the human chimpanzees I saw along that hundred miles of horrible country . . . . But to see white chimpanzees is dreadful; if they were black, one would not feel it so much, but their skins, except where tanned by exposure are as white as ours" (qtd. in Loomba 109).

18   This history is remembered in Quebec writer Michèle Lalonde's famous 1968 poem "Speak White."

19   See also Lauren Berlant's trilogy on national sentimentality and citizenship in the United States: *The Anatomy of National Fantasy: Hawthorne, Utopia, and Everyday Life*;

Affect in Ricardo Bracho's *The Sweetest Hangover (and Other STDs)*," Muñoz argues that, similarly to a nation's official language laws, there are unofficial but just as powerful laws of national affect (68). This national affect in the United States, which is racially coded as white, "reads most ethnic affect as inappropriate" (69). In relation to English Canadian affect, French Canadian affect was likewise coded as excessive and unassimilable often in racial terms. In part due to this French Canadian racialization, French Canadian activists, including the writers of *Parti Pris*[20] found special inspiration for the Quebec independence movement in the anticolonial writings of Frantz Fanon and Jean-Paul Sartre as well as in the civil-rights movement and *Négritude*.[21] The most famous example of the comparison between the Québécois liberation movement and black liberation movements is Pierre Vallières's controversial

---

The Female Complaint: The Unfinished Business of Sentimentality in American Culture; and *The Queen of America Goes To Washington City: Essays on Sex and Citizenship*.

20   A 1960s socialist—and specifically anticolonialist—journal, *Parti Pris* was one of the key early texts for the production of cultural memory and national identity in Quebec. The journal was started by a group of graduate students from UQAM, and contributors sought to emphasize Quebec's national self-fashioning and quest for independence from Anglo Canadian and Anglo American hegemony as situated within an international conjuncture of decolonization struggles. In a 1967 article, Gilles Bourque writes of similarities between black American identity and Quebec identity: "Les Noirs américains ont ceci en commun avec les Québécois qu'ils sont des colonisés de l'intérieur. Ils héritent donc la tâche commune au sein du même monstre, celle d'amener son pourrissement en agissant en son cœur même." [Black Americans and Québécois share this in common: they are colonized from the inside. They thus inherit the common burden from within the same monster, to bring about its destruction by striking it at its heart.] (10).

21   As Québécois writer Jacques Godbout wrote in a piece on Quebec's historical memory in *L'Actualité* in 1999, in the 1960s in Quebec, "[T]ous les soirs, au petit écran, défilaient les images du mouvement des droits civils des Noirs, réprimé par la police du sud des Etats-Unis, les combats de liberation du Viêt Nam, les assassinats en Irlande, les bombes de l'OAS, Che Guevara en Bolivie, l'Algérie ensanglantée" [Each night, on the small screen, a stream of images of the civil-rights movement disciplined by the police in the southern US, the liberation struggles of Vietnam, the assassinations in Ireland, the bombs of the OAS, Che Guevara in Bolivia, Algeria steeped in blood]. Certain *engagés* writers in Quebec saw in these struggles and movements an analogy for those of French Canada.

1968 book *Les nègres blancs d'Amérique* (*The White Niggers of America*), which
positions French Canadians as North America's "white niggers" because of
their disadvantaged socio-economic position and the racism directed at them
by Anglo Canadians.[22] But as David Austin points out, black nationalism in
1960s Montreal was ultimately perceived as competing with both Canadian
and Québécois nationalisms. The failure of Quebec history and cultural memory to imagine itself in relation to local black history (without converting it
into analogy) as early as the 1960s begins to explain the current lack of signifi-
cation of blackface as part of francophone Quebec's iconographic reservoir.

This short history of the very complicated dynamics of blackness in
Quebec helps to show, on the one hand, that a performance of blackface will
enact different political and cultural work in Quebec than it will elsewhere
in the world. It illuminates how *Québécité* (Quebecness) might be disclosed
precisely through the performance of blackface even as this performance is
a potentially injurious act of imitation. This history of blackness in Quebec
also demonstrates how, even within Quebec, spectators sensitive to and conditioned by different histories might feel differently about such a performance,
and therefore judge it in heterogeneous manners. Some Québécois will partake
in a cultural memory that is transnational or diasporic rather than limited
to the national territory. Paul Gilroy's groundbreaking concept of the black
Atlantic, a time-space of black diasporic cultural formulation as opposed
to strictly national cultural formulation, is particularly resonant here. So,
too, is the work of black Canadian writers such as Dionne Brand (*Rivers
Have Sources, Trees Have Roots*; *Bread Out of Stone*; *A Map to the Door of
No Return*), M. NourbeSe Philip (*Zong!*), George Elliott Clarke (*Fire on the
Water*; *Odysseys Home*; *Directions Home*), and Wayde Compton (*Performance
Bond*; *After Canaan*), whose writing has done so much to chart the local as
well as diasporic histories of black Canada. As David Austin, writing of the

---

22   The metaphor became somewhat contagious within the public sphere in Quebec,
being taken up by many writers for *Parti Pris*, but also spreading into a broader collective
imagination. Indeed, in the online comment sections under YouTube clips of Jean's use
of blackface as well as under articles and op-eds on the incident, Quebec's status as *Les
nègres blancs d'Amérique* was once again invoked.

importance of black diasporic memory, reminds us, "[T]he struggle between the state and Black popular narratives, identities, and experiences was local, international, and transnational, with repercussions not just in Canada but in the United States, Britain, and the Caribbean" (28).

This deterritorialized and transnational history of black peoples and black oppression contrasts importantly with the territorializing impetuses of French Canadian historical narratives. Indeed, Quebec historiography and national identity has relied heavily on tropes of territorialization, specifically *le terroir*. *Le roman du terroir*, or the country novel, was an important part of the French Canadian literary tradition from the mid-nineteenth century until the advent of the *roman urbain*, the urban novel, with Gabrielle Roy's *Bonheur d'occasion* in 1945. Louis Hémon's *Maria Chapdelaine* (1913) is one of the most iconic examples of the *roman du terroir*, a genre which promoted four primary values, namely the land, the family, the language, and religion.[23] However, the history of deterritorialization articulated in black Canadian writing is also accompanied by a reterritorializing impulse. The work of Clarke (*Fire on the Water* and his ongoing work on Africadia) and Compton (*Bluesprint*) especially territorializes blackness in regional geographies, on Canada's east and west coast respectively, from which it has been absented. In fact, the claims that blackface is an "American phenomenon" that has nothing to do with Quebec is an excellent example of the erasure of blackness, or rather a relation to blackness from a regional history. The reterritorialization of blackness in a region or nation, like the territorialization of French Canadian history in Quebec, far from fixing cultural memory to place, unsettles the fixity of this relationship. Because one never knows what absented histories might at some future date return, or what new forms of territorialization the future might bring, the national present (and presence) is unsettled, suspended between what might have been and what might be. The nation is provisional. While there has been a strong drive to root cultural memory in Quebec in national territory, the very necessity of this endeavour, as well as the diasporic nature

---

23   For a longer description of this tradition see Réjean Beaudoin's *Le roman québécois* and Antoine Sirois's *Mythes et symboles dans la littérature québécoise.*

and reterritorializing work of black Canadian writing, means that many of Quebec's spectators either already partake in, or might partake in at some point in the future, a cultural memory and history that cannot be limited to the territory or nation of Quebec.

The comedian who was the subject of Jean's contested imitation, Boucar Diouf, is a case in point of a cultural memory that exceeds Quebec. The francophone Diouf wrote a response in *La Presse* and was later interviewed about the incident on the television show *125, Marie-Anne*. In his article, Diouf ridicules those who would be offended by Jean's performance, calling them "constipated in relation to intercultural joking." In the later interview, Diouf is visibly and vocally torn up. He speaks slowly and sadly—entirely unlike his usual, happy, bubbly self. He had received a huge backlash (including death threats) from members of the black community in Quebec. Diouf tells the show's host that he was pressured by l'Association des professionnels de l'industrie de l'humour (APIH) as well as by *La Presse* to take a side regarding Jean's performance following the publication of Dauphin's piece, despite his own desire not to take sides. He didn't want to suggest in any way that there wasn't racism in Quebec. Clearly he was upset at having given this impression. "Racism is the most shared thing in the world," Diouf says. As for many others in Quebec, the relationship between blackface and racism was not an obvious one for Diouf. He explains that, coming from a black francophone, Senegalese culture, blackface was not a familiar form to him, but he now understands that for other members of Quebec's black community it opens painful wounds. The fact that Diouf did not foresee the reaction his response garnered from so many members of Quebec's black community speaks to the possibility that in a lifetime shared between Senegal and Quebec, one might not have experienced the minstrel form of blackface.

Diouf's interview is saddening to watch, and one of its most potent effects is to show heterogeneous reading practices for the complicated sign of blackface across various black communities. Jean's public disclosures of feeling return us to the questions of what feelings and whose feelings get legitimated within the public sphere and what types of patterns these repeated acts of legitimation and delegitimation create over time. For, when evaluating Jean's performance in blackface, the question is not—and cannot be in an Arendtian account—"Who has the accurate reading of the performance?" The question instead is, "Which readings will society choose to collectively care about?" And "What are the stakes, and who the beneficiaries, of these choices?"

FEELING-ACTIONS AND NATIONAL AFFECT

Muñoz's understanding of national affect must also be understood in the context of affective legitimation in the contemporary blackface scandal. Muñoz ultimately deems national affect a truth game, which is rigged "insofar as it is meant to block access to freedom to those who cannot inhabit or at least mimic certain affective rhythms that have been preordained as acceptable" ("Feeling Brown: Ethnicity" 69). To read the responses of the journalists (largely, though as outlined earlier not exclusively, members of the dominant white francophone public) who were critical of those who would be offended by Jean's impersonation as "better capturing" the intention of the performance, and then to disregard the feelings of injury that some of the spectators experienced upon its viewing would correspond to the affective truth game described by Muñoz. This is even more clearly the case when those who criticized the performance were accused of Quebec-bashing, when Dauphin and many of the people who spoke out against the show were Québécois themselves. This suggests that to be inside of *Québécité*, one must fulfill certain emotional credentials and scripts involving nationally appropriate manners of responding to the representations of racialized groups. If talk about the (sometimes denounced as extreme or ridiculous) actions of Quebec's language police is familiar, Quebec also has feeling police. Mathieu Bock-Côté, who is an extreme rather than a representative voice in the Quebec media, but one who nevertheless is given an enormous amount of media space,[24] responded

---

24   Bock-Côté is a blogger for *Le Journal de Montréal*. He regularly writes op-eds in *La Presse* and *Le Devoir* and makes regular radio and television appearances on *Radio-Canada*, *Télé-Québec*, and *Le Canal Nouvelles*.

to the backlash against Jean's performance in his *Journal de Montréal* blog with "Retour sur la querelle du 'blackface.' " Bock-Côté evokes the image of a feeling police, but here a specifically anti-national feeling police, in a creatively alarmist manner. He writes:

> Antiracism misunderstood is a dangerous *weapon of mass intimidation*. It allows *fanaticized morons*, certain of their rights and convinced of the virtue of medio-juridical persecutions, to *hijack the public space* and to *take the population hostage*, imposing upon it a strange form of *censorship*: that of enraged ideologues who have no humour and whose ideological stubbornness is equal only to their closed-mindedness. (emphasis added)

The characteristically polemical Bock-Côté frames the critics of Jean's performance (who, as we have seen, are predominantly people of colour) ambiguously as *terrorists* (the public sphere has been taken *hostage* by fanaticized terrorists from its rightful owners) or police (they are *censoring* the public sphere). In a post-9/11 age, the language of terrorism is itself racially coded, as the word "fanaticized" is haunted by evocations of (Muslim) religious fanaticism. The strange terrorist/police hybrids are here construed as criminal and they are not only non-national, they are also counter-national. Note that secularism is here linked to the ability to laugh off a potentially racist action, whereas the expression of offence taken at an action understood as racist verges, in Bock-Côté's language, on fanatical religious piety.[25] This is an example of the equation of secularism with whiteness that was discursively articulated in many of the debates about the Charter of Quebec Values. Here, Bock-Côté codes (religious, racialized) feeling-actions regarding the use of black face paint on a white performer as injurious, as counter-national at the same time as he codes their opposite (secular, white) feeling-actions as national.

---

25   I wonder if, less extremely, expressions of offence taken at actions deemed to be humorous within a national tradition might be experienced as a failure to embody a Québécois joie de vivre.

But if we have established that spectators are likely to judge actions in ways that are conditioned by individual histories, and we have also established that an important portion of Quebec's public partakes in a transnational black history and cultural memory that might include blackface both in Quebec and abroad as a painful symbol, then it seems that the courage and risks involved in feeling in public are unequally distributed between various types of feelers. In this case, one of the risks for those who are not regarded as national a priori (white francophone Québécois) is national belonging itself. Acting and feeling in public, for a traditional cultural outsider, is made more difficult when either her emotional rhythms or objects of cathexis do not correspond to those already nationally legitimated. In her writing about citizenship as "the right to take up soundspace" (*Cruel Optimism* 231), Lauren Berlant argues that "melodramatic political performance sometimes claims to perform the scale and measure of just legitimacy and sometimes claims that an Other suffers from aural bloat that is out of control" (230). The emotional rhythms performed in Dauphin's and Bock-Côté's responses are not so different from one another; they are both rhythms of anger, frustration, and dismissiveness, and both rely on hyperbolic, provocative language. Both also reify an us-vs.-them structure. Dauphin's piece is about herself and those who would be upset by the use of blackface vs. Quebecers who would not. Bock-Côté's response is about himself and those Québécois who would see nothing wrong with blacking up vs. those who do. Dauphin also positions herself within the English language, whereas Bock-Côté positions himself within the French. It seems that the comparison between Dauphin's response and Bock-Côté's is an example of the differential coding of what is actually a similar affective rhythm, according to both the feeler and the object of cathexis. Dauphin, a black, anglophone woman, is angered by Québécois performing in blackface. Bock-Côté, a white, francophone man, is angered by Dauphin's anger. Despite the similar affective rhythms of each actor, the risks involved in their emotional coming-outs were not the same. When acting in the public sphere, one of the risks Dauphin took was coming up against the stereotype of the "angry black woman,"[26] a racialized and gendered subject whose anger and sentimentality are deemed a threat, and "a sign of weakness that needs to be regulated" (Berlant, *Cruel Optimism* 230), rather than a sign of moral virtue.

The fact that Dauphin "came out" in English in Quebec increased the possibility of the dismissal of her feelings about blackface from a legitimated national affect, which is coded as francophone Québécois. As Maryse Potvin has pointed out, "[F]or a long time, in the various halls of government, recognizing the existence of racism through public policy seemed tantamount to admitting the Quebec model of integration [that is, Quebec's management of two-thirds of its immigration policies] had failed" (273). Pointing out racism in Quebec then comes with the added risk of being read not only as oppositional to national policy and values but also as Quebec-bashing. But the risks for Dauphin exceeded even this. In one particularly shocking response to Nydia Dauphin's op-ed, Dauphin was met with a public ridiculing and shaming by the brown comedian Rabii Rammal. In a post in the indie magazine *Urbania* entitled "Chère Nydia" [Dear Nydia], the face of a smiling Rammal, a Montreal comedian of Lebanese origin, is smothered with Nutella in a comic denigration of Dauphin via the application of black face paint. If Jean's performance reads ambiguously as participating in a tradition of blackface rooted in derision, Rammal's reads much less ambiguously. As for Boucar Diouf, he has been accused, as he shared in his letter and interview, by members of Quebec's black community of being a "house negro." These forms of national or communal disavowal that Dauphin and Diouf encountered following their feeling-actions within the Quebec public sphere call for a supplementation of Arendt's account of risk with an account of its unequal distribution amongst diverse sorts of actors and actions, feelers and feelings. As seems to happen strangely often with Arendt, this necessary supplementation is offered elsewhere in one of her own insights: that retrospective storytelling imbues action with meaning. Different stories about

---

26   See Harris-Perry. The "angry black woman" stereotype places black women in a deadlock in which both not speaking and speaking in anger, however righteous, risks stifling their voices altogether.

Quebec's history, in all of its Indigenous, colonial, and diasporic complexities, can result in the arrival of new—and hopefully more egalitarian—structures of feeling and stages for action.

This essay has taken up several tasks. Following Hannah Arendt's thinking about political action as that which creates a space of appearance, I have proposed the notion of "feeling-action" as a way of conceptualizing risky forms of appearing and feeling in public. I suggest that the concept of feeling-action provides a useful framework for thinking about what Stephen Johnson calls "the complexity of intention and reception" regarding blackface, which "builds up in layers over time" (3). The paper has sought to call forth, in particular, the different historical conditionings of the various spectators, feelers, and actors involved in the recent media scandal about blackface to begin sketching a history of racial and national feeling in Quebec, thereby joining scholarship reckoning with blackface in hitherto uncharted moments and locations. The forms of reception that the performance of blackface met in contemporary Quebec suggest that there are affective requisites for belonging to the large, happy, (somewhat) racially diverse family staged on the Québécois comedy scene, a scene which has been a vital matrix for national performance.[27] One of these affective requisites involves being a good sport and, in fact, aligning oneself with a national humour in the very moment one feels hailed and injured as the butt of its joke.

---

27   See my essay "Not Just For Laughs: Sugar Sammy, Stand-Up Comedy, and National Performance" for an account of the centrality of Québécois comedy to national fantasy.

BECOMING-IMPERCEPTIBLE IN THE STUDIO: DELEUZE, POSTIDENTITARIAN AFFECT, AND "IMMANENT EPIC THEATRE"

DAVID FANCY

French philosopher Gilles Deleuze's (1925–1995) thought lends itself well to the purpose of discussing performance and theatre practice for a variety of specific reasons. Not least among these is Deleuze's affirmation that the relationship between theory and practice can best be understood as a series of mutually constitutive exchanges: "Practice is a set of relays from one theoretical point to another, and theory is a relay from one practice to another" (Deleuze and Foucault 206). Deleuze's *immanent* approach—one that privileges process rather than transcendent anchors as integral to the emergence of representation, subjectivity, and ontology—asserts that thought is not a suspension of action, embodiment, affect, and creation, but rather a continuation of these via other means. The engagement by theatre/performance artists and scholars with Deleuze's writing has occasionally lapsed into uncritical celebration of the aleatory and disruptive potentials that result from this emphasis on process and emergent systems in such a way that might suggest his ideas to be irrecuperable to politically informed discussions of identity. While Deleuze's work can be understood to be "postidentitarian" in orientation, given that it explores the constitutive and generative dynamics that precede and subtend normative concepts of the "self" (rather than presuming the givenness of its human form as a starting point for analysis or creation), it by no means necessarily follows that his work is apolitical. In fact, Deleuze's commitment to understanding the genealogy of self is precisely what can provide room to negotiate new manifestations and assemblages of what we call subjectivity and identity—both on stage and off.

What I would like to do here with this particular relay—one that finds itself moving both away from and back toward my own artistic practice—is brave the risks of solipsism by discussing how Deleuze's concept of "becoming-imperceptible," generated in collaboration with frequent writing partner and theorist Félix Guattari, has been useful for my work as a writer, director, and acting trainer. The idea, elaborated upon in their text *A Thousand Plateaus*, addresses a particularly fulfilled moment on the trajectory of "becoming-minor," a trajectory that they describe as veering away from majoritarian and stratified structures (of bodies, institutions, affects) that would inhibit the continued emergence of new possibilities for living. Although not always unbeneficial, when not being regularly countered by various kinds of becoming-minor, stratification can lead to the calcification of structures and concepts in a way that obfuscates their origins and influences and thereby in turn foreclose possibilities for future change.

For example, we could describe the way in which Lee Strasberg takes up and promotes a certain limited aspect of Stanislavsky's work on psychological realism to evidence a problematic *stratification* given that Strasberg's "Method" acting presumes human beings to have "essential" cores bound by discernable parameters of ego and memory that can be drawn upon in a predictable fashion for the purposes of generating specific and repeatable acting effects on stage or on film. The becoming-minor of Strasberg's Method acting would involve recognizing that human beings are much more complex phenomena than his method presumes in addition to proposing ways of liberating energies and pathways of expression that would otherwise have remained occluded or unrecognized. It is in this sense that becoming-minor can be understood to be an ethical act given that it is pursued in contradistinction to "becoming-fascist," which Deleuze and Guattari describe as the binding together of differences in a fashion that constrains institutions, bodies, and identities (or any other coherence enduring for a period of time) to serve the purposes of a power that would dominate it. The potential inclusiveness arrived at by a more comprehensive understanding of the expression and potential of human performance as it varies across cultures and time would be central to the ethical implications of any becoming-minor of Strasbergian Method acting.

For its part, becoming-imperceptible occurs when the coherence in question—such as a human actor—takes destratification further and in some fashion accesses the pre-individual (asubjective) and pre-representational (asignifying) affective substrate that constitutes it. For example, I have found that work in the studio with choreographer Rudolf Laban's motion factors and effort actions allows actors to explore the ways in which all of their actions (be they verbal, physical, or inner—to use the Stanislavskian designations) are comprised of various mixes of weight, space, time, and flow rather than necessarily being entirely recuperable to realities of the bound bourgeois subject. Actors I train with this kind of approach frequently speak in terms of "going beyond themselves" or "opening up to a much wider sense of connection and relationship" to what is around them.

Such destratifications, however, given that they are still prompted by engagement with objective and measurable qualities and quantities (weight, space, time, flow), might only go so far in helping actors experience a constitutive outside of the inherited stands of normative subjectivity that are arguably integral to approaches to acting like Strasberg's. A more thorough manifestation of becoming-imperceptible in my own studio work involves the affective engagement with the impulses and tendencies that can be understood to be constitutive of weight, space, and flow in their own right. I undertake this kind of exploration by drawing on elements of Jerzy Grotowski's *plastiques* (lines of non-representational action that aim to fully engage an actor's organism), for example, while at the same time challenging some of Grotowski's own problematic and essentialist assumptions about selves having cores that need to be exposed. I also draw on aryurvedic medicine and chi kong practices to mobilize the awareness of the actor's breath through his or her body (without necessarily privileging mystical and possibly apolitical understandings of "energy" and "chakras") with a view to providing an intensification of affective experiences that can allow them to pursue with ever-increasing subtlety and refinement an apprehension of the constitutive dynamics that comprise their own experience as coherent organisms. Inducing moments of becoming-imperceptible with these techniques ultimately also provides the actor with an ability to more accurately engage and resonate with the comparable constitutive dynamics that inform the characters they are working to inhabit, contributing in turn to a non-mimetic understanding of what "becoming-character" can mean. "We fall into a false alternative if we say that you either imitate or you are," write Deleuze and Guattari: "What is real is the becoming itself, the block of becoming, not the supposedly fixed terms through that which becomes passes" (238). "The actor Robert De Niro walks 'like' a crab in a certain film sequence" they state in *A Thousand Plateaus*, "but, he says, it is not a question of his imitating a crab; it is a question of making something that has to do with the crab enter into composition with the image, with the speed of the image" (274).

Deleuze and Guattari also remind us that "[b]ecoming-imperceptible means many things," but is most certainly "the immanent end of becoming, its cosmic formula" (279). When human actors pass through such a moment, it does not necessarily follow that chaos, lack of structure, or even death will result, although becoming-imperceptible can lead to such ends if pursued without any regard to preservation of one's coherence. We can imagine for example that the kinds of affective and performative experiments undertaken by Artaud in his attempts at becoming-imperceptible extended far beyond those of Laban, Grotowski, or Maria Knebel and contributed to the wild destratification of his "madness" (Artaud, *The Theater and Its Double* 64–65; Goodall 67–68). Becoming-imperceptible, when undertaken cautiously and methodically in creative and pedagogical settings, in or out of the studio, can be an affirmational (though not always unpainful), ethical, as well as pragmatic process insofar as it invites—and indeed *insists*—on experimentation with different ways of constituting subjectivity, permitting in turn increased possibility for intervention into the micropolitical realities of everyday life.[1]

---

1   For a thorough articulation of becoming-minor or becoming-minoritarian and associated processes see Deleuze and Guatarri's "1730: Becoming-Intense, Becoming-Animal,

Actors or audience members who have developed increased resonances with coherences other than themselves might be more liable to respond to future manifestations of difference with openness rather than ignorance, censure, or violence.

In that becoming-imperceptible "is to world, to make a world or worlds, in other words, to find one's proximities and zones of indiscernibility" (Deleuze and Guattari 280), I've used the concept both to help understand and further extend moments when actors working on characters in my texts have arrived at certain points in their character trajectories when they appear to be in a state of both chassis and potential. At the risk of sounding somewhat disingenuous I'll say that as I was preparing to write this piece I noticed that in three of my recent plays (two of which I've produced and the other I will produce in the coming months), at specific junctures when characters could be described in classical terms to be experiencing recognition and/or reversal, moments of becoming-imperceptible seem to arise. That is to say their development as characters is fuelled by levels of realization, of intensive moments of becoming-minor, that cause a sudden and significant increase in self (and other-than-self) awareness.

The first of these is from a text called *That Woman* that I wrote in 2010 and staged the following year with my neXt Company Theatre. Amongst other things, this text explores various pathways between objectification and sexualization and how these kinds of representational violence contribute to forms of physical and institutional violence. The story revolves around the way in which a character entitled "*that* woman" gradually finds her way into prostitution by initially simply enjoying her sexuality, and then how this unapologetic commitment to pleasure is exploited by the less-than-salubrious and fully patriarchal behaviour of her former employer ("the husband") with whom she had been a lover. The character of "the wife" only meets *that* woman on one occasion earlier in her life, but holds her responsible for the seduction of "the husband." The wife has a moment toward the end of the play

---

Becoming-Imperceptible" in *A Thousand Plateaus* 231–309. For a useful summary of the ethical and political implications of such projects, see Braidotti.

where a rupture of her sense of self is brought about by the realization that her adopted daughter Casey—the biological daughter of *that* woman whom she and the husband have raised—has been sexually assaulted by one of *that* woman's former johns. In this moment the wife appears to be overtaken by thoughts and memories that belong to other women. This ultimately causes her to begin to recognize the contradiction in her judgment of *that* woman being responsible for Casey's violation. In an elegiac moment of becoming-imperceptible she says:

the harder I try to forget,
the more I remember things that didn't happen to me
things I haven't seen
what others saw but didn't speak of
couldn't speak of

Lord let me forget
Let me forget
her face when she left me
Casey in the kitchen
at the door
Casey in the car
the car going down the street
lord please let me sleep and forget

Lord why am I dreaming of women working in fields
women in factories and forests
women lying under strange men
pieces of women in the earth
lord please let me sleep and forget
these women under sheets
legs stuffed under beds
and in drawers
hands in fine perfumed linens

feet in jeweled boxes
I don't want to see it any more

I just want Casey like she was
before the kitchen, the car, the street,
just her and I, mother and daughter,
a happy conspiracy of two women against the world
this fucking crazy place

why can't I remember that?
What's happening to me?

I cast actor Monica Dufault in all three roles in a bid to mobilize alienation effects that would work to destabilize any naturalized assumptions about the relationship between gender and violence. Rehearsals involved the exploration of a substantial number of Brechtian feminist distantiation effects in order to suggest that each character was always already in a state of constructedness. However, in the moment above not only was the impermeability between that play's characters suggested to have been breached, but the affective presence of the many women who appeared in the wife's consciousness also found their way into the playing space. The wife's neat categorization of women according to the schema of mother, virgin, prostitute that Luce Irigaray proposes to be site of the birth of capital itself is suddenly ruptured by the becoming-imperceptible of the wife and the emergence of her first painful steps toward solidarity with women marginalized by patriarchy and capitalism. The kinds of studio work with Dufault that involved generating a sufficiently strong and receptive container for this laterally shifting affect was facilitated by engagement with my own acting training introduced above, which draws on postidentarian aspects of Grotowski and Knebel's taking up of the late Stanislavsky's active analysis. Extensive warm-up activity using Grotowski's *plastique* work, careful and playful exploration of the interaction of textual valence and multi-level expression of the actor (the "physical" body, the "breath" and "energetic" bodies, the "voice body," etc.), and a relentless and intensive generation of the affective realities comprising the universe of the play made for a satisfying collaborative environment for Dufault and I, resulting in the complex production we were ultimately able to share with the audience.

The second moment of becoming-imperceptible text is from a play entitled *Khalida* I wrote for a friend who was, for a period, Saddam Hussein's favourite actor, Addil Hussain (no relation). In this text the actor once again plays a variety of other characters as the central figure of Said recognizes the extent to which the food, mores, and lifeways of the new country in which he is an immigrant are disturbing him on a profoundly affective level. Said speaks to the ghost of his wife who returned to their country of origin and perished in political struggle while he stayed in their adopted country to try to make a life as an artist and to raise their son. The play is set in an oil-producing country somewhere in the economic north and toward the end of the story Said has an encounter with a new potential partner that he has met while delivering parcels to her house. She compares his brown skin to the "oily" land that they are in, and the "oily" country from which he has come. This induces the strong affective response that drives Said careening toward an intensive moment of becoming-imperceptible. He realizes he does not want to be party to the seduction and leaves the woman's embrace:

I run from the house
laughing like I am crazy
I do not shut the door
(she did not sign for her parcel!)

"Delivery?"
Fuck you!
Fuck you and your delivery!

and running
away from the car
into the morning the late afternoon the night
each of my organs darkening

from the body's colours
colours of
bone white
lymph yellow
blood red
vein blue
colours draining away
until
by the time I arrive
they are all as black as night
—and I am no longer myself—

[Flower,
tree,
nectar,
love.]²

these dark pieces of me
they too desire to drain away and
secrete themselves to become
part of this greater body of lightness and darkness
with no territory
ever-flowing
angelic
this endless place of
infinite liquid flexibility
connection and variation

2　These square brackets invite the director and actor to recognize that this language, brought forward from some of the earlier scenes of the play, has gained an additional and subterranean resonance that flows underneath Said's more conscious articulations of his state of mind.

[force,
fire,
violence,
lust.]

All that remains is
the oldest body of all
that came before everything
—before man desiring woman
before woman desiring man
and woman desiring woman
and man desiring man—
waiting jealously under the earth
in this place with no law
except
the law of movement
the law of the flammable
of the law of that which has no choice but to burn

[Birth,
blood,
mind,

death.]

and here
I wait for the dark flash
the explosion
and then:
and then:

The incantatory and transportive quality of the text is a manifestation of Said's
own awareness and indeed embrace of his becoming-imperceptible. He races

beyond restrictive forms of identification projected on him by his adopted culture and experiences a complex new set of relationalities that significantly expand his basic understanding of what constitutes subjectivity. As did Dufault before him, actor Jason Jazrawy talked about accessing a certain kind of "place" beyond his experience, one not qualified by a reliance on fixed human forms, sources, or essences that would precede and presume certain norms of character identity, but rather a generative dynamic space of sensibility and affect that in some cases initially felt outside his creative experience. When stimulated via the textual work and then focused through the specific form of actor training we undertook in rehearsal, Jazrawy's becoming-imperceptible was induced along with that of the character of Said. Indeed, I understand my work as a director in such instances, through the pairing of the simultaneous and co-emergent pathways of becoming-imperceptible (that of the actor and of the character), to create circumstances where this affective process can be generated from scratch each rehearsal and each evening of the performance "as if for the first time."

Too much emphasis on what we might call "transcendent" anchors in the studio work (such as the overdetermination of the significance of blocking, or attempts to repeat and reproduce the affective *results* of a generative process rather than induce the process itself) only leads to the suppression of the immanent potentials available in the moments of the actor's and characters' co-becoming-imperceptible. In a related fashion, given that the materials and the characters in the plays under discussion here are beyond my own literal lived experience (as a white, middle-class, heterosexual subject living in the economic north), the kinds of sensitivities induced by my own experience of becoming-imperceptible throughout the creative process (from writing, to training, to directing) are essential to attempting to live beyond my own experience and relative privilege and in the process generate complex solidarities with other types of identities and lifeways.

The awareness of the constructedness of character and actor on even the subtlest and "foundational" of affective levels—as well as the way this awareness can be harnessed throughout the process to resonate with subjectivities beyond our own—might be described to be moments of an "immanent epic theatre." Such a theatre aims to extend the practice and thought of those such as Bertolt Brecht, Erwin Piscator, Joan Littlewood, and Elin Diamond by pairing cognitive and critical self-awareness—key to existing articulations of epic theatre—with the occasionally violent falling away of affective habituation central to becoming-imperceptible. Such combinations can serve as affective and critical bases for visions and actualizations of increasingly equitable futures between and among various human subjectivities and even other-than-human life forms. Of course, even separating affect from cognition for the purposes of methodological musing necessarily reminds me of their quality of inseparability that Deleuze invites us to consider. It's clear that further relays through this material are necessary for a more thorough articulation of how they might operate and be extended.

Perhaps theory has come to a standstill in this moment, and it may be best if I end with an affective journey born of practice, a moment in a text called *CUT* when a woman named Fatima seems to harness moments of becoming-imperceptible and direct them toward another character named Colin, a failed psychiatrist who has caused unnecessary suffering for both her and his own family in part as a result of his own inability to access the kinds of complex interrelationalities that becoming-imperceptible can permit. Over the course of the play Fatima has developed a close bond with Colin's estranged daughter and has reconciled herself to the fact that she can no longer love her traumatized husband, whom Colin has unsuccessfully attempted to cure. She seeks out Colin at the end of the play, with the others looking on, and takes him to task for having tried to turn her husband into a pathological curiosity as well as for his abject negligence of his daughter. In this moment of the play, Colin has just accused Fatima of hiding a knife, but she has no actual physical weapon, only her adroit use of language and Colin's own fearful imagination that she wields against him. Her capacity to invoke broader if unconventional solidarities with all manner of affective flows and diversities of bodies is a threat to his own very constrained mode of living his subjectivity. At the end of Fatima's speech to Colin featured here, the threat posed by her evocation of moments of becoming-imperceptible has reduced him to a catatonic state:

I'm telling you with warm breath
on the edge of your ear
that houses and rooms are full of perfume
and unlike you
when I inhale the morning
I am satisfied—I see, dance, laugh, sing;

I'm gently reminding you that
I know the role I've played
that my sisters and brothers and I have played
how we've been here forever
your child, my husband, myself and all the others

simple things:
that we are all the colours of the day and night
that we have pissed the stars and shat the earth
and for some reason
this knowledge
burns in your throat
for some reason known only to you but still
in fact unknown by you
these simple things
freak you out beyond belief

I'm whispering softly
right into your brain
and with my knife hard to your throat
to remind you
how we welcomed you with open arms
arms around arms embrace

but you never came

we welcomed you:
in the fields
at the gates of the desert
inside the ships
on the long forest paths
we've welcomed you in the streets
we've welcomed you into our beds
but still you never accepted

I'm pressing the knife through the soft flesh now
and telling you that
we've seen you struggle with your demons
while we threw off our shackles
and you took your children away to war
but still you don't know who we are
your brothers and sisters
your friends, fathers and concubines and lovers
you have no idea who we are

you are simply afraid,
unlike us you are
wandering in graveyards,
sobbing and spitting out your teeth on the grass
unlike us
you are simply afraid.
if you could only
see us for who we are

HIGH EMOTION—RASABOXES IN THE EMO LAB: EMOTION TRAINING FOR ACTORS IN THE TWENTY-FIRST CENTURY

URSULA NEUERBURG-DENZER

> Each box of emotion gives me a different "feeling" in my body, breath and [of] location in my body. Disgust is very centered in my gut, but I think that is probably for a lot of people. Grief is in my mind, gut and a general "shiver" that extends [to] my entire body. Anger makes my breath fast and heavy and my face hot. I "shoot" anger out of my eyes. Love is light. Joy and love are similar, though love carries an accent of sexual arousal, at least in the sense that I have been using it. Love for my mother is more pure and protective. Fear brings my body alive and I have the flight or fight sense. Aware. Joy is pure euphoria, makes me want to jump, twirl and play. Awe is pure wonder.
> —Graham Berlin

As an empiricist and practitioner, I focus on the embodied emotion of the actor—specifically in the context of theatrical performance. As such, the affected as well as the affective body of the performer is my locus of inquisition. At the same time, as a scholar, I am researching actor training with regards to emotional expression and management. At the core of my research-creation practice are the "rasaboxes" exercises devised by Richard Schechner for his company East Coast Artists. Since being first exposed to the exercises in 1994 as a member of the company, I have been using rasaboxes in a number of settings, but mostly as a teaching tool in university-level acting classes.

The rasaboxes exercises[1] are in part inspired by the emotion theory laid out in the *Natyashastra*, as well as by Antonin Artaud's call for the actor as an "Athlete of the Emotion" (*Theater*) and the facial-expression studies of basic emotions by psychologist Paul Ekman (Ekman and Davidson). Borrowing the nine basic rasas from the *Natyashastra*, Schechner devised a set of exercises intended for performers trained in contemporary Western acting methods. Some of the goals of the exercise are to clearly differentiate between emotional states, to investigate different means of performing such states, to recognize the different ingredients of mixed emotions, and to apply them to the performance flow. In the basic layout of the exercise the workspace is divided into distinct spaces—"boxes"—each one reserved for one rasa (see fig. 1). The rasaboxes grid is then used for a number of different exercises. But to what degree is the term rasa useful to the exercise?

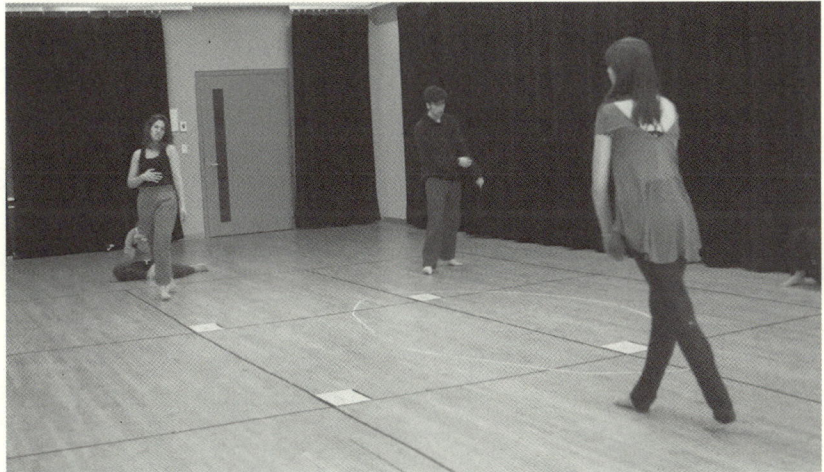

Fig. 1. Rasaboxes taped out on floor. With Sheila Higgs, Roxane Loumede, Oliver Price, Alexandra Goldman.

---

1   In recent years, the rasaboxes exercises have been further developed and trademarked by two company members: Michelle Minnick and Paula Murray Cole. They offer regular summer intensives at NYU and Ithaca College. Aside from Richard Schechner, there are currently six certified teachers of rasaboxes: Minnick, Cole, Rachel Bowditch, Marcia Moraes, Fernando Calzadilla, and myself. See www.rasaboxes.org.

Within the class or lab context students often question whether or not the experience of rasa can be stripped of its cultural context and applied to an historically and geographically different actor training and audience-performer relationship. Why do we talk about "rasa" rather than "emotions," "affect," or, to stay within the Sanskrit framework, the performer's conventionalizing of emotion through "bhava"? The answer lies in the fact that the concept of rasa presents a much broader, multi-layered, and at the same time more specific perspective on the phenomenon of emotion than the other terms imply. Rasa refers to the artistically expressed emotion, emotion mediated for performance and experienced through performance, rather than to just the actor's expression or to emotion in general. In his 2001 article, "Rasaesthetics," Schechner elaborates on his adaptation of those philosophies to Western actor training. Although often criticized for his cultural borrowing, Schechner is not attempting to create or imitate a codified body language for the rasaboxes exercises as the precise poses and gestures that are described in the *Natyashastra*. He is primarily interested in the exchange between performer and audience, the experience of rasa, which is why the training is called rasaboxes exercises. "In the rasic system, the emotions *in the arts, not in ordinary life* are knowable, manageable, and transmittable in roughly the same way that the flavors and presentation of a meal are manageable by following recipes and the conventions of presenting the meal" (32).

In the context of the emo lab, the borrowed term "rasa" functions more as a catalyst of ideas than a historically or culturally specific concept that is applied directly to the work. For my purpose, I mostly translate rasa as "performed emotion," although its meaning is closer to "performed emotion experienced by performer and observer." It seems to me that the performer first has to learn to differentiate between emotion and performed emotion and then begin to hone her craft before actively pursuing rasa. Rasa needs to be understood as artistically shaped emotion performed to move both performer and observer. Rasa implies not only the knowledge of craft but its mastery and ultimately its sublimation. What takes place in the lab could be called something like "dirty rasa," an as-of-yet unshaped, accidental experience that nevertheless touches both participant and observer. The performers feel and are affected by the emotions; they experience, invent, and rid themselves of them. The work is intense and exhausting but in the end very powerful and astoundingly simple.

In what follows, I will outline the key practical and theoretical influences on the rasaboxes system, detail its practice, and suggest the possibilities and challenges of the psychophysical alphabet it cultivates, interspersed with examples from my experience as performer and lab leader. But first, some definitions toward building a shared vocabulary.

While a performer can be affected during a performance and while the performer can certainly affect someone else (i.e., the audience member), s/he does not perform an affect but an emotion. In the theatrical context affect should be understood as the most immediate reaction to a stimulus before that reaction is mediated into a readable and possibly felt emotional expression. Affect is thus not a "manageable" process that can be rehearsed, practised, conditioned, or repeated like an emotional response, but rather is a spontaneous occurrence. The emotions on the other hand are visible and invisible bodily changes in reaction to some kind of trigger event that can reach from biochemical processes to skin coloration and facial expression. The triggered emotion may or may not result in the performer's feeling of these changes but result, rather, in what I call "performed emotion." In his research on skin conductivity, neuroscientist Antonio Damasio found out that *changes in skin conductance always preceded the signal that a feeling was being felt. In other words, the electrical monitors registered the seismic activity of emotion unequivocally before the subjects moved their hand to indicate the experience had begun"* (101, emphasis in original). In biological terms the body's reactions start before they are consciously registered, which means feeling is a kind of knowing that follows the emotion process, i.e., the conscious awareness of an emotional process. How does this play out in performance? The actor can show signs of emotion (for example, the widened eyes of a startled response or a small smile of joy) without feeling them herself or endowing them with her own feeling. But for the actor, who performs emotion, this is a question of choice, of choosing how to enact an emotional sequence within the given circumstances and aesthetic parameters of a production.

Due to this element of choice, theatre scholar Rhonda Blair in *The Actor, Image, and Action*, applies the term "feeling" rather than "emotion" to the actor's work. Her application of neuroscientific principles to several strands of twentieth–century actor training (particularly the Stanislavskian systems) implies that only in the state of feeling can the actor make conscious decisions: "Being aware of feelings—the conscious registration of emotions—allows us to be innovative and creative in our responses to the thing causing the emotion, for, at the level of consciousness, choice and decision-making can finally come into play" (68). Although working with some of the same principles, I am arriving at just the opposite conclusion. While I concur with Blair in the goal of reaching a place in actor training where decisions about emotional expression can be made consciously, in my experience the actor's work on emotion may or may not be endowed with feelings.[2] Emotions themselves fall into conscious and preconscious reactions to a trigger (LeDoux 64, 163–65). It seems to me that in Blair's model the actor is expected to be feeling, to be in some kind of authentic state of not only performing emotions but also feeling them, beyond the cognitive process of knowing. "What is authentic about weeping, if it is generated solely through physical self-manipulation?" Blair asks. "And should this matter?" (48). To this question I would answer, no, it does not matter as long as the "physical manipulation" fits the desired effect and style of performance. The performer's *techniques* of performing emotion have more to do with the bodily expression of emotions and the mental and physical triggers that activate or imitate the emotion process than does the resulting "mind process of feeling," as Damasio calls it (70).

Richard Schechner confirms this stance in his work on the rasic system of Indian performance, which undergirds the systems that I deploy in

---

2 For example, I recall a moment many years ago, that after I had completed an emotionally loaded scene, my director wanted me to freeze and maintain the moment. I stayed in the physically alive freeze, breathing, but in order not to let my focus wander, began counting bricks on a chimney I could see through the studio's window. Afterward my director expressed his amazement about my deep focus and emotionally strong performance during the freeze. This moment made me realize that a performer's work and the audience's perception are two very different things.

my artistic and teaching practices: "In the rasic system, there are 'artistically performed emotions' which comprise a distinct kind of behavior (different perhaps for each performance genre). These performed emotions are separate from the 'feelings'—the interior, subjective experience of any given performer during a particular performance. There is no necessary and ineluctable chain linking these 'performed emotions' with the 'emotions of everyday life'" ("Rasaesthetics" 32). The stress here is again on the fact that there is no necessary relationship between performing and feeling, but that it is both a matter of aesthetic choices and subjective experiences. There is a clear distinction between emotion in real life and in the context of performance.

In 2012, a full semester-length class based on the rasaboxes exercises was added to our BFA acting curriculum at Concordia. Like my previous research labs at Concordia University, I called the class "Emo Lab," in order to signal to the students that while this is a class with clear learning goals, the students are also part of an experiment where the process of discovery is more important than the result and that the learning path is evolving according to the work of the students rather than following a preset course. My objective was to teach the students a firm understanding of the differences between the distinct, fundamental emotions of the rasic system (see fig. 2)—some of which correspond with what Ekman and others call "basic emotions" (Ekman, "Basic" 46)—as well as a knowledge of mixed states and levels of intensity in performance. To me, the exercise serves as a means to the training of the nuanced and conscious performance of emotion and strengthens the performer's ability to differentiate between the immediacy of affect, the visible and performable signs of emotion, and the conscious experience of feeling the performed emotion. Beyond that, I wanted to find out if the rasaboxes exercises are as flexible and easily adaptable to different acting styles and aesthetics as I have been arguing over the years (Neuerburg-Denzer, "Emotions" and "Faking"). It seems that today, not so differently from the past, our ideas about the nature of performing emotion are coloured by the aesthetic or style that we are most familiar with or that is predominant in our different cultural and historical settings.

Fig. 2. Sophie Nation in karuna (grief), France Maurice in bibhatsa (a very low level of disgust), Roxane Loumede in shanta (bliss).

For instance, in Sanskrit drama, a strongly conventionalized performance style, the performed emotion is called rasa and is a shared experience between performer and audience ultimately for the purpose of enjoyment. Rasa can be understood as a third dimension in which both performer and audience member are transported to the experience of aesthetic pleasure. In an Aristotelian dramaturgy, however, the performed emotion is to be mimetically co-experienced by the audience in order to induce pity and fear and ultimately catharsis. The audience member is led to this cathartic reaction but it does not need to be shared with the performer. Contemporary Western realism is still widely based on the principle of mimetic co-experience resulting in the audience's cathartic relief. Different again, in a Brechtian context the detached presentation of emotional behaviour shows how behaviour is culturally and socially determined. While Brecht did not specify in acting-technical terms how emotions should be performed, a number of his exercises clarify the distance between performer and performed, or actor and role. In a postmodern setting the fracturing of the emotional score underlines the precariousness of identity in an art form that is based on embodiment. This approach requires a heightened athleticism from the actor, being able to play a wide palette of styles in quick order. Part of the work in the lab is to differentiate between and learn some of these emotional styles in relation to different aesthetic and training styles. Whereas it has become common practice within the realm of American realism to train internal triggers that are based on memories or on narrative imagination related to text or story (in other words on psychological means), in the rasaboxes exercises the trigger can be a number of different things, varying from physical to mental cues—for example, specific breathing patterns, a physical pose or sequence, a facial expression, a memory, text, an imagined situation, or anything else proven repeatedly successful.

INFLUENCES 1: IS THERE RASA IN THE RASABOXES?

> For wherever the hand moves, there the glances follow;
> Where the glances go, the mind follows;
> Where the mind goes, the mood follows;
> Where the mood goes, there is the flavor (rasa).
> —Nandikeśvara, *The Mirror of Gesture: Being the Abhinaya Darpaṇa of Nandikeśvara*

Rasa can be translated as "that what is being tasted or enjoyed," but also as "flavor, essence, and emotion" (Muni 1951, 105–07).[3] The *Natyashastra*, the ancient Sanskrit text on the performing arts, is regarded as the primary source for the study of rasa. Originally a Vedic text ascribed to the mythical sage Bharata Muni, the *Natyashastra* is now regarded to be a conglomerate of writings by a number of scholars over a period of several hundred years. The Sanskrit word *natya* means dance drama, and *shastra* stands for treatise or scripture, referring generally to knowledge, which is based on principles that are held to be timeless (Olivelle 169). Using literary style and textual references as indicator, core parts of the *Natyashastra* (*NS*) are dated as early as

---

3   Rasa is also sometimes translated as "feeling" or "sentiment" instead of "emotion." Different commentators focus on the different aspects of meaning of the word rasa.

500 BCE and later parts could have been added until about 400 CE (Singal 17–21), though some scholars date it between 200 BCE and 200 CE.[4] The *NS* is a comprehensive compendium of the performing arts: practical, theoretical, and religious. Everything that comprised Sanskrit drama, from poetry to music to architecture, from devotional practice to acting, costume, make-up, and audience involvement is considered here. All performative elements together shape the encounter between performers and audience in order to achieve the "multisensorial, heightened aesthetic and emotional state" called rasa (Chakravorty, "Dance" 6).

When asked to explain rasa, Bharata answers:

> Because it is enjoyably tasted it is called rasa. How does the enjoyment come: Persons who eat prepared food mixed with different condiments and sauces, etc., if they are sensitive, enjoy the different tastes and then feel pleasure (or satisfaction); likewise, sensitive spectators, after enjoying the various emotions expressed by the actors through words, gestures and feelings, feel pleasure, etc. This (final) feeling by the spectators is here explained as (various) rasas of natya. (Muni, 1996 55)

In the performance context rasa stands for that which is communicated between the performer and the audience through means of a highly conventionalized system of signs. Theatre historian Erika Fischer-Lichte suggests that rasa might be "a human disposition activated by the sign" ("Performing" 1). A similar notion is voiced by Coomaraswamy and Duggirala in the introduction to their 1917 translation of the *The Mirror of Gesture*. They state that "according to the Indian view, the power to experience aesthetic emotion [rasa] is inborn, it cannot be acquired by mere study" (6).[5] Here, rasa is translated as

---

4   This timeline is given, for example, by Sanskrit scholar Kapila Vatsyayan in the foreword to his translation of the *Natyashastra* and in Zarrilli et al.'s "Early Theatre in Court, Temple, and Marketplace."

5   Nandikeśvara's *The Mirror of Gesture* is compared to the *NS* as a much-abridged treatise on gesture, which is supposed to be based on the *Bharatanatyam*, another ancient treatise on dance that may have preceded the *NS*.

aesthetic emotion—a form of emotion specific to performance and the aesthetics of a specific performance style. In its highest form during the Sanskrit period, rasa was considered to be a blissful state of union between humans and gods, rooted in the very bodily sensations of flavour and taste. This "human disposition" for aesthetic pleasure in the performing arts that Fischer-Lichte refers to ("Performing") is triggered by the combination of physical signs as the ingredients for the emotional "meal"—rasa.

The *NS* differentiates between eight natya rasas, that is, rasas that are the effect of conscious performance (Pande 311):[6] sringara (love), hasya (humour), karuna (pathos, sorrow, compassion), raudra (anger), vira (heroism), bhayanaka (fear), bibhatsa (disgust), and adbhuta (wonder, surprise). Some hundred years later, after the arrival of Buddhism in India, a ninth rasa, shanta (white light, bliss, or nothingness) (Schwartz 15), was added to the first eight by scholars, who argued that Bharata had indeed already mentioned shanta in an early version of the text.

In order to achieve rasa the performer expresses the corresponding sthayi bhavas (conventionalized emotional states) by means of abhinaya (acting) in a combination of highly differentiated facial and body movements. Language, music, makeup, and costume are also contributing elements to the rasic experience. In the *NS* the bhavas concern the actor's technique, specifically a technique that is rooted in traditional Sanskrit drama, which has carried over to many of the classic Indian styles of dance drama practised today. Bhavas, then, are the elements a performer uses to compose an emotional state; the corresponding rasa is the experience of this state by both performer and spectator.

As opposed to the Sanskrit context, when working with Schechner's rasaboxes exercises the meaning of rasa and bhava is somewhat conflated. The boxes are identified by the Sanskrit term for the basic rasas, but when the rasas are translated for the participants, the English translation of the corresponding

---

6   Pande elaborates: "It is worth noting here that the terms vibhava, anubhava and vhyabhicaribhava refer to stage representations, not to the realities of life. It follows therefore, that the rasa they produce must also be a stage effect rather than some aspect of real life. That is why the rasas are called natya-rasas" (311).

sthayi bhava is used; i.e., the rasa "bibhatsa" is translated as "the odious," while the corresponding bhava "jugupsa" is translated as "disgust." In the performer's vocabulary "disgust" can be played as an action; "the odious," however, is the rasa produced through the enactment of disgust. Thus during the work sessions we will translate bibhatsa as "disgust" and skip over the differentiation between bhava and rasa.

When further defining rasa, it is stated in the *NS* that "rasa is the cumulative result of vibhava (stimulus), anubhava (involuntary reaction) and vyabhicari bhava (voluntary reaction)" (Muni 1996, 55). This dictum on rasa or "rasa sutra" does not only lay out how Bharata analyzed the emotion process, which is very similar to a contemporary cognitive definition, but also details the performative ingredients for this process. Neuroscientists define emotion processes as induced by a trigger event, which can be followed by two differing processes. One includes the cortex and thus a process of cognition, while the other, shorter pathway circumvents the cortex and could be considered precognitive. Both pathways result in physical changes and a goal-directed action (LeDoux 164). In other words, the different kinds of bhavas—vibhava, anubhava, and vyabhicari bhava—combined in performance endlessly reiterate this emotional process of stimulus, involuntary reaction, and voluntary reaction. The cause for the ensuing emotional state, vibhava (stimulus), is often embedded in the story or text of the performed play, but also in the performed actions themselves. Anubhavas are the "involuntary" physical reactions to a stimulus; sometimes these are simply translated as "consequences" (Vatsyayan 87). The vyabhicari bhavas describe the "voluntary" reactions, the consciously chosen gender-, age-, and status-appropriate outward signs of the emotional state. There are thirty-three vyabhicari bhavas described in the *NS*. In addition, there are eight sattvika bhavas, such as tears, change in skin colour, or shaking. These bhavas could also be identified as an involuntary response[7] and are performed with the help of stylization; the

---

7   In the *NS* and in the commentary the exact relationship between the different kinds of bhavas, such as vyabhicari and sattvika, is not completely clear, thus commentators have debated these interrelationships. The sattvika bhavas also correspond to what is called in

Sanskrit performer was not expected to actually cry or change the colour of his/her skin. So, even though there is a clear differentiation made between two kinds of emotional reaction to the stimulus, involuntary and voluntary, as can be observed in the emotion processes in everyday life, in performance both types of reaction are performed using conventionalized means of expression. All types of bhava are performed through words, gesture, and facial expression—that is, through the means of abhinaya.

But how does one learn to express rasa in performance? The contemporary Odissi dancer Nandini Sikand responds:

> Within the performing arts, there is this idea of riaz or sadhna, the repetition of a performed activity that is routine like. But it is not simply bodily habit but rather this bodily practice is necessary to get to the evocation of rasa. And unlike other schools of acting where the actor or performer draws on similar emotional experiences to bring out a particular emotion during performance, in this context the sheer repetition will ultimately result in emotion.

This brings up the question of whether this physically learned behaviour and the resulting emotional reaction is another form of the performer's self-conditioning. In the Lab we have been talking of creating triggers, which work similarly to a conditioning process à la Ivan Pavlov, who inspired both Constantin Stanislavsky and Vsevolod Meyerhold. The performers come up with specific body poses, expressions, and/or short movement sequences for each rasabox. They keep repeating these now-conventionalized forms until the form itself becomes the trigger for an emotion. Anthropologist, practitioner, and teacher of Kathak, Pallabi Chakravorty points out that these artistically performed emotions are not automated or void of feeling but, on the contrary, evoke intense joy in the performer through the medium of riaz. "The feeling of rasa creates deep self-enjoyment within the performer,

---

current North American psychology somatic or somatovisceral events. See Cacioppo et al. and Prinz, *Gut Reactions* 212–13.

which prompts her to engage in play and improvisation" ("Dance" 11). It is understood that a more mature performer with a greater realm of emotional experiences will be able to achieve greater depth in expression. This suggests that the performer supplements the emotion triggered by riaz in classical Indian dance theatre forms with his/her increasing personal experience of emotional states (Chakravorty, "Dance" 6–8).[8]

INFLUENCES 2: EKMAN, ARTAUD, PAVLOV

In addition to the practice and aesthetic of rasa, Schechner cites the emotion studies by behavioural scientist Paul Ekman ("Magnitudes" 30–37) and Antonin Artaud's concept of the actor as the "Athlete of the Emotions" ("Rasaesthetics" 43) as his other most influential sources in developing the exercises. Ekman's work on basic emotions[9] and the accompanying facial expressions explores the so-called hard-wired, early evolutionary patterns of emotion processes. His findings resonate with the ideas of conventionalized expressions of emotions as described in the *NS* in that he has mapped specific facial expressions linked to each of the "basic" emotions, i.e., the engagement and contraction of muscles or muscle groups distinctive of an emotional state such as anger.[10] But rather than investigate the performed emotion as the *NS* does, Ekman looks at emotional expression in everyday

---

8   In addition, these notions were discussed at the Performing Ecstasy symposium, co-convened by Chakravorty, in which I partook as participant/observer.

9   Several researchers past and present (i.e., Silvan Tomkins, Carroll E. Izard, Jaak Panksepp, Robert Plutchik, Ekman) suggest that there is a set of so-called "basic emotions," also known as primary emotions, which are recognized by peoples around the globe. While the total number of the basic emotions has been challenged and changed over the years, repeated claims have been made to consider fear, anger, joy, disgust, and grief as "basic," with all other emotions being understood as mixed states. The debate about basic emotions, their definition, and which emotions are falling into that contested category is ongoing.

10   Ekman has worked on facial expression for five decades now. A good overview and reference article for his work is "Facial Expression of Emotion," written with Dacher Keltner.

life. Michelle Minnick and Paula Murray Cole, who have collaborated with Ekman on several occasions in their further development of the rasaboxes technique, work occasionally with his facial-expression charts. They use the specific muscle contractions he suggests for each of the basic emotions to introduce new participants to the work. In Ekman and Wallace V. Friesen's *Unmasking the Face*, a book geared toward readers such as nurses or police officers with a specialized interest in reading facial expression, there is an exercise in which the reader can look at a series of photographs and herself guess what particular emotion is portrayed. When I experimented with the exercise, I found that my relative success was based on my ability to imitate the expression in the photograph, and through that process of imitation and the resulting physiological changes in my expression, I triggered an internal "reading" of the emotion. Through a process that might be linked to the activation of mirror neurons, I can imitate the outer signs of the emotion, arouse the emotion in myself, and identify it. A similar process is in action during a Lab session, when my facial muscles involuntarily imitate a student's expression in one of the boxes close to me (see fig. 3). This internal reading allows me to decide on further steps in coaching the student.[11]

In the Lab itself the facial expression between Lab participants working on the same emotion varied considerably. It quickly became clear that it was not in our interest to find conventionalized forms of expression, but instead to work on differences, or, in other words, on specifics relating to a role or a part. Each lab participant had chosen different triggers and goals for their emotion, different levels of intensity and outward expressiveness, thus the expressions varied widely. It seems that in order to achieve similar expressions not only does the theatrical situation need to be very similar—by that I mean

---

11   In a historical study of performance of affects, and specifically the investigation of seventeenth- and eighteenth-century acting manuals and performance descriptions, Fischer–Lichte discusses the phenomenon of emotional contagion (Ansteckung) of the audience member by the actor. Especially in the eighteenth century the combination of vocal expression and gesture in conventionalized forms lead to a deep sympathetic contagion of the viewers, to the extent that audiences get up and break out in crying, hugging, etc. ("Theater als 'Emotionsmaschine'").

Fig. 3. Ursula Neuerburg-Denzer, Oliver Price, Vanessa Blais, Sheila Higgs, and Alexandra Goldman. Coaching.

the given circumstances that are triggering the emotion—but also the level of performed intensity, and consequently the importance of the goal needs to be the same. For example, in the lab we discussed different imaginary triggers for fear and found that fear is expressed very differently when you are trying to be quiet so as not to be detected, as opposed to when you are running away screaming from, say, an animal attack.

Artaud suggests in his essay "Affective Athleticism" ("Un Athlétisme Affectif") that the performer has "a kind of affective musculature which corresponds to the physical localization of feelings" (*Theater* 133). He stresses the practice of specific breathing patterns for the performer as described in the Cabbala. In his opinion, the expression of emotions in performance can and should be trained, in ways analogous to the athlete's training of the muscles. In the Emo Lab we experimented repeatedly with rasa-specific breathing patterns and found them both powerful and easily accessible. When the participants in the emotion lab each had established clear, repeatable breathing patterns for the different rasaboxes, we sat in a circle and demonstrated these patterns, observing our own reactions to each other's examples. We then proceeded to repeat some of those patterns as a group and found that we could stimulate emotive responses in ourselves. These responses, triggered by breathing patterns that were not our own, often called up a kind of variant of that emotional state that might not have been part of our "personal" realm of experience or imagination, thus opening up each person's emotional repertoire:

> I think that in this exercise I understood more deeply the concept of creating triggers. . . . Very much like Pavlov's dogs responding to a bell, the actor can respond to imagined stimuli as if it were their own life when the trigger has been appropriated from more personal sources. (Perry-Fagant)

A goal of the exercise itself is that through practise and repetition, and the mapping of their individual techniques and triggers, the actors learn to immediately create distinct emotional states. The physical or mental triggers can be minimized over time. The actors can then infuse these states into a theatrical situation by calling up the now-minute trigger. The technique of developing triggers through repetition is loosely based on the Pavlovian principle of conditioning reflexes wherein an emotional state can be reached by using a specific "trigger," the final influence on the rasaboxes system (see fig. 4).

About stimuli and triggers, Pavlov wrote:

Fig. 4. Sheila Higgs, Roxane Loumede, and France Maurice working with personal objects in a Sense Memory Exercise.

> Conditioned reflexes are phenomena of common and widespread occurrence: their establishment is an integral function in everyday life. We recognize them in ourselves and in other people under such names as "education," "habits," and "training"; and all of these are really nothing more than the results of an establishment of new nervous connections during the post-natal existence of the organism.

Of Pavlov's influential studies on the conditioning of reflexes, his most famous is his experiment conditioning the dog to salivate. First the dog is exposed to two stimuli, both the conditioned (food) and the unconditioned stimulus (bell). After a certain period of time the conditioned stimulus (food) would be removed and the conditioned dog salivated when hearing the bell alone. Techniques based on this principle of conditioning and reflexology have been used by Stanislavsky, Meyerhold, and most prominently in the US by Lee Strasberg in his sense-memory exercises. For instance, in the Strasbergian sense-memory exercise the actor (subject) imagines "sunshine" (the unconditional stimulus); through exploration of a related sense memory the actor will also arrive at a previously undetermined emotional state (i.e., the memory could cause a sense of longing, sadness, or intense happiness). The actor can then relate his/her specific memory of an experience of sunshine with precise physical and sensual qualities attached to a feeling without having to call up the complete memory again. Some of the questions asked to make the memory very specific and located in the realm of sensory experience are: what type of sun are you experiencing? Can you tell the time of day, time of year, the sun's colour, its intensity, etc.?

EXPERIMENTS IN THE EMO LAB: RASABOXES MEET STRASBERG, BRECHT, AND LABAN

During our exploration of twentieth-century acting styles, Strasberg's chair relaxation and sense-memory exercise are just one set of preparations to work in the boxes. When the students enter the rasaboxes exercises with this preparation, the exploration of the boxes takes on a distinct flavour. The student is both very relaxed and sensually alert. The approach to the different rasa states is consequently less physically conventionalized but more subtle and driven by sensual experiences (hearing, smelling, tasting, touching, etc.). When the Strasberg preparation is followed by text work, the delivery is often quiet and very intense, less outwardly directed but with a strong internal focus. And to refer to Blair's terminology, more feeling-driven.

This is very different from a preparation with Laban's effort actions. When the performers in their preparation are experimenting with Laban's three categories of time (quick/slow), weight (light/strong), and space (direct/indirect), which in their eight possible combinations result in the movement-quality-based archetypes, the work in the rasaboxes leads to extreme character building (Newlove and Dalby 129–40). For example, Danielle Woodman worked on the character of Strophe from Sarah Kane's *Phaedra's Love*. Strophe is Phaedra's daughter from an earlier marriage who previously had an affair with her stepbrother Hippolytus and knows of her mother's infatuation with him. For her effort action Woodman chose the "flicker" (the flicker combines: quick/light/indirect). When she layered these physical characteristics on "Strophe" in a scene with Hippolytus using the rasaboxes, Strophe suddenly turned into a junky-like character whose inability to connect with her relatives seemed to stem from her level of self-abuse within an abusive environment. Not only did Woodman find a powerful physicality for her character, but also a lens through which to read the play and her character's relationships to the other figures.

Another example of using a different approach to the boxes was our investigation of Brechtian distancing effects. While here we didn't work with a warm-up or preparation specific to Brecht's techniques, the distancing exercise was layered onto scenes previously prepared within the rasaboxes and then taken out of the physical environment of the boxes and blocked in a scene-appropriate setting (i.e., using chairs, a wall, props, etc.). The actors would run their scenes and then layer in the "he says—she says" exercise with the addition of naming the rasa in which they were saying the line. For example, the actors Brefny Caribou Curtin (Phaedra) and Mitchell Cohen (Hippolytus) would run their rehearsed physical score, adding the following lines before saying their text:

> COHEN: "Hippolytus says in bibhatsa (disgust): 'Hate me now?'"
> CURTIN: "Phaedra says in karuna (sadness): 'Why do you want me to hate you?'"
> COHEN: "Hippolytus says in raudra (anger): 'I don't. But you will. In the end.'"
> CURTIN: "Phaedra says in sringara (love): 'Never.'" (Kane 78)

They were also asked to stop the action and look out to the audience while they said "s/he says in . . . " This exercise was perceived by all class members as extremely difficult, but opened up some surprising insights once the actors were able to actually do the switches wholeheartedly. They found that they were able to drop into the emotion with an even higher level of intensity, as if the constant switching between distancing and immersion allowed for even more commitment to the emotional state. The principle of freedom within confinement, be it the physical confinement within the rasaboxes themselves on the grid or the temporal space between lines of self-distancing, was both challenged and explored through these exercises. Once the student was able to accomplish the principle, he or she tremendously advanced as a performer.

To me, both the excitement and conundrum inherent in the rasaboxes exercise is the possibility of working with diverging techniques. On the one hand, the exercises allow for a detailed analysis and practice of performed emotions, using the findings almost like a new psychophysical alphabet that allows for affective resonance in both performer and observer. Here the work is based on a system of physical signs that, when acted out fully, results in an emotional state via a process that could be linked to Meyerhold or Sergei Eisenstein's reading of Pavlov's reflex conditioning. On the other hand, through repetitive motion, sound, or breath this same grid of boxes can become the gateway to ecstatic or trance-like states.[12] Or the grid can be a place for scene work and realism-based character work, befitting American realism. When exploring the grid with a comedic mindset the possibilities for comic enlargement and overemphasis of the emotional state and those for parodic reversal between trigger and reaction become eminently apparent. In the end the exercises, simple but powerful, offer the performer multiple possibilities to practise and expand their range, and to reach, when called for, the climactic moments of high emotion.

---

12   This process resonates more with the ecstatic transformation in the Indian Bhakti tradition. The Bhakti movement flourished in Hindu devotional culture during the early Middle Ages as a countermovement to the Sanskritized Vedic culture, co-fertilized by the increasing influence of Islam. Kathak dance was very much influenced by the Bhakti tradition. Its influence can be seen, for example, in the footwork and twirling typical for Kathak. See Chakravorty, *Bells* 35–39.

ARTIST STATEMENT
MONSIEUR ARTAUD AND I: PEYOTE HAS A LASSO

F.P. FAVEL

Peyote can make you into an artist.
—Leonard Crow Dog, Lakota Medicine Man

1. TRADITIONS

Every person finds a medium in which to express his or her humanity and all of its striving toward some understanding of one's place in the world, in society, within one's tribe or nation. Theatre as a medium is not unique in that regard; all are relative, we could say, not worth more nor worth less than any other medium.

Theatre is many things to many people—entertainment, a diversion, a career like any other career, or an expression of a culture and of a People— and all ways are valid. For some, the need to do theatre can arise from an indescribable angst, a feeling of fracture from one's being or cultural history, from the sacred environment, and from modern society. In these cases, such as my own and that of Antonin Artaud to which I'll turn below, we could say that the impulse to do theatre or any art form is an impulse to psychological wholeness and integration. Or, to frame this process in a traditional Cree world view, we do theatre to bring us back to Creation as a Human Being balanced in Mind, Body, and Spirit, the way the Creator of the Universe originally intended when Creator first created the Human Being in the month of the Frog Moon.

Theatre and our Indigenous traditions have a lot in common; indeed, we can say that when theatre arrived on our shores over five centuries ago on a rat-infested ship, it became the younger brother of Indigenous tradition. Our people very quickly saw the possibilities and genius of this younger brother and it was not long before they adopted this foreign brother, and soon colonists were treated to performances of Native songs and dances in their colonial markets and town squares. Famous Lakota visionary Black Elk travelled to Europe as a young man to perform, and then, as an old man, continued to do shows in the Black Hills for tourists. In addition to the entertainment value, his purpose was to teach. "Watching these traditional rituals, spectators would judge for themselves their moral worth. This was the logical extension of Black Elk's wish to make his vision 'go out,' to share the traditional ways with white men" (DeMallie 66). I see my own work as part of this vision, one that was also prompted in a letter to me from the great twentieth-century director Jerzy Grotowski, with whom I had trained in Italy for two years.

In this letter Grotowski outlined my destiny, recommending I work with my mother culture and find my own way of working. This advice led me to begin to think of allying theatre with Indigenous culture and tradition. This is what I have done and along the way I gradually began to form my own way of working, developing a theatre process based on Indigenous techniques and systems present in social and ritual activities.[1] Through my research, I found concrete and precise starting points that can be repeated and followed. For instance, after breaking down Indigenous songs and dances to their technical structure, I have used these structural elements as starting points for creative explorations. The Lakota Winter Count system—a narrative action pictographic record of the years—allows for explorations into dramaturgy,

---

1   I would describe my years in Canada since I left Europe as a form of exile or imprisonment, due to the fact that the arts were divided up into Kafkaesque categories for different types of ethnicities, and we even had our own category as Aboriginals. It was these same types of oppressive rules that originally had made me escape to Europe, and now these rules were part of artistic policy and very often managed by people with limited Aboriginal ancestry and experience. Yet they were making the rules about and for us. The theatre, indeed, is a nightmare from which I am struggling to awake.

choreography, montage of body and image. I also developed a schema for the analysis of Indigenous performance, one that I used in imagining a show about Antonin Artaud, French playwright and director.

Polish writer and philosopher Czesław Miłosz wrote, "[P]oetry is constructed out of the remnants found in ruins" (97). This statement, I feel, is what developing a theatre process based on Indigenous cultures is all about. The process is the poetry, and its details are the remnants of Indigenous civilizations of this hemisphere—that is, the ruins. Like all processes, it is very personal; one begins with one's own life and family, immediate surroundings. I propose that this development, this search, is a healing journey.

2. PROCESSES

In the shadows of experimental theatre of the twentieth century there is the gaunt, tortured figure of French director, writer, and actor Antonin Artaud. He has been called many things—a failed theoretician, an opium addict, a great actor, a lost soul. But the main point is that his search for techniques and methods to bring theatre back to its ritual roots was intimately related to his search for wholeness, for healing. This search led him into the wilds of north-central Mexico amongst the Tarahumara, Indians from this Island, North American—Indians very much like myself.

Cree peyotists say that peyote has a lasso that ropes in wayward souls— souls such as Monsieur Artaud, for example. Artaud suffered from a feeling of disassociation from society, of not being balanced in his mind, heart, and body. Old Cree Indians say that when one feels like that, one is not connected to one's Spirit. Maybe the Spirit was left somewhere due to a trauma, a sin, illness, or even due to sorcery, and some of the symptoms are moodiness, irritability, inability to focus, or a feeling of being disassociated from society; that is exactly how Artaud felt. The task then becomes to reconnect to your Spirit.

Some time in 2006 I decided to create a show about Artaud's journey to the Tarahumara Indians of Mexico in 1935. The Tarahumara are an Indigenous nation, a tribe that live in north-central Mexico and are famed for their long-distance races. Shortly after Artaud's theatrical expedition, his seminal book, *The Theater and Its Double*, was published, which included an essay about his experiences in Mexico entitled "Peyote Dance." In *The Theater and Its Double*, Artaud left us visionary spiritual writings; of these, Grotowski has said, "[H]is writings have little methodological meaning because they are not the product of long term practical investigations. They are an astounding prophecy, not a program" (*Towards* 24). I, however, was interested in a program that might lead to healing.

The program looks like this: Tr (traditions) + Pr (process) = Th (theatre, public performance).

For the Artaud production, it looked like this: Tr (peyote ritual) + Pr (research into Anaïs Nin's diaries, Artaud's writings, Tarahumara studies, modern French theatre, etc.) = Th (public performance—lights, sound, money and grants, applause).

As I submerged myself fully into the Process (research) and Tradition (peyote ritual), however, the schema reversed itself and forgot about the show. In this case the schema turned into a life-enhancing journey that took on this appearance:

Th (public performance—lights, set, music, etc.) ↔ Pr (literary research and research into that peyote ritual) → Tr (active participation in peyote milieu-leadership, service, cutting wood, learning creation stories, healing, self-development, developing relationships with my children, forgiveness of sins and past wrongs, no applause nor money, etc.).

Artaud had proposed that theatre has as its Double, the shadow, the mysterious imbued with magic and the hidden nature of humanity capable of shocking society into a form of catharsis that forces society to look at itself and perhaps be cleansed. This was a noble attempt and I think that in order for this to be achieved, a personal healing of the practitioner must take place, such as the one I have described in the above paragraph. In order to do this, one has to make one's way back into the theatre.

Tr → Pr → Th2 (theatre and its double).

3. PEYOTE

From the 1870s onward, the peyote ceremony spread from the Kiowa and Comanche until it reached our area of Saskatchewan in the 1930s (Stewart 257–59).[2] Its first apostle was an Assiniboine from Mosquito First Nation, George Lightfoot, who learned the ceremony from the Shoshone and Bannock tribes of Idaho. Here this story intersects with Artaud's, who was in northern Mexico attempting to kick his opium addiction and seeking a sacred theatre, and he too made contact with peyote (Artaud "From"). In the peyote way they say that peyote picks the people who will meet you. In the 1930s, this area of Idaho was accessible only by rail and horseback and Lightfoot most likely, like Artaud, arrived on horseback to this mountainous region. Here their journeys diverge. Artaud spent a few weeks amongst the Tarahumara, whereas Lightfoot spent six years eating medicine and learning the ways before he brought the ceremony north. He was given a water drum, gourd, a staff, and some medicine and they say he came walking and hitchhiking home, carrying his ritual paraphernalia and the sacred medicine in a gunny sack. Lightfoot told the people when he came home two thousand kilometres north, "I found a way, a good way." He taught this new way to the Cree and Assiniboine People of the Eagle Hills, raised a family, and in his old age was kind to children and drove the reservation school bus (Daniels). Artaud, when he came home, was arrested and placed in a straitjacket and spent the rest of his life in an insane asylum in Rodez, France.

2　Much has been said and written about peyote; that small unremarkable sacrament that grows in the desert regions along the Rio Grande has generated a lot of misconceptions and controversy. It is not a drug, and this was proven in the 1950s; in fact, there was a peyote meeting in Fort Battleford, Saskatchewan, in 1956, attended by world-renowned scientists and researchers, including Dr. Humphry Osmond who coined the term "psychedelic" in the 1950s. He came to the conclusion that "all the evidence that we have suggests that Peyote is wholly beneficial and in no way a drug of addiction. It cannot even be defined in such a way since it does not have the essential compelling qualities or the withdrawal symptoms" (Stewart 263).

In the early days of peyote in Saskatchewan (the 1930s to the 1950s), the leaders were young men and women in their twenties and thirties. Persecuted by the law, they held their ceremonies in secret in the coulees of the Eagle Hills south of Battleford until peyote was deemed legal in Canada in 1954. They endured the scorn and ridicule of traditionalists from their home communities, but they continued, bringing a type of cultural revolution to the province and the country, a way of singing, drumming, different ceremonial and musical instruments, a peculiar ceremony from the southern regions of Turtle Island. Prior to the 1930s, this ceremony did not exist in our area. But by the 1970s the people of the Battlefords had developed their own unique style of singing and drumming; it had taken forty years—two generations—for this to happen; people had to be born into it, from their mother's womb they absorbed the music and eventually made it their own. Art emerged from their ritual practices.

In the early days of the reservations in Oklahoma, where many tribes had been forcibly relocated, Geronimo and the Comanche Quanah Parker used to sit together and eat the holy medicine. They would pray, talk, share, and sing, and sometimes they would use a bow and hit the bowstring with an arrow to accompany their singing. The same vigilance and awareness they needed in their warrior ways were utilized in the ceremony. It required stillness—no coughing out loud, no clumsy footfalls, no laughing—as this would scare the spirit and make it fly away. The spirit, which is characterized as a bird and is as fast as the speed of light, might descend and transmit some blessing. Reaching for that spirit is what peyote ceremonialists say is the goal of the ritual. Once, as I sat in a tipi contemplating, I asked an elder why we have ceremonies. Why must we pray, why must we work hard to make the ceremony look nice, why must we impose rigour upon ourselves? He said, "To prepare us for death." Maybe this is one of the meanings of the "poor theatre" that Grotowski wrote about: the solitude and aloneness when all you have and depend on is the spirit, the creative spirit, the Holy Spirit. For true art, like ritual, comes from a place with severe rules; one must create one's own art with one's own visions, one's own theories and ethos, one's own hand, one's own body.

4. TEACHERS

Artaud came to our Turtle Island, cultured, sensitive, and unwell. He did not come to colonize or enslave the People. This white man from the East, his hand extended in peace, came searching for a deeper meaning to theatre, a theatre that could express the mystery of life and the forces of the world. In my journey to find the true art within me, out of the ruins of my culture, I remember the stories told of Lightfoot, of Artaud, and of their healing journeys. As for my show on Antonin Artaud, maybe I will never write it. It is no longer important.[3]

It is important, though, to remember performance pioneers like Black Elk, whose intent was to create understanding, to build bridges. I have created a system of theatre creation based on the ruins of my culture, created out of a search for wholeness and origin and feelings of fracture and angst. The next step is to share this with our younger brothers and sisters, the white people, and all of the other strangers who followed them. I think that deep down we have the same goal, which is to live in a natural manner with Creation and to find the meaning of art within ourselves.

It is the beginning of winter 2013. The old beaver who lives at the creek has dammed it and created a large pool of water; he has chopped down the poplar trees almost to my doorstep. The beaver tells me it is going to be a long and cold winter with deep snows all around the world. I think back over the past to Grotowski and his message to me: Work with your mother culture. And I think, yes, I did; I was always going to do this anyways, so what he told me had already been within me. That is a great teacher.

---

3   I had wanted to write the show from the perspective of the Tarahumara and their thoughts and impressions of this strange Frenchman who arrived on horseback. Perhaps there are oral stories about him still being told in the Sierra Madre? No doubt they saw in him the search for the sacred and metaphorical frame of mind.

FEELING (TOO) CLOSE

A GAY OLD TIME:
JILL JOHNSTON, 1975[1]

SARA WARNER

"I was flattered that somebody wanted to make a movie of me. If Andy Warhol wanted to make a movie of me, I wouldn't be flattered, you understand . . . but a woman in Canada wants to make a movie of me, this is very flattering" (*Jill Johnston*).[2] These are the final lines of the film *Jill Johnston: October 1975*, a thirty-minute cinéma-vérité documentary by two novice feminist filmmakers, Lydia Wazana and Kay Armatage, that chronicles four days in the life of its titular American subject at a pivotal point in the women's liberation movement and in her own career as a writer. Johnston, a dancer turned art critic at New York's underground weekly paper *The Village Voice*, caused a sensation with the publication of her 1973 book *Lesbian Nation: The Feminist Solution*, a polemical tome credited with sparking the separatist movement. Insisting upon the political and tactical significance of lesbians to the project of women's liberation, Johnston convinced females—gay, straight, and experimenting—on both sides of the forty-ninth parallel that sapphism was the

---

1   I would like to thank Lydia Wazana and Kay Armatage for talking with me about the making of *Jill Johnston: October 1975*. I would also like to thank Kyla Tompkins, Mary Jo Watts, and Erin Hurley for their comments on various versions of this essay.

2   All subsequent quotes from the documentary are taken from the film. Johnston is being coy here. Andy Warhol did make a documentary, unreleased, titled *Jill Johnston Dancing* (1964), in which the titular artist prances around the Factory. After becoming radicalized in the late 1960s, Johnston came to see that while Warhol's films effectively employ cinéma-vérité techniques to trouble social constructions of gay men and male-to-female transgendered subjects, they are deeply misogynistic and reinforce negative stereotypes about women and lesbians.

vanguard position. *Lesbian Nation* had such a profound impact on Canadian feminists that Johnston was invited to guest lecture at Innis College, where a collective of graduate students, Armatage among them, were leading the University of Toronto's first women's studies courses.

When the mercurial Johnston returned to campus two years later for the premiere, at the fourth annual Women's International Film Festival, she was anything but flattered by the image on the screen.[3] The filmmakers were visibly shaken when, after the credits rolled and the auditorium erupted in applause, Johnston rose out of the audience to denounce the project, personally disparage Armatage, and threaten to sue anyone who attempted to distribute the documentary outside of Canada. Though Johnston had no legal grounds for censoring the film, her shaming remonstration ensured that the work would not circulate. This painful, humiliating, and deeply divisive incident thwarted a potentially vivifying transnational dialogue between North American feminists and it engendered dissent among the Toronto collective, manifesting in a decades-long rift between co-directors Wazana and Armatage. As a result, *Jill Johnston: October 1975*, which is widely regarded as one of the first experimental feminist films by an all-female crew in Canada, has rarely been shown to anyone anywhere, and, to the best of my knowledge, it has never been screened in the US.

This little film and the enormous social drama it engendered are events of great historical significance, not because they index the devolution of radical energies into a lifestyle politics, as critiques of second-wave feminism lead us to believe, but because they underscore the fact that any attempt to make and document history happens in tandem with forgetting—a forgetting that is both calculated and strategic. The emotional baggage surrounding cultural productions from the women's liberation movement dictates to a great extent how '70s feminism is understood and remembered today. In *Feeling Women's Liberation*, Victoria Hesford argues that artifacts of this epoch remain subject to intense feelings of attachment and disidentification that both contribute

---

3   Founded in 1976, the Festival of Festivals was renamed the Toronto International Film Festival (TIFF) in the mid 1990s.

to and occlude the moment's historical complexity. Attention to the fraught reception of *Jill Johnston: October 1975* reveals the influence this buried relic has not only on how we feel about the past but what we sense as the future of feminist and lesbian studies.

CULTURAL CONTEXTS: STUDIO D AND THE CREATION OF A FEMINIST PUBLIC SPHERE

In the same year that Johnston published *Lesbian Nation*, the United States Supreme Court granted women the right to control their reproductive destiny in the landmark legal case Roe v. Wade and Billie Jean King defeated Bobby Riggs in a televised tennis match promoted as the "Battle of the Sexes." In that same year, 1973, female traders were allowed on the floor of the London Stock Exchange for the first time, and in Canada a group of ambitious artists and activists organized the nation's inaugural women's cinema festival. That event, titled Women and Film 1896–1973 International Festival, evidences the dual aims of many feminist projects, including this essay: historical recovery—the recuperation and revaluation of women's art—and epistemological inquiry—a critical analysis of the discourses and practices of knowledge production. The hope was that the festival "would contribute to the evolution of constructive theories and criticisms of film by women" (Armatage et al. 3; see also Pallister; White; and Waugh). It was staged in conjunction with lobbying efforts for the formation of Studio D, a women's production unit at the National Film Board, that would give women artists access to material resources, allow them to tap into established distribution networks, and promote the Women's International Film Festival.

The first publicly funded women's film unit in the world, Studio D changed the face of global cinema through the creation of a state-supported agency for the production and dissemination of work by, for, and about women. Studio D produced more than one hundred and twenty-five films before its dissolution in 1996, many of which were cinéma-vérité documentaries that used realist techniques to convey previously unexplored and under-examined

facets of women's lives. Sharing personal stories in the context of larger socio-political issues, feminist filmmakers used cinema to construct a female
gaze they hoped would balance asymmetrical power relations between the
sexes, thereby enabling women to understand and alter the representational
practices through which they had been excluded and marginalized. Studio
D documentarians did this by capitalizing on the medium's affect-inducing
techniques, namely lean-ins, close-ups, and reaction shots that capture the
authentic feelings of female subjects as well as emotional cutaways to scenes
that have recognizable sentiments built into them, such as a crowd of angry
protestors or a solitary woman walking down a lonely path. These affective
techniques marshalled and mobilized spectators' feelings, fostering attachments and identifications between and among audiences and the women on
screen. These tactics constitute what Erin Hurley calls art's "emotional labour,"
investments that make sense (affectively and cognitively) of what individuals
and collectives value, desire, and dread (10).

While the promotion of a multiplicity of voices and visions was the expressed goal of Studio D, there is definitely a particular *feel* to the projects
produced under the auspices of this entity, which, like many national feminist
organizations in North America, was directed primarily by white, heterosexual, middle-class women who were more interested in liberal aspirations,
in assimilation and sharing the wealth, than they were in a radical restruc-
turing of society. "Canadian women's cinema," note the editors of *Gendering
the Nation*, "is not necessarily an equitably shared tradition. Its tremendous
range and diversity owe much to circumstance; birth, economics, geography,
language, funding institutions, and most importantly, the prevailing attitude
toward women in each particular decade inform what films get made and
what cinematic conventions will shape them" (Armatage et al. 4; see also E.
Anderson). *Jill Johnston: October 1975* illustrates this inequitably shared tradition. Armatage, a straight, Anglo feminist of means, went on to become one
of the nation's most venerated scholars of cinema and women's studies (and an
editor of the anthology just cited) in addition to being a senior programmer
for the Toronto International Film Festival for nearly a quarter of a century.
In contrast Wazana, a Moroccan immigrant and single mother without an

advanced university degree, not surprisingly, found mainstream institutions less welcoming. Moving in and among a number of feminist and queer communities, as well as avant-garde circles—she worked with David Cronenberg, Robert Clouse, and Andy Warhol—Wazana eventually left Canada to pursue a successful career as a restaurateur in the Dominican Republic.

Critics have charged Studio D with reproducing the status quo and with reinforcing hegemonic narratives about women and gendered forms of oppression, narratives shaped ideologically by a particular stream of universalizing, moralizing, and pro-censorship liberalism within the North American feminist movement. Rooted in polarizing conceptions of gender, including conservative—some might call phobic—views on the sex industry and non-normative modes of intimacy, many Studio D productions depict participants in these activities as helpless victims in need of deliverance. The paradigmatic example of this is perhaps *Not a Love Story: A Film About Pornography* (1981) by the American expatriate Bonnie Klein, who immigrated to Canada with her husband, a conscientious objector against the Vietnam War. This film, in which the director successfully shames a burlesque performer, Linda Lee Tracey, into leaving a lucrative career as a sex worker, was one of the most important and controversial artifacts of the Culture Wars. It would be a mistake, however, to categorize Studio D as anti-sex or homophobic. To do so would be to ignore the many films it produced that explore in nuanced ways the complex nature of female desire and eroticism, including the collaborations between Holly Dale and Janis Cole and the work that concerns me here, *Jill Johnston: October 1975*.

This film would not have been possible without the creation and support of Studio D. A wry and irreverent portrait of a lesbian separatist, this documentary eschews the earnest, didactic, and sentimental tone typically associated with Studio D films and with cultural feminism generally speaking. Women's cultural productions sought to engender new affinities and identities, political constituencies and aesthetic practices, and they helped make women's liberation a nationally mediated event. Many of us have mixed feelings about the assumptions, associations, and essentialisms undergirding these world-making projects. These ambivalent feelings produce circumscribed interpretations of history that define, to a great extent, the ways in which this sphere of '70s feminism is understood and remembered today.

Women's cultural production has yet to be given its due, argues Jill Dolan, because it was "caught in the crosshairs of political and academic history, falling victim to the poststructuralist theoretical critique and becoming a scapegoat for a new academic field trying hard to establish itself as legitimate and serious" ("Feeling" 205). Wedged within and warped by "this constellation of historical pressures," feminist cultural productions—which include women's cinema, the women's music scene, women's coffee houses, women's theatre, and women's periodicals, "in all of which 'women's' was a thinly veiled substitution for the less easily spoken 'lesbian'—were too quickly dismissed as essentialist and retrograde by . . . [later] feminist and queer theorists who adopted post-structuralism's suspicion of experience and identity politics" (205). Part of the reason women's cultural production has been so maligned and neglected is because it is often associated or conflated with cultural feminism, which certain women in the 1980s—including those trying to assimilate into the academy—considered a travesty of radical politics. "With the rise of cultural feminism," laments Alice Echols, "the movement turned its attention away from opposing male supremacy to creating a female counterculture . . . where 'male' values would be exorcised and 'female' values nurtured" (5). While some feminists supported the creation of women's spaces, they feared that this would too easily devolve from a sphere of active political resistance into "a place of emigration, an end in itself" (Echols 105). Echols roused a chorus of critics who singled out cultural feminism as precipitating the demise of the women's liberation movement and the devolution of Leftist ideology into a lifestyle politics. While her taxonomy of feminisms helps historians think about the nuances and vagaries of second-wave politics, this vertical economy advances a perniciously distorting set of political, theoretical, and institutional antagonisms that contribute to our bad feelings and sense of historical amnesia about the era.

In retrospect we can see that the social actors Echols tries to compart-mentalize into tidy categories and neat little boxes borrowed freely from a variety of methods, tactics, and strategies in ways that defy easy categorization.

Johnston's *Lesbian Nation,* for example, with its galvanizing rhetoric—its insistence that "the lesbian is *the* revolutionary feminist"—and its call for "the
creation of a legitimate state defined by women," is often cited as a paradigmatic example of the trappings of essentialism and the pitfalls of identity politics
that plagued cultural feminism (Echols 156, 277). In reality, however, lesbian
nationalism, as Johnston initially imagined it, had less to do with withdrawing
from society than it did with mapping out alternative public spheres—such as
Toronto's LOOT, to which I turn momentarily—where women could trouble
the codes and conventions that confer identity, govern expressivity, and establish the categories of intelligibility through which citizenship is defined,
regulated, and protected, by law.

In *Acts of Gaiety,* I suggest that Johnston's vision of separatism had less
to do with the formation of an actual geopolitical landscape than it did with
fostering affective states of rapture and joy (105–38). The felicity of the performative utterance "I am Gay," as far as she was concerned, had as much to do
with coming out as a lesbian as it did with "coming into that abnormal condition known as elation" (*Lesbian* 122). Sue-Ellen Case convincingly argues that
such "incantations, vocalized for political effect were what we now term 'performative' language rather than, as they have been termed, 'essentialist'" (3).
Far from a declaration of fixed ontology, *lesbian* was for Johnston a practice,
an erotics, "a linguistic tool to break through the centuries-long tradition of
patriarchal, unmarked language" (Case 3). Johnston's primary preoccupation was with what it *feels* like to be gay, not what it *means* to be gay. In other
words, the project of lesbian nationalism sought to promote and proliferate
gayness—as both a sexual politics and an *élan vital*—through the cultivation
of a separatist sphere, an ambient environ predicated upon and open to different sets of affects and affections, to modes of attachments that offer more
capacious sexual and identificatory possibilities for being and belonging. By
rehearsing dramatically different ways in which women produce themselves
as subjects, *Lesbian Nation* challenges our reductive understanding of identity politics, separatist experiments, and cultural feminism.

Lesbian Nation came to serve as a blueprint for the formation of women's
communities across the globe, including LOOT, the Lesbian Organization of

Toronto, which referred to itself as "the house that Jill built" in homage both to Johnston and to the "do-it-yourself" spirit of women's collectives (as in, "Hit the road, Jack," we can erect our own structures and institutions) (Ross). The epicentre of women's cultural production in Ontario, LOOT (1976–1980) consisted of a multi-use community centre located in a house on Jarvis Street that it shared with the Other Woman, a feminist press, and the Three of Cups Women's Coffeehouse, an important locus for women's music. The members of LOOT developed their own rules and regulations, norms, and conventions. As with any other community, they also fostered antagonisms and prejudices that led to exclusionary practices and elitist policies. Whatever failings cultural feminism had, it helped engender vital and viable alternatives to a misogynist, capitalist society and to develop forms of resistance to conformist lifestyles.

Dolan, who in her first book *The Feminist Spectator as Critic* allied herself with Echols in disparaging cultural feminism, has come in recent years, and for a host of reasons, to rethink this position: to question the "usefulness of parsing 'the feminisms'" into a taxonomized hierarchy and to re-evaluate the significance of women's cultural productions by trying to evoke what it feels like to take part in these events and activities ("Feminist" 434). Dolan's work and her own vexed relationship with cultural feminism provide an opportunity and an occasion to think about the emotional draw of women's cultural productions and why it is that "the sharp feelings that motivated" lesbian and feminist politics "have been discounted before scholars really had a chance to analyze what all those heightened emotions . . . accomplished," or to consider what those intense feelings thwarted, stalled, or silenced ("Feeling" 206).

REEL FEELINGS: CINÉMA-VÉRITÉ

Jill Johnston: October 1975 is a prime example of, and features a number of sites associated with, women's cultural production in Toronto, sites integral to the formation of a feminist and lesbian public sphere. It follows Johnston and her lover Ellie during four days of interviews, public readings, consciousness-raising sessions, communal meals, and house parties with local activists and artists. The idea to make the film came from Wazana. Hired to videotape Johnston's lectures at Innis College, she made cinematic history when she suggested to her roommate Armatage, one of the event organizers, that they make a documentary of this important visit. With a largely volunteer crew, borrowed equipment, and five thousand dollars in seed money from Armatage's family, these women—who had absolutely no experience as film directors or producers—created a "creditably professional and feminist 30-minute *cinéma-vérité* documentary" (Armatage 49). (see fig. 1)

Fig. 1. Members of the cast and crew of *Jill Johnston: October 1975*. Bottom left: Kay Armatage, Jill Johnston, and to the far right, Lydia Wazana.

Cinéma-vérité is a particular style of documentary filmmaking that came into prominence in the early sixties and soon dominated television and commercial-movie production. The premise is simple: the camera rolls, "objectively" recording what happens in front of it. The lens, the women at Studio D knew, is not a neutral instrument. Rather, it functions as an operative technology of discipline and domination—or subversion and sedition in the hands of feminist filmmakers—in a complex visual regime of knowledge and power. Female artists and amateurs alike were drawn to the aesthetic and political potential of cinéma-vérité, which they believed would enable them to reveal if not the truth about women's lives, then the lies that pass for truth.

While feminists quickly came to question whether cinéma-vérité actually captures "reality" and whether anything like a female gaze is possible or even desirable, these experiments were a way of staging powerful acts of resistance that disrupted the assumptions and contingent foundations of a heteronormative, patriarchal culture. Close readings of key sections of *Jill Johnston: October 1975* show how dominant epistemologies that conflate knowing with seeing are blind to entire registers of perception, to vast repertoires of gendered and classed forms of expressiveness that camouflage, mask, and veil fugitive forms of communication and feeling. Taking as axiomatic the salience of affect and emotion as operative categories for feminist cinéma-vérité I detail specific strategies this film employs to expose the ways in which mainstream representational strategies induce a wilful amaurosis of the senses.

Jill Johnston: October 1975 was conceived and executed in a feminist manner through collaboration, flexibility of roles, equality of participation, and active engagement of spectators' emotions. It employs a variety of cinematic techniques, including the use of hand-held cameras, jump-cuts, voice-overs, and the filming of real people in uncontrolled situations. Like many Studio D documentaries, it features actual women, not actors playing parts or performers engaged in a masquerade, who, unencumbered by the constraining facade of scripted gender roles, are, at least theoretically, free to tell the truth of themselves. The ways in which women, as social actors, are forced to wear a mask in public is dramatized in the opening sequence of the documentary. In it, Johnston is seen in the makeup chair being powdered and primped for a television interview with Reiner Schwarz. The camera moves from behind the scenes to the set where host and guest meet for the first time. Schwarz has not prepared for the interview. Not only is he unfamiliar with his subject's work—he asks her to list the titles of her three books, as this will "take a load off [his] back"—he mispronounces her name, calling her Johnson (*sans* "t") several times until Jill, politely but firmly, corrects him. Schwarz brushes aside the error only to add insult to injury when he launches into the introduction he plans to use on the air: "If the name Jill Johnston is familiar to you, it may be familiar to you because one day [she] took [her] bra off." No, Johnston corrects him; he has her confused with someone else. At this point an exasperated Schwarz spins around in his chair and exclaims, "Well, obviously I've been misinformed. I'm going home." What I love about this scene is Johnston's masterful control of the terms of the interview. This merry prankster had, in fact, taken off her bra in public at a women's liberation event, and this act had been documented in detail in the press, but Johnston refused to let Schwarz, who knew nothing about her save for some sensational media image, categorize her as an angry, militant dyke, and certainly not at the expense of talking seriously about her literary achievements (Curtis).

The film's opening sequence—of Jill Johnston behind the scenes on Schwarz's show—illustrates a central tenet of feminist cinéma-vérité: telling the story of how a work is produced is as important as the subject of the film itself. This emphasis on reflexivity over narrativity was seen as a way to dissolve, if not eliminate, the art-life distinction in order to educate the public about the theatricalized deceptions daily practised on them by political leaders and media outlets. Wazana and Armatage display an investment in process over product and the act of creation over the created object. The directors expose the means of production and the hidden labour of women's emotional work while at the same time staging an inquiry into how identities (both hegemonic and oppositional) are constructed, sustained, and made legible within different representational and affective economies. This point is further emphasized in the sequence that follows the Schwarz interview. Flashing back to Johnston's arrival in Toronto, we watch Jill and Ellie arriving by plane then car to Wazana and Armatage's apartment, an expansive industrial loft above a bank. As the Canadian feminists welcome the American visitors with warm smiles and hugs, we notice the directors have made a conscious decision to include, rather than disguise, the camera operators, sound engineers, and photographers documenting this moment. Audiences in the 1970s would have been surprised, if not delighted, to see women seizing the means of cinematic production.

The soundtrack for this sequence consists of dialogue interspersed with a voice-over of Johnston talking about women's struggle to individuate from men but also from "tribal mothers" whose labour supports the patriarchy by keeping females bound to a biological imperative and embedded in normative kinship systems. Voice-overs, consisting primarily of Johnston's Steinian-inflected prose and her stream-of-consciousness musings on life and art, punctuate the entire film, thwarting rather than ensuring clarity. Intent on disrupting any semblance of plot or linear narrative structure, the film begins and ends *in medias res*. Less concerned with creating a didactic, consumable political message than with exploiting film's affective dimensions, the directors capitalize on the cinematic image, which, like Johnston's poetry, is experienced through multiple senses.

HOSTILE VIBES: TELLING IT LIKE SHE FEELS IT

The most dramatic scene in the film takes place at a public reading where Johnston, unnerved by a group of men in the back of the auditorium who refuse to take a seat, tells the crowd: "I feel a hostile male element in here. . . . I don't mind guys being here, but I feel a hostile male element that I don't like and that's making me agitated." This declaration escalates rather than diffuses the tension Johnston intuits. "Not all men are hostile," a young man seated in the front row proclaims, oblivious to the fact that his misinterpretation of Johnston's comment and his commandeering of the lecture constitute acts of aggression. Accustomed to male hecklers, Johnston snaps back: "You're making a generalization, man. . . . See, I'm feeling your hostility. . . . You better get the fuck out of here or I'm going to kick you right in the balls and get you out of here so fast, man. You better get the fuck out of here right away because I don't like it." Divided shouts from the spectators accompany this threat. A number of women yell "yeah" and "right on" while clapping loudly in support of Johnston. Others groan "come on" while booing and hissing the speaker. (see fig. 2)

Springing to his feet to challenge Johnston, the heckler moves toward the podium, smirking with his right hand on his hip and his left hand waving in a gesture of dismissal. "I don't feel any hostility," he says with authority. To which Johnston replies, "I said *I felt* a hostile male vibe in here, and *I* don't like it. You don't feel. *I* feel it. You feel something different than I feel." A woman seated on the floor in the front row of the audience attempts to quell the commotion. As she speaks, her voice is eclipsed by an audio splice of Johnston saying, "I think we've just reached the limit of what the male ego can and wants to do possibly, and there's going to be a kind of glacial change." The voice-over ends here, and we return to the scene, to Johnston listening to the woman and smiling. "I'm telling you how I feel," she says. "Ain't that fabulous? You got somebody here telling you how they feel."

Fig. 2. Jill Johnston feels hostile vibes from male members of the audience. *Jill Johnston: October 1975*, directed by Lydia Wazana and Kay Armatage.

In this exchange, Johnston attempts to explain the "*mise-en-scène* of feeling-understanding-knowing" constitutive of a feminist consciousness and how this is radically different than the affective-apprehensive-interpretive field of the patriarchal imaginary (Conquergood 149). Instead of listening, affirming, and sympathizing with Johnston, the protester disrupts and discredits her while the other men in the room stand apart and aloof, complicit in what they witness. This scene dramatizes what Johnston called the "corrective rage" that accompanies and seeks to counteract displays of sexism and misogyny (*Gullible's* viii). Her outburst conveys a sense of urgency about the need for gender equity and social reform, and it hails the women in the audience into an affective economy, Sara Ahmed's phrase describing the ways in which emotions mobilize and marshal constituencies (*Cultural Politics* 20–42). Long before the "affective turn" in critical theory, '70s feminists engaged in and elaborated a passionate politics in which feelings were understood as vital for refashioning subjectivities and reordering society (Clough and Halley).

The affective economy of '70s feminism was fuelled by anger, but also by hope and love, among other emotions. Intense and sustained participation in the struggle for social change entails a tremendous expenditure of emotional, intellectual, and manual labour. Women's spaces and cultural productions provided a healthy respite for players swept up in the *sturm und drang* of politics. Women's music, theatre, and dances provided balm for battle wounds and encouraged the kind of emotional connections and affective bonds that enabled activists to keep fighting the good fight. After a day or night of activism—protesting, canvassing, or staffing a rape crisis hotline—social gatherings in an intimate setting allowed women to blow off steam and recharge their batteries, but more importantly they nurtured people's faith in the validity and efficacy of their labours. House parties, especially in communities without a women's centre, were an important part of the affective economy of '70s feminism.

Jill Johnston: October 1975 features a number of women-only spaces, including a consciousness-raising session about sex work, in which Johnston shares what it felt like to attend a strip club in London with Kate Millett, and a party at Wazana and Armatage's loft. In contrast to the public events, which were somewhat formal and consisted of sizable crowds of men and women, many of whom were strangers to one another, the party was a private affair for intimate associates and the guests of honour. The camera pans the room to show a group of revellers, Maenad-like, talking and laughing, drinking and smoking pot, playing drums and dancing. Their body language, proximity to one another, and gestures of physical affection indicate a relaxed, almost euphoric atmosphere. People engage freely in public displays of affection—snuggling, kissing, and holding hands. Johnston—dressed in a yellow T-shirt, plaid flannel shirt, patchwork dungarees, and knee-high leather boots—works the room, cavorting with several members of the collective as she struts her stuff across the living-room dance floor. Ellie, Johnston's lover, appears nonchalant about Jill's flirtatious exploits and seems as accustomed to sharing Jill with other women as she is with sharing her bed. In stark contrast to the mood in the lecture hall, there's not a hostile vibe in the room.

The soundtrack for this sequence consists of a voice-over in which an inebriated Johnston waxes philosophically about the differences between men and women, about how her writing style, which tends to be circular in its logic with no paragraphs or punctuation, is tied to her biological rhythms, and about her thoughts on bisexuality (she thinks it "causes lots of trouble"). Audible alongside this besotted disquisition is the soundtrack. It features Carole Pope, a new wave Canadian chanteuse with a penchant for bondage wear who became one of the first openly lesbian artists to achieve international fame. As the lead vocalist for Rough Trade—a sexual reference for a casual or anonymous erotic encounter—Pope would write and record one of the first explicitly themed lesbian Top 40 hits in the world, "High School Confidential" (1981). The song in the film soundtrack is titled "Footless Dancer," which, because of the competing sonic tracks, sounds as if Pope is singing "foolish dancer." The song appears again at the end of the film as the credits roll, leaving audiences with the image of Johnston as a "foolish [sic] dancer, a well-paid prancer."

MOOD SWINGS

These lyrics accurately describe the Jill Johnston who visited Toronto in 1975. The self-appointed court jester of '70s feminism, Johnston was as famous for her dance criticism as she was for her alcohol-induced escapades, shameless sapphic spectacles, and piercing polemical diatribes. Her gay exploits were legendary, and she treated her antics as artistic events, reviewing them as performances in her weekly *Village Voice* column alongside concerts, happenings, and Fluxus experiments. Because of her platform at the *Voice* and her savvy upstaging of mainstream media events, Johnston was one of the most famous activists of the 1970s, and, within the context of movement politics, one of the most controversial. Her national presence and self-conscious fashioning of a sexually deviant celebrity persona meant that her opinion carried a great deal of weight among artists and activists. Hence the filmmakers' shock and dismay when she lobbed a bombshell at the premiere of *Jill Johnston: October 1975* and denounced the picture.

Neither Wazana nor Armatage could have imagined that Johnston would criticize the documentary for making her look foolish, not when the joker was a persona she had spent years cultivating through carefully choreographed acts of gaiety. Nor could they have predicted that America's first "shameless public lesbian" would object specifically to the scene in which she aggressively confronts men who disrupt her public reading (Solomon). "I feel it's like someone not taking herself seriously," Johnston complained to the directors. Saying "she couldn't relate to the film" and that the image it created—"the flipped out lesbian, the performing-seal commando"—would "harm her aspirations as a serious writer," Johnston took umbrage with the lack of attention to her creative process, which was the reason she thought she was invited to Toronto (Gilday 57). When the directors attempted to refute Johnston's charge that the film was exploitative or sensational, things really heated up. Johnston launched into a vitriolic personal attack, levelling charges of homophobia and elitism against members of the film collective and threatening legal action against anyone who distributed the movie. Lacking any juridical authority, the writer's bellicose posturing was intended not to frighten the filmmakers but to guilt them into submission, and it worked. The directors felt so bad about disappointing their feminist icon that they publicly agreed to Johnston's terms. Not only have they refrained from showing the documentary outside the country, they have rarely screened it in Canada.

We have yet to take a full account of the effect such impassioned scenes had on second-wave feminism or to explore how and to what extent activists' feelings about the past (pride, embarrassment, anger, joy, etc.) affect their— and by extension our—interpretation of the historical record. In the case of *Jill Johnston: October 1975*, emotional dynamics dictated what materials got put into circulation and what objects and artifacts got archived. If we want to make sense of this pivotal moment in transnational relations between Canadian and American feminists, we need to understand what precipitated Johnston's change of heart about the film, and specifically how, in a span of just two years, she went from being flattered to furious, lustful to litigious, and shameless to chagrined in her feelings about the project. Attention to the affective dynamics of the film's reception challenges received wisdom about the pitfalls and possibilities of cultural feminism, the ethics and efficacy of separatist political projects, and the devolution of radical energies into conservative aspirations that portend the rise of neo-liberalism.

Crestfallen and publicly humiliated by Johnston's reaction to their film, the collective's stunned silence at the premiere was countered by vociferous outrage on their behalf by members of the feminist press, who penned caustic reviews not of the documentary but of its subject's opprobrious behaviour. In *Cinema Canada*, Katherine Gilday accuses Johnston of hypocrisy, of censuring the documentary not because it was a misrepresentation "but because it didn't portray her as she *wanted* to be seen." Gwen Hauser, writing for *The Body Politic*, Canada's premiere lesbian and gay publication, said Johnston's rant against the film constituted "some of the most patently reactionary anti-woman statements ever heard in [such a] setting." Hauser expressed shock that the American was able to get "away with it without being skewered by the lesbian community."

Gilday and Hauser were not alone in judging Johnston's performance at the Innis College film forum a treasonous act, one that set the women's liberation movement back. I want to argue that Johnston's tantrum in Toronto set movement politics *forward*, by which I mean it pushed them *ahead*, away from the gay old time of cultural feminism and toward the sobering straight time of sexual neo-liberalism. A normative and normalizing form of political optimism characterized by a demobilized and depoliticized constituency, sexual neo-liberalism is predicated on the notion that women's happiness, security, and freedom come not from forging alternative public spaces or separatist spheres such as LOOT but from embracing the cultural dictates and socio-economic principles of mainstream society. Buying into the notion that individual fortune and minoritarian progress necessitate an investment in free-market capitalism and the discriminatory workings of the nation-state, neo-liberals do not contest dominant heteronormative forms, but uphold and sustain them. Johnston's surprising rejection of the documentary presages the neo-liberalization of sexual politics that takes root in the mid 1970s and very quickly effects the domestication of revolutionary aspirations, the commodification of activist energies, and the erosion of cultural feminist practices that might have helped thwart this assimilationist-oriented mode of consumer citizenship.

By the time of the film's premiere in 1977, Johnston had left movement politics. She felt that feminism and gay liberation had failed to bring about the emancipation and empowerment of women, herself included. At best, it reinforced lesbians' position at the margins of cultural intelligibility. The inquisitive spirit and utopian impulses that crowned Johnston a culture hero and made it possible for her to live and write as an out dyke were quickly dissipating in a backlash of conservatism. Whereas *Lesbian Nation* was a critically acclaimed bestseller, the manuscript Johnston was invited to Toronto to share had been rejected by multiple publishers and was unsigned at the time of the film's premiere. Neither lesbians nor experimental prose were in vogue by the late 1970s. To complicate matters, *The Village Voice*, under new management, notified Johnston that it was cancelling the column she had penned since 1959. The founders of the *Voice* had given Johnston complete artistic licence to write about whatever she wanted and in whatever way she wanted. Not only had they encouraged her queer art of high amusement and contempt for authority, they had supported her through nervous breakdowns, incarceration, and phases of mental instability (*Admission* ii). Johnston had never imagined that "her fame (infamy to some) and wide berth for both political and literary outrage would ever end," and she never stopped to think about what she would do when her cultural capital as North America's first public lesbian threatened to bankrupt rather than bankroll her career (ii).

In need of work and seeking the security of steady income, Johnston felt it necessary to improve her reputation and to distance herself from behaviour that might dissuade potential employers from hiring her. She saw *Jill Johnston: October 1975* as yet another millstone around her neck, a "giantess misshapen profile rigged up in the glare of [inter]national publicity" (iii). In renouncing the jester who appears in the documentary, Johnston rejects the ludic politics of lesbian nationalism and recants any faith she once had in cultural feminism and separatist political projects to create alternative worlds governed by obverse arrangements of affects and identifications. Fuelled by fear and anxiety about the future, her performance at Innis Hall marks a hastened retreat from the pleasurable and playful spirit of *Lesbian Nation* and heralds the abstemious approach to social equality that undergirds sexual neo-liberalism. This episode shows that, contrary to what critics like Alice Echols have argued, it was not the turn toward cultural feminism that precipitated the devolution of progressive politics but the turn away from it.

I am less interested in judging whether Johnston's rejection of the film makes her a sellout—she saw it as a gesture of self-preservation—than I am in the deep and profound sense of shame the documentary elicits, and which she projects onto the filmmakers. In her memoir of the *Lesbian Nation* years, Johnston confesses to being mortified when she reflects back on the rabid militancy that engendered her celebrity and endeared her to women across the globe. "Nothing . . . relieves a certain embarrassment I can have over a lack of detachment in my political diatribes," she laments (vii). The "[t]ones of unvarnished rage, of didactic hyperbole, and of unapologetic disregard for every conventional nicety in the political pieces were never pretty," Johnston concedes, "and much less attractive than ever at this remove in time" (i). The sense of shame Johnston felt about her political exploits increased rather than decreased with age. My goal here is not to speculate as to why this was the case but rather to indicate the extent to which Johnston's feelings about the past shaped her writing, colouring her interpretation of history (and by extension ours), while simultaneously circumscribing or circumventing the documentary's future (not to mention access to and knowledge of this volatile period in history).

Feelings of attachment and disidentification circulate—long after events conclude, artifacts have been put away, and unpleasant experiences are forgotten. On the fortieth anniversary of *Jill Johnston: October 1975*, which was oft-cited at the 2013 Toronto International Film Festival but not screened, we can see that Armatage and Wazana didn't simply record history; they created a time capsule. My goal in picking the lock of this buried treasure has not been to produce more tchotchkes for feminism's cabinet of curios or more emotional baggage for its archive of feelings. Rather, I have sought to stage an affective encounter with a freighted moment in feminism in order to understand how feelings illuminate and obscure historical complexity about social movements. The trajectory of this ill-fated celluloid artifact reminds us that we have forgotten much more than we remember about women's liberation, and about cultural feminism and lesbian nationalism in particular, including details that, after all these years, are still capable of disturbing the atmosphere.

THE SECRETS OF OTHERS
JULIE SALVERSON

I've always been attracted to catastrophic events. Joseph Campbell says to "follow your bliss" (113), and while others respond by pursuing love or fulfillment, I'm drawn to tragedy and the fault lines in the psyche of a culture, the secrets that fester in families, leak quietly into communities and sometimes explode. I grew up listening to other people's secrets. Vicarious suffering helped me weep.

"I woke in bits, like all children, piecemeal over the years," writes Annie Dillard. As time went by, "awake more often than not . . . I predicted with terrifying logic that one of these years not far away I would be awake continuously and never slip back, and never be free of myself again" (11). I spent decades avoiding this kind of imprisonment. I hated confessional memoirs, particularly about childhood. I have few conscious memories of my own early years. I know that I cringed every time my mother assured friends that her daughter was the world's best babysitter. I hated being left alone with other people's toddlers. When the visiting parents disappeared for a stroll through my mother's blossoming garden, I would half-heartedly roll a ball across the floor, or comb a doll's hair, feeling miserable and confused. Something mysterious was expected of me. I had no idea how to play.

When I was in grade nine, some friends let my mother and me stay alone in their cottage on Georgian Bay. One night she went to sleep with candles burning. I was in my usual spot out on the rocky cliff watching the stars. I came back around midnight to burning curtains. We drove home in silence and my parents talked quietly in the kitchen about a trial separation—between me and Mom's drinking.

Dad was packing for Montreal to spend a few months writing a science-fiction television series so a neighbour let me live with her. Sylvia's old farmhouse was calm and I loved chatting with her while she made dinner. I admired her graceful hands as she taught me to chop garlic. "Vigorous, be vigorous!" she said, standing back to coach as I pressed hard on the flattened knife.

Sylvia treated me like an adult. She had been a dancer when she was young and she now helped young women get abortions by driving them across the American border. I thought this secret rescue was even more glamorous than ballet. Sylvia did something in the world about real problems. Not like the neurotic problems at our house. Perhaps that was when I decided to become an activist and save the world.

"What goes on with your parents isn't your fault," she assured me. "You'll be an adult soon, everything will be fine. You'll be fine." Her tanned face crinkled when she smiled. I think Sylvia really believed that growing up would offer me refuge. But Annie Dillard got it right. Eventually you catch up with yourself.

***

Not long ago a friend pushed a newspaper under my door. "The Day The Sky Exploded" says that scientists have discovered all there is to know about what happened when an atomic bomb fell on Hiroshima. It was almost seventy years ago; time to close the book and move on. "All uncertainties must be ironed out." I'm sure this is reassuring to some. But certainly makes me nervous. I'm not easily reassured. I'm the person who hears something like this and buys a plane ticket to Japan. The trip to Hiroshima is the culmination of a ten-year journey that begins, in strictly geographic terms, with a uranium mine in northern Canada and an invitation. In personal terms, it starts in the shadows of an atomic childhood.

One Saturday night in Toronto in 2002 I walked into my apartment carrying a bouquet of daffodils. It had been a long winter and I was recovering from a busy teaching term. The phone rang. It was my colleague Peter van Wyck, a professor who writes about disaster and nuclear threat.

Peter has a low baritone. "Did you know that the uranium used to develop atomic bombs dropped on Japan came from a uranium mine in northern Canada?" I didn't. Nor did most people I later would ask. Somehow this was left out of our public-school curriculum. "The mine was shut down in the sixties," said Peter, "but the site is still there, on the edge of Great Bear Lake, in the Northwest Territories. It's about five hundred kilometres north of Edmonton, near a town called Deline."

The opening lines of a play I wrote flashed through my head: "What would you do," the teacher asks the student, "if I told you something you don't want to know?" The student thinks. "I guess it depends what happens after you hear a bad story. Do I have to feel bad?" The teacher smiles. "Oh, you'll feel bad when you hear about this!"

Witnessing is the trendy term when it comes to talking about loss. I've written carefully about the kind of responsibility and qualities of attention it demands. For over thirty years I've worked with survivors of violence—refugees, victims of assault, marginalized youth—to create theatre. I become a witness when people tell me their experiences and we create a play. Meeting people under these circumstances is never dull and helping them stage their experience is rewarding, even pleasurable. What isn't fun is listening to accounts of abuse, aggression, and cruelty.

Lately I've felt exhausted and ill. Am I taking this concept of witnessing too far? What kind of person pursues trauma like a thrill-seeker chasing storms and then agonizes over not being able to help? I once told my therapist I couldn't do anything for a friend who was going through cancer. "All I can do is listen." My therapist shook his head and looked at me sadly. "You think listening is a small thing?"

I've never believed that listening was enough. What do I *do* with what I hear? I didn't grow up with organized religion, but my father would tell stories about how his Icelandic grandfather in Winnipeg carried food to other new immigrants. They lived in tents by the Red River at forty below zero. The city had organizations that the old Icelander could have worked with, but that wasn't my great-grandfather's way. You didn't trust charities or groups to do your job for you. You paid attention and rolled up your sleeves. I developed an even more urgent sense of witnessing and responsibility in graduate school. It isn't only passing on a story that matters; I have to let the story change me. That's where the bearing of the witness—the carrying of the event—comes in.

On the day that Peter called, I had decided that I shouldn't do this work anymore. My first impulse, as he crooned on about atomic bombs and Canada was to slam the phone down. I'd sent out a kind of force-field announcement to the universe: "Enough is enough!" Of course, when you do that kind of thing, the opposite tends to happen. But I had a legitimate reason. I was following professional advice.

My doctor's acupuncture office is a corner suite at the end of a luxurious hallway of old oak and refurbished copper. One week before Peter's call, I lay on a high, flat table beside a river overflowing from the previous night's rain, listening to geese through the open window. My doctor is competent and kind. Her white coat sparkles in the sunshine. She bends over and I wince as each acupuncture needle enters my aching back. "You are exhausted," she says.

I tell her that I came back from Germany a month ago and have been tired and listless ever since. "You haven't fully returned," she mutters. "Your physical body is here but not your ethereal body. Part of you is still over there, the part that isn't yet finished with the journey. What were you doing in Europe?"

I sigh into her lavender pillow. This sounds New Age to me, but the woman is right, to say that I am not "all here" feels accurate. "I work as a playwright with people who've survived trauma. I help them tell their stories. I've been visiting memorials and museums about the Holocaust."

There is a pause while strips of paper are efficiently ripped from needles. She plunges them into the bottom of my spine. My doctor is German. "This treatment will make you feel better. Help you return. But it is not enough."

The geese honk furiously. She strides to the window and slams it shut. "Next time, you must study something else." I feel a gentle hand on the back of my neck. "Next time, why don't you research paradise?"

My work has allowed me to briefly glimpse the secrets of others. It is often after the fact that I understand how some gesture, something I've seen or heard, teaches me. I recall one now, told to me by a South African friend. For the Sangoma people, spirits in the body travel different routes and carry a person's history through the body. When that spirit, or history, is blocked—not told—illness occurs.

Getting sick scares me. I don't want it to happen again. I listen while Peter describes a black-and-white documentary called *Village of Widows*. "The director, Peter Blow, went with them to Japan!" "Japan?" "Yes, yes, this is the reason I'm calling!" I twist the plastic phone cord as Peter tells me that when the Dene on Great Bear Lake found out about the connection between their land and the bomb, ten of them got on a plane and went to Japan to offer the *hibakusha*—the atomic-bomb survivors—an apology.

As soon as I hear this, I'm hooked. All my resolve goes out the window and I'm asking question after question. Why would they do that? What kind of responsibility are they taking, these Dene from northern Canada who surely are the victims in this situation, not the perpetrators?

Within weeks Peter and I are writing a grant proposal to the Canadian government. We want to follow the path of Canadian uranium and its stories, and write about what it means to bear witness to a route, an historical account, and an archive. We will both produce scholarship about this, and it is my hope to write an opera libretto. Even as I draft my pages I am conflicted. How did my doctor put it? *Next time, why don't you research paradise?* Shouldn't I be finding hopeful stories to write about, not flying to a uranium mine? My mind churns *No!* while my fingers type *Yes!*

I state reasons why I must do this project: I can be a witness, I can write about it, I have a track record as a scholar and a playwright. I've become too good at generating ideas, they rush out in a torrent of explanation. Do I really want to immerse myself in another disaster? Like an addict on a hit, I type furiously—arguments, rationales, possibilities. I print the pages and admire their tidy lines, the smell of fresh ink.

I pore over scholarship and writing that inspires me, framing my part of the research proposal in terms of what it means to bear witness to historical memory. I find a spiral notebook from a graduate-school ethics class and read a passage I have written and underlined heavily: "In Jewish tradition, there is the path (*haggadah*) and the law (*halakhah*). *Halakah* is from the root *halakh*: to walk, to go. It is about what is binding, commanded, permitted, forbidden. The *haggadah* is from the root *higgid*: to say, tell, narrate. It is about stories, legends, witticism. The path is not something followed, it is something transmitted, passed on, listened for. It is dangerous when the requirement to pass on is forgotten. Or lost."

I am not Jewish but this tradition captures something important. Suddenly I have a gut sense that this trip might be just what the doctor ordered. For once the destination is my own country, but it's more than that. I have been obsessed with nuclear war and atomic bombs all my life; maybe it's time to ask why. I decide to write my way through my own haunting. I won't only travel the path of Canada's connection to the atomic bomb. If I'm lucky, I'll unravel my own.

COMPLICATED FEELINGS: *TECUMSEH* AS LITERARY LAND CLAIM

HEATHER DAVIS-FISCH

It is autumn 1885. Charles Mair suffers from writer's block, unable to finish his drama *Tecumseh*, which "depict[ed] dramatically the time and scenes in which the great Indian so nobly played his part—at first independently and in his own country, and afterwards in alliance and leadership with General Brock in the War of 1812" (Mair, Preface 4). Mair began the play's final act, in which Tecumseh heroically died, months earlier, but was interrupted on March 27 when he learned of the Battle of Duck Lake, the skirmish between North West Mounted Police and Métis militia that marked the beginning of the Northwest Rebellion. A mere ten days later, Mair was aboard a train, determined to help put down the uprising (Shrive 172–76). When he returned to Windsor, Ontario, in July of that same year, having seen no military action, Mair remained in a state of heightened anxiety: "Most significant of all obstacles was the tension created in him by Riel's trial and the subsequent delay in carrying out the sentence. . . . [U]ntil Riel was hanged in November Mair seemed to undergo a strain that only an execution could relieve" (Shrive 176).

Charles Mair had a troubled history with the Métis leader, whom he first encountered while he was paymaster for the construction of the Fort Garry Road and moonlighting as the *Globe*'s first Northwest correspondent (Bumsted 41).[1] In the summer of 1869, the men met several times, most

---

1 Mair's published letters in the *Globe* quickly got him into trouble at Red River: he became notorious for criticizing "half-breed women" (Shrive 70) and suggesting that "'halfbreed' indolence" caused famine in the region (Bumsted 41). "L.R."—Louis Riel—responded by disparaging Mair and protesting that he gave "the impression elsewhere that there was no need of relief in Red River" (qtd. in Bumsted 43).

notably when Riel visited Pointe des Chênes, Manitoba, to observe Mair's road party (Shrive 87). The animosity that developed must be understood against the backdrop of the transfer of the Northwest Territory from the Hudson's Bay Company (HBC) to the Dominion of Canada, scheduled for December 1, 1869. Métis saw land-survey crews as examples of Canada exercising illegitimate authority in the territory (Ray 197); annexationists, in contrast, did not believe that the Métis "had any valid rights to land" (Ray 177). During the Red River Rebellion, Riel imprisoned Mair and, in late December 1869, his provisional government sentenced Mair to death; Riel apparently told Mair, "[W]e can't save you, you must prepare to die" (qtd. in Bumsted 109). Mair narrowly escaped to Ontario and devoted much of his career to promoting the western settlement to which Riel was opposed.

Mair held complex views on Riel and the Red River and Northwest Rebellions. He saw the first conflict as a "struggle between Canadian national expansion" and the "greedy monopoly" of the HBC; to Mair, the Métis were pawns in this struggle (Shrive 173), but Riel was a murderer (Bumsted 171). His feelings about the Northwest Rebellion were equally mixed: as a businessman, he sided with the Métis in their demands for the federal government to provide land titles (Shrive 154), yet he continued to see their leader as "a horrible villain" and hoped "to make Riel [his] captive!" (qtd. in Shrive 176, 175). These inconsistencies are representative of Mair's often contradictory sentiments and experiences. As a passionate patriot, he was a founding member of the nationalist Canada First group.[2] As a journalist, he established the *Prince Albert Times and Saskatchewan Review* to promote western settlement, advocating "a specifically Protestant immigration that would sweep aside the Roman Catholic Métis as well as the natives" (Latham). As a romantic conservationist, he "bewail[ed] the imminent demise of the First Nations" and "condemn[ed] the railroad for the extinction of the buffalo" (Grubisic 72).

---

2 Canada First was a nationalist group founded in Ottawa in 1868. The group hoped to lay the intellectual foundations of the new nation and combined recognition of Canada's Anglo-Saxon heritage with a desire for increased Canadian autonomy. They were firmly opposed to American influences and feared American annexation of territories in what is now western Canada (Vigod).

By the late 1870s, he had come to believe that "although the old way of life on the prairie was doomed by settlement, there was much more that was good" about Métis life than he had believed as a young man (Cogswell 9).

In contrast to his shifting views of Indigenous peoples who were his contemporaries, Mair's opinion concerning the historical Tecumseh was un-ambiguous:[3] he had long admired his "transcendent ability" and his "genius and self-sacrifice at the most critical period of [Canada's] history" (Mair, Preface 5).[4] By writing about Tecumseh, Mair hoped to "urge by means of literature . . . a recognition of Canada's heroic past and of her potentiality for a magnificent future" (Shrive 157–58). Norman Shrive, Mair's biographer, suggests that Mair's emotional investment in Tecumseh even led him to move his family to Windsor because of its proximity to places where Tecumseh fought during the "critical period" of the War of 1812;[5] while living there, Mair "immers[ed] himself in the atmosphere and history" of the region (Shrive 161), visiting the Thames battleground where Tecumseh died and fruitlessly searching for Tecumseh's unknown grave (Shrive 162).[6]

There is something uncanny in imagining Mair at his desk in Windsor in 1885. Fascinated with a charismatic Indigenous leader who united the tribes

---

3   Tecumseh was a Shawnee leader whose people traditionally lived in the Ohio Valley, but had moved northwest to present-day Indiana as Americans expanded their territory.

4   Mair imagined writing a play about Tecumseh as early as 1868, when he published "Prologue to Tecumseh" in his collection of poems, *Dreamland* (Shrive 157).

5   In August 1882, Mair felt that Prince Albert (in present-day Saskatchewan) had grown too dangerous for his family and decided to relocate them to Ontario. Shrive argues that although the move to Windsor satisfied his wife's desire to be near her mother, who lived in Amherstberg, Mair's decision was "almost entirely determined" by his interest in Tecumseh (160–61).

6   Mair's script indicates his belief that Tecumseh's followers buried his body and kept his final resting place a secret (127). Arthur Ray points out, however, that Shawnee oral history actually includes "conflicting stories" about what happened to Tecumseh's body after his death (139).

of the Western Confederacy[7] against Americans who refused to recognize Indigenous rights when they impeded western expansion, Mair desperately wanted to finish his play. Unable to overcome his anxiety about Riel, a charismatic Métis leader who united his people against a government set on expanding the Canadian frontier, Mair could not complete the script until his enemy was executed. The ghost of the not-yet-dead Riel haunted Mair, preventing him from dramatizing Tecumseh's death. Because of *Tecumseh's* literary "weaknesses," it is often characterized as a closet drama (Goldie 48), "the work of a poet who had no experience of the theatre" (Carson), and as "virtually unactable" (Benson and Conolly 13).[8] I propose considering *Tecumseh* not as a failed performance but as the textual remain of an actual performance executed by Mair himself. Arlie Russell Hochschild uses the term transmutation to describe how emotional work—private acts of emotion management—is mapped onto emotional labour—public acts of emotional management (*Managed* 7, 19). In the autumn of 1885, Mair was unable to adequately transmute his feelings in order to complete the play that would

---

7   The Western Confederacy was a pan-tribal group that formed to oppose American expansion into the Northwest Territory at the end of the American Revolution; Tecumseh attempted to reunite these tribes in the early nineteenth century in order to convince American authorities to renegotiate treaties that had been signed with illegitimate Indigenous leaders (Ray 135–37).

8   Shrive argues that Mair was "unfamiliar with dramatic creation" and claims that because of this "inexperience or because of his following the examples of a host of nineteenth-century writers . . . he decided upon the 'literary' or 'closet' drama" (163). Alan Filewod points out that this is a problematic characterization, as "[c]loset dramas were verse plays that weren't produced, and when poets wrote verse plays that were, they were no longer 'closeted'" ("National" 74); in other words, had *Tecumseh* been performed, it would no longer be characterized as a closet drama. Questions about performance intentions are complicated further by Shrive's note that, as he completed the play, Mair had a "growing conviction that the work might actually be staged" (171). Filewod notes that material conditions could have prevented a staged performance, even if Mair desired it ("National" 74). Filewod argues it is more productive to set questions of performance intention aside and instead consider the play as a "metahistorical nationalist fantasy" written for an "imagined theatre—the theatre that *ought* to do *Tecumseh*" (*Performing* 6, 10).

frame Tecumseh's death as a tragedy that laid the groundwork for the birth of Canada. The play that Mair wrote following Riel's November execution retains strange traces of this incomplete transmutation, signalling his melancholic engagements with both Indigenous leaders.

These failures come into focus most clearly in the ways in which *Tecumseh* proposes but fails to consistently operationalize what Daniel Coleman, following Margery Fee, calls a "literary land claim." Coleman explains that in many works of Canadian literature:

> What may appear as sympathy for Indigenous peoples . . . often represents what Margery Fee has called a "literary land claim" . . . insofar as the apparently civil act of memorialization premises itself upon a claim of intimacy with Natives who are figured as approaching the verge of extinction, leaving their memorializers to inherit their words and land. (196, quoting Fee 17–18)

The literary land claim performs an "ideological function" and is "analogous to the historical territorial take-over" (Fee 17). Although Coleman suggests that Mair's *Tecumseh* is a literary ancestor to contemporary literary land claims (196), I contend that the play is actually an early example of this phenomenon, whose "mixed feelings" on the subject resonate for both the play's contemporaneous and contemporary audiences. In *Tecumseh*, Mair discursively constructs the inevitability of racial extinction while evoking sympathy for Tecumseh's desire to help his people survive, introduces a civil white figure—the poet-warrior Lefroy—as Tecumseh's legitimate heir, then generates tragic catharsis to allow characters and readers to mourn Tecumseh's regrettable but ultimately productive death. At the same time, however, Mair undermines his own ideological work, suggesting that Indigenous extinction was not necessitated by progress but was the result of human weakness, introducing American characters as shadow heirs, and reminding readers that Tecumseh's demands were ultimately unresolved. *Tecumseh* not only demonstrates how the emotional labour of the literary land claim is enacted but also, through problematic moments that cannot be fully assimilated into the literary land claim, reveals Mair's inability to fully transmute his various emotional attachments into an ideologically coherent script.

EXTINCTION AND SURVIVAL: "ALL ARE DRIVEN FROM THEIR HERITAGE"

Tecumseh appears to present Indigenous extinction as a sad necessity but actually problematizes this necessity in significant ways. Mair explicitly introduces the idea of racial extinction early in the play, when Tecumseh's niece Iena tells her white lover Lefroy that "[t]he Long-Knife strengthens, whilst our race decays" (23) and predicts how colonizing forces would facilitate this extinction:

> So melts our heedless race! Some weaned away,
> And wedded to rough-handed pioneers
> [. . .]
> Some by outlandish fevers die, and some—
> Caught in the white man's toils and vices mean—
> Court death and find it in the trader's cup.
> And all are driven from their heritage[.] (23–24)

Iena precisely articulates how Indigenous ways of life were being challenged: through intermarriage,[9] the spread of diseases, and access to goods

---

9   Intermarriages between European men and Indigenous women often took the form of *mariages à la façon du pays* or "country" marriages, common-law unions performed outside the official sanction of the Catholic or Protestant church. Despite clerical disapproval, French authorities encouraged these unions in the seventeenth century (Ray 61–62) and these relationships were common between North West Company and Hudson Bay Company employees and Indigenous women until the mid-nineteenth century (Ray 104–05, 174–76). When the first Indian Act was passed in 1876, it included the provision that Indigenous women who married non-status men lost their Indian status and all its associated rights, "violat[ing] long-standing post-contact marriage practices" (Ray 203). Iena's comment, in the context of her romantic relationship to Lefroy, would have had particularly contemporary connotations in the 1880s.

like alcohol. Iena's prediction, however, is undermined by Lefroy's reply: he assures Iena that he will defend her and her race, promising, "My love is yours alone, my hand I give, / With this good weapon in it, to your race" (24). Lefroy's promises, linking romantic love and military defence, suggest the generative potential—both sexual and political—of interracial relationships. The scene pronounces then dismisses the inevitability of Indigenous extinction. Although critics have remarked upon how Tecumseh embodies the necessity of extinction—Filewod calls him "the heroic figure of a doomed race" (*Performing* 31)[10] and Coleman claims that in death "Tecumseh finally resigns himself to the ideology of the waning race" (63)—the vacillation around extinction in Iena and Lefroy's conversation recurs throughout the play, most notably in Mair's characterization of his title character. Tecumseh, far from accepting that his race is tragically doomed, is motivated by an overarching desire to prevent its "waning" by securing the land and rights necessary to ensure its survival. Although Mair ultimately frames Tecumseh's struggle as a tragic one, the impassioned speeches he gives Tecumseh problematize the idea that racial extinction was a fated necessity by consistently reinforcing a causal link between gaining land rights and racial survival. Mair, furthermore, affectively legitimizes the challenge Tecumseh poses to tragic extinction discourses by representing him as a just leader whose noble motivations generate sympathy.

In the first three acts of the play, Tecumseh attempts to politically unite the Wyandot, Miami, Delaware, Kickapoo, and Dahcota tribes in order to force American authorities, represented by General Harrison, to open treaties negotiated in bad faith with illegitimate Indigenous leaders. Tecumseh expresses his grievances most eloquently in the final scene of act two, when he and Harrison meet at Vincennes.[11] Tecumseh tells Harrison "reason was

---

10   Filewod's comment arises from a comparison of Tecumseh to the character of Thayendanegea (Joseph Brant) in J.B. MacKenzie's 1898 *Thayendanegea*, which is generically and ideologically similar to Mair's *Tecumseh*.

11   In August 1810, Tecumseh, accompanied by a large party of armed warriors, met with Harrison at his Vincennes, Indiana, home. There are competing accounts of the meeting, but most include mention of Tecumseh making what was construed as a physical threat

the snare / Which tripped our ancestors," leading them to mistake "your fathers' vows for truth"; the wrongs of these treaties "live with the living, who are here— / Inheritors of all our fathers' sighs, / And tears, and garments wringing wet with blood" (44). As the scene continues, Tecumseh's rhetoric grows more passionate; accusing the Americans of crimes of "broken faith" (50), he cries, "There is no hand to help, no heart to feel, / No tongue to plead for us in all your land. / But every hand aims death, and every heart, / Ulcered with hate, resents our presence here" (50). Tecumseh's rhetorical power generates sympathy for Indigenous peoples' suffering and anger at American colonists.

Although Tecumseh is rhetorically and affectively compelling in this scene, at times his anger with Harrison gets the best of him; these "outbursts" remind white readers of Tecumseh's racial difference because of how they contrast the emotional control displayed by both Harrison and other officers, American and British, throughout the play. Indeed the only other male character who openly displays emotions to the extent that Tecumseh does is Lefroy, a character marked by his indigenization. The first time that Tecumseh's surplus of emotion becomes dangerous occurs when he threatens Harrison: "The injuries which you have done to us / Cry out for remedy, or wide revenge. / Restore the forests you have robbed us of— / Our stolen homes and vales of plenteous corn! [. . .] Ere the axe rise!" (44). Later in the scene, Harrison's implacability leads Tecumseh to erupt: "[W]e shall strike you to the ground! / Pour flame and slaughter on your confines wide, / Till the charred earth [. . .] / Reeks with the smoke of smouldering villages, / And steam of awful fires half quenched with blood" (48). Although Tecumseh's threats are not backed by action, these lines would have reminded readers—with the memory of the Northwest Rebellion still fresh in their minds—of the violent potential of such conflicts. Mair appears to oscillate between representing Tecumseh as just and as capable of "savage" violence; however, the relationship between Tecumseh's righteous anger and its potentially violent effects is somewhat more complicated than this. Donald Grose's discussion of stereotypical representations of

---

to Harrison (see accounts by Benjamin Drake; Edward Egglestone and Lille Egglestone Seelye; H. Marshall; and B. B. Thatcher in Klinck 66–74).

Indigenous masculinity in nineteenth-century American drama is instructive here. Tecumseh's rhetorical power and moral authority mark him as a noble savage, "filled with an intuitive knowledge of nature and its secrets, elegant of speech, stoic, and totally loyal to friends, relatives, and loved ones" (Grose 186). Grose explains that when the noble savage was "brought into conflict with white civilization, three possible methods of adjustment were available: willing victimization, acculturation, and extermination" (186). Extermination results from a rejection of white society that causes the Indigenous figure to relinquish "his natural nobility. Unwilling to go gently into oblivion and equally unwilling to acknowledge his inferiority, the Indian assumes the guise of the red devil," who "thrives in an environment of . . . violence . . . towards well-meaning whites," and whose "savagery grew as much out of his failure to be white as out of his deeds" (187). Grose highlights how these apparently contradictory stereotypes are actually mutually dependent. It is unclear whether Mair was familiar with John Augustus Stone's 1829 play *Metamora*, Grose's main example; however, Mair's representation of how Tecumseh temporarily transforms from powerful and sympathetic rhetorician to violent "red devil" demonstrates how porous the boundary between these two literary stereotypes was.

Presenting a literary land claim that relies upon generating sympathetic feelings about an Indigenous character's fight for fair treaties is a risky move. Mair is careful though: he allows readers to sympathize with Tecumseh by making his motivations emotionally comprehensible and morally laudable but, by directing his frustration at Americans, Mair avoids positioning Canadian readers as perpetrators. Furthermore, his representation of slippage from "noble savage" to "red devil" prevents audience members from fully identifying with Tecumseh. This ambivalent slippage reflects Mair's own experiences. Coleman argues that Tecumseh's nobility acts "as a foil for the treachery of Riel, as a demonstration . . . of how a 'good Indian' should behave" (61). The final moments of the second act, however, suggest how easily a "good Indian" could become a bad one. Mair was certainly anxious about this, believing "[t]he greatest danger" to western settlement "lay . . . in the unpredictable character of the Indians" while also acknowledging that "the

brutal outrages of American frontiersmen . . . gave rise to" this violent potential (Shrive 138–39).[12] The final scene of act two stages the consequences
of failing to negotiate, legitimizing Tecumseh's motivation for land security
but also suggesting that the violence arising from conflicts over land was so
dangerous that, once unleashed, it could only be contained by extermination.

When the action of the play moves north of the border in act four, it appears that alliance with the British will enable Tecumseh to secure land, thus
preventing the extinction Iena feared. In contrast to the contested American
lands described in act two, Upper Canada is explicitly identified as already
British territory, demonstrated in General Brock's use of possessive pronouns
in the lines "We can defend our forest wilderness, / And spurn the bold in-
vader from our shores" (73).[13] Mair also uses Brock to quickly establish the
difference between American and British attitudes toward Indigenous peoples; he, for example, benevolently calls them "[p]oor injured souls, who but
defend their own" (81).[14] Mair then attempts to elide differences in power
by presenting Brock and Tecumseh as what Daniel Coleman terms "brother officers" (Mair 87; Coleman 46–80). When the two men meet, Tecumseh
asks Brock to recognize "that a portion of our own [land] / Is still our own"
and to confirm this recognition through a "sacred treaty to our tribes" in

---

12   In the 1870s, the Plains nations remained a "powerful military threat" (Ray 210),
leading Alexander Morris—the Lieutenant-Governor of the Northwest Territories from
1872–76 and of Manitoba from 1873–78—to caution Ottawa that he believed the Cree,
Siksika, and Assiniboine nations posed a real threat and to encourage the federal government to negotiate treaties quickly.

13   The attitude behind Brock's possessive reflects the perception of many United Empire
Loyalists who, because they "believed land was owed to them in appreciation of their
loyalty . . . did not feel bound by the provisions of the Royal Proclamation," the 1763 act
that asserted Aboriginal title as central to the process of land transfers (Ray 142). Brock's
words are dangerous in their insidiousness, demonstrating that the attitudes held by early
nineteenth-century Loyalists held purchase at the end of the century.

14   The benevolent attitude Mair ascribes to Brock suggests that alliances were established
out of altruism; however, British "benevolence" predated the war as a strategic policy that
used "traditional avenues of trade and gift giving" to "guarantee British control of the upper Canadian peninsula" in the case of conflict with Americans (Ray 136).

exchange for military alliance. Brock agrees, promising that any peace treaty will "bear a seal that doth . . . guard your rights" (87). Brock appears to give Tecumseh what he wants, but the alliance requires Tecumseh to concede to the British title of the territory (rhetorically extinguishing Aboriginal title) and recognize Brock's ability to distribute lands. Both Brock and Tecumseh also ignore the fact that any lands Brock promises would have been far from Tecumseh's traditional territory and, in reality, would likely have belonged to another Indigenous nation.[15]

The hope, problematic as it may be, introduced by Brock and Tecumseh's alliance is ultimately an impotent one. After Brock's death at the end of act four, it becomes clear that treaty settlements and the recognition of Aboriginal rights depend on the whims of individual whites. With the war progressing up the Thames River toward Tecumseh's base at Moraviantown, Tecumseh asks General Proctor, Brock's successor, to help him fight: "We have fought [. . .] Our promise is redeemed! but what of [Brock's]?" (108). When this plea fails, Tecumseh asks Proctor to give him "[t]he arms our father furnished for our use" (108), but Proctor again refuses to help. Tecumseh's only recourse is a heroic last stand during the Battle of the Thames. When he is mortally wounded at the end of the act, Tecumseh's final words are for his people. Asking, "Who now will knit them?" he calls on "the Mighty Spirit" to "shelter—save—my people!" (126).

Tecumseh's death can be interpreted, as it is by both Filewod and Coleman, as a sign that racial extinction is certain; I would argue, however,

---

15   This concession of British ownership, essential to the strategic military alliance that propels both the play's plot and the British war effort, was not shared by all Indigenous leaders when Mair wrote the play. For example, in 1874, Cree leader Pitikwahanapiwiyin (Poundmaker) complained that "[t]he governor mentions how much land is to be given to us. He says 640 acres . . . he will give us. This is our land! It isn't a piece of pemmican to be cut off and given in little pieces back to us" (qtd. in Ray 210). Brock's assumption that all of the "forest wilderness" was British territory and Tecumseh's willingness to negotiate with Brock on these terms cannot be read, then, merely as Mair's effort to accurately represent their historical relationship but must be strategically located within the political frameworks surrounding treaty negotiations in the 1870s and 1880s.

that the ending is slightly more ambiguous and creates space in which the necessity of extinction can be challenged. First, Tecumseh's death does not arise, as it would in an Aristotelian tragedy, from the necessity of internal dramatic circumstances but from human weakness: Proctor's cowardice and disloyalty. His death generates recognition, but this recognition occurs among audience members and is not of the sad historical necessity of his death but of the fact his fate could have been changed. Reading Tecumseh's death metonymically, then, suggests that Indigenous extinction was not a foregone conclusion but could, through civil intervention, be reversed. Second, Tecumseh's final words certainly demonstrate his fear that his people were doomed, but they also underline that his people indeed survived after his death. The real effect of the War of 1812 was not extinction but political and physical displacement (Ray 140–41), which continued to affect Indigenous and non-Indigenous peoples throughout the century. Any suggestion in the play's final moments that Indigenous peoples were close to extinction must be read historically: it is impossible to imagine that anyone reading the play in 1886 could imagine Indigenous peoples as extinct. Indeed, in the wake of Riel's execution, Indigenous peoples were likely a more potent political force than at almost any moment in recent memory. The inconsistency of Mair's representation of extinction—his apparent acceptance of extinction as necessity combined with the play's almost constant reminders of Indigenous presence in 1886—suggests the extent to which he could not completely manage, either discursively or affectively, the relationship between his idealized vision of Tecumseh's role in forging the Canadian nation in the 1810s and his first-hand knowledge of the realities of settler-Indigenous relations in the 1880s. The ambivalence preserved in the text is the consequence of Mair's incomplete transmutation of his own feelings.

LEGITIMATE AND SHADOW HEIRS: "WHO NOW WILL KNIT THEM?"

The literary land claim nominates an heir, a white but "indigenized" surrogate who merges civil and primitive values; Canadian identity, according to Alan Filewod, emerges in this figure at the "interstice of aboriginal Nature and the British monarchy" ("National" 73). Daniel Coleman argues that such forms of indigenization play a significant and strategic role in settler colonies like Canada: "[T]he settler must construct, by a double process of speedy indigenization and accelerated self-civilization, his priority and superiority to latecomers; that is, by representing himself as already indigenous, the settler claims priority over newer immigrants and, by representing himself as already civilized, he claims superiority to Aboriginals and other non-Whites" (16). Indigenization separates Canadians from Britons, particularly in military contexts in which the "faithful brother's indigenous expertise distinguishes his particularly Canadian virtues of virile action and adaptability from the impractical niceties that impede English officers" (Coleman 75). Lefroy, as both Alan Filewod and Terry Goldie note, emerges as precisely this kind of "romantic" indigenized figure (Goldie 32), and this qualifies him as Tecumseh's heir. Filewod argues that Lefroy, "a Byronic Poet 'in love with the woods'" and with Tecumseh's niece Iena, is "transformed from prisoner to disciple, first of Tecumseh and then of Tecumseh's British avatar, Isaac Brock" ("National" 75); at the end of the play, Lefroy emerges "as the prototype of the ideal Canadian" (81) who can fuse "Brock's political philosophy and Tecumseh's natural spirituality" (80).

Lefroy's romance with Iena situates him as Tecumseh's potential genealogical heir. Although Tecumseh is initially opposed to their relationship, proclaiming "Red shall not marry white" (16), he is impressed by Lefroy's courage and his love for Indigenous culture and decides to respect the young lovers' desires (26–27). Since Tecumseh has no children, Iena is like a daughter to him; the early scenes imply that Lefroy and Iena will continue Tecumseh's bloodline. Iena's untimely death, however, eliminates the possibility of literal miscegenation. Instead, Lefroy is transformed into Tecumseh's political heir, the man who can unite not the tribes of the Western Confederacy but Indigenous and British values in the new post-war nation. This is clear when an American officer accuses Lefroy of being "soulless" for leaving his "place in civil, good society / To herd with savages" and Lefroy replies, "My genius leans, like Nature, to all sides, / Can love them all at once, and live with all" (123). Lefroy is the implicit answer to Tecumseh's rhetorical question, posed in his dying speech: "Who now will knit them? who will lead them on?" (126).

It is relatively straightforward to claim that Lefroy emerges as Tecumseh's heir, playing a key role in the play's work as a literary land claim. But what do we make of the candidates for heir the play apparently rejects? In other words, how do we assimilate American characters who "inherit" traditional Indigenous lands in considering Lefroy as Tecumseh's heir? The second scene of act two, which immediately follows a scene in which Tecumseh scathingly indicts American treaty processes, appears to provide comic contrast by introducing four American "yokels" and to alienate civil Canadian readers from the characters by underlining the immorality of American attitudes. The scene begins with the yokels criticizing the belief that Indigenous peoples "shouldn't be meddled with on their resarves, and should hev skoolin'" and arguing that they should be relocated to give "reliable citizens a chance" (37). The conversation then turns to an explicit endorsement of violence: Slaugh says he wants to give Indigenous people "Kernel Crunch's billet" and explains that this Colonel "killed a hull family o' redskins, and stuck 'em up as scar'-crows in his wheat fields" (37). The characters' lowbrow qualities, signified through their debased language, suggest that readers were not meant to identify with their sentiments; it is, however, possible that readers could initially dismiss them as mere comic relief. In contrast, the disturbing story that follows this exchange highlights the legitimacy of Tecumseh's grievances. Twang, discussing a Moravian mission church nearby, describes how "Kernel Crawford" had his militia surround the church "when the Injuns was all a-prayin'" and then "put a squad o' melish' at each winder with their bayonets pinted and sot fire to the Church, and charred up the hull kit, preacher and all!" (38). For readers who missed the point of the story, Twang describes how survivors "got lands from the British . . . and founded what they call the Moravian Town" (38).

Twang's glorification of genocidal violence establishes the British obligation to protect Indigenous peoples from Americans. At the same time, however, Mair's depiction of this overt racism potentially overshadows the subtle, institutionalized racism that underlay settlement policies and treaty negotiations in Canada, distracting readers from recognizing that their own perspectives might fall on this spectrum of racism.

In the next scene, Mair appears to contrast the "yokels" with civilized Americans, but ultimately suggests that American leaders are little more than educated versions of Twang and friends. Barron, an Indian agent, tells General Harrison about Tecumseh's complaint that treaties are "heavy loads" that do not reflect how "[a]ll lands . . . are common to his race" (40). Harrison calls Tecumseh's demand "[a]bsurd!" because it would prevent "[a]ll purchase and all progress" (40). Harrison echoes the yokels' complaints about reserves and land use, although he expresses them more articulately. Harrison's speech also provides Canadian readers emotionally affected by Tecumseh's arguments and offended by the preceding genocidal sentiments with a rational argument against Tecumseh's demands. Although Harrison speaks from an American perspective, he describes the economic complexities faced by the Canadian government, which had just finished negotiating numbered treaties one through seven.[16] By the 1880s, it was becoming clear that the treaty process was more expensive and complicated than Sir John A. Macdonald's government had anticipated. The sympathetic Harrison[17] subtly validates concerns about the cost of these settlements and delicately allows Mair's readers to displace explicit questions about treaty negotiations across the American border.

The second act of *Tecumseh* elides cultural similarities between the United States and British North America, figuring the United States as foreign

---

16   Treaties one through seven were signed between 1871 and 1877 and gave Canada title to most of the land in Manitoba, Saskatchewan, and northwestern Ontario.

17   Mair recognized that his sympathetic portrayal of Harrison was potentially problematic, but when his friend George Taylor Denison objected to his characterization, Mair replied that he could not "falsify history for the sake of dramatic effect" (qtd. in Shrive 171).

"other" in order to distinguish British-Canadian identity. Lefroy emerges as Tecumseh's symbolic heir, a uniquely "Canadian" figure who merges
Tecumseh's natural nobility and Brock's civilized vision of the future. But
the American characters who appear in act two—both the yokels and the
civilized gentlemen—were Tecumseh's literal heirs: they inherited, through
illegitimate treaties and war, lands traditionally occupied by Tecumseh's people. If the United States acts as a screen on which Canadian concerns were
projected and explored, these characters are shadow heirs, representations
of the desires—for erasure, for displacement, for genocide—that had to be
deliberately forgotten in order for Mair to nominate Lefroy as the progenitor
of modern Canada.

MOURNING AND MELANCHOLIA: "SLEEP WELL, TECUMSEH, IN THY UNKNOWN GRAVE"

Terry Goldie identifies *Tecumseh* as an example of the "Indian heroic tragedy" (173), a genre that dramaturgically and affectively relies, I would argue,
upon the death of the doomed Indigenous male hero. In order for *Tecumseh*
to perform its emotional and cultural work as a literary land claim, it must
first generate a particular and admittedly partial form of catharsis, allowing
the audience to pity Tecumseh and mourn his death, then providing paths
to emotional closure, allowing the audience to move forward and forget. In
contrast to Aristotelian tragedy, which generates pity and fear and then purges
these emotions through catharsis, in Indian heroic tragedies like *Tecumseh*,
there is no fear, only pity. In *Rhetoric*, Aristotle explains that pity arises in
response to an evil that "appears . . . to befall one who does not deserve it"
(60); in these tragedies, Indigenous characters were frequently figured as characters unfairly but necessarily harmed or destroyed by the forces of western
expansion and colonization. Aristotle then differentiates between fear and
pity, explaining that "whatever people *fear* in their own case . . . they pity as
happening in the case of others" (61). While both feelings emerge in response
to a tragic hero with whom the audience identifies emotionally, something

Mair's depiction of Tecumseh largely affords, fear arises from the recognition of personal similarities to the tragic hero's particular circumstances. Aristotle's definitions of pity, fear, and catharsis are still hotly debated;[18] however, this particular differentiation between pity and fear is helpful in explaining tragic feelings aroused in *Tecumseh*: Mair's ideal Anglo-Saxon reader might feel pity for Tecumseh, even identifying with his feelings, but could never fear that he might experience the same fate as Tecumseh.

The final scene of the play appears to perform the affective labour of the "Indian heroic tragedy," generating pity for Tecumseh and allowing for purgation of that pity through mourning his death. Harrison and the captured British Colonel Baby[19] enter together, Harrison praising Baby for supporting Tecumseh's last stand. Harrison's acknowledgement validates Tecumseh's death as a just defence of his people. Baby tells Harrison that he is in mourning for "the death of one— / A soldier—and a savage if you will—able and honourable, valiant, pure, / As ever graced the annals of the earth" (126). Harrison tells Baby that his men, at that very moment, are searching for Tecumseh's body and that he hopes "to give him fitting burial" (126); although the two were enemies in life, Harrison wants to recognize Tecumseh's heroism in death by providing a fitting, that is Western, burial. When Harrison's soldiers return, unable to locate Tecumseh's body, one eulogizes Tecumseh, claiming, "All will mourn for him" and discursively constructing him as an ahistorical and naturally wise "noble savage": "To be free / required no teacher, no historic page . . . For such things were himself, and, as his breath, / Instinctive, pleaders 'gainst the fears of death" (127). The final lines of the play belong to Harrison, who memorializes Tecumseh:

---

18   In *Rhetoric*, Aristotle also comments that pity can arise in response to an evil "which one may himself expect to endure, or that someone connected with him will" (60), which appears to contradict his later differentiation between the two emotions. See Gobert for a discussion of how catharsis has been interpreted over time.

19   While living in Windsor, Mair became friends with William L. Baby, the son of Colonel Baby in the play (Shrive 161–62).

Sleep well, Tecumseh, in thy unknown grave,

Thou mighty savage, resolute and brave!

Thou, master and strong spirit of the woods,

Unsheltered traveller in sad solitudes,

Yearner o'er Wyandot and Cherokee,

Couldst tell us now what hath been and shall be! (127)

The final moments of the play stage a "surrogate audience of survivors on stage," providing readers with an "indispensable frame of social response from which the new and presumably wiser order will arise" (States 171, 172). Harrison's final lines allow readers to weep for Tecumseh's death, but require them to identify with the circumstances of their onstage counterparts, the white characters who pity Tecumseh and mourn his death.

The final lines also signal the strange temporal alienation of this performative moment. Harrison's comment that Tecumseh can somehow see both past and future marks him as, in death and perhaps because of the somewhat mystical and mysterious circumstances surrounding the location of his body, outside the flow of history represented on stage. Readers and imagined audience members in 1886 were, like Tecumseh, outside of the historical moment of the play: they already know a future that remains unknown to the characters. The ending of the play, Filewod argues, operates as "a triumphant reminder of historical adversity, an anglo-Canadian 'je me souviens' framed by the memory of the ensuing victory that is the pre-condition of the play itself" (*Performing* 25). The audience, unlike the characters on stage, understood the future significance of Tecumseh's death and the strange temporality of Harrison's final lines about Tecumseh remind them of this. Readers, then, could simultaneously experience the emotional engagement of catharsis, mourning the loss of Tecumseh through identification with the onstage mourners, and emotional alienation, stepping back from the affective power of the scene through its reminder of their historical perspective—a perspective that permitted them to not only mourn but also celebrate Tecumseh's death as nationally significant.

The workings of catharsis are further complicated by noting that although the final moments of the play allow for pity to be purged through mourning, they also remind readers that Tecumseh's circumstances—that is, his demands for fair treaties and land security—are left unresolved: while the ending appears to provide emotional closure, it circumvents political closure. Tecumseh's death, like Brock's that precedes it, occurs off stage, yet readers still witness what are apparently Tecumseh's last words. The mortally wounded Tecumseh, recognizing he is close to death, laments:

> Oh I have loved my life,
> Not for my own but for my people's cause.
> Who now will knit them? who will lead them on?
> Lost! lost! lost! The pale destroyer triumphs!
> I see my people flee—I hear their shrieks—
> And none to shield or save! My axe! My axe—
> Ha—it is here! No, no—the power is past.
> O Mighty Spirit, shelter—save—my people! (126)

Tecumseh's final lines link questions of physical shelter and cultural survival, suggesting that the Indigenous people united under his protection will be landless and powerless without his leadership. In the play's final scene, Baby acknowledges Tecumseh's unfulfilled hopes and the widespread prejudice against Indigenous peoples, asking Harrison to protect them:

> They are men
> Much hated by the small and greedy mind—
> [. . .]
> And some there be who coldly pass them by
> As creatures ruled by appetite, not law;
> Yet, though to such they seem but human beasts,
> They are to those who know, or study them,
> A world of wonders! I entreat you, sir,
> To make right use of your authority,
> And shield them if you can. (126–27)

Harrison's response to Baby is positive but noncommittal: "I shall, I shall. / Right feeling tends this way, though 'tis a course / Not to be smoothly steered" (127). Although Harrison implies that he pities Tecumseh's people, he is cautious—perhaps rightly so in the worldview of the play—about committing to political action, reiterating the tension between the emotional and political domains that arises at the end of the play. In the same way as readers knew, through historical hindsight, that the war would turn in favour of the British, they also knew—whether they acknowledged it or not—that the end of the war had devastating effects for Indigenous peoples.[20] The increase in immigration to British North America and the decrease in the strategic military importance of alliances with Indigenous peoples that followed the signing of the Treaty of Ghent, which ended the War of 1812, led to treaties that were too frequently negotiated in bad faith and the displacement of Indigenous peoples from their traditional lands. Readers knew—or should have known—that Baby's request and Harrison's promise went unfulfilled. The closure that the play's tragic ending attempted to produce, which depended on a retrospective understanding of the past, is potentially undermined by the very knowledge upon which it relied.

Although the characters on stage in the final scene of the play are represented as mourning Tecumseh's death, Bert O. States's comments on the phenomenology of witnessing at the end of tragedy complicate matters. States asks readers to "imagine what would happen if you were to think away the chorus of saddened survivors at the end of a Shakespeare tragedy (the most cathartic point of our involvement) and allow the hero to die alone and unattended, like a great tree falling in an empty forest" (172). Although Mair allows readers to witness surrogate mourners grieving Tecumseh's death, he does not allow his characters or the audience to witness Tecumseh's actual death or to see Tecumseh's body. The impossibility of witnessing evidence of Tecumseh's death is problematic, suggesting that the emotional closure

---

20   Historian Arthur Ray summarizes this: "After almost one hundred years of intermittent warfare, they had managed to secure only widely scattered tracts of land in British North America" (141). Tecumseh's death, in particular, "crippled the Western Confederacy" (Ray 140).

tragedy should provide is actually incomplete. This failure to witness and thus incorporate an event in the moment of its occurrence produces not a tragic but a traumatic relationship to the past (Caruth 4), complicating the operations of mourning so crucial to the literary land claim, since traumatic knowledge suggests an ongoing affective engagement, rather than a closed relationship, with the past.

PAST IN PRESENT

The bicentenary of the War of 1812 is being celebrated as I write this, making questions of how and why the war is remembered relevant again. In 2012, the Canadian government released a short video titled "The Fight For Canada." Bearing a resemblance to Canadian Heritage Minutes[21] and feature-film trailers, it begins with a grim narrator, his voice underscored by beating drums, reminding viewers that "[t]wo hundred years ago, the United States invaded our territory." The video then introduces the "stars" of the conflict in familiar poses: Major-General Isaac Brock, standing backed by soldiers; Shawnee leader Tecumseh, nodding approval, presumably of Brock; Lieutenant-Colonel Charles de Salaberry, shouting orders; and Laura Secord, running through thick woods. The action ends with British and American soldiers lined up against one another and a British officer yelling "Fire!" The video then directs viewers to an informational government website, which reinforces the video's message by including images of the four "heroes" at the top of its homepage. The four figures function metonymically, signifying the military contributions of not only French and English troops but also of women and Indigenous warriors; this is underlined by Prime Minister Stephen Harper's official message on the site, which describes 1812 as "a war that saw Aboriginal peoples, local and volunteer militias, and English and French-speaking regiments fight together to save Canada from American invasion" (Harper).

---

21   Canadian Heritage Minutes are short films that illustrate significant moments in Canadian history and were shown on Canadian television and in Canadian movie theatres.

The video and website attempt to motivate Canadian viewers to feel pride in their ancestors' ability to defend "our territory," despite the fact that Canada did not exist as a nation until 1867. And while the government's recognition of the role of Indigenous peoples in the war is commendable, their contributions appear to be cited in an attempt to promote a nationalist, inclusive interpretation of "Canada's" war. Not only do the bicentenary promotional materials erase historical alliances between Indigenous peoples on both sides of the border, they also forget the consequences of the war. The official forgetting involved in bicentenary commemorations has not gone unnoticed; John Allemang comments, for example, "Despite their fierce contribution . . . these trusting natives were big losers. The best we could now say is that it could have been worse."

Rebecca Schneider, drawing on Fred Moten and John Donne, uses the term "inter(in)animation" to describe how cross-temporalities or syncopations inform performances across media, times, and spaces (163). Considering *Tecumseh* and "The Fight for Canada" cross-temporally, as mutually constitutive texts, foregrounds the powerful ideological work performed by the literary land claim and demonstrates the strange complicity of memorialization and strategic forgetting at work in accounting for Indigenous involvement in the war. Furthermore, the two performances, read together, highlight how individual affective engagements operate politically and historically and suggest that the relationship to the past suggested in each performance is not the closed relationship of mourning but the ongoing relationship of melancholia.

David Eng and David Kazanjian problematize the relationship between mourning and melancholia, suggesting that "the politics of mourning might be described as that creative process mediating a hopeful or hopeless relationship between loss and history" and to argue that the "pervasive losses of the twentieth century"—and I would argue the nineteenth as well—"need to be engaged from a perspective of what remains" (2). Attention to remains "generates a politics of mourning that might be active rather than reactive, prescient rather than nostalgic . . . social rather than solipsistic, militant rather than reactionary" (Eng and Kazanjian 2). This materialist approach to history arises through a melancholic engagement with the past, in which the past is not closed but "remains steadfastly alive in the present" (Eng and Kazanjian 4). I have suggested that Mair's play serves as a performative remain, a relic of the affective labour involved in producing a literary land claim. Eng and Kazanjian shed light on the political and social implications of recognizing Mair's emotional work in transmuting his private feelings into public emotional labour. Their call for a melancholic and politicized engagement with the past is a provocation to inter(in)animation, suggesting the need to link past (1886) and present (2012) commemorations of history in interrogating the politics of memorialization.

AWKWARD FEELINGS

WHOSE AWKWARD MOMENTS? AFFECT, DISABILITY, AND SEX IN *THE BOOK OF JUDITH, TIME TO PUT MY SOCKS ON,* AND *THE GLASS BOX*

KIRSTY JOHNSTON

Theatre criticism often turns on how successfully or unsuccessfully feelings are marshalled among theatre's participants, with the many related awkwardnesses prompting theatre and affect theorists Nicholas Ridout and Robin Bernstein to argue in different contexts for the centrality of awkwardness, queasiness, embarrassment, and, importantly, shame, in theatre experience. Describing theatre as an affect machine, one "that sets out to undo itself," Ridout explores stage fright, corpsing, embarrassment, and other theatre predicaments to demonstrate how scholars gain a more precise sense of theatre's economic and political conditions when they attend to theatre's affective undoings as constitutive rather than aberrant features of the machine (*Stage Fright* 168). Similarly, in her recent article calling for greater integration of theatre history and affect studies, Bernstein argues for shame as a "crucial motor on par with death in much theatre," particularly, as her case studies demonstrate, in the method-based realism that animates much twentieth-century theatre (215). In a related vein, and with reference to a specifically Canadian context, Christine Kim has pressed for more investigations of the feelings and affects at play in Canadian theatre's "awkward multiculturalisms," particularly those that bring racialized bodies' intimate stories into the public sphere. She champions theatre that [pushes] for a reworking of the dominant public by refusing to move the work of discomfort and minor narratives into "private" spaces. This kind of obstinacy is necessary if counterpublics are to be more than simply publics that others do not want to engage with, let alone care about. (193)

While Kim's many compelling arguments take up theatre that involves performing and witnessing bodies marked as racially or ethnically different, I am interested here in theatre that involves performing and witnessing bodies marked as disabled. Thus, while I am inspired by Kim's insistence on the productive work of discomfort and minor narratives in theatre to fashioning a more inclusive public sphere, I explore similarly productive obstinacy in theatre that turns on narratives of disabled sexualities. Pushing me in this direction are several recent Canadian theatre productions that shared the intimate details of disabled sexualities in theatrical events that included both performing and witnessing bodies marked as disabled. In Toronto, Die in Debt Theatre, Absit Omen, and Theatre Centre's 2009 production of *The Book of Judith* was prompted by a discussion concerning inclusion activist Judith Snow's sexuality as a quadriplegic woman. Calgary's Stage Left and Ottawa's Smashing Stereotypes's production of *Time To Put My Socks On* follows the underwear-clad character Marc, a mid-life professional with cerebral palsy, as he reflects on his increasingly serious romantic and sexual relationship with Linda, a non-disabled woman. In Vancouver, Theatre Terrific's *The Glass Box* explored the sexualities of three different characters described as "a 55 year-old wife and mother, a 23 year-old woman living with quadriplegia, and a 32-year-old man with Down Syndrome."[1] Although they did so differently, each of these productions used theatre to bring specific narratives of disabled sexuality into the public sphere. It is my hope that these examples will have critical relevance for Canadian theatre and affect studies because their collective refusal to, in Kim's words, "move the work of discomfort and

---

1   This quote derives from the company's press release for the production's January 2009 premiere at the Intrepid Theatre Club in Victoria, BC.

minor narratives into 'private' spaces" (193) aligns with a significant challenge posed in the broader affect studies field by disability theorist Tobin Siebers (*Disability Theory* 193).

In his "interrogation of shame and the sexual experiences of people with disabilities," Siebers presses affect theorist Eve Kosofsky Sedgwick's highly influential and generative accounts of shame to ask who gets to feel it (159). Sedgwick argued extensively and persuasively for shame's distinctive and socially critical capacity to bridge human feelings across difference. Indeed, in *Shame and Its Sisters: A Silvan Tomkins Reader*, she and Adam Frank cite Tomkins's formulations concerning shame that place it among the basic set of affects while also distinguishing its special power to, in their words, "enable or disenable so basic a function as the ability to be interested in the world" (5). Siebers notes that for Sedgwick "shame is the queer emotion by which we put ourselves in the place of others" (158). While this account of shame helps us to make sense of why Ridout, Bernstein, and others insist upon its central importance in the theatrical event, an event that frequently turns on actors and audiences putting themselves in the place of others, Siebers argues that any understanding of shame, including Sedgwick's own, must examine how it might be shaped by the ideology of ability or "the belief that the able body defines the baseline of humanness" (Siebers, *Disability Theory* 159). To this end, he explores Sedgwick's own illustrative examples of shame's ethical usefulness and discovers a series of occlusions that position disabled people as objects for empathy or catalysts for non-disabled people's feelings of shame rather than subjects who might feel shame themselves in distinctive ways that need to be more fully articulated and considered. How, for example, are feelings like shame sometimes understood in ways that replicate ableist ideology concerning public and private bodily functions or resonate only with what disability theorist Rosemarie Garland-Thomson has described as normate corporealities?[2] Like Bernstein in her analysis of shame's central role in

---

2   Rosemarie Garland-Thomson has coined the term "normate" to suggest the figure constructed in contrast to the disabled person "through which people can represent themselves as definitive human beings" (8).

method-based theatre realism, Siebers builds from shame's etymological roots in a pre-Teutonic word for "cover[ing] oneself."[3] Finding in the literature on shame a recurring emphasis on the public confession of shameful emotion, Siebers notes how shame pivots on "the movement between private and public realms," a fact that he argues has several implications for people with disabilities in that it relies on access and mobility and implies both access to the public sphere and the possibility of privacy (*Disability Theory* 163). If shame is a primary human affect, then it is important to account for how shame is felt by the full spectrum of human experience, including those bodies whose interests in and capacities for "covering themselves" and navigating public and private spaces are diverse. Siebers provocatively considers how

> the ideology of ability shapes not only the existence of human beings and their susceptibility to shame but also whether a person becomes a person at all. It controls the capacity of disabled and nondisabled people to live independently and to act, and whether they have agency, sexual or other, in their own life. It defines the spheres of existence in which they dwell, determining how they have sex and when they pass between the private and public realms. It exerts enormous pressure on the assignment of gender and on whether a body is viewed as having sexual properties. (*Disability Theory* 175)

Siebers's arguments prompt theatre and affect scholars to seek out those moments in the public space of theatre when disabled performers hold artistic agency and use it to elucidate their particular body's sexuality. Although they did so very differently, *The Book of Judith*, *Time To Put My Socks On*, and *The Glass Box* turned precisely around moments in which disabled performers' bodies confronted the ideology of ability informing normate sexual standards and practices. Comparing these works, it is striking that, to varying degrees,

---

3   In support of her broader analysis of shame's constitutive role in theatre, Bernstein notes that "the word 'shame' derives in part from the Gothic words *Scham* and *skaman*, which refer to covering the face—a performative gesture of shame and also a fundamentally theatrical action of masking, of producing that which is a sham" (215).

each brought into public light details of how particular disabled bodies both feel and prompt feelings of shame, esteem, awkwardness, and desire.

All three productions involved artists with ties to a growing disability arts and culture movement across Canada. Although many Canadian artists disagree about best practices for Canadian disability theatre, in their different ways each of these productions sought to unsettle common prejudices related to disability experience and challenge the ideology of ability, not least by bringing disabled performers onstage and sharing intimate narratives related to disabled people's lives and sexualities. Thus while the particular production circumstances varied, each had a sense of a broader cultural context shaped by ableist ideology in which disabled people's perspectives, particularly in relation to sexuality, are either excluded with indifference or encountered awkwardly.

In 2009, the specific question of how one paraplegic woman's sexuality makes other people feel was the animating principle behind *The Book of Judith*. Starring co-creators Michael Rubenfeld and Sarah Garton Stanley, Canadian disability arts activist and performer Alex Bulmer, a choir of disability artists, and the eponymous inclusion activist Judith Snow, the show was first produced in Toronto, toured around Ontario, and was invited to several UK venues.[4] Toronto's *NOW Magazine* theatre reviewer Jon Kaplan began his 2009 preview of *The Book of Judith* with the question

> How do you feel when you meet someone with a disability? Probably as awkward and uneasy as writer/actor Michael Rubenfeld did. Rubenfeld didn't know what he was getting into when a good friend, personal assistant to quadriplegic Judith Snow, asked him to help find a lover for Snow, an advocate for inclusive community living.

Kaplan's phrasing and assumptions about his readership's familiarity and comfort with disability add further examples to the arsenal in support of Siebers's claim that "[d]isability is properly speaking an aesthetic value, which is to

---

4   The play has been performed in Toronto, Kingston, St. Catharine's, Aurora, and Peterborough. See Bower.

say, it participates in a system of knowledge that provides materials for and increases critical consciousness about the way that some bodies make other bodies feel" (*Disability Aesthetics* 20). Kaplan's assumption that his readers are neither disabled themselves nor familiar with disabled people and disabled people's sexualities helps to highlight how ableist assumptions shape public discourse. Indeed, in a CBC Radio *Metro Morning* interview related to the show, Judith Snow explained the prevalence of unacknowledged prejudice:

> I think all of us are stuck in it. It's not just that we think a person is disabled, like me, but we have that concept of disability. It affects everybody whether you actually are labelled yet or not. You don't see it because it's like water to a fish.

A growing disability performance scholarship concerning Canadian professional performance criticism tries to account for this "water" and the related economies of affect in which onstage performances of disability circulate. In Carrie Sandahl and Philip Auslander's *Bodies in Commotion: Disability & Performance*, for example, Owen Smith cites Canadian dance critic Michael Scott's review of British dance company Candoco's 1999 performance in Vancouver: "There is a horrific, Satyricon quality to Candoco that heaves up in the chest—nausea at the moral rudderlessness of a world where we would pay money to watch a man whose body terminates at his ribcage, moving about the stage on his hands." Scott's very terms invoke feeling as the basis of aesthetic criticism and Smith uses this review as an example of "conservatism and normalizing tendencies in the dance establishment" (Smith 85). More recently, Rachel E. Hile has investigated critical responses to Irene Poole's performance of Kate with a limp in the 2008 Stratford Shakespeare Festival production of *Taming of the Shrew*, directed by Peter Hinton. For example, she cites *Toronto Star* critic Richard Ouzounian as mocking the decision in his review:

> On the strength of one line in the text ("Why does the world report that Kate does limp?") which most scholars usually accept as a joke inspired by some physical business (a kicked leg, a broken shoe),

Hinton has decided that Katherine has an actual physical deformity and has her hobbling across the festival stage as though she were Richard III instead of Katherine I.

Hile argues that "the nearly unanimous disparagement of Hinton's decision suggests a profound discomfort with the idea that a heroine in a romantic comedy could have a disability." Drawing from a disability-studies perspective, Hile pursues the question, "[W]hy did that performance have such an unsettling effect upon reviewers?" As these examples suggest, in a range of different directions, scholars are interrogating how disability performances raise critical consciousness of how some bodies make other bodies feel.

I cite these reviews beyond *Book of Judith* to make clear that Kaplan's assumptions and the kinds of feelings he describes reviewing the production are hardly a rarity in contemporary Canadian culture or its attending theatre-review practices. However, they are striking and instructive to note here in relation to a production that explicitly aimed to feature artists with disabilities, challenge ableism, and accommodate more patrons with disabilities.

As Kaplan's review suggests, *The Book of Judith* follows Rubenfeld's affective journey from feelings of repulsion to celebration, bewilderment to enlightenment, awkwardness to dignified calm in response to meeting Snow and being asked to find her a lover. The blogspot for the production describes this central narrative as follows:

> The Book of Judith, created by Michael Rubenfeld and Sarah Garton Stanley, is a musical play about a self-annointed [sic] preacher man who is passionately driven to change the lives of others. After a chance meeting with a quadriplegic woman named Judith Snow, theatre artist Matthew Goldberg believes he has "seen the light." With the help of his director, Shauna Coupland, and her best friend, disabled artist, Pippa McLaren, Matthew has managed to coral [sic] a fully integrated group of choristers with and without disability, to help him tell, for the first time, his inspirational, maniacal and deeply suspect tale of Judith Snow. The Book of Judith takes us from

innocence to ignorance and through to the other side—a truer place
of transformation. (*Book*)

The Book of Judith was actually the second production created by Rubenfeld
and Snow following their initial meeting; the first, *Suck and Blow*, was produced as part of Toronto's Rhubarb! Festival in 2006. This production aimed
to emphasize Snow's sensuality and involved Rubenfeld and Caleb Yong,
Snow's former personal assistant, silently dressing Snow onstage (Bower).
Formally, *The Book of Judith* is very different from this antecedent. Snow
does not appear unclothed on stage at all and she appears as herself only at
the play's end. In *The Book of Judith* it is the character of Matthew Goldberg
as played by Rubenfeld who undresses and dresses. Indeed it is his personally
transformative yet flawed and "suspect" journey that provides the play's narrative arc and structure. As Rubenfeld explains of his character, "He talks to
people about how to get beyond their own fears but in reality, he doesn't recognize his own flaws" (qtd. in Bower). Co-creator and director Sarah Garton
Stanley emphasizes the importance of this tension and the feelings it provokes both for the character and the audience: "[T]he idea of discomfort is
central to what the production explores. . . . It's Michael who confronts his
own fear, self-loathing and concern about how he's perceived by others, but
we can't help but be implicated in the same feelings" (J. Kaplan). Goldberg,
fashioned as a revivalist preacher, begins by expressing his bewilderment and
awkward feelings of discomfort with Snow's request to help him find her a
lover. Described by its poster tagline as a "Healing Crusade," the play then
charts this moment's place in his personal history, interspersing his experiences with passages read from Snow's communications and publications. He
shares with increasing evangelical fervour his growing love and appreciation
for Snow's perspectives and philosophies and, like a revivalist preacher, urges
all present to adopt these as gospel.

Although the production centres around Rubenfeld's highly emotive and
energetic performance, a hagiographic image of Snow is ever present both
on the stage's large church-style banners and on the cover of the audience
programs that contain lyrics that audiences are encouraged to sing along

with during the production. In Toronto, audience members were invited to sit on flexibly arranged folding chairs or wheel into spaces among these, gathering beneath a big tent designed to feel like a simulated site for a religious revival meeting. A gospel-style choir of artists with various disabilities lead by award-winning playwright and disability-arts advocate Alex Bulmer sang songs written by Andrew Penner that amplified Rubenfeld's emotional delivery. Costumed in choir gowns and singing in rich emotional tones, their work was critical in amplifying the emotional qualities of the performance.

The role of Bulmer as choir leader and a major figure in the production's development and public presence online and in media interviews is worth considering further. Well-known in Toronto's professional theatre, drag king, and disability-arts-and-culture scenes, Bulmer is also a professional voice instructor. She has an exceptionally strong vocal and physical presence on stage. Nearly ten years earlier, her Floyd S. Chalmers Canadian Play Award–nominated play *Smudge* had followed the awkward and intimate dating and sexual details of a central female character, Freddie, who, like Bulmer, had been diagnosed with a degenerative eye disease, retinitis pigmentosa. Despite her many professional successes like *Smudge*, Bulmer had left Toronto several years earlier for the UK, where more inclusive policies and a program to support artists with disabilities had allowed her to act as a professional dramaturg and to develop a comedy series for Channel Four, *Cast Offs*. I emphasize these aspects here as Bulmer's role in *The Book of Judith* was not incidental but rather a pivotal aspect of the production's means of connection to broader principles of disability theatre. Bulmer explained why she returned to Toronto for the production in an interview with Diane Flacks for *The Toronto Star*:

> "My God, talk about a strange universal answer to what I was looking for."
>
> Bulmer's friend, theatre director Sarah Stanley, asked her to act in a project inspired by its author, disability rights advocate Judith Snow, who is quadriplegic.
>
> "That's it!" I thought. "That's my reintroduction."

"The show, *The Book of Judith*, is inclusive. It's a show with an integrated choir of disabled and nondisabled people. I play the choir-master." It is comic, dark but sincere, and she couldn't say no.

Sarah Stanley has noted that many of the songs Bulmer and the choir sing are indeed dark and in a minor key. She argues that they contribute a sense of lamentation: "They're moody and evocative, and mirror the script's yearning for more in life, for connection with others" (qtd in J. Kaplan).

The drive for connection is a cornerstone of Snow's international inclusion activism and aim to move beyond ability/disability binaries. To keep pace with her ideas, the production as a whole attempted more inclusive staging practices. Explicitly protesting widespread inaccessibilities for both audiences and performers in Toronto's professional theatres, the production created a revival-style white tent on the lawn of the Centre for Addiction and Mental Health on Queen Street West. It had flexible audience seating and a ramp that bisected the audience space and allowed performers to wheel directly up onto the stage. The choir and, ultimately, the much-heralded and anticipated Snow herself, made striking entrances this way.

While the production's drive to create and publicly insist upon more inclusive production choices aimed in part, following Snow, to make Canadian theatre's fish more aware of the water in which they swim, it is useful to consider how they also functioned within the scenography's mock-religious revival invocations. The fact that Snow, other performers in wheelchairs, and audience patrons in wheelchairs were more easily able to navigate the space underlined how spatial choices inform feelings of agency and inclusion. Goldberg's performance of awkwardness at being asked to find Snow a lover, in a space where inclusive staging practices drew both performers and audience members who were also quadriplegic, resonated differently than it would have at one of the city's inaccessible venues. In this context, we might ask differently Kaplan's question: What precisely is experienced as awkward in this minor narrative of soliciting a lover for Snow, now amplified with a revivalist setting and choir comprising many disabled performers and an audience inclusive of disabled people? Where religious revivals have traditions that invite faithful people with physical impairments to cast off their crutches and walk, or visually impaired people to open their eyes and see, their transformed bodies upheld as evidence of faith-based delivery from what is read as an entwined spiritual and physical deficit, here performers in wheelchairs and performers with vision impairments navigated the space, shaped the performance, and did not seek such ableist framings of transformation. The character whose awkward, suspect, and flawed transformation audiences witnessed instead was a charismatic, avowedly non-disabled man. It was this man whom audiences followed on his journey from shame to redemptive pride, from awkwardness in the face of Snow's sexuality to heightened appreciation of her whole being. It was his romantic foibles and sexual promiscuities that were charted in the production, not Snow's. Following the amplified emotional registers of Goldberg's journey, the arrival centre stage of the comparatively quieter, less frenetic, and more dignified Snow herself acted as a kind of emotional salve to awkwardness. Thus, while Snow and her inclusive ideology were exalted, her own more detailed journey and, importantly, her body, its specific sexuality, desires, agency, relation to public and private realms, as well as her feelings of awkwardness and shame were comparatively muted. It is through the gamut of Goldberg's emotions that the dramatic arc ran—formal choices that established his full humanity—while the emotional range of the putative subject of the performance, Snow herself, was less embodied on stage.

Several of the performance choices in *The Book of Judith* that shaped how feelings about disabled sexuality circulated among audiences and performers stand in contrast to other roughly contemporary Canadian productions involving sexuality and disability. *Time To Put My Socks On*, co-written by Alan Shain and Michele Decottignies and first co-produced in 2008 by their respective companies, Smashing Stereotypes Productions and Stage Left Productions, offers the sequel to Shain's internationally acclaimed touring solo show *Still Waiting for that Special Bus*.[5] The sequel again hinges on Shain's

5 The production played to sold-out audiences at Calgary's Balancing Acts Festival in 2008 and 2009, and in Ottawa in 2010. It was also mounted as part of the Fringe Festival in Toronto and Montreal in 2008 ("Production document"). *Time To Put My Socks On* was "[d]eveloped by Alan Shain, Michele Decottignies, Nicole Dunbar, and Rachel Gorman"

charismatic portrayal of Marc, now at the critical moment of his first anniversary with Linda, a non-disabled woman, who is keen to take things to the next level and move in together. In their production materials, the show's creators offer the following précis:

> [*Time To Put My Socks On*] presents a naked, crippled guy having raucous sex with a non-disabled, typically "hot" woman (something that is entirely unprecedented in Canadian theatre). It invites audiences into the heart of Marc's world by dropping them into his adapted and expensive man cave/bedroom, where he crawls on his hands and knees, moshes with his walker, and twirls around in his underwear. And where he makes us laugh out loud over his slightly-biased version of relationship fights over seemingly silly things like toothpaste. This show also filters Marc's concerns around losing his independence through the perspective of a man who was made to spend 20 years in physio-therapy learning to do everything for himself. In this way, *Time To Put My Socks On* shifts the source of Marc's interpersonal struggles with Linda from individual insecurity to a shared response by many disabled men to internalized oppression—all the while offering a totally unique and utterly hilarious perspective of life within universal human stories of masculinity, dating, relationships, sex, love, marriage . . . and socks! ("Production" 3)

As this promotional summary suggests, the show's creators were driven to invest audiences in Marc's narrative and the intimate details of his body,

---

(Shain). Citing himself and Decottignies as the production's co-creators, Shain goes on to explain that "*Time to Put My Socks On* represents a unique three year collaboration which has been supported by the Canada Council for the Arts, the Ontario Arts Council, and the City of Ottawa. The development of this show was also supported by disabled artist/activist, Rachel Gorman, who provided movement direction and character decorum considerations, and by nondisabled artist Nicole Dunbar, Stage Left Production's former Associate Artistic Director. Dunbar provided dramaturgical, directing, and acting support, and [is] who plays Linda in the voice overs and video montages."

sexuality, and emotional journey. Details of Linda and Marc's sexual history were mostly shared in a series of short scenes within a video projection. These included, for example, a scene of them playing the game Twister naked and romping around in candlelight. Linda also leaves a raunchy message on Marc's answering machine that alludes to their recent sexual activities. Listening to it along with Marc, audiences heard both her message and his private reflections on the anxieties their relationship was raising for him—they were wholly aligned with his perspective and shared in the space of his private world throughout the production. This intimate bond between performer and audience was amplified by the fact that he was the only performer to interact live with the audience. Further, he interacted with them clothed only in his underwear, laying bare his body, its distinctive features, and his emotions throughout. Like Matthew Goldberg in *The Book of Judith*, the nearly nude Marc shared with audiences his romantic and sexual activities and anxieties in relation to an offstage woman. Indeed, in contrast to Snow's ultimate and exalted appearance in *The Book of Judith*, the audience never saw Linda fully embodied on stage. Instead, in *Time To Put My Socks On*, through direct address from the masculine environment of his "man cave," Marc shared his many anxious, frustrated, and, ultimately, loving feelings about Linda. He emphasized how his and Linda's different experiences of banal objects like toothpaste and socks created physical and emotional awkwardnesses between them. As the title suggests, the play pivoted on the details of Marc donning his socks. He prefers tube socks to the fancier, more-awkward-to-wear socks Linda favours. When I saw the Calgary version of the production in 2009, audiences were clearly and audibly delighted when Linda was revealed to have understood this—evidence of their emotional investment in Marc's particular corporeality and narrative. Like the theatre Christine Kim champions in praise of awkward multiculturalisms, *Time To Put My Socks On* built a public forum for audiences' emotional investment in the banal and awkward features of a minor narrative, in this case one focused on disabled sexuality, masculinity, and identity.

Although I have considered some of its features elsewhere (*Stage Turns* 143–50), it is useful here to look briefly at Theatre Terrific's 2009 production of *The Glass Box* to demonstrate how thinking through feelings about per-formances of disabled sexualities uncovers critical aspects of the work. *The Glass Box* brought intimate details of specific disabled sexualities into theatre's public spheres and hung on feelings of awkwardness. Starring Kyla Harris, Watson Moy, and the company's artistic director, Susanna Uchatius, *The Glass Box* was produced at the Playwrights Theatre Centre on Granville Island in Vancouver and developed collaboratively by the performers with dramaturgs Jan Derbyshire and Joanna Garfinkel. Like *The Book of Judith*, *The Glass Box* was inspired by a discussion about sexuality between a disabled woman who has rarely performed in theatre and a non-disabled theatre artist. In this case, visual artist Kyla Harris, who is quadriplegic, and Theatre Terrific artistic di-rector Susanna Uchatius discussed Harris's frustration with having regularly to explain to others that "just because I am in a wheelchair doesn't mean I am no longer a sexual being. Yes, I can have sex" (Litwin). Like Snow's con-versation with Rubenfeld and his friend, Harris's conversation with Uchatius provided the original impulse for performance creation. Neither Snow nor Harris were professional theatre artists prior to their involvement in the re-spective productions but both are visual artists who were willing to bring their conversations about sexuality and their bodies onto the stage.

While *The Book of Judith* invoked the sense of a big-tent religious revival of heightened emotion and *Time To Put My Socks On* the private, confessional intimacy of Marc's "man cave," *The Glass Box* presented in close proximity to the audience a tidy cube of light that was variously configured to seem at different moments like the focused lights of a game show, a celebrity confes-sional program, and a clinical encounter. In this bright, intimate space, each performer answered questions aimed at illuminating details about their re-spective sexual experiences, worries, regrets, and dreams. Although sometimes hailed by their own names, each answered mainly as a performing body cast as an iconic and hypersexualized figure: Harris as Cleopatra, Moy as Brad Pitt, and Uchatius as Sophia Loren. This doubling highlighted the intimacy of the characters' minor, private stories with those of the hypersexualized iconic public figures they played. The doubled characters received game-show points in response to questions concerning "sexual worth," a concept the play connects to formal questions Harris had to answer for insurance purposes as a fifteen-year-old, following the school trip diving accident from which she became quadriplegic. The ableist assumptions at play in the idea that a person's sexual worth can be determined through clinical questions and measures, measures shaped, as Siebers might suggest, by "the belief that the able body defines the baseline of humanness," were shown to be ridiculous (*Disability Theory* 159). However, near the play's end, Cleopatra/Harris addressed their effects in a more serious and revealing way:

> CLEO: I'm worth it. I know I'm worth something. It's just so much easier to see what I'm not. It's easy for me to not place anything on what I've done or who I think I am. That's one of the reasons I'm so attracted to Cleopatra; she became known for what her sexuality could get her, how it enhanced her reign over Egypt. I want to feel the kind of extraordinary pride and strength of self that I imagine her to have had. I want to feel the strength of who I am and I want people to see that . . . but reading the binder, if you read the binder, you'd realize I'm normal and I don't feel normal, so I don't want to be seen as normal. I don't want people to see me the way I see myself; I don't want people to know just how normal I am, because if I was, how would I be able to conquer my own Rome?
> SOPHIA: Kyla, conquer yourself.
> CLEO: I'm sorry. I'm so sorry. (192–93)

Differentiating how she is seen and measured from how she feels in relation to the term "normal," connecting her feelings to ideas of social worth, pointing to what she would like to reveal and cover about herself and indicating where she has been and would like to be, the doubled figure of Cleopatra/Harris shares feelings in tension between desire and fear, confidence and awkwardness, self-esteem and shame. Offered in combination with the other doubled characters' conversations that take up similar feelings and tensions, the production as a whole built public space for investment in disabled characters' feelings concerning their respective sexualities.

When Christine Kim championed theatre that inserted intimacy and awkwardness into racialized bodies' public conversations, she argued that such performances compel "us to contemplate how we might occupy a public that is intimately invested in racialized subjectivities and what kinds of conversations might subsequently be able to emerge" (183). All three of the productions cited here drew intimacy and awkwardness into disabled bodies' public conversations, generating public investment in specific disabled subjectivities and attending to their particular feelings of sexual desire, shame, esteem, and awkwardness. Moreover, all aimed to raise public critical consciousness of these feelings. In each case, the productions involved fictional characters. In *The Book of Judith* and *The Glass Box*, performers also referenced autobiographical details. Each also brought on stage and into the public sphere the very bodies whose feelings and particular embodiments provided the original impulses for production.

While the parallels between the shows are clearly many, there were also significant differences in the kinds of feelings, narratives, and embodiments each shared. For example, while Harris/Cleopatra revealed her feelings about formal sexuality assessments and the idea of "sexual worth" and Marc in *Time To Put My Socks On* was seen cavorting sexually with a woman on film and discussing his sexual history directly with the theatre audience, much of Snow's sexuality, beyond the initial request for a lover, remained an enigma. While most of the intimacies shared in *The Book of Judith* pertained to Goldberg, the production as a whole did invest audiences in Snow's sexual subjectivity. The range of disabled subjectivities engaged across these productions might be read as productive within an emerging scholarship concerning disability and sexuality that holds, as Michael A. Rembis argues, that "a multiplicity of voices will be needed to rearticulate and reconceptualize (dis/abled) sexualities" (Rembis 58). One way to invest publics in listening to such rearticulations and reconceptualizations is through intimate, awkward theatre involving disabled performing and witnessing bodies. Indeed, such productions build from what Ridout has determined to be theatre's basic awkwardness to raise questions and public concern for who gets to feel included, shamed, desired, or awkward.

When Siebers asks who gets to feel shame, he acknowledges that the question is both political and potentially strange; surely to be human is to be susceptible to shame (*Disability Aesthetics* 159). Siebers's question has parallels, however, with those asked by affect and performance scholar José Esteban Muñoz in "Feeling Brown, Feeling Down." Here Muñoz builds from Gayatri Chakravorty Spivak's highly generative question, "Can the subaltern speak?" to ask "How does the subaltern feel? How might subalterns feel each other?" ("Feeling Brown, Feeling Down" 676, citing Spivak, "Can"). Engaging with different psychological and phenomenological discourses, Muñoz seeks to "theorize affective particularity and belonging" (676). Thus, though they draw from different kinds of affective particularity and interests in belonging, both Siebers and Muñoz challenge affect and performance theorists to rethink the universal subject. Where Muñoz hopes to break from past aesthetic and hermeneutic approaches that conformed to a "crypto-universalism associated with the universal white subject" (678), Siebers is interested in breaking from a universal able-bodied subject to find out how disabled subjects feel and prompt feeling.

The inclusive staging practices and relatively intimate scales of the productions of the theatre I have analyzed here (Marc, semi-nude in his apartment; game-show contestants baring all in the tidy cube of light; Judith Snow's wheeling through the performance tent's audience to arrive, much-anticipated, on stage) invested audiences in the particular, minor narratives of how disabled subjects feel and prompt feelings about sex. The awkward intimacies shared in *Time To Put My Socks On*, *The Glass Box*, and *The Book of Judith* also built public space for investment in disabled bodies as subjects, rather than simply objects of emotion.

MEET ME AT THE BORDER: THEATRE REPLACEMENT'S *BIOBOXES*

KIM SOLGA

BIOBOXES: Artifacting Human Experience is a group of six immersive, one-on-one shows created in 2006–2007 by Vancouver-based Theatre Replacement; over the past several years it has toured across Canada, to Germany, and appears as a short video on the Internet.[1] Theatre Replacement describes the piece as "a collection of short one-person shows for one-person audiences that take place in a very intimate theatre: a box worn on the actors' shoulders" (Theatre Replacement, *BIOBOXES* 132). It is, at its most basic, a migrant show about migration, based on interviews with a series of first-generation Canadians living in Vancouver, channelled through the creative work of a group of artists of similar ethnic background and translated into what Theatre Replacement calls "a new form of documentary performance" that has more in common with the "museum" and the "photo album" than it does with the proscenium arch stage (Theatre Replacement, Program Note).

As this description suggests, *BIOBOXES* is generically and formally mixed, both in the several styles of live and visual art it references—the boxes can be characterized as interactive photo booths or puppet shows and classified variously as intimate theatre, documentary theatre, performance art, or installation art (see Levin et al.)—as well as in the aesthetic and social goals of its broader *mise en scène*. Audiences enter the "host" theatre space (an unadorned black-box stage on both occasions I saw the show) in small

---

1 *BIOBOXES* was created by Anita Rochon, Marco Soriano, Paul Ternes, Cindy Mochizuki, Donna Soares, and Una Memisevic. I saw it for the first time at the Dorothy Somerset Studio on the University of British Columbia campus in Vancouver, BC, on 1 June 2008. I saw it again at the Theatre Centre in Toronto, Ontario, on 2 May 2009.

groups and sit on the periphery of the playing area, in the middle of which the boxes and their apparatuses are positioned in orderly rows. A video of interviews with the performance's documentary subjects—the migrants to Vancouver on whose stories each box's performance is based—plays on a screen behind the installations while spectators sit or chat quietly, anticipating their turns with the performers. The scene is lively, active, at turns evoking a working rehearsal, a trade conference, or even something of the civic "heritage fair" with which many Canadian spectators will be familiar.[2] While we wait, the six actors in charge of animating each box prepare their miniature stages for a fresh round of play; they are dressed in white lab coats, projecting from a distance a slightly clinical air. When they approach their audiences en masse, though, calling spectators by name and offering a warm handshake, this sense of scientific distance dissipates. Their welcome is sincere yet also theatrical: while the performers are clearly "on," they are also clearly not yet "in character." They tell us their (real) names; they seat us in the auditorium for one contained within each box; they explain the features of their boxes so that we understand how the performance will proceed. They make us as comfortable as possible. Then they disappear around the back of their boxes, pop their heads uncannily into their own, tiny puppet spaces, and begin.

These are the bare facts of *BIOBOXES*, the "clinical" view: what it looks like from the outside. In keeping with this volume's focus on the affective freight of Canadian performance, however, in this essay I will dive inward, into the boxes and into my own sometimes very awkward interactions with them in order to think in detail about the ways in which *BIOBOXES*'s aesthetics might make participants *feel*, and about how that feeling might be politically productive for contemporary intercultural (as opposed to *multi*cultural) Canada. For Ric Knowles, following Julie Holledge and Joanne Tompkins, "interculturalism" differs from its cognates (including cross-culturalism, multiculturalism, and transnationalism, among others) in its spatial dimension, its "focus on the contested, unsettling, and often unequal spaces *between* cultures,

---

2   Theatre Replacement's YouTube video advertising *BIOBOXES* captures clearly the aesthetic of the experience; see Andrade.

spaces that can function in performance as sites of negotiation" (4, emphasis in original).[3] Knowles defines "interculturalism" as an ethics of engagement with difference that demands physical and imaginative proximity *as well as* respectful distance—a fluid, elastic, heterotopic space that Gloria Anzaldúa has famously characterized as "the borderlands." For Anzaldúa, the borderlands open up "whenever two or more cultures edge each other, where people of different races occupy the same territory, where under, lower, middle and upper classes touch, where the space between two individuals shrinks with intimacy" (19). Anzaldúa's borderland—like Knowles's interculturalism—is a contact zone, and marked as such by internal contradictions that can seem terrifying, but may also register, under the right circumstances, as full of potential. In the borderlands, different cultures find themselves simultaneously pushed together and pulled apart, intimate yet foreign; in their awkward proximity they risk "violent clash" (23) but also useful ambiguity as each steps carefully toward one another's ideologies, prejudices, strengths, and goals. In the borderlands cultural boundaries may be aggressively policed, but cultures may also press up against one another, *impress* upon one another (to use the language of Sara Ahmed), perhaps begin to open one another, to *affect* one another (*Cultural* 6 and passim).

Keeping Knowles and Anzaldúa close, but bearing Ahmed in mind, I'd like to suggest that *BIOBOXES* is a performance of and in the borderlands: a work that not only invokes, but in its unusual physical form (the box on the actor's shoulders, weighty but fragile) and structure (the series of tiny spaces in which performer and spectator huddle close, face to face) deliberately *embodies* the loaded space of cross-cultural encounter in order to generate what I will call an *intercultural affect*. I imagine intercultural affect to be unsettling but also thoughtfully contestatory: not necessarily aggressive (though, as Anzaldúa reminds us, it might be), but persistently demanding *as well as*

---

3   Lo and Gilbert offer a related definition: "The term 'intercultural' suggests an exploration of the interstice between cultures; it draws our attention to the hyphenated third space separating and connecting different peoples. The act of crossing cultures . . . should ideally activate both centrifugal and centripetal forces in the process of mutual contamination and interaction" (44).

pleasurably inviting. In Kelly Oliver's terms, intercultural affect might evoke a "response-ability" *and* an "address-ability" at the border with difference: the sense of being responsible *to* an other, alongside the parallel sense of being visible to, and addressable *by*, that other (7 and passim). While these notions of responsibility and addressability may be intellectually recognizable to most Canadians steeped in the anti-racist discourse that has emerged alongside the language of official multiculturalism since 1988, I would argue that they are also unlikely to be *affectively* familiar for those spectators whose experience of cultural difference has been mediated primarily by the Canadian government's official multicultural apparatus (and I include myself, a first-generation Canadian who grew up on the prairies, in this group). This apparatus deploys the language of cultural difference as social good and political currency; it fetishizes the separate-but-equal notion of many cultures living side by side in harmony, courts members of "minority" cultures as voting blocs and gateways to new economic markets, and encourages those marked by cultural difference to perform that difference in exchange for (limited) power and recognition from the state. In turn, it encourages white and predominantly anglophone or francophone cultural majorities to consume performances of difference at a relatively safe distance from the implications of *lived* difference, the day-to-day experiences of those marked as non-white, non-majority Canadians.[4] What would it mean if the distance on which official multiculturalism hinges were compromised? If the power of cultural "others" was not contingent upon majoritarian recognition, but perceived as a given, as socially and politically

---

4   I don't have space within this short piece to explore in detail the strengths and weaknesses of multiculturalism as Canadian public policy, and much excellent work has already been done on this topic. See Bannerji and Gunew for two thoughtful critiques of hegemonic multiculturalism in Canada and Australia; for a usefully historicized overview of the modern "politics of recognition" in a multicultural context, see Charles Taylor. Norma Alarçon, meanwhile, deliberately figures multiculturalism under late (neo-liberal) capital as consumption-driven, "the discourse of choice for a multiplicity of national and transnational agendas to name the traffic in goods and peoples, the referential subjects of this complex discursive economy" (139). This is a quality of Canadian cultural policy that has become increasingly prominent in recent years as successive federal parties divide Canadians along ethnic lines and tailor political and economic messages accordingly.

non-contingent? How would it feel to *feel* difference as a source of pleasure but also as a site of labour, messy and awkward but worth working through together, rather than to perceive difference as part of a binary framed by self and other? These are the questions intercultural affect impresses upon bodies, and these are the questions *BIOBOXES* provokes for me.

"The space between two individuals shrinks with intimacy": a perfect description of what happened when I stepped inside Cindy Mochizuki's Japanese/English box for the very first time. I felt a mix of pleasure, light claustrophobia, anticipation, and mild anxiety, looking first around at the gorgeous design of the box, a city skyline in cardboard as seen from above (see fig. 1), and then straight into Mochizuki's eyes. The boxes' dimensions position their performers only a foot or so away from spectators' bodies, the latter perching on stools in front of the tiny proscenium arches framing each box-stage. The decoration in most boxes is extraordinary, at times breath-taking: several are cluttered with stuff, glorious and colourful miniatures that set a playful scene and encourage spectators to *take in* their surroundings, unabashedly to enjoy the display (Stephenson 129–30). The proscenia are all decorated, too, adorned with curtains (French/English box, Cantonese/English box), drawings (Japanese/English box), arches and pillars (Italian/English box), and surgical masks (Cantonese/English box). And they each bear small, Velcro-backed cards to mark the languages spoken in each box: one says "English" and the other is labelled with the language representative of the box's documentary subject. Spectators are meant to switch the cards at will, pressing the box's storyteller into service; each performer knows his or her text by heart in two languages (though, in only one case, in two *official* languages), and as the card switches the language of delivery changes (quite uncannily) on a dime.[5]

---

5   I have described the language cards as I remember them functioning during my two viewings of the show. Theatre Replacement's Maiko Yamamoto notes that the cards were originally standardized across the boxes as two signs, one that read "English" in both of the box's languages, and another that listed the other language in both English and that language. However, "eventually [the performers] found their best way to get the audience to indicate the switch. Some just simply asked their audience member to say 'English' or

Fig. 1. Writer/performer Cindy Mochizuki in the Japanese/English box.

The language cards are key to the virtuosic pleasure of *BIOBOXES*, fore-grounding the extraordinary skill of each box's creator/performer/caretaker, but they are also the things that make each biobox explicitly into a border space, a contact zone: they demarcate the edge at which spectators may approach, may virtually touch individual performers, may invade their performance space, may propel their labour (and make them work harder). They also, as I will argue, offer the performance a way to unsettle spectators' experiences, to change the terms of engagement between self and other, actor and auditor, at the border. Even though the cards appear, in their passive request that we choose our preferred language of communication, to defer to *our* choice, *our* power, *our* comfort as spectator-consumers, they are *trompe l'eoil*; my choice exposes me to my performer's gaze, indeed to the *performance*'s gaze. In the borderlands, remember, distance requires proximity, productive

---

'Cantonese' [for example], and others just used one of the signs as a kind of lever that they could see [and] when the audience member pushed the lever in, the language switched. By the end, I think everyone had a variation specific to their performance, as it should be" (Yamamoto).

encounter requires tension; the language cards enact both, operating as the fulcrum of contradiction at the edge-space of cultural encounter. Their invitation (to get comfortable in the language of my choice) is also a dare (to chance the other language, with which I am likely not very familiar, if at all);[6] in turn, that dare stages *BIOBOXES*'s two linked research questions (perhaps questions formulated long in advance of my arrival by those white-coated scientists, the performers' alter egos?). What will happen if I switch the card? What will happen if I *don't*?

Only one box—the French/English box—embeds both of Canada's official languages, conjuring something of the bitter language politics that have plagued the nation since at least 1976 (when the Parti Québécois was first elected to office) if not since Confederation in 1867; as a unit, however, the six boxes both hail and sideline official bilingualism, querying its continued relevance in a state where, today, multiple languages compete for public space and validity. Insofar as *BIOBOXES* is at its most basic a show not about bilingualism, nor biculturalism, nor even multiculturalism, but about *migration*, the language cards also raise another anxious ghost: the spectre of arrival at the international border, that ultimate, high-stakes contact zone in which the productive contradictions of Anzaldúa's borderland and Knowles's interculturalism are resolved into strict rules of engagement, tensions that can prove literally dangerous, and in which "choosing" a language of communication (if there is a choice at all) is as fraught as trying simply to *appear*, to look the part of someone who is *supposed* to be there. While there is, of course, nothing of the tension or the genuine stakes of the international crossing in the tiny, charming puppet theatres that comprise Theatre Replacement's installation, that absence, too, is a kind of fairground trick—for the stakes of crossing live on in the show's documentary matter (the real-life stories of its

---

6   I do not assume spectators' language skills or lack thereof, and I recognize that the pleasure of hearing a box's story in two familiar languages affords an altogether different spectatorial position from the one I describe here. The diversity of the boxes and the episodic structure of the piece, however, ensure that an auditor familiar with English, French, and Italian, for example, will eventually encounter unfamiliar languages, and thus the double edge of the language card.

migrants), in its physical shape (the booths for two, just a bit too close for comfort), and in the surprising difficulties and awkward self-reflections its language cards can present.

WELCOME TO CANADA/BIENVENUE AU CANADA

> Threat is ultimately *ambient*. Its logic is purely *qualitative*.
> —Brian Massumi, "The Future Birth of the Affective Fact"

> As you move from one state to another, you "play" yourself, and hope you are convincing.
> —Sophie Nield, "On the Border as Theatrical Space"

What does a border *feel* like? The answer to this question depends on context: where in the world you are, which nation you are trying to enter, how you look and sound, what's in the trunk of your car. As Anzaldúa well knows, writing from the zone of hyper-surveillance that joins the US with Mexico, borders evoke concrete state authority as they project the threat of detention or even armed intervention, all in order to draw an unmistakable line between "us" (those permitted in) and "them" (those denied entry). Border guards sit behind glass at airports; they carry guns at checkpoints. Their unflinching gazes demand your passport. In monotones they query your business. Maybe they fingerprint you. They do not smile. All the while "the border" (that oversized lettering above the guard booths that reads "UK Border" or "Bienvenue au Canada," the queues marked "Citizens" or "Foreign Nationals," the miles of rope) acts, too. It requires you to stay behind the yellow line until called forward. Its signs tell you to turn off your mobile phone. It diagrams words and actions that will not be tolerated. It asks you to have your documents ready.

Sophie Nield argues that "[t]he border, and the refugee, are both products of the 'theatrical'" (69). The border divides us into characters—the "citizen," the "visitor," the "alien"—and its space is "organized in such a way as to compel

certain kinds of appearance" (64), requiring those who approach it to conform
to what theatre students will recognize as a particular brand of *emotional*
realism. At the border, "one must simultaneously be present and be represented. The issue is not whether a person is there. A person is clearly there.
The issue is precisely 'who is there?'—whether the person who is there *is* who
they *represent* themselves to be" (65, emphasis in original). At the border, to
seem "fake" is to risk being stripped of passport and, with it, personhood; to
seem "real," on the other hand, to compel true belief in one's life story from
the "observers, inspectors, judges—audiences" charged with authenticating
one's performance and conferring the legal right to remain, is to achieve access and status, a quality of "belonging" (65, 67).

There's always a subtext to emotional realism, of course: the state requires
us to perform ourselves at the border in order that it may produce its own
self, invoking, via the bodies of both citizens and aliens, a sense of national
interiority. It requires each of us to feel the border's threat and check ourselves accordingly, so that we may finally inhale the palpable relief of passing
through the gates, passing *into* the nation. Nield's borders are not just theatrical, in other words, but performative in Judith Butler's sense (see *Gender*;
"Performative"): the border establishes the categories of citizen and "other,"
and marks the difference between them, by classifying human behaviour at
the border as normative or not. To be naturalizable, to be admissible to the
class of citizen (or potential citizen, or welcome guest), I need to *act* natural. But "natural" always has a particular flavour: as José Muñoz has argued,
the conflation of "normal" affect with legal status has been one of the levers
by which minoritarian subjects have historically been excluded from full
personhood in North America. Positing "ethnicity as 'a structure of feeling,'
as a way of being in the world" ("Feeling Brown" 79), Muñoz contends that
"[c]itizenship is negotiated within a contested national sphere in which performances of affect counter each other in a contest that can be described as
'official' national affect versus emergent immigrant" (69). For Muñoz, one
figures as uncomfortably "ethnic" (or "immigrant") when one stages one's

"affective difference" (70) from the dominant (white)[7] culture's norms; in practice this might mean acting "too loud" or "too excitable" (too jumpy at the border?), speaking too emotionally in an unfamiliar language or accent, seeming somehow "excessive" in public spaces. The quality of being "ethnic" is often stereotyped as overly theatrical; another way to describe its affective difference might be to say that it appears to stage "private matters" in "public space"—to the embarrassment, the story goes, of everyone around.[8] Arriving at the border, the migrant consequently needs to moderate his or her affective difference, to shift into the register of nationally sanctioned emotional realism. The border demands that the migrant be tacitly ashamed of what he or she *was*, so that he or she may perform (as) someone new.

Shame is the border's affective lever, for migrants and citizens and visitors alike; it is the ghostly partner of the fear, the nerves we all (naturally) feel as we approach the guard's booth. To be nervous, even fearful at the border is to be always already *potentially* ashamed of oneself: the border compels me to fake outward calm so that I can seem who I believe myself to be—or who I hope to become—and this inevitable fakery is both affectively and etymologically linked to an experience of shame. As Elspeth Probyn notes, "[S]hame comes from the Goth word *Scham*, which refers to covering the face. The crucial element that turns sham into shame is the level of interest and desire involved. There is no shame in being a sham if you don't care what others think or if you don't care what you think" (72–73). The border invites the sham: hinging on an essentially performative encounter that is nevertheless *disguised* as authentic, unmediated, real, the act of border crossing requires

---

7   Muñoz defines whiteness not as skin colour nor ethnic marker but as "a cultural logic that prescribes and regulates national feelings and comportment"; he notes that "some modes of whiteness—for example, working-class whiteness—are stigmatized within the majoritarian public sphere" and "do not correspond with the affective ruler that measures and naturalizes white feelings as the norm" ("Feeling Brown, Feeling Down" 680).

8   Christine Kim argues that *BIOBOXES* makes its major contribution to Canada's multicultural performance canon as it deliberately spotlights the personal, the mundane, the banal—the unabashedly private—experiences of Canada's ethnic "others," the kinds of things one goes out of one's way *not* to perform at the border (191).

our *enactment* yet delegitimizes the very idea that we might be performing *for*, rather than simply *appearing naturally at*, the border. Thus the fear of being "caught out" at the border—having brought foreign food or too much alcohol or simply having the wrong kind of document—translates quickly, as we approach the guard's booth, into fear that I might be a sham, that I might be *acting*: the sense I get as I shuffle through the line that I must have done something wrong somewhere, which I now must work to hide. The border compels my fear; my fear compels a performance. The performance is the stuff of the border—and it hinges on the possibility, indeed the likelihood, that I should be ashamed of myself.[9]

Probyn's work on shame, however, is not pessimistic, because shame is no simple feeling: it "cannot be conceived of as an external object that could be dispassionately described, nor is it a purely personal feeling. Shame is subjective in the strong sense of bringing into being an entity or an idea through the specific explosion of mind, body, place, and history" (81). At the border, shame's rich intersubjectivity—the entanglements between differently empowered human beings standing on either side of a glass screen—as well as its political, cultural, and historical dimensions (the material history of every border as a contested, shifting, geographic terrain), is disguised; it exists as "affect," never as "idea" (79), and as such can only be felt and passed through, never parsed. What might happen, though, if the border's abiding theatricality were to be brought into view? By unmasking and playing within the border's theatrical frame, we might begin to generate what Probyn calls an "ethics" of shame: to "[reconfigure] how we think about [shame] and about the bod[ies]" on which shame acts. An ethics of shame might allow us, further, to explore "expressions of shame" (81) as not personal but shared, social experiences from which we might derive more productive, collaborative, intercultural affects. Returning "sham" to "shame," we might think critically about affective differences, plural, and examine the expectations of shaming buried in the

---

9   My thanks to Nicholas Ridout for insights in this paragraph into the relationship between fear and shame at the border (and at the theatre).

normative division of multicultural space into "self" and "other." Returning sham to shame, we might begin to shift the border, expose its borderlands.

Inside Theatre Replacement's bioboxes, every border is always already a theatre: the proscenium arch every spectator meets as s/he sits down in its tiny, darkened cubicles at once constitutes the magical promise of the puppet show and the disquieting configuration of the guard booth: I face the individual on the other side of the barrier who looks at but also *through* me, and I see the card that asks me to stake a claim to a particular language in order to proceed. The freight of border shame, too, comes specifically into view via that language card, as it concretizes the border's distributive function: either I choose "same"—the language of familiarity to me, the language that will allow me to absorb, consume, move through the performance seamlessly, the language that will allow me to perform my reactions authentically *for* the performer just inches away from me—or I choose "other"—the language with which I am less-, or un-, familiar, the language that will alienate me entirely from the performance's narrative, the language that will mean my performance as spectator will necessarily be a struggle, an awkward sham. In both cases, the card crystalizes a sense of loss—my recognition of the Catch-22 of this binary option.

In the remainder of this essay, I would like to explore in some detail the potential of *BIOBOXES*'s shame ethic by ruminating on two difficult encounters I had with its language cards on two separate occasions. I invoke the personal here not to indulge myself (although indulgence is no bad thing, especially for subjects often told to indulge themselves less, to be quieter, more decorous, to check their emotions at the border), but specifically in order to discover the *transactive* function of shame in the box. In one instance, the language card gave me, like the proverbial border patrol, momentary power over the performer in front of me, reducing that performer to object; on another it predicated my total loss of control, leaving me feeling sick and inadequate as I found myself unable to navigate an environment that should, in theory, have felt very familiar to me. In both cases, the shame that rises at my memory of these encounters has encouraged me to reflect on what, exactly, I did when I switched the language card: what I accomplished and for whom, whether or not I allowed myself truly to become addressable by as well as responsible to the performer in front of me.

JUNE 2008: CINDY MOCHIZUKI, JAPANESE/ENGLISH BOX

Cindy Mochizuki's Japanese/English box was the first in which I sat on my very first visit to *BIOBOXES*; it constituted my formal introduction to the work, and has remained for me one of the most memorable of the six pieces in the show. Inspired by the unsettling effect it had on me, I quickly wrote a review essay about *BIOBOXES* that used Mochizuki's work as exemplary. The review begins by reconstructing (imperfectly) my initial reaction to my and Mochizuki's close, disquieting proximity inside the box, and then details what I remembered at the time (even more imperfectly) to be the gist of the box's narrative. I then confessed:

> As I record these disconnected memories I know I'm not painting a very good picture. The truth is I don't remember much of Cindy's performance, in part because I chose to listen to half of it in Japanese, a language I don't speak at all. The option was there: affix the language card and hear her words in English or Japanese, switching at will. I'm not entirely sure why I kept switching into Japanese. I think I felt bad that the character in the narrative, still so unsure in her English,[10] should have to keep using it just for me. Or perhaps I sensed it would be somehow more respectful to hear the performance

---

10   I'd misconstrued the narrative as the story of an immigrant girl who had lost a loved one. In fact, Mochizuki's narrative, titled "Flight," is based on an interview with the male international student Yoshiyuki (Kim 184). Mochizuki's translation of the interview into monologue form explores, in Christine Kim's words, "among other things, the desire not 'to be a bird but . . . to be *like* a bird,' the struggle to pose appropriately for photographs, and the anxieties associated with speaking imperfect English" (184; see Theatre Replacement, *BIOBOXES* 142–45).

in its "native" language. In hindsight, I know I was wrong: my choice might have seemed somehow generous at the time but it proved unhelpful, provoked by my useless guilt as an English-speaking, native born Canadian. Ultimately, the language barrier stopped me from experiencing Cindy's performance fully. Now I barely know enough of it to pass on. (161)

Responding to my words in her thoughtful analysis of *BIOBOXES*, Christine Kim cites the above passage as "an ideal enactment of what Charles Taylor calls the 'recognition of difference,'" something Taylor invests with value in a multicultural framework but about which Kim asks we think again, querying what "recognition" actually means under multiculturalism, and who it actually benefits (188). Taking my failure in the Japanese/English box perhaps too lightly as a form of recognition, late in my review I claim that, ultimately, the story I missed did not really matter all that much to me (166); I perceived the performance's value elsewhere, in the contradiction it produced between my pleasure in its intricate miniatures (the cardboard skyline, a hand-held camera and a parcel of photos, incense, a charm I got to keep) and my cognitive disturbance in not having actually understood what was going on. As I have repeatedly revisited my memory of Mochizuki's box since writing those reflections, however, I have come to realize that the box's story in fact matters a great deal. For Kim, *BIOBOXES*'s small, intimate, even mundane narratives constitute an attempt to shift what qualifies as recognizably "multicultural" in the Canadian public sphere (190–91). Similarly, for me, in their indelible links to their language cards—which signal first and foremost their status as oral texts, but also embed their inherent bilingualism—these narratives pose a challenge to spectators to figure out how best to encounter the stories they surrogate: that is, to do the affective work required to "recognize" what it takes to hear these "immigrant" stories (or not to hear them) at all.

All the *BIOBOXES* language cards are set to "English" to begin; the performance in this way assumes an audience that is at least functionally fluent in English, and thus that English will be the common language of experience for all spectators, regardless of other (and varying) language ability (and regardless of whether or not spectators more comfortable in another language represented in the show—say, Italian or Serbo-Croatian—will choose to switch immediately into that language upon entering its box). This is also the border's assumption: that we will all communicate using the lingua franca of the nation for which it stands, unless we explicitly request otherwise (often a daunting proposition). And yet *BIOBOXES*'s point is not to be exclusive in this way; after all, it does frame language *as choice*. More significantly, in that choice it signals both shared address-ability (everyone with some English can enjoy each box) and audience response-ability: we are invited actively to decide on a "common" language for each performance, and implicitly (though not necessarily consciously) we must thus recognize communication, miscommunication, and mis/understanding as equally possible (even planned) outcomes inside each box.

When I chose to switch from English into Japanese fairly early in Mochizuki's narrative, several things happened. First, I felt delight; Mochizuki made the switch virtuosically, without skipping a beat. Second, I chose to value delight in her virtuosity and pleasure in hearing her speak Japanese over the content of her narrative, a story based on the experiences of an international student called Yoshiyuki. Third, I became slowly aware that I had no idea what was going on in the story, and after coming to this awareness I switched back to English again. I left with my souvenir, all smiles; then I went back to the edge of the stage and sat with my friends, who had visited different boxes. They asked me what I had seen and heard, and at this point I began to doubt the nature of my experience. What did I remember about the box? Not a lot. I remembered my affect; I remembered how Mochizuki's labour had made me feel. I remembered enjoying it all, mostly. I did *not* remember the narrative, except in tiny, inaccurate scraps.

Over time, my failure to understand Yoshiyuki's story/Mochizuki's narrative, which prompted my first written reactions to *BIOBOXES*, has deepened into a sense of shame. Faced with the choice to understand the content or to "experience" the spectacle of the Japanese/English box, I chose the latter, acting as a consumer rather than a listener; I chose to "recognize" Mochizuki, her work, and her documentary interlocutor as pleasurably other, rather than to allow myself to engage with these things more deeply and, arguably, more meaningfully. This is not to say there was no depth or meaning in the encounter I had with Yoshiyuki/Mochizuki in the box; in my memory the experience is profoundly moving, and Mochizuki's skill as a performer and as the beautiful box's creator in particular stays with me. Nor is it to say that the option I did not choose was the "correct" one. Had I acted more passively and stuck with English I would still have missed a crucial aspect of the Japanese/English box: the feeling of vertigo that accompanies hearing words spoken quickly in a language completely foreign to my ear and then trying to react to those words in a meaningful way, the experience of disturbance that came from my own work in navigating Yoshiyuki's/Mochizuki's difference on its own terms for a time. Both choices are plentiful but incomplete without the other. Both promise misses and losses—and perhaps that's the point. Each experience of each box, for spectators fluent or capable in only one of its languages, will be a failure one way or another, and that failure has the power to produce—for those (like me) who are uncomfortable with, but nevertheless entangled in, the consumer-driven, self/other-based model of multiculturalism the tiny, delightful box sets cheekily recall—some level of shame. As Probyn reminds me, this shame is not unproductive, nor is it *my* shame alone. *BIOBOXES* stages the shame of imperfect choice in the moment of cross-cultural encounter, demands it from us in order *simply to begin*; in its gorgeous theatricalizing of that choice, however, Mochizuki's box also prompts me to reflect on shame's intersubjectivity. How does my shame in front of her—specifically, my worry over how to *play* the kind of spectator to difference I think I *should be*—impact those who share borderland spaces with me? Having recognized *not* the other in the frame, but rather the colossal failure of the binary choice the tiny proscenium border demands of me, what do I do next?

MAY 2009: PAUL TERNES, GERMAN/ENGLISH BOX

I was a different kind of spectator in Paul Ternes's German box, which I did not visit until my second time at *BIOBOXES*, in 2009. I am ethnic German, the first generation daughter of two immigrants who arrived in Canada in the late 1950s. They embraced the call to integrate, learning English in (still strongly anglophone) Montreal when they first arrived, and we spoke English at home throughout my childhood. I have some German but not a lot, gained mostly on trips to visit family in Europe. I know more French; like many Canadian kids I learned French at school. Although I'm by no means fluent (again, like many Canadian kids who learned French at school), I did pretty well in Anita Rochon's French box; I felt both nervous and excited before I stepped in, as though I was back in school and about to take a test I was fairly sure I could pass. By contrast, I wholly dreaded visiting the German box.

Ternes's story is titled "A Modernist Nightmare," and it is strangely familiar to me. Its first half features a mother and child (both played by figurines) as the former tells the latter something of her earlier life in Bavaria; at the narrative's midpoint the story shifts and a narrator (unnamed and not gendered, but played by Ternes) recounts being "there when the wall came down" (Theatre Replacement, *BIOBOXES* 153). The narrator then describes a dinner party s/he held at home in Canada after German reunification, and the feeling of desolation that hit when the guests asked whether s/he could recognize the sentiments of those back in Germany "who were now sort of asserting their German-ness," and whether s/he too could now "embrace my nationality" (153–54). Feeling "utterly alone" in the face of this query, posed by well-meaning friends at a friendly social gathering, the narrator concludes: "[I]n some strange way I became German after that" (154).

My mother, too, told me endless bedtime stories of her home in Germany, the land and the smells and the activities that traced her days; my father wasn't at the Wall when it came down, but he was raised partly in East Germany and made a point of visiting Berlin shortly afterward. I don't know how German my parents feel today, or if they could even put that feeling into words, though I suspect that, like Ternes's narrator, they have had to become both more and less German in their leaving—that the act of migration likely precipitated for them a series of tiny crises in the performance of self both at and beyond the border. As for me, I hold two passports but don't have any idea how to feel

German, and I'm always afraid that my persistent affective failure will show itself when I approach the German border.

The uncanny likenesses between Ternes's narrative and my own history have, ironically, only become visible to me after reading his script; they were not available to me in his box because I knew that in order for the box to *feel* right—in order for me to feel "same" enough, *German* enough—I would need to switch the language card immediately and listen in German for as long as I could reasonably pretend that I was following the story. Unlike in Mochizuki's box, where the switch into Japanese seemed first thrilling, then discombobulating, and later troubling to me, the provocations of its "soft" borders becoming apparent only after my visit had ended, in Ternes's box the pressure to switch came hard and fast from inside my own body and provoked a strong sense of the fear of failure I often feel when I cross the German border on my German passport. I felt the anxious pressure to perform my legal as well as my cultural legitimacy long before I sat down in Ternes's space, and even though the stakes at *BIOBOXES*, as I suggested earlier, are comparatively low, I felt that pressure at a level familiar to me from much higher-stakes situations.[11]

In Probyn's words, I knew before I entered the German/English box that I was a sham. But the box did not bury my shame; instead, it staged the national border—as physical barrier, as site of confusion and loss, as locus of uncertainty and embarrassment and even fear—more directly than any of the other boxes in the show. The German/English box is comprised primarily of a Styrofoam wall that separates Ternes from his audiences (150); the mother and child figurines appear in front of the wall, manipulated by Ternes from behind, and as the narrator describes the fall of the Berlin Wall, Ternes drills through the Styrofoam and then begins tearing it apart with his hands (153).

---

11   Although the risks I face at international borders are not the same as those faced by refugees or other vulnerable travellers (including non-white travellers), because I currently work in the United Kingdom as an EU national my livelihood is directly tied to how well I "pass" as German at the UK border, where now-electronic gates offer all instructions to me in German. The requirement to perform my language ability is literally (and worryingly, for me) encoded on my EU travel documents.

Pieces of it float into our laps on the other side of the box's proscenium, and suddenly Ternes and his audiences come face to face (see fig. 2). Audience members spend the first part of the performance staring at this (rather ludicrous) barrier, wondering amidst the figurines' domestic story what it could possibly mean, and the other half brushing bits of it from clothing, all too aware it is the Berlin Wall and yet forced to reckon with the fact that it is, literally, just plastic. At turns isolating, sinister, charming, and funny, the smallness and flimsiness of the Styrofoam wall (at one point Ternes's script reads "*The performer softly blows away the last piece of wall debris*" [153] in a gesture I remember as weirdly delicate) deliberately contrast with the strength and tenaciousness of the concrete, supposedly unassailable borders between nations and individuals Ternes's narrative invokes. For me, struggling to follow Ternes in German, feeling more and more gut-wrenched and missing the vast majority of the story as a result, the real/fake, powerful/breakable, intimidating/ridiculous wall/border disrupted, perhaps even mocked gently, the tension and embarrassment and shame I felt during my few minutes in the box. Rendering both (hard) international and (soft) interpersonal borders

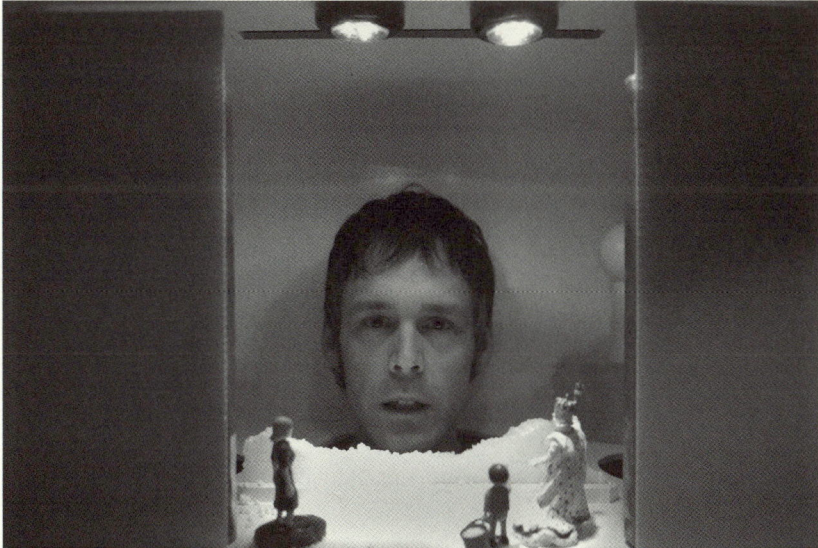

Fig. 2. Writer/performer Paul Ternes in the German/English box.

literally at puppet scale, Ternes's DIY barrier offered me a salient reminder of how much of the border zone we each carry inside of our bodies and brains— and thus of how much national borders literally, physically, indeed *concretely* depend on our willing, performed co-operation with state authority in a space that is in fact comprised of intensive, mutually constitutive, vulnerability.

***

In their now canonical essay on shame, Eve Kosofsky Sedgwick and Adam Frank quote Silvan Tomkins:

> Like disgust, [shame] operates only after interest or enjoyment has been activated . . . Such a barrier might be because one is suddenly looked at by one who is *strange*, or because one wishes to look at or commune with another person but suddenly cannot because he is *strange*, or one expected him to be familiar but he suddenly appears unfamiliar, or one started to smile but found one was smiling at a *stranger*. (500, emphasis added)

Shame mediates all potential encounters with strangeness, and as we are accustomed to pathologize shame we pathologize the different, the strange. Yet as Sedgwick and Frank, perhaps anticipating Probyn, note, "Without positive affect, there can be no shame; only a scene that offers you enjoyment or engages your interest can make you blush" (520). The theatre is that place where strangeness enchants me, where I take pleasure in the weird; shame hovers at the edges of all theatrical encounter, bereft there of any connotations of badness or wrongness (though I may well be embarrassed at the theatre for the actors or for fellow spectators or because of my own imagined engagements). Where the border meets the theatre, might shame risk its own vulnerability, become something more socially productive, more collectively empowering? In this essay I have placed Probyn's shame ethic in conversation with the intercultural theory of Anzaldúa, Knowles, and others in order to reimagine the theatricalized border zone as "a precarious hyperreflexivity" where one may be turned "inside out—or outside in" (Sedgwick and Frank 520). *BIOBOXES* may seem a too-small and too-charming site for such an upheaval, but just as Sedgwick and Frank explain how shame requires the promise of joyful engagement, Christine Kim reminds us that the signifying potential of the small is routinely underestimated. Charming is also disarming: the powerful, contradictory feelings and lingering uncertainties with which *BIOBOXES* still haunts me attest to its critical potency. I no longer see a point in resolving those contradictions; I do, however, hope to continue to engage with them.

TAKING *NANAY* TO THE PHILIPPINES: TRANSNATIONAL CIRCUITS OF AFFECT

CALEB JOHNSTON AND GERALDINE PRATT

INTRODUCTION

16 November 2012. We were ushered into the dean's office at the GT-Toyota Asian Cultural Center, a new multi-million dollar complex at the University of the Philippines Diliman in Manila. The dean was running late but her two associates were available and welcoming. Introductions were formal and business cards were exchanged. In ice-breaking preliminaries, Professor Reuben Cañete, responsible for cultural programming at the centre, told us about the migration of his family members to Vancouver fifteen years ago. When Dean Carolyn Sobritchea arrived we learned that she was a former visiting professor at the University of British Columbia and that she possesses a keen interest in Vancouver; she spoke at length about the Philippines's special relationship with Canada. She presented us with her latest publication—*Health of Our Heroes*, a study aimed to assess and improve women migrant workers' access to sexual and reproductive health services and information. Funded by the Canadian International Development Agency, the publication is both evidence and product of her long-term involvement within an extensive policy-making network in the Philippines and beyond. The atmosphere eased. Chocolate cake was served.

We were in Manila planning the tour of *Nanay*, a testimonial theatre play designed to stimulate public debate about Canada's Live-In Caregiver Program (LCP)—a labour visa program through which many Filipina women migrate each year to Canada to care for Canadian children and the elderly. Migrant workers admitted through this program must complete twenty-four months of live-in care work within forty-eight months to qualify to apply for an open visa and then permanent-resident status in Canada. Their contract is with a single employer and they must live in that employer's home while registered in the LCP. Since the mid 1990s the majority coming through the program have been Filipina women, reflecting a long history of American imperialism in the Philippines. Western education and English-language instruction were central features of the US "civilizing mission" in the Philippines through the early decades of the twentieth century and have been key to the production of a vast migrant labour diaspora and culture of out-migration, first institutionalized by President Marcos in the 1970s as the Labor Export Policy (LEP) and expanded by subsequent administrations, in large part because of the significance of remittances for the Philippine economy (Guevarra; Rodriquez).

The numbers of Filipinas admitted to Canada through the LCP expanded exponentially through the 1990s and 2000s; from 2,684 in 2000 to 9,819 in 2009, with a high of 13,775 entries through the LCP in 2007 (Kelly, Park, de Leon, and Priest). With the downturn in the economy, numbers dropped to 5,882 in 2011 (P. Kelly), but the LCP remains a significant component of Canada's care strategy and has been a defining feature of Filipino migration to Canada. In 2009, for example, forty-nine percent of all Filipino immigrants to Canada came through the LCP (TIEDI). The program is thus embedded within a long history of transpacific movement between North America and the Philippines, a culture of out-migration, a political economy of labour export from the Philippines, a dense web of discourses about Filipinas' capacity for care and sacrifice (Cruz), and a great need for high-quality child and elder care in Canada. The LCP is by no means the worst program of its kind; it is almost unique in the world among migration programs for domestic workers because of the opportunity it affords for permanent migration and family sponsorship. For all of these reasons the issues are complex and require full and nuanced public debate.

Documentary theatre seemed the right vehicle for staging this debate. It would allow us to bring individuals with different relationships to the issue into the same intimate space to hear and feel the issues from different perspectives. It would present "evidence" that could not be discounted, embodied by professional actors so as to be felt as well as thought. It would create an occasion for conversation between those who do not normally converse on an equal footing: Filipino domestic workers with Canadian employers, policy makers with grassroots activists, Filipino children with their Canadian teachers. At the time of conceiving the play we were not yet reading Jacques Rancière's work on politics and aesthetics and the potential of theatre as an emancipatory space, but it is now clear that our thinking is in line with his theorizing about theatre and politics (*Disagreement*; *Politics*; *Emancipated*; *Dissensus*). We were hoping that our theatre piece could draw the audience close enough to different dimensions of the debate so as to scramble existing identifications and open a space for new ideas and political alignments.

In 2007 we began working on this project, which was developed in a multi-year collaboration that brought together geographers ("Translating"), professional Vancouver theatre artists, and community activists from the Philippine Women Centre of British Columbia (PWC).[1] In creating the play as documentary theatre, we translated scholarly research into drama, which is to say, we transformed conventional social science interview transcripts into a verbatim script. From Pratt's research archive, collected over the past fifteen years, we gleaned compelling narratives that spoke to the complicated politics and ethical dilemmas of Canada's LCP. From a series of interviews conducted with Filipino domestic workers, their children, as well as Canadian employers and nanny agents, we edited extracted transcripts into a number of testimonial monologues. In the summer of 2008, these were developed in a workshop led by Vancouver director Alex Ferguson at Chapel Arts, a former funeral home recently transformed into an arts centre in Vancouver's Downtown Eastside.

In January 2009, we carried out a three-week rehearsal and production process with a cast of professional actors and a full slate of designers and crew.

---

1 We co-wrote the script and the work was produced through Caleb's performing-arts society. See "Nanay."

Nanay premiered at Vancouver's 2009 PuSh International Performing Arts Festival, and, later that same year, we toured the project to Berlin's Hebbel am Ufer Theatre as part of their Your Nanny Hates You! Festival. We constructed *Nanay* as a site-responsive performance installation of monologues and other scenes, in which small audiences of fifteen are guided through a series of rooms where they encounter different characters with different relationships to the issues of care and need in Canada. Each and every performance of the play has moved seamlessly from performance into an hour-long facilitated public forum in which audience members are encouraged to examine their own entanglements, complacencies, and complicities and to discuss the issues staged in the play. These forums have provided the setting for some remarkable conversations across substantial difference, especially in Vancouver where we were able to ensure that at least five Filipino domestic workers or their children were at each performance (for details, see G. Pratt 111–12; Johnston and Pratt 124; Pratt and Johnston, "Translating" 130–32). We have turned to theatre to put disparate experiences of care and need into public dialogue; we have looked to harness the affective impact of theatre to put these issues into greater visibility, to greater public effect.

Our experience of staging *Nanay* in Vancouver and Berlin stimulated our desire to take the play to the Philippines. Some of this can be expressed in the language of scholarly debate. Citing Nancy Fraser's argument that deliberations of justice are often misframed geographically and existing territorial arrangements (of nation-states) exclude those who should be heard, we are arguing for the opportunity that our play affords to recalibrate the scales of justice by generating transnational public dialogue and debate (76–99). Theories of global care and ethics also imply Canadians' obligation to understand the implications of the LCP from the perspective of those living in the Philippines; *Nanay* could help Canadians fulfill this obligation.

Our desire to take *Nanay* to the Philippines came from other sources as well, more heart than head. In assessments with our community collaborators after the Vancouver performances, domestic workers who participated in the play's design and performance said that the play moved them to want to tell their stories differently to their families in the Philippines, to be more explicit about the everyday traumas that they experience under the LCP. Like many migrants, Filipina domestic workers often feel obliged to construct narratives for their families in the Philippines that accentuate their success in order to shelter themselves and their families from the pain of migration and family separation. *Nanay* tells nuanced but painful stories of coming to Canada; our hope is that it can shoulder some of the burden of circulating the stories and emotions that migrants have difficulty expressing themselves. We were equally spurred by a spirited post-performance talkback discussion in Berlin with several members of the Philippine embassy who attended the play. They told us, "And to the gentleman who has been asking that you must see that the social cost is so great, of course we do. Canada did not need to make this study or this play for us to know the problem that we have. It is everywhere [in the Philippines]. It is something that is even in the [news]papers and in countless studies. We knew before we came today that the problems and the social costs are stupendous . . . But these are things that we are already working towards solving" ("Talkback" Berlin). The conversation spilled into the bar after the talkback and the embassy representatives were both engaging and dismissive—frustratingly and enticingly so, in ways that fuelled our desire to push further and to insist on continuing the conversation in the Philippines.

But what does it mean to travel with the play and continue the conversation in the Philippines? For Canadians the play brought into presence an issue that many can comfortably ignore: this is Canada's reliance on a type of indentured servitude to address national child- and elder-care needs. In the Philippines most everyone has an intimate personal connection to the struggles of migration. Within the first hour of arriving in Manila on our planning trip in November 2012, our driver from the airport spoke about his own experiences as a migrant worker in Dubai, those of his relatives in Vancouver, and his hopes that his children might migrate to Canada through the LCP; we knew even then that we had entered into a radically different emotional and political landscape and began thinking about its implications for reshaping the script and production. Rather than a lack of feeling and visibility, in the Philippines migration is hypervisible, and complex affects, which articulate as hope, fear, and sacrifice, circulate widely. And though so many we met in Manila had direct connections to Canada, it is facile to expect that the play will move easily or evenly across transnational space. We write at the start of a process of transnational translation, with the understanding that there is a geography to the circulation of affects and that different affects travel differently in different contexts, with different political effects. We use this as an opportunity to share some of our deliberations and present several scenes and strategies through which we hope to move *Nanay* into a new emotional, affective, and political terrain. We will be returning to the Philippines in November 2013 to put them into practice through performances at the Philippine Educational Theater Association (PETA) in Manila.

WORN-OUT AFFECTS AND TIRED DEBATES

It was Michiyo Yoneno-Reyes who first greeted us at our meeting with Dean Sobritchea. As an academic at the University of the Philippines, her work focuses on Filipino migration to Japan. But her knowledge of migration to Canada is intimate as well; members of her husband's family have settled in Toronto. In the Philippines, "migration," she noted, "is part of everyone's everyday life." As we presented the concept and intent behind the play, she picked up and ran with our desire to tell complicated, messy narratives about migration experiences. She spoke of a generalized fatigue within the Philippines about the ways that migration stories tend to be narrated: migrants portrayed either as victims of abuse and exploitation or as heroes of the nation (see also Gibson, Law, and McKay). The stories that need to be told to advance political debate, in her assessment, are the complicated, nuanced ones that neither celebrate nor condemn labour migration but convey the complexity of affective investments, attachments, and outcomes.

We already had heard this concern in Canada but for somewhat different reasons. Martin Kinch, the dramaturg from the Vancouver Playwrights Theatre Centre with whom we worked in 2007–08 when writing the script leading up to the Vancouver production, was determined that we include testimonial material from a domestic worker who embodied a more positive experience of migrating to Canada as a live-in caregiver. His concern was not that audiences would be exhausted by stories of victimization, but that inclusion of a positive story would make *Nanay* more credible. If monologues from domestic workers told of only negative, exploitative experiences he felt that middle-class Canadians could dismiss the play as biased and disengage.

Nevertheless, as difficult decisions were made in the Canadian production about which monologues would be kept and discarded, the more positive monologue was cut and the migration experiences of Filipino domestic workers and their families were told through the following five scenes: an ebullient monologue at the moment of leaving the Philippines in which a domestic worker describes the economic pressures to emigrate and her great optimism about overseas live-in domestic work, an angry monologue of exploitation within the LCP, tearful recorded accounts of domestic workers leaving their children in the Philippines, a largely depressed account of family separation and reunification from the perspective of a child who had been left behind and then reunited with her mother in Vancouver, and a replica of a domestic worker's cramped Canadian basement bedroom.[2] Staging domestic workers as neither heroes nor pure victims, the monologues and scenes nonetheless drifted toward the negative, the angry, the hopeless, and the sad (see fig. 1). Canadian audience members' reactions indicate their receptivity to this emotional range: "[M]y son said that for him the one that impacted him the most was going into that bedroom because he felt it was so heavy"; "I felt a dreaded sense of hopelessness looking through the nanny's room"; "the little room was so very sad."[3] The Children's Choice Award determined that *Nanay* was the "Saddest" of the seventeen plays presented at the PuSh Festival in 2009.

Traditionally liberal thinkers have had a great deal of faith in the capacity of stories of pain and suffering to create emotional proximity that can powerfully disrupt and transcend social and geographical distances. In his 1993 Oxford Amnesty lecture, for instance, Richard Rorty argued for how essential the telling of and listening to sad stories has been for the

---

2   For full scripts of the first two monologues, see Johnston and Pratt.

3   The first statement comes from a forum held within the Filipino community after the Vancouver performances; the remainder are from audience surveys.

Fig. 1. Photograph of Filipino-Canadian actors in Vancouver production, *The Georgia Straight*, 2009.

emergence of a human rights culture that pushes the boundaries of who counts as fully human: "We pragmatists," he declared, "argue from the fact that the emergence of the human rights culture seems to owe nothing to increased moral knowledge, and everything to hearing sad and sentimental stories" (118–19). Sympathetic to Rorty's general point, feminists and others nonetheless have raised hard questions about the politics and geopolitics of empathy and spectacles of suffering. Rather than disrupting the status quo, familiar patterns of who tells and who receives stories of pain and suffering can reinscribe hierarchies of privilege: the privileged listen and watch, the marginalized tell. The capacity to empathize with the suffering subject is often taken as a hallmark feature of the liberal bourgeois subject, which simultaneously reinforces their sense of liberal goodness (e.g., Berlant, *Subject*; G. Pratt 79–81). On the other hand, third-world women and other marginalized peoples are frequently staged as agentless suffering victims who exist without the complex and contradictory subjectivities or emotional depth of the privileged (Chow; Mohanty). As bell hooks wrote of the representations of African Americans so many years ago, "Tell me your story. Only do not speak in a voice of resistance. Only speak from that space in the margin that is a sign of deprivation, a wound, an unfulfilled longing. Only speak your pain" (152). Equally, transnational encounters run the risk of retracing long-standing neo-colonial trajectories; Françoise Lionnet and Shu-mei Shih, for instance, are critical of the ways that binaries of north/south persist in even critical post-colonial and transnational studies. Theories and practices of transnationalism, they argue, tend to focus on the most dominant and the most resistant in ways that simplify and essentialize subjectivity and power relations and foreclose possibilities for ethical transnational encounters and constructive political debate.

As we met with academics and theatre artists in Manila the reasons for exploring complex and contradictory feelings and affects multiplied beyond this generalized (albeit extremely important) critique of hegemonic Western white representations of marginalized and/or non-Western people. In one of our first meetings with Dennis Gupa, a theatre director and dramaturg based at the University of the Philippines Los Baños, he said quite simply that he would not tell these stories: "Life is hard. We know suffering." One way of thinking about this statement is to recognize that different affects and emotions are normalized in different places. In Canada, suffering is not assumed to be the norm and—rightly or wrongly—there is national pride in Canada's success as a multicultural nation and its role as alleviator of world suffering (Razack). There are different registers of normalcy in the Philippines as compared to Canada and a theatre piece that simply reproduces the norm does nothing to disrupt it. In the Canadian context (where "we alleviate the world's suffering"), stories of suffering as a result of Canadian immigration policy are genuinely disruptive. In a context where "we know suffering," a theatre piece about Filipina suffering may reproduce norms rather than disrupt them. Given the normalization of different affects and emotions in different places, productive disruption will happen differently in different places.

We need also to consider that in the Philippines stories of victimization in Canada are not necessarily arresting or welcome stories for three reasons. First, many people who we met there told stories of raw, physical, sometimes life-threatening abuse in nearby countries—a brother-in-law who narrowly escaped being raped in Dubai, the body of a domestic worker returned from Mongolia without her heart (Ellao). Arlie Russell Hochschild has coined the term "global heart transplant" to describe the affection that migrant domestic workers develop for children that they care for when they work overseas in countries such as Canada ("Love and Gold" 22). Relative to the actual removal of bodily organs, this metaphorical heart transplant seems relatively benign (see also Kittay). The monologue of poor treatment under the LCP and the small basement bedroom that evoked such emotions of sadness and pity in Vancouver may be received very differently in Manila. Second, and related, Canada is imagined as a place to escape from suffering. It is a dream desti-nation for many Filipino migrant domestic workers because of the unusual opportunity the LCP affords to migrate permanently. Whereas middle-class Canadians seem to have a voracious appetite for stories of victimization of others (especially ones that reinforce rather than disturb their sense of good-ness), narratives of suffering in Canada are unlikely to be as compelling or as popular in the Philippines. They close off a fantasized route of escape. Third, we are keen to invite family members of domestic workers in Canada to attend the play and associated public forum. These family members may not be willing or able to hear stories of difficulties in Canada. Our role—as white middle-class Canadians inducing shame and worry in family mem-bers who benefit from the remittances sent to them by loved ones working as domestic workers in Canada—is an ethical situation that demands careful consideration.

For our project, we have the desire and responsibility to anticipate and engage possible blockages to affective engagement with *Nanay* and the issues that it attempts to raise, and to consider how certain emotions such as shame may circulate in problematic ways that cause pain and close down in other ways productive areas of affective engagement and public discussion. The blockages to and the circulation of feelings likely work differently in different contexts. Liberal assumptions about universal or shared emotions miss the possibility that sadness or pain, for instance, emerge and take shape differently within specific contexts. Discourses of suffering and empathy may not work in universal ways and may be more or less possible and/or politically productive in some situations rather than others. In her discussion of a transnational politics of empathy, Carolyn Pedwell poses a series of challenging questions: "What is empathy? What does it do? Who does it serve? What are its risks? And, crucially, how might it become otherwise?" (25). How might empathy be rethought, not as a remedy to injustice but as a space of mediation, not only as a structure of feeling but as a means of feeling structural relations? The answers, she argues, are likely to vary in different times and contexts.

As we plan to take the play to the Philippines, we are keen that it engenders nuanced debate rather than sloganeering at the extremes: migrants are heroes, migrants are victims; the LCP is good, the LCP is bad. And so we are re-examining our script in preparation for its translation into a new emotional and political landscape. As one aspect of this we have reinserted the more positive migration story that was earlier discarded to facilitate a more emotionally ambiguous exchange. This is a story of a self-scripted go-getter who extols the virtues of her entrepreneurial individualism while telling a larger tale of community suffering and uneven capitalist development, speaking of loneliness and homesickness in the language of personal triumph. She is unsettling: hard not to simultaneously admire and argue against; she is difficult to ignore.

PERFORMING JOVY

[My name is Jovy.] I'm from Laloma, Quezon City, the hometown of the famous *lechon*! [Before leaving to Canada] I graduated [with a] Bachelor of Science in Mathematics in the Polytech University of the Philippines and I was able to get a job in . . . BPI, one of the biggest banks in Manila.

I went to Makati and readied my resume. I had 10 resumes. My first stop was BPI. When I had my screening, they already gave me the schedule for exams, and I made it. I came in the next day. They sent me for an interview and I made it! The next day I was already hired! I didn't have time to distribute my resume. It's a waste of resume and picture!

I wanted to get a job that was prestigious. It was a bank, right? *Ayun ang*, prestigious job back then.

The job is very good . . . [but] when I got married and I got 2 kids, then it's a different story altogether: milk, diapers, vaccinations, and all that. You receive your pay and that's it—the money is just enough. There is no savings. And pretty soon, my kids are going to school, right? What are our options? It's to go abroad. But how? So I heard about this Live-In Caregiver [Program from a newspaper ad]. They said that after 2 years you can get your family. So I took the training.

[To tell you the truth, originally] . . . I don't want to go anywhere because *masaya ang buhay ko sa*. I am happy in the Philippines . . . I have a good job, I have good friends, my family is there, so that's it. It was only when, sort of, the necessity of money came that I decided that this was the only option. But I don't want to go to the Middle East or Singapore or Hong Kong because I have [heard] lots of stories from . . . domestic helper[s]. They just work there for ten years, 15 years, 20 years, until the kids grow up and then they grow old and they're still working there as domestic helper[s]. [Me], I don't mind working as a domestic helper but only for such a time. I know once *ma-establish, ko ano man yung kung* goal, because I know once I establish my goal, I can move [on]. I [was] willing to put my [office] career aside for as long as I have a goal and I have something to look forward to. [My husband and I] dreamed about this.

[How many years was I separated from my kids?] Four years. When I started in 2003, [how we communicated], it's all phone cards! Oh my gosh. I should've been a millionaire by now if I saved all that money. Everyday, *siguro*, maybe ten dollars. It's an everyday thing. Those are the days when I still don't have my own PC . . . [Finally] I got my own computer. So it's the internet now. Webcam. Everyday *din yon*, we webcam! There are even times that the webcam is turned on and [the kids] are just about. It is me who . . . listens to what they are doing . . . When I get homesick I just listen to the little noises they make, what conversations they are having, when the kids are playing even if the camera is not focused on them—I could still hear what they are doing around the house . . . That's all. I just listen.

After the 24th month [of work in the LCP in Canada I] immediately applied for my Permanent Residency, and I got my open visa. So it means I'm no longer restricted to the caregiver job. [At] the same time, the papers [for my family]—the embassy [in Manila] is already working on [them] . . . All in all, [I was separated from my family] for four years.

[After the LCP] . . . then that's the time that I got two jobs, three jobs. It's pretty good earning but my body is worn out and tired . . . [But] I wasn't disappointed. I was content because . . . I found a job at a carpet manufacturer and it is like a Filipino family . . . Oh, we are really happy. So . . . [it's like] my future is being designed so that I won't get shocked when I am done with the LCP.

[At this business] little by little Filipinos are being employed! The Caucasians are the minority because [the bosses] like the Filipino work ethic . . . It's like they saw that it's harmonious. How come the Filipinos are always happy, do not complain, [and are] fast learners? So then they looked for more Filipinos! So now we're all Filipinos there including the warehouse.

[When I was in the LCP,] my employers knew . . . my plan. I told them after the 24 months . . . "I will not work for you anymore as a caregiver."

[Now I have] office work in a cargo service facility. I was sent there to teach the cargo system—the computer system. It's so happy . . . I'm okay here, but [is] there something more[?] I am being prepared for the next step . . . It's like everything is falling into place. Thank God!

[I came to Canada because] you have a lot of opportunities when you grow up, you can have everything you want when you have a job. [My nine-year-old daughter], she wants to design clothes. That's good. If you excel in that you can have your own business. I told her: this is the land of opportunities! There's nothing impossible here. [It was easy for me to find a job right after the LCP because I am a] go-getter . . . Despite the circumstances . . . I never lose hope. [It's just] a matter of mind conditioning. If I say I can do it, I can do it. You know. It's a combination of personality plus your experience, plus your confidence . . . That's what I learned.

[Do] you know how many people from the Philippines get disappointed when they get here? They can't do what their true job is. It's hard to adjust. Me, I'm really sure that I will face difficulties. I prepare my heart for that. I actually put my pride aside. Because if one just has blind hopes, things won't happen that way. You'll get disappointed. When you get disappointed, you go very, very low. You're lonely . . . you cry. What will happen to you? That's why so many of us caregivers who are first timers going abroad, end up going back [to the Philippines].

We learned about those cases. There are *a lot*. Either they commit suicide here from being so depressed or go crazy [or] return after eight months. [Or] it's almost at the end of their 24-month term and [they] couldn't make it and so went back. It's like, why? Almost 24 months and you quit? Types like that. If you're not strong here [*points to head*] and you're not strong here [*points to heart*], you'll have a hard time. [*crosses herself*] (Pratt and Johnston with the PWC, *Nanay* 7–9)

***

Jovy is negotiating between discontinuous frames of meaning and affect, only some of which are anchored in experiences of suffering. She tells her story with great energy and optimism but she nonetheless tells an incoherent story that moves between emotional registers. Furthermore, as we work with this monologue for the Manila production we are returning more and more of it to Tagalog and Taglish, to the mixture of the languages used in the original interview (some of which was translated for research purposes and for the Vancouver production). It was the Filipino Canadian actor who workshopped the monologue with us in Vancouver, Lissa Neptuno, who drew attention to the way in which Jovy's mode of storytelling changes in the original untranslated transcript (not shown here) as she moves in and out of Tagalog, English, and Taglish. Her mode of storytelling is very different in English and she is more likely to use this language, for instance, when she answers a question as "a research subject." We are hoping that the violence of colonialism and Western knowledge production can be opened up and explored through a careful scripting of the movement between languages and modes of storytelling. In other words, there may be ways of communicating affective relations in the form as much as the content of the story, and in ways that leave the contradictory range of emotions in tension and in play.

FEELING FOR THE EMPLOYERS

There is second track of monologues in *Nanay* involving Canadian employers and a Canadian nanny agent. In the Canadian production, staging these monologues was a source of much disagreement and debate. What did we want audience members to feel about and toward Canadians who hire Filipino domestic workers: empathy, disdain, hostility, moral superiority, or some mixture of unsettled emotions? Further, the middle-class employers were interviewed in very different circumstances than were the domestic workers (the former interviewed in their homes by a university researcher, the latter at the Philippine Women Centre in the context of activist research). Did their research-interview transcripts and script give the director and actors enough to work with to find a complicated emotional range? We eventually created three scenes. One was developed from an interview with a couple that hired first a Filipina and then a European nanny. Their dialogue, in which they express a sense of self-congratulatory paternalism toward the first and then make invidious comparisons between the Filipina and European nanny, lends itself to satire and the dialogue was staged in Vancouver to exaggerate their racism and privilege through casting, costumes, setting, and actors' demeanour (see fig. 2). A second scene was created from two separate interviews with Canadian women who were trying to cope with finding home care for their children within the existing Canadian labour supply of mostly young and older women caregivers, almost all undependable in the short or long term. Their experiences of hiring and firing or being let down by these workers thread in and out of each other, and the staged "dialogue" is an exhausting repetition of stories of stress and frustration. Unable to find an interview within the existing research transcripts with someone who had actually hired a Filipina nanny for childcare that elicited empathy, we interviewed a close

Fig. 2. Staging of Canadian employers in Vancouver production.

friend who told of her experiences hiring a Filipina live-in caregiver for her mother, who had had a stroke and has advanced Parkinson's disease; this was worked up as a third employer scene.

Responses in a community forum held by Filipino Canadian community collaborators after the Vancouver performances suggest that it was the second scene that created the most emotional connections for at least some Filipino audience members. A Filipino Canadian activist, himself the father of two young children, spoke of

> being surprised to like parts that I didn't think I would like, in particular the two women in the kitchen. I don't know why it resonated so much but I think it was really seeing the Canadian issues collide with the Filipino community's issues. As two mothers—I guess they were single moms, I'm not sure—but just talking about their difficulty finding childcare as a family. My reaction was really surprising to me. ("Talkback" Vancouver)

Finding this ground for empathy seems like an important step in shifting the focus away from identity politics and from good and bad employers to more complicated and nuanced discussions of Canada's "care crisis" and toward building strands of solidarity among those who otherwise see themselves on opposite sides of this issue. It might create the means toward different attachments and for coming together in new ways.

When we began discussions about *Nanay* in Manila we assumed that the employer scenes would be of less interest to audiences there. We were very quickly told otherwise and this has prompted us to think carefully about whether and how these scenes will need to be reworked as well. In the first instance, we want to counter the misconception that Canada "is heaven" by including a monologue of a nanny agent that was not treated as a separate scene in the Vancouver production. This is a difficult monologue to listen to because the agent is so explicitly and brutally racist in the distinctions that he makes between European and Filipino domestic workers. For instance:

You ask other people, they'll tell you the same thing about Filipinos. Depends what you're looking for, what you want. My personal view, if you have a baby and you want someone to lick your home clean: Filipino girl. Go for that. If you have kids three, four years of age, and you want interaction, you want them to go to the park, arts and crafts, do things, you're better off with a European. (Pratt and Johnston, *Nanay* 60)

Presenting this monologue in the Philippines runs the risk of subjecting Filipinos to Canadian-based hate speech. On balance, we have decided that this shockingly overt racism—located in a verbatim monologue—brings the issue of systemic racism in Canada into the public conversation in difficult but important ways. It disrupts naive fantasies of Canada as a place of hope and opportunity to create space for other animating fantasies of the good life, including ones in which staying in the Philippines is a viable life choice. Closing off fantasies of Canada as "heaven" might open room for—and even force—a more probing discussion of the Philippine Labor Export Policy and its associated culture of out-migration.

As we rethink the play we are attempting to disrupt other aspects that were reductive and arguably replay Western-centric logics. In the first instance, we have recast one Filipino Canadian actor who played a domestic worker in the Vancouver and Berlin productions as an employer and have auditioned and hired actors in the Philippines for the domestic-worker roles. It is a simple point perhaps but in retrospect it is worth examining how easily we cast Filipino Canadians in the role of victimized domestic workers[4] and how commonsensical it seemed to cast white Canadians as employers. More and more

---

4   When representatives of the Philippine embassy attended the play in Berlin they angered the Filipino Canadian actors because, in conversation after the talkback, they seemed to systematically disqualify these Filipino Canadians as Filipinos. (One was told that "your accent doesn't sound Filipino," another that "you don't look Filipino, you look Chinese.") At the time we interpreted this as a power play to discredit the critical message of the play. From the vantage point of the Philippines, such an interpretation seriously misreads and trivializes relations and tensions between and among diasporic and national Filipinos.

sponsorship through the LCP involves Filipino Canadian families as employers and casting a Filipino Canadian actor as an employer complicates (in a way that is actually more accurate) the racialization of employers and employees in Canada and opens up for discussion the complex class dynamics within many transnational Filipino families. This will also involve pulling out and working with aspects of the script that receded in the Canadian production. For instance, in the third monologue, about eldercare, the Canadian employer comments that her Filipino domestic worker was in the first instance "invited to come from the Philippines to stay with her husband's family and take care of his grandparents." The audience is told that "one of them had Alzheimer's. She took care of them twenty-four hours a day, seven days a week. For two years. And it seems they never gave her any relief at all. And they didn't give her any pay. So she'd basically never worked before in Canada except for taking care of her husband's grandparents" (Pratt and Johnston, *Nanay* 83–84). This prompted virtually no commentary or discussion in Canada for reasons that we failed to investigate. But it should cause discussion and commentary because the heavy reliance on the LCP among Filipino families increasingly draws the attention of Canadian policy-makers and points to complicated relations within Filipino families in Canada and transnationally. Eliciting a fulsome discussion about the way the LCP functions within Filipino families from the perspective of the Philippines could be a significant contribution to public debate in Canada and likely in the Philippines as well.

POLITICS, THEATRE, AND AFFECT

Throughout *Nanay* we have turned to theatre as a vehicle for circulating affect in unpredictable ways; we have sought to stage a range of affective tonalities—sadness, hope, fear, frustration—in order to push audiences to feel the issues differently, to enter into risky public conversations, and to prompt them to take (even in some small way) action within their everyday lives. "[L]ive performance provides a place," argues Jill Dolan, in her search for hope at the theatre, "where people come together, embodied and passionate, to share experiences of meaning making and imagination that can be described or capture fleeting intimations of a better world." She calls these moments of affective intensity among audience members "utopian performatives" and she especially treasures those in which audience members feel allied with each other and grasp the potential of "how powerful might be a world in which our commonalities would hail us over our differences" (*Utopia* 21).

We hold Dolan's hopefulness in tension with Rancière's skepticism toward the ideal of theatre as a space of communal feeling; he finds hope in the possibilities it affords for active disagreement and for redistributing the senses so as to feel, hear, and see the world differently. Attunement takes shape as politics when participants engage and attach outside and beyond their existing social identities; this is the difference, for Rancière, between the political and politics. In the Vancouver production, *Nanay* was self-consciously created as an intercultural space in which those who are positioned very differently in relation to the LCP were brought into discussion and possible disagreement. We endeavoured to produce spaces for middle-class Canadians to hear the emotions of migrant women coming through the LCP and of families who experience long periods of separation, and, in doing so, prompt audiences to reflect on their own unconscious complacencies in a system that exploits so-called Third World women. We also worked hard to create a space for Filipino audiences to hear the emotions of Canadian families—the deep frustration of women struggling to secure childcare and the desperation of those labouring to care for their ailing parents. We wanted everyone to feel—really feel—that something is genuinely awry in the world and to be sufficiently distanced from their default social identities to open possibilities for new solidarities, new political attachments, new ideas, and new life trajectories and aspirations.

Lauren Berlant argues that the contemporary moment is one of impasse in which new idioms of politics and public attachment are needed. Existing practices of politics and attachment function as a mode of "cruel optimism" insofar as they are obstacles to rather than a means toward fulfilling the wants and desires that bring forth that political engagement or attachment. We need, she argues, to detach "from the life-destructive forms of the normative political world" (*Cruel* 229) and to pay close attention to art (and other) forms and practices that provide "atmospheres and spaces in which movement happens through persons" often as "a space of abeyance," "a habituation without edges, a soft impasse" (230). We argue here and elsewhere (G. Pratt) that theatre can work formally as this kind of space of abeyance, a temporary suspension from everyday life, in which new relations can come into being. In line with Rancière, it can be a space to model a different, more vulnerable and egalitarian mode of relating to dissimilar others. It might also create a time-space to "slow things down and to gather things up, to find things out and to wonder and ponder. 'What is going on'" (Berlant, "Thinking" 5). If, as Berlant claims, politics is always in the first instance affective, the affective engagements and atmospherics created through and within theatrical performance open opportunities for new ways of relating and contemplating new practices of politics.

We are reasonably familiar with the lines of political debate and the forms in which social identities and politics have become stuck in Canada; we are less certain of this in the Philippines and of how *Nanay* can do the work of politics there. Rather than the LCP, the focus of debate will likely be the LEP, the other end of the "care chain" and migration process. One thing is clear: in order for the play to do the work of politics in the Philippines we need to be attentive to the context and to a radically different political and emotional terrain where most everyone shares an intimate knowledge of migration. With the help of colleagues there we have been pushed to begin reshaping and recontextualizing *Nanay* to open opportunities for domestic workers in Canada to narrate their experiences differently to family members, to disrupt notions of Canada as heaven, and to prompt a public dialogue that moves beyond dualistic representations of overseas workers as either purely the victims of structural violence, or, conversely, as the saviours of the nation and the Philippines as a culture in which temporary labour migration is taken as the norm.

We continue the process of thinking through this translation. Here, we have presented several strategies through which we are reshaping *Nanay* as the project engages the possibilities of a transnational circulation of affects. We are conscious of being in a kind of soft impasse in which our movement can only happen through persons; that is, a close engagement with others who are positioned in the world differently than ourselves.

ARTIST STATEMENT

EMOTIONAL AND RELIGIOUS LANDSCAPES: THE MAKING OF THE DOCUMENTARY FILM *A PIECE OF PARADISE*[1]

PATRICK ALCEDO

Recent studies on transnational economic integration, with emphases on labour conditions and class identities, have contributed much to the strengthening of scholarship on Filipinos now living in Canada. My forthcoming documentary film, *A Piece of Paradise*, builds on these works that reveal pressing issues in immigration experiences such as dislocation, alienation, and quasi-citizenship status. Through the lens of the religious Ati-Atihan Festival, it will offer an original cultural understanding of the complexity of immigration experiences, which are replete with varying degrees of nostalgia for one's original home and of a desire to be assimilated into a host country. By concentrating on religion, performance, and emotional labour, *A Piece of Paradise* deepens the scholarship on Filipinos in Canada that has heretofore focused predominantly on demographic spread, intergenerational conflicts and differences, and the deprofessionalization most highly educated Filipinos face when they land in Canada (see Chen; Coloma et al.; Kelly, Astorga-Garcia, Esguerra, and the Community Alliance for Social Justice; and Laquian and Laquian). Putting Toronto Filipinos centre stage, I structure the ethnographic

1   Funding for the production of *A Piece of Paradise* comes from the Social Sciences and Humanities Research Council of Canada's Research/Creation Grant. I would like to thank SSHRC's generosity, without which the film would not have been brought to fruition.

film's narrative using the stories participants have told me about themselves, their families, employers, and communities "here" in Toronto as well as those "there" in Aklan. Each of the women's stories is punctuated by emotional high points that link their private lives with their public participation in the Ati-Atihan Festival. In what follows, I draw out some of the more affecting elements of their stories.

The film takes for its focus the quotidian and festival lives of four Toronto women who all hail from the province of Aklan on Panay Island in the Visayas region of the Philippines. We have this in common, as I grew up in Kalibo, Aklan, before joining the Aklanon community of Toronto as a fellow immigrant in 2008. They immigrated to Toronto either by way of family sponsorship or Canada's Live-In Caregiver Program (LCP), which offers Canadian permanent residency to foreign workers after two consecutive years of providing care to children, elderly persons, or persons with disabilities in private homes (see also Johnston and Pratt in this volume). Age, class, and immigration status differentiate Femme Carrillo, the sisters Betsy Relente and Norlyn Relente Maravilla, and Janice Zarate from each other. Yet receiving remuneration to care for the elderly and children who are not their own, annual participation in the Ati-Atihan Festival, and a strong devotion to the Santo Niño (the Holy Child Jesus) link them in the diaspora. *A Piece of Paradise* illustrates how various affective environments and practices created by these four women have become spaces where they negotiate the work of their everyday and extraordinary lives and where they slowly build a community in a foreign country. At the heart of the film is their religiosity, a folklorized Roman Catholicism they have brought with them from Kalibo, the capital of Aklan province, and that they continue to practise in Toronto. For them, faith is best expressed through street dancing during the festive Ati-Atihan season and through the love they give to the Santo Niño during that time and throughout the year.[2] Introduced to the Philippines by Europeans in the early part of the sixteenth century as a symbol of Christianity and as a marker of the Spanish Colonial

---

2   To reflect oral custom among this group of Catholic Filipinos, the Santo Niño statue is referred to throughout this piece as "he" or "him."

Period, he is a wooden statue wearing vestments, carved and constructed after the Infant Jesus of Prague. As a foreigner requiring care as a condition of devotion, Santo Niño resembles those that Femme, Betsy, Norlyn, and Janice care for in Toronto as a condition of work.

Due to the steady and intense fusion of cultures in the diaspora, accelerated in the twentieth century by waves of migration and the huge popularity of Canada's LCP—which has seen almost half a million Filipinos living in Canada as of 2012 (Statistics)—the religious practices that immigrants bring from their home countries inevitably take on different religious and emotional registers. For instance, because the Ati-Atihan Festival season occurs in the third week of January, it is held inside a building when celebrated in Toronto. Back in Kalibo, in that part of the world that is close to the equator, Ati-Atihan is held out in the streets. The diaspora has thus moved Ati-Atihan from its original "public" environment to a "private" domain of devotion. Such an environmental difference leads to a much more contained expression of feelings toward the Santo Niño in Toronto in comparison to those expressed in the streets of Kalibo. In Aklan, Ati-Atihan is celebrated by participants dancing in the streets with hundreds of Santo Niño statues. In Toronto, Ati-Atihan is centred on a single, life-sized Santo Niño that is paraded around a rented social hall. (In the early 1980s, an Aklanon couple and long-time residents of Toronto brought over this particular statue from Kalibo.) But if their affective piety is contained spatially, it is much less restricted temporally. For it has become a tradition among Aklanon families in Toronto to take turns caring for this image, whom they fondly call "Niño," throughout the year. Every two weeks Niño is transported to a host family that takes responsibility for dressing him up and praying novena and offering food to him. Because of these daily rituals and the warmth they shower on Niño, he becomes a member of the family until such time as he is again moved to a new home. During the night of the Ati-Atihan Festival, the families that have taken care of him gather together to decorate his float, provide him with an expensive set of clothes, and dance with him until the festivity ends.

A Piece of Paradise documents the effects of these differences that emerge in diaspora that can have an intimate and powerful impact on religious and emotional life. By way of ethnographic research mainly conducted in Toronto and secondarily in the Philippines and Hong Kong, my findings zoom in on the kind of Roman Catholicism that the four women and their Aklanon community practise in Toronto. *A Piece of Paradise* locates the diaspora as a site of origin rather than simply as an angle of juxtaposition to the Roman Catholicism and the Ati-Atihan Festival observed in the Philippines.

The Ati-Atihan, celebrated by Filipino immigrants in Toronto—specifically the ones from Aklan in the central Philippines—is a textbook case for transnational religious mixture and hybridity. Given that the centre of my research project is a festival event, articulating it through a visual medium brings to the viewers an immediate experience of Ati-Atihan's movements, sounds, music, colour, costumes, choreographic design, and heightened atmosphere. These festival elements, which a written text is challenged in capturing, coalesce to generate a feeling of exhilaration and sheer happiness to be in an event with loved ones, friends, and community members, and literally to be dancing close to Santo Niño, the devotional subject of the festival.

From 2011 to 2013, my collaborator, Fruto Corre, who is the videographer for *A Piece of Paradise*, and I followed Femme, Betsy, Norlyn, and Janice during their travels with Niño as he migrated from home to home. We recorded instances when they asked permission of the United Aklanon Association of Toronto, the organization in charge of Niño's schedule, to host him to mark special occasions like birthdays. These are joyous moments where the women gathered their friends and relatives to help them welcome Niño and to pray to him, offering their thanks, wishes, and petitions. Their journeys with and ministrations for Niño move the film forward, as the four women care for their own families, the families of their employers, and work hard in Toronto so they can send money back to the Philippines.

In addition to the critical presence Niño plays in the film, another of the film's structural devices is the change across time seen in the lives of the four women. For example, when I started the project in 2011, Femme Carrillo was a live-in nanny for a Jewish family with two young daughters. The film captures her participating in the festival as that year's holder of the Miss Ati-Atihan title, representing the Aklanons of Toronto in events such as the Filipino Mabuhay Festival at the Metro Toronto Convention Centre, and turning over her crown to Miss Ati-Atihan 2012. In 2013, after finishing the mandatory two-year residency under the LCP, she finally received her permanent-residency status. Gaining this status firmed up Femme's plan of starting her own family; it has always been her dream to settle down for good in Toronto. That year she decided to tie the knot with Joerene Teruel, her fiancé of many years, who was working as both a restaurant and funeral manager in Mindanao in the southern Philippines. After the wedding—a highlight of the filming—Fruto and I met Joerene and Femme at the country's capital of Manila to bid Femme farewell before she boarded her flight back to Toronto. Femme promised Joerene that when she arrived in Toronto she would immediately work on their spousal sponsorship papers. In return, Joerene promised to be always in touch through Skype and Facebook. In the film, Femme's story ends with her entering the gates of the airport for her long flight back to Toronto, with Joerene outside already missing her.

Betsy Relente had always wanted to work abroad. Her meagre salary as a police officer in Aklan could not support the needs of her parents and younger siblings. In 1980 she moved to Singapore to work as a domestic helper. Although her salary there was better, it was still not enough. Four years later, in the depths of winter, she immigrated to Canada through the LCP. In my first interview with her, she recalled how difficult it was during her first months in Toronto. For anyone from the tropics, Toronto's winter can be harsh and alien. It was the friendship of the Aklanons, she fondly remembered, that helped her cope with the strangeness of her new environment. They gave her winter clothing and blankets to keep her warm. "They really 'adopted' me. They even raised funds when I competed for Miss Ati-Atihan that year," she attested. Canada, Betsy explained, will always have a special place in her heart, for not only did it provide her with the economic prosperity she had aimed for all her life, but it was also in this adoptive country where she met Ravi Naipaul, her husband of Guyanese descent. Santo Niño also played an important role in their family life. It was her faith in the Santo Niño, she said, that helped her survive the pain of several miscarriages and then blessed them with a baby boy after continuous fervent prayers. Thus every year on the birthday of her only child, Nicholas, nicknamed "Bimboy" ("little boy"), Betsy makes sure that Niño takes residence with them for a few days.

When I first I met Norlyn Relente Maravilla in 2008, I was amazed at how she managed to keep a full-time job while single-handedly taking care of her then-ten-year-old son, Darryl. In my estimation, one of the strongest moments in *A Piece of Paradise* is the day when Norlyn, as a Personal Support Worker (PSW), was filmed at an elder-care facility attending to a female patient, a woman she lovingly addressed as "Mother," with advanced Alzheimer's disease. Norlyn put makeup on Mother's face—softly applying lipstick to her lips and gently stroking a light blush on her cheeks—with warmth and without any sense of hurriedness. At that day's end, Fruto and I drove with Norlyn to pick up Darryl at a nearby middle school where mother and son greeted each other with excitement.

To share their blessings with their family and help weave affective bonds between family "here" and family "there," Betsy and Norlyn went home to the Philippines for the 2012 Ati-Atihan in Kalibo. They brought with them their sons Bimboy and Darryl so they would know where they came from— their "roots" in Betsy's words—and so that they would learn to love their cousins and relatives. In December 2011, Fruto and I travelled with them, documenting their travel from Toronto to Manila and then finally to Kalibo. By combining Norlyn's savings from her PSW profession and Betsy's from her jewellery business, they threw a grand reunion for their family and sponsored a band for their family's street dancing at Ati-Atihan. Before the festival, Bimboy and Darryl visited the Santo Niño in the Kalibo Cathedral. As of this writing (December 2013), Norlyn and Betsy are busy preparing for their trip once again to Kalibo for the 2014 Ati-Atihan. For them going home is about saying thanks to the Santo Niño, too. But this time it will be specifically about Norlyn expressing her gratitude for bringing her fiancé, Melchor Carillo, an Aklanon United States citizen residing in New Jersey, into her life. For Betsy, who has recently been diagnosed with breast cancer, this trip is about the Santo Niño helping her throughout the gruelling chemotherapy and radiation treatments, and for gifting her a new lease on life. I anticipate that in *A Piece of Paradise* the story of these two sisters will end with Norlyn and Melchor's engagement party and Betsy's thanksgiving luncheon.

Unlike Femme, Betsy, and Norlyn, Janice Zarate entered Canada from Spain. While making Spanish paella for our lunch, Janice shared with Fruto and me the story of her early years in Madrid:

> It was like the *Sound of Music*, you know. I took care of twelve children! How could my female employer bear that many children? It's simply incredible! Thank goodness the husband had a very successful textile business, so they were able to afford to raise those children and to run a huge household.

Because the Spanish government had no provision for foreign workers like herself to gain citizenship, she decided to immigrate to Canada in 1980, where she gained Canadian residency and married Peter Sazon, a Filipino from Batangas, a city on the northern island of Luzon. In contrast to her Spanish employer's impressive fertility, she and her husband were unable to have children.[3] In *A Piece of Paradise*, Janice consistently talks about how thankful she is that Niño is in Toronto. She has taken it upon herself to take care of him. There is footage that shows Janice treating Niño like her own child: praising how handsome he is, putting food on his altar, saying goodbye to him when she leaves the house and greeting him hello when she comes home. Among the Aklanons in Toronto, it is Janice who best knows the whereabouts of Niño, where he is and which household is taking care of him at the moment.

At the 2013 Ati-Atihan Festival in Toronto, Janice was Niño's *hermana mayor*, the female in charge of Niño that year. In the deep winter, Fruto and I shot, sequence by sequence, Janice bringing Niño to their car with help from Peter; driving him to the Cultural Centre in Scarborough, the festival's venue; unloading him in a parking lot covered in snow; and slowly placing him

---

3   When the husband of Janice's niece died from a typhoon that devastated Aklan in 2008, Janice and Peter offered to send their children to school. When we began filming Janice's life, she constantly talked about their plan of eventually adopting their grand nephews and nieces, so they could immigrate to Canada in the future.

on his carriage in the middle of the centre's social hall. The affection Janice showered Niño with was so infectious that other women joined her in dressing him up for the occasion and decorating his carriage for this festival that, for Janice and other Aklanons, is his most special day. I imagine that in my documentary Janice's story will culminate in this festival, with her dancing with her much-beloved Niño.

A Piece of Paradise offers the viewer an experience of the Ati-Atihan Festival with all its aesthetic, performative, embodied, and affective dimensions. The festival's energy, sounds, colour, and dancing bodies unite to bring a feeling of bliss to the participants. The film foregrounds such a feeling, one that is expressed by the four women I have just described. But in following the lives of Femme Carrillo, Betsy Relente, Norlyn Relente Maravilla, and Janice Zarate, their families, their communities in Toronto and in the Philippines, together with the travels of Niño himself, *A Piece of Paradise* also foregrounds less positive emotions. It highlights the women's affective ties to the Philippines as their home country and the emotional complications attending intense investment in their own families while performing domestic labour for others. It is this combination of feelings that I hope my documentary film captures and elicits in viewers when it is released in 2015.

BRIDGING SAINT-BONIFACE TO WINNIPEG AND "VICE VERSA"

NICOLE NOLETTE

"Can hope be disappointed?" asked philosopher Ernst Bloch in his inaugural lecture at the University of Tübingen in 1961. Yes, he answers, and it must be *unconditionally* so, as "it holds the condition of defeat precariously within itself"; this is what distinguishes it from confidence (341). As he explains, "[N]ot only hope's affect (with its pendant, fear) but, even more so, hope's methodology (with its pendant, memory) dwells in the region of the not-yet, a place where entrance and, above all, final content are marked by an enduring indeterminacy" (341). This anticipatory region of the "not yet" where hope dwells structures the affect temporally: hope endures as a perpetual promise that is also perpetually disappointable.

As Canadians, we are familiar with both hope's affect and with its enduring "not yet" temporal structure. In fact, one of the country's defining features, official bilingualism, relies on a variation of the not yet. The promise, as what "has not yet been defeated, but likewise has not yet won" (Bloch 341) of Canadian official bilingualism, hinges not on heightened individual linguistic capacities, as is usually assumed. Rather, this promise depends on concrete translation policies and practices that criss-cross between—or bridge—speech communities, allowing these communities to maintain their official language. In this sense, the resurgence of the bridge metaphor, used again and again to qualify literary translation in Canada—though usually from the English side—is telling. As Kathy Mezei reminds us,

> It is precisely the desire for a visible figuration of the interplay between separation and connection so critical to Canadian cultural

politics that has elevated the bridge into a powerful metaphor in discourses about translation between the two charter cultures and languages from the mid-nineteenth century through to the late 1990s. (28)

Centred on the metaphor of the bridge, these discourses about translation between French and English in Canada have often emphasized liberal ideals about national unity and peaceful cohabitation. These already "hopeful," "utopian" ideals were at the root of the Official Languages Act, which came into effect in 1969 and effectively validated the separate-but-joined approach to cultural politics. Yet by placing French and English on two equal, divided-yet-communicating sides, the metaphor of the bridge of translation shifts away from concepts of diglossia and of unequal power dynamics between speech communities. Scholars of comparative literature and translation—Mezei, but also comparatist E.D. Blodgett—have thus repeatedly sought to debunk the bridge metaphor for the linguistic and cultural difference it obscures as it moves across, joins, and appropriates the shores of the two objects it references (see Blodgett). But the bridge metaphor recurs, still, because it sets up affective conditions for *hope*.

Taking up the bridge metaphor and its hopeful affect, Franco-Manitoban playwright, director, actor, and translator Marc Prescott joined forces with long-time collaborator and actor/director Alain Jacques to create Théâtre Vice Versa Theatre (TVVT), Winnipeg's first self-proclaimed bilingual French and English theatre company. From its very beginnings this theatre company's mission was to work in French and in English, in Winnipeg and Saint-Boniface, in creation and in translation. Its mission statement takes up the figure of the bridge as translation:

Théâtre Vice Versa Theatre is dedicated to the development and production of original scripts and of original translations whether it be from French to English or « Vice-Versa. » [sic] Théâtre Vice Versa Theatre is the *bridge* between French and English theatre in Canada. ("TVVT," emphasis added)

In practice, for TVVT, "bridging" French and English theatre in Canada has so far meant two modes of performance. The first of these is to produce the same play in French and in English on alternate evenings, with the same bilingual actors and crew every evening. Marc Prescott's *Fort Mac* was presented in this way in June 2011. Prescott's bilingual play *Les disparus/The Disappeared*, co-produced with the Festival du Voyageur in 2012, also held different proportions of French to English depending on the evening it was presented. Michael Nathanson's *Talk*, translated by the ever-present Marc Prescott, was scheduled to be produced in the same manner—French on one evening, English on the next—in June 2013. Secondly, Théâtre Vice Versa Theatre holds a salon-style series of readings of plays from Quebec in Winnipeg, including Evelyne de la Chenelière's *Bashir Lazhar* and Carole Fréchette's *Jean et Béatrice*.

If theatre and translation practices, for TVVT, serve as urban "bridges," how do they cross the Red River from Saint-Boniface to downtown Winnipeg and back? In this sense, Winnipeg could be considered as a linguistically divided city, a "city in translation" like Montreal, Trieste, Barcelona, and colonial Calcutta, cities where creativity blooms from zones of possible linguistic conflict (Simon). Scholars specializing in the literary and cultural production of Montreal, regrouping under the banner of a research team called Zones of Tension, have recently shifted their focus on the city as a "zone of contact" (Leclerc and Simon 24). This term, which they borrow from Mary Louise Pratt, hones in on the sometimes consensual, sometimes conflictual spaces of individual interactions *between* speech communities—"spaces where cultures meet, clash, and grapple with each other, often in contexts of highly asymmetrical relations of power" (M. Pratt, "Arts" 34). Inviting us to hope along with her, Pratt asks that we imagine

> a linguistics that decentered community, that placed at its centre the
> operation of language across linguistic lines of social differentiation,
> a linguistics that focused on zones of contact between dominant
> and dominated groups, between persons of different and multiple
> identities, speakers of different languages, that focused on how such

speakers constitute each other relationally and in difference, how
they enact differences in language. ("Linguistic" 60)

Following Pratt's lead and envisioning Montreal as a zone of contact and a
zone of tension has enabled the Zones of Tension team to interpret shared
grounds across the city, even if these shared grounds proved to be territories
of linguistic and cultural warfare. In this sense, they have undertaken an in-
depth investigation of the urban conditions of hope and of its inner defeat, of
"conflicting loyalties" (Harel) and of "affective dislocations" (Lane-Mercier),
an investigation that is already critically *hopeful* as it looks upon tensions and
defeats as affective, creative, and productive.

In light of their findings on Montreal, I ask how, in the zone of contact,
conflict, interaction, and non-interaction between downtown Winnipeg and
Saint-Boniface, the bridge of translation is performed, felt, transmitted, received. I argue that the TVVT initiative, as a "critical utopia" (Muñoz, *Cruising*
11) of a bridge of translation within the city of Winnipeg, builds with hope
upon historically distant and conflicting linguistic zones. As we shall see, the
hopeful bridge enacted by TVVT works to level out culturally specific emotions and spectatorial loyalties, as well as to dislocate emotional geographies
through linguistic and theatrical crossings. Such bridges can break down,
however, as they hinge precariously upon their own conditions of defeat. By
zooming into TVVT's first public production, *Fort Mac*, and particularly into
a monologue by actress Alicia Johnston in French and in English, I round out
my examination of the hopeful affect of the utopian project of TVVT with its
precariousness, asymmetries, and disappointments.

1. BRIDGING RED RIVER

TVVT's bridge of translation enacts the critical form of hope that José Esteban
Muñoz, following Bloch's historically situated and collective-related "concrete
utopias," finds particularly relevant to queer performances (and performances
of queerness). Muñoz's critical utopianism differs from Jill Dolan's emphasis

on live theatre as a place for "utopian performatives" in *Utopia in Performance: Finding Hope at the Theater*. The locus of hope in his study of queer performances is not in "small but profound [live] moments" between the actors and the audience (Dolan, *Utopia* 5); rather, for Muñoz, "hope as a critical methodology can best be described as a backward glance that enacts a future vision" (*Cruising* 4). In the context of Théâtre Vice Versa Theatre's work, a palpable affective vision of the bridge of translation might be an experience of the city as harmonious; as a place where language doesn't hinder the circulation of theatre creation, production, labour, and reception; as a city where Franco-Manitoban and "Anglo-" Manitoban authors, directors, and actors alike could find work on both banks of the Red River—a vision of a city, moreover, where audiences would be receptive to local theatre, no matter which language group may have originated it. TVVT's affective vision is thus a utopian project for—an approach toward—a linguistically reconfigured Winnipeg.

As a concrete—and critical—basis for this affective vision, Blodgett's concerns about the bridge as a possible conduit for assimilation seem to capture the very geography of Winnipeg's traditionally anglophone and francophone communities, historically divided by the Red River. A "backward glance" through historical maps of the area clearly show Winnipeg's Broadway Avenue and Saint-Boniface's Boulevard Provencher as a straight line bisected only by the river, yet connections and bridges have been less than straightforward. Sporadic and often purposefully cut off, attempts at bridging the Red River have also been, to some at least, hopeful and profitable. Until 1879 ferries linked the two shores, and although plans for the railway to cross from Provencher over the Red River to Broadway lost out to other such dealings for the Louise Bridge location (Coutts and Stuart 36), a "Broadway Bridge" was finally built in 1881–1882. The 1882 spring flood wiped out this new bridge three days after its completion, but reparations were quick to be made and traffic kept crossing the Red River (Coutts and Stuart 36). According to local paper *Le Manitoba*, in 1908 municipal officers in Winnipeg and in Saint-Boniface dreamed of

[u]n pont, frappant en plein centre commercial de Winnipeg, et qui compterait un espace pour les voitures, et pour le tramway, et

qui aurait en outre une passerelle pour les piétons, [ce qui] nous
contribuerait puissamment au progrès des deux villes

(a bridge, hitting Winnipeg's downtown business core, which would
include a space for cars and for the tramway, and which would also
include a passageway for pedestrians, which would contribute greatly
to the progress of both cities). ("Le pont du Transcontinental," qtd.
in LaCoste 66)

Countering these hopes and dreams, the construction of Union Station on
Main Street between 1908 and 1911 cut off any circulation east of Broadway,
thus dooming the first Broadway Bridge. A second bridge, built for vehicular
traffic in 1918 and opened to tramways in 1925, would link up to Winnipeg
five hundred metres north of Broadway. And, more recently, the Provencher
Bridge, constructed between 2001 and 2003, realized the hopes of 1908 as it
paired a vehicular bridge to a footbridge (l'Esplanade Riel). The construction
of this vehicular and pedestrian bridge establishes conditions for circulation
between Saint-Boniface and Winnipeg that make possible the kind of future
hoped for by translation and in the practices of TVVT.

The dreams of 1908 may seem to have been fulfilled a hundred years later, especially since Franco-Manitoban architect Étienne Gaboury designed
the pedestrian bridge. However, the esplanade became contested grounds
when the mayor of Winnipeg first insisted on getting full utilities installed
on site at the cost of one million dollars ("Toilet"), then superseded plans for
a bilingual bistro in its centre by leasing the space to local chain Salisbury
House instead ("New Restaurant"). In her barely fictionalized account of the
devolving tensions, Janis Locas writes that "le charmant bistro bilingue que
la communauté avait imaginé en plein centre du pont neuf s'est métamor-
phosé, en passant par le bureau du maire, en projet de toilettes géantes" ("the
charming bilingual bistro imagined by the community for the centre of the
bridge morphed, while passing through the mayor's office, into a project for
giant toilets," author's translation, 64). This decision led to a mass mobilization
by francophone youth in 2004. Far from simply being anecdotal, these lived

experiences of the tensions of a bridge between Winnipeg and Saint-Boniface give historical and social density to the metaphor. Keenly aware of these tensions between metaphor and referent, Alain Jacques and Marc Prescott located a Radio-Canada radio interview for Théâtre Vice Versa Theatre's inaugural production on the Provencher Bridge (Freynet-Agossa).

2. HOPE AND THE BRIDGING OF SPACES

Théâtre Vice Versa Theatre's "bridge" project is interesting not only because it seeks to make bilingualism its working order and artistic licence, but also because it puts forward the bridge metaphor as coming *from the other side*— the francophone side. As Mezei observes, the bridge metaphor usually serves national ideals from English Canada, whereas

> the bridge of translation between French and English Canada was interpreted by many Québécois as a barrier to sovereignty. From the 1960s through to the 1990s, Québec attitudes to translation and to bicultural relations were less inclined to invoke bridges because the traffic seemed weighted towards Anglophone agendas and domination. (30)

If francophone communities across Canada have not had the same objectives of sovereignty as the Québécois, they have also been historically wary of anglophone domination. But as hope's "backward glance" *also* enacts visions of the future, recently, and as evidenced by TVVT's project, francophone theatre companies have partly let go of these historical tensions and have been opening up to their geographic and linguistic localities. In Saskatoon since the 1990s, as Louise Forsyth describes, francophone professional theatre company La Troupe du Jour has been exposing the ways in which language and directorial choices introduce varying affects by holding plays in French and their translation in English "on alternate evenings, with different directors but with the same cast" (135). Contrary to La Troupe du Jour's bilingual experimentation, which involves an author separate from his or her translator, as well as two different

directors, Théâtre Vice Versa Theatre's work conflates the author and the translator, as well as the direction for both linguistic versions. The formula TVVT
depends on involves the same cast, the same director, and a playwright whose
translation work reverberates on his or her writing practice. Even the blocking
remains the same on both evenings. Through this exacting similitude, TVVT's
productions reduce the possibility of cultural variation in affective intensity.

Moreover, through the selection of criss-crossing, translational performance venues, TVVT dislocates the language loyalties that typically reside in
certain places. In his seminal 1953 study on languages in contact, linguist Uriel
Weinreich qualified language loyalty "as a principle . . . in the name of which
people will rally themselves and their fellow speakers consciously and explicitly
to resist changes in either the functions of their language (as a result of language
shift) or in the structure or vocabulary (as a consequence of interference)" (99).
The language loyalties described by Weinreich as resistant to change are firmly
situated on two sides of the river: francophones in Saint-Boniface, anglophones
in Winnipeg. On the other hand, the performance of "bridges" and of "crossings" in TVVT's marketing plan involves performing plays in both languages in
locales where they would have typically been performed in one *or* the other. In
this way, TVVT programs a circulation of hope within the divided geography
of the city. The inaugural production, *Fort Mac*, was performed in French and
English at the Canwest Centre for Theatre and Film (400 Colony Street); *Les
disparus/The Disappeared*, a bilingual production in conjunction with Festival
du Voyageur (January 2012), at the Franco-Manitoban Cultural Centre (340
Boulevard Provencher); and the Carol Shields Festival reading of Prescott's
French translation of *Talk*, by Winnipeg Jewish Theatre artistic director Michael
Nathanson, at the Colin Jackson Studio of the Prairie Theatre Exchange (Portage
Place, 4 May 2012). Cultural affect is not invested in a permanent infrastruc-
ture on either side of the river, neither in the place where francophone theatre
historically would have situated itself in Saint-Boniface, or in Winnipeg's independent theatre scene. Instead, Théâtre Vice Versa Theatre rents space on
both sides of the river, in established theatre centres, criss-crossing the city and
dislocating loyalties—and affections—among different audiences toward its
utopia of the bridge of translation.

3. *FORT MAC*: A BRIDGE BETWEEN HOPE AND DESPAIR

TVVT's production of *Fort Mac* itself involves a figuration of space as a bridge, separate and connected at once. Incidentally, the play already focuses on hope and its downfalls, following the downward trajectories of four characters, newly arrived from other regions of Canada, in an uneven topography of hopes and dreams that is Fort McMurray (Dorow and Dogu). Jaypee, a small-time crook from Quebec, and his ambitious girlfriend Mimi arrive in Fort McMurray in search of the quick fortunes to be made in the tar sands. Mimi's younger sister Kiki tags along and meets Maurice, a local who has seen it all before. Predictably, Jaypee's fortunes decline as he sinks deeper into illegality, sinking Mimi along with him. Kiki, however, will be the true victim of the spectacular crash of their collective—if short-term—hopes and dreams: she offers up her body to rows of blue-collar workers for a few dollars to pay back Jaypee's debts. After this long ordeal, Maurice will, as promised, assist her in her death. Concurrent with the characters' self-destruction is a recurrent discourse on the demise of the natural world (Mother Nature) by human hands.

Of these characters, Jaypee, the man in search of better fortunes who ends up selling drugs and owing money, best impersonates the migrant worker population for whom "Fort McMurray is where hopes for other places, times, or people are enabled or frustrated" (Dorow and Dogu 273). He also stands at one end of the distinction made by philosopher Gabriel Marcel between desire and hope. Marcel argues that hope, as opposed to desire, is neither covetous nor egoistic; rather, it waits, patiently, for a collectivity—for "us" (Marcel). As the young and naive ingenue who first appears on stage wearing a white wedding dress, Kiki symbolizes hope's project "for us" as well as its inner defeat. Prophetically, she foresees both an end to hope and her own tragic end. Taking on the analogy of Mother Nature, Kiki exclaims, "If Mother Nature could see what was going on here [in Fort McMurray], she would cry rivers, rivers of tears. Wow, that's pretty. I could cry a puddle, she could cry an ocean." (Jacques, *Fort Mac, English version* 2:10–2:25). Just like the tears caused by ecologically devastating economic development in Fort McMurray, Kiki's fate is inextricably linked to that of Mother Nature. Her countless wishes, because they are never shared by a collectivite, never end up as more than an overflowing collection in a well; even ashes are more easily shareable. As Kiki tells Maurice,

> There was a well in my backyard. Well not really a well, it was just a rusted bucket. But I thought of it as a well. Every night I'd throw a penny in the well and make a wish. And then, one day, the well got full. And there was no more room for wishes. But I don't really feel like throwing pennies right now, I'd like to throw ashes. My mother's ashes. Would you like to spray my mother's ashes with me? (Jacques, *Fort Mac, English version* 6:36–6:59)

The two other characters, Mimi and Maurice, are dragged along in the downward spiral and ultimate disappointment of Jaypee and Kiki's hopes. The first becomes a pregnant pole dancer and then prostitutes herself to pay off Jaypee's debt. The second slits Kiki's throat at her request to appease her suffering from a series of violent abuses and rapes. *Fort Mac* concludes on this seemingly definitive destruction of both hopes and dreams, yet Maurice seems ready to resurrect Mother Nature symbolically in a poetic passage following Kiki's death, where he evokes "rose petals raining from the sky, for three whole days, in Fort Mac" (Jacques, *Fort Mac, English version* 45:15–45:20). The plot's trajectory from a reduction of hope to its timid resurgence confirms Marcel's assertion that "the conditions that make it possible to hope are strictly the same as those that make it possible to despair" (101). To this, Ben Anderson adds that becoming hopeful emerges "from the context of specific diminishments" and thus that "hoping abandons the existent" and that "some types of hope can also feed back to *continue* relations that diminish even as we are attached to them" (743, emphasis in original). Echoing these concerns about the concurrence and commingling of hope and despair, Kiki's death (and by extension, Mother Nature's) causes as much despair as it puts forward hopes for a better future for *Fort Mac*.

4. *FORT MAC*: A BRIDGE BETWEEN FRENCH AND ENGLISH

Fort Mac is also a bridge between Alberta and Manitoba—Marc Prescott was first asked to write the play by Daniel Cournoyer, artistic director of L'UniThéâtre, Alberta's professional francophone theatre, as a way to promote local playwriting around the issues involved with the economic development of the oil sands. Relocated to Winnipeg for the TVVT production, *Fort Mac*, its problems, and its possibilities seem at once near and far, a bridge in itself to another place. Prescott's play, produced in 2007 in Edmonton and published in 2009 by Les Éditions du Blé, was considerably modified to fit its new production locale, Winnipeg, in 2010. Chief among these modifications was the origins of the characters. The back cover of the published version describes the play and its characters:

> Jaypee, petit magouilleur québécois, et Mimi, son ambitieuse conjointe, ont installé leur roulette sur le premier terrain venu et se préparent à plonger dans le trou noir de l'or noir. Sous le regard mélancolique de Maurice, un Franco-Albertain enlisé sur place, leur destin se désagrège cruellement, magnifié par la présence mystérieuse de Kiki, soeur de Mimi, étrange enfant-femme, dont le trajet illumine, comme la brève lueur d'une étoile filante, la folie d'un lieu abusé et désabusé par l'argent.

> (Jaypee, a small-time crook from Quebec, and Mimi, his ambitious partner, have set up their trailer on the first available plot of land and are getting ready to dive into the black hole of black gold. Under the melancholic gaze of Maurice, a Franco-Albertan stuck in one place, their destiny cruelly disintegrates, magnified by the mysterious presence of Kiki, Mimi's sister, a strange girl-woman whose trajectory illuminates, like the brief glimmer of a shooting star, the folly of a place abused and disabused by money.)[1]

---

1   Unless otherwise noted, all translations are by the author.

The interactions between the Québécois characters and Maurice, their Franco-Albertan counterpart, are predicated upon a hierarchical rapport between the two and upon the clichés by which both are characterized. For the Québécois characters, this means aggressiveness, crudeness, and ambition; for Maurice, it means conservatism, prudishness, and reserve. These internal zones of cultural tension are often made invisible to the anglophone eye (Leclerc and Nolette), and the difficulty in understanding these differences means that translation often diminishes their effect. Prescott's translation into English, as well as his reworking of the French text for TVVT, glosses over these disconnects. Jaypee is still from Quebec, but the sisters Mimi and Kiki are now from Sudbury, Ontario. This allows them to be Franco-Ontarian in the French version of the production (and thus closer to the Franco-Albertan character and the Franco-Manitoban audience members, as Sudbury is a major centre of francophone culture outside Quebec), as well as Anglo-Ontarian in the English version. In French, situating Mimi and Kiki's origins in Sudbury allows Prescott to trace his literary lineage in the footsteps of Governor General's Literary Award–winning playwright (and translator) Jean Marc Dalpé, known for his characterization of Sudbury oral speech patterns in plays such as *Le Chien*. In English, the sisters' origins in Sudbury allow for alliances with anglophone audience members who might identify better with the play if not all characters are francophone. In this version, the characters' linguistic positioning is elaborated on in the second scene, when they meet on the piece of land where the sisters and Jaypee are squatting.

> JAYPEE: Who's that?
> MAURICE: Maurice. Plaisir.
> JAYPEE: Ah bien! Un Québécois à Fort McMurray!
> MAURICE: Je suis pas Québécois.
> MIMI: You're not a Quebecer?
> MAURICE: No, I'm from around here.
> JAYPEE: From Fort Mac?
> MAURICE: Non, Plamondon.

JAYPEE: Plamondon? Where's that?

MAURICE: À une couple d'heures au sud.

JAYPEE: And you speak French too?

MAURICE: C'est pas ça que je fais?

JAYPEE: I didn't know there were francophones out here.

MAURICE: Well there are. I'm the living proof.

JAYPEE: I just can't get over it. There are francophones out here.

(Jacques, *Fort Mac, English version* 13:19–13:37)

This moment, through synecdoche, performs the hopeful utopia sought by TVVT: characters speak in French and in English yet some of their differences are brought to the forefront. Moreover, Jaypee situates these linguistic differences in a separate-yet-connected space, "out here." Also bridging these differences, Mimi's reply changes from one night to the other, from "Il a pas l'accent acadien" (Jacques, *Fort Mac, French version*) to "You're not a Quebecer?" in English. Translation enacts these characters' flexibility and polyvalence of origins as a bridge toward the linguistic profiles of its different audience members. In both versions, these characters' origins enact a diasporal sense of place for Fort McMurray as well as a sense of an interprovincial national Canadian space for Manitoban audience members.

5. UNHINGING THE BRIDGE: THEATRE CULTURES AND ACTING STYLES

The focus on hope of TVVT's *Fort Mac* production hedges its bets on similarities that unite, rather than on dividing differences. Writer-translator Marc
Prescott is the first to mend differences into similarities, and the characters
of Mimi and Kiki are also called upon to bridge dissimilarities in culture.
Spectators are then expected to cross geographic distances and invest urban
spaces in ways not predicated by linguistic loyalty. Some other proceedings
of Théâtre Vice Versa Theatre, however, call into question just how fraught
the metaphor of the bridge can be and how "some types of hope can also feed
back to *continue* relations that diminish even as we are attached to them" (B.
Anderson 743, emphasis in original). The utopian moment of bilingualism
mentioned above, for example, is the only such instance of a true incursion
of French into the English performance. The French performance is equally
hermetic to a crossing over of English, except in scenes like the one where
Kiki practises for her job as a cashier at Tim Hortons. In their preoccupation
with finding bilingual actors and crew, Prescott and Jacques were unable to
find a bilingual stage manager for the production of *Fort Mac*. Consequently,
as I witnessed during my brief observation of rehearsals (14–15 June 2011),
much of the workings behind the stage took place in English, bringing up
once again the asymmetry of the languages in the bilingual project undertaken by Théâtre Vice Versa Theatre, especially as they try to produce work
in downtown Winnipeg.

As we zoom in on the actors on whom this bridge also relies, hope's affect
and its inner defeat become less easily orchestrated by TVVT's project. At a
level that is felt by the spectators, including me, some actors are noticeably
uncomfortable with the language change on alternate evenings. I first noticed
these differences between actors' performances while attending the final rehearsals for *Fort Mac* in June 2011, and these intuitions were confirmed when
I combed through and compared specific moments of the actual production captured audiovisually. The actor's "capacities to affect and be affected"
(Deleuze and Guattari 261) vary according to their linguistic capacities and

their training in different acting styles. In fact, the variability in linguistic capacity was part of the reason for modifying the text of *Fort Mac* and its translation. As director Alain Jacques explains,

> Alicia Johnston, Mimi, trained at the National Theatre School, on the English side. Nadine Pinette, Kiki, graduated from a theatre program at the University of Winnipeg. She is from St. Claude, a Franco-Manitoban town with a particular accent. According to the text, the girls are from Quebec but because the two had such accents, we decided to adapt the text so that they would be from Ontario, which might explain their partly Anglicized accents. Yvan Lecuyer [Maurice] trained in improvisation in Vancouver. Gabriel Gosselin [Jaypee] learned on stage with the Cercle Molière. Gabriel can imitate a Québécois accent so we kept the idea that he met the girls on the road westward while going through Sudbury, if I remember correctly. Yvan played a Franco-Albertan so kept his Western Francophone accent. In English, there were no problems with accents. Gabriel has a slight accent when he speaks English but since he played the Quebecer, it worked well. He added on to it though, as it made the Anglos from around here laugh. ("Rep")

Jacques points out two discomforts for the actors: first, unevenly distributed linguistic abilities; second, training in theatre cultures that criss-crosses expected associations to language.

Canadian theatre, as prolific theatre translator Linda Gaboriau argues, is marked by two dominant cultures of actor training. In English Canada, actors "receive training which is distinctly North American and which is often, in terms of contemporary theatre, more psychological than it is in Quebec. They are not as comfortable, for instance, with flights of language, with poetry, or lyrical, rhetorical material" (84). Gaboriau adds that this qualification of the Canadian acting style as "psychological" must be seen as an "orientation," not an absolute, as it does not "go as far as the naturalistic, kitchen-sink drama that you have in some North-American theatre" (85). Indeed, Anna Migliarisi has detailed the sometimes-covert historical dissemination of Stanislavsky's ideas about actor training in Canada, noting that "Stanislavskian praxis has been naturalized by Canadian actors" (31). Though psychological realism is subtler in English Canadian than in American acting styles, its prevalence provides a sharp contrast with the "theatrical style nourished by classical rhetoric and lyricism" (Gaboriau 85) found in Quebec. Jean-Michel Henry / Mike Henry, a francophone actor trained in the English section of the National Theatre School, elaborates on these divergent styles and approaches to training in a 1992 interview with Denis Salter:

> Whereas generalized emotion and imagination are big words for the French, for the English, specific internal needs, as defined by the "method," matter more. There's nothing better than imagination and method working together; that's the amazing thing that would happen if you could actually bring together the best of both worlds . . . (qtd. in Salter 12)

According to Gaboriau, however, these different approaches rarely "work together." Rather, their jarring dissimilarities often mean that English Canadian productions of translations of French Canadian or Quebec plays "can be quite awful, something like the effects of a dubbed movie, when the gestures don't always match the intonations of the language. The audience is seeing one play and hearing another" (84).

Indeed, in the performance of translations, the marked differences between theatre cultures in French and English Canada hinder actors' capacity to affect and be affected. Théâtre Vice Versa Theatre, however, seeks to bridge over these two theatre cultures: *Fort Mac* is written in French in a genre that is supposed to work in English Canada, that is to say, dramatic realism. The play offers mimetic views of the regional dialects attributed to the characters and of the constant cycles of hope and disappointment of migrants and locals in Fort McMurray. As in Chekhov's plays, the characters' psychology—their hopes, dreams, and failures—is revealed through slightly more poetic monologues. As the French version of *Fort Mac*, with its realism, is already a bridge across theatre cultures, its translation into English and its performance style should therefore not be as "awful" as the "dubbed movie" effects of Quebec theatre in translation. TVVT's transmission of hope depends on this successful (affective) performance of realism's dramatic, technical, and theatrical conventions across language communities. Following the same blocking and direction every evening, no matter what language they are speaking, actors must perform convincingly, without discomforts around linguistic ability. In so doing, they project the palpability of the possible world proposed by TVVT.

As Jacques suggests, the actors of *Fort Mac* are already performing a form of stylistic hybridity in their professional careers. Their training often belies their first language or expands on a first theatre culture: francophones Nadine Pinette (whom theatre critic Alison Mayes called "luminous") and Yvan Lecuyer trained in English, the first at the University of Winnipeg and the second in a Vancouver institution. Like Jean-Michel Henry / Mike Henry, they have approaches that could "bring together the best of both worlds." Gabriel Gosselin's practice-based learning in a small francophone theatre in Manitoba could perhaps also be seen as a bringing-together of worlds. Theatre critics have unanimously praised his recent work on productions in French and in English, on both sides of the river (see for example Rivers; and Prokosh). The fact that he played up his accent for an extra laugh from anglophones, however, hints at the problematic aspects of a bringing together of worlds where one side must caricature itself and elicit a laughing *at* rather than a laughing *with* in order to fit into the other. In these cases, what results from the bringing together of worlds is not the best of either.

6. ALICIA JOHNSTON AND THE UNHINGED PERFORMANCE OF A CROSSING

Of these four actors, Alicia Johnston's uneasy crossover from English into French reveals the greatest physical unease. TVVT's hopeful vision falters in the live performance of her acting in French. After a French-immersion program, she pursued training in the English section of the National Theatre

School, an institution where the language divide between sections is rarely crossed. In fact, according to Denis Salter in 1992, the English section still has to find an ideological (read to mean national) orientation. Very few of its teachers, except for Richard Fowler (from the Odin Teatret), proposed politically charged training that went "to the heart of the colonized sense of insecurity which gets bred, from birth onwards, into the language of the English-Canadian body, to the ways in which it has allowed itself to relate to the space around it" (Salter 11). Although the NTS was not the same institution in Salter's 1992 study as it was during Alicia Johnston's training there from 1997 to 2000, it maintained its two-pronged approach—"deux écoles sous un même toit" ("two schools under one roof," author's translation, Jubinville 136)—the French and the English sections using different teaching methods, aesthetics, and, more importantly, different sources for movement and emotion. Salter goes on to quote movement teacher Bryan Doubt, who states that from his experience the movements of English Canadian students at the NTS could be

> shy, isolated, small, contained, tentative; there was a lack of the instinct that comes from pleasure in the body; they were very tentative with touch, overly polite, not daring enough, not provocative enough, too constrained, too intellectual, pale . . . you had to teach them to play, that it was all right to experience pleasure. (qtd. in Salter 11)

The tentative movements described by Doubt are not present in Johnston's English acting; the "colonized sense of insecurity" seems to have been worked through during her training at the NTS. In fact, her capacity to affect and be affected makes her performance a brilliant standout in the English *Fort Mac*. Her Mimi is hopeful, gritty, and increasingly in despair over her circumstances. Critic Alison Mayes, watching Johnston in her English-language performance, says that she "holds nothing back in her raw performance as Mimi." Her second monologue occurs when there are signs that the family's hopes will be disappointed: Jaypee already has money problems, but he insists he has found a job; he teases Mimi about becoming a dancer, but still mostly as a compliment to her body; Kiki and Maurice are getting to know each other and fall asleep, hopeful and trusting, on a picnic table. While Mimi's first monologue gave the audience insight into her abusive father, her second monologue speaks to her mother's solitary death. Both are highly affective moments, but the second ends on a generalized note of unhappiness that foreshadows the tragic denouement of the play. The Christmas lights of the camper glowing behind her, Mimi sits alone in a spotlight, hunched on a lawn chair, wearing a tank top branded "Hustle," and holding a beer in her right hand. As she explains to the audience:

Mom died, what . . . four years ago now? Really? Four? No, it's five. Five years, fuck, time flies; Mom died five years ago. She died alone. I should have found her. Hmm.

Mom loves Christmas. She just fucking loves it. I was supposed to go see her but I don't know . . . I didn't go. I know I should have. I promised. I lied, and I didn't go. Just like that. But I was too damn busy, okay? And maybe I didn't want to go; I mean, what do you want me to say.

Mom hadn't paid the electric bill. That's how they found her. Hadn't paid in months. She wrote postdated cheques for the rent but she paid the electric month to month. When they found her, they had to pry open her door. There was so much mail on the floor. Magazines, mostly. Fucking magazines. And stacks of electric bills. They found her right in the middle of the living room. Right in the middle of summer with a set of Christmas lights in her hands. Can you fucking believe it? Anyway, I mean. She died with everything she held most dearly to her heart right next to her. Fucking Christmas decorations.

Ah, well, luckily there's the electric company, huh? If it weren't for them, she'd probably still be lying there. Dead as a dog, eyes wide open, tongue hanging out, right in the middle of summer. Right in the middle of the living room with a set of Christmas lights twin-kling in her hands.

It's not a very graceful way to go.

Here's what life has taught me. We are all unhappy in our own way. We're all happy in the same way. Happiness is unorigi-nal. Misery is unique. No one chooses to be born. And we all die alone. (Jacques, *Fort Mac, English version* 38:01–40:58)

Ma mère est morte il y a . . . quoi? Quatre ans maintenant? (C'est-tu déjà ça? Quatre? Non, cinq! Cinq ans! Eille! Le temps passe vite.) Ma mère est morte il y a cinq ans. Elle est morte tu-seule chez elle. (Tu-seule comme un chien. *Shit.* J'aurais dû trouver ma mère, estie.)

Ma mère adore Noël. Elle a-dore ça! J'étais supposée aller la voir mais je sais pas . . . J'ai pas eu le temps. Je suis pas allée. Je sais. J'aurais dû. J'avais promis. J'ai menti, pis je suis pas allée. C'est comme ça. J'étais trop occupée. Pis je voulais pas y aller! O.K.? C'est comme ça aussi, des fois, la vie. Ma mère avait pas payé l'Hydro. C'est comme ça qu'ils l'ont trouvée. Elle avait pas payé depuis des mois. Elle faisait des chèques postdatés pour le loyer mais elle payait l'Hydro au mois. Quand ils sont rentrés chez elle, il paraît qu'ils ont eu de la misère à ouvrir la porte tant il y avait de la poste par terre. Des magazines, surtout. (Ses maudits magazines à marde. En tout cas . . .) Pis une pile de bills d'Hydro. Ils l'ont retrouvée au beau milieu du salon, en plein été, avec un jeu de lumières de Noël dins mains (*Shit.* Peux-tu croire?) en tout cas, elle est morte avec toutes ses choses préférées autour d'elle . . . Ses maudites décorations de Noël.

Heureusement qu'il y a l'Hydro . . . Si c'était pas pour Hydro, elle serait probablement encore là. Morte, tu-seule comme un chien, la gueule pis les yeux grands ouverts, au beau milieu de l'été, au beau milieu

de son salon, avec ses décorations qui clignotaient encore dans son
sapin de Noël artificiel.

C'est pas élégant.

Voici donc mes quatre vérités . . .

On est tous malheureux à notre propre façon, on est tous heureux
de la même façon, personne a choisi de naître, pis on meurt tous
seuls. (Jacques, *Fort Mac, French version* 38:51–41:45)

In the English version of this monologue, Johnston's efficacy in affecting and in
being affected rests on a repetition of movements and vocal inflexions linked
to emotions. She oscillates between Mimi's waning hopes and increasing
despair, between her bravado (grand gesturing with her hands, knee kicks,
beer-can pointing, shrugs, and sideways head shakes) and her pain (inwards
head bob and sideways glances). When Mimi speaks of the time that has
elapsed since her mother's death, she raises her eyebrows several times, turns
her head and shakes it sideways three times, then lifts up her left hand. An
eye rub, a downward-cast face, and a small laugh accompany the admission
that Mimi should have been the one to find her dead mother. At the words
"Mom loves Christmas," Johnston punctuates each word with her left hand,
then slices the air sideways from her mid-body when she repeats how much
her mother loved it. Her head bobs inward and she glances sideways as she
admits that she was supposed to go see her but didn't. While this first part of
her monologue is constantly punctuated by the left hand and by shrugging
shoulders, the second part involves the right, beer-holding hand coming
forward for emphasis. The final part of the monologue features Johnston al-
ternating between the left and the right hand, her right leg crossing over the
left as she announces: "Here's what life has taught me." She nods several times
while recounting these teachings, ending her monologue with the same left-
hand air slice she used at the beginning. It is Johnston's connections between
gesture, text, and emotion in the English version of *Fort Mac* that garner her

praise for her "raw performance" as Mimi. The character's specific internal needs, emotions, and motivations are met by gesture in the actress's performance style; the actress is thus able to affect and be affected, and to enact some of TVVT's posturing around the bridge.

Paradoxically, it is in French that Johnston's ability to affect and be affected is hindered by the "language of the English-Canadian body." Johnston sits in the same lawn chair, holding her beer with the same hand under the same spotlight, but her right leg crosses over her left at the beginning of the scene, blocking off the transmission of affect to the audience. During the performance this leg fidgets, revealing unease that is also evidenced in recurrent hand movements to hide the actress's face. In moments where Mimi reflects on the Christmas lights and Hydro payments, which in the English version were characterized by laughter, head bobbing, and hand movements, Johnston even rests her face in her left hand, which she uses to stretch her mouth and jaw. The left-hand air slice is the same for "Ma mère adore Noël" as it was for "Mom loves Christmas," but she then brings both hands to the beer can as she speaks to the audience, eyes cast down and head bent into her chest. As she shakes her head sideways, she fidgets with her right, crossed-over leg. When her left hand leaves her face, it is clenched like a moving fist at hip level as she shakes her head sideways once again. Her major hand gestures are reserved for the discovery of her mother's dead body lying in Christmas decorations in the middle of summer—she alternates between the left (index and thumb held together) and the right hand at mid-body to punctuate her words. Her final words of the monologue, which ends with the Tolstovian "on meurt tous seuls," is preceded by a sideways head shake, a head bob, and a moment where she lifts her beer can as if for a toast. As the spotlight fades, Johnston finally uncrosses her legs. In this performance she moves inwards rather than oscillating between the outer bravado and inner pain as she did with her English Mimi. Moreover, in the French version, Johnston relies on many objects: her right sandal, her armrest. As a result, she appears to be fidgeting rather than conveying any depth of emotion, as she did in the English version. In Stanislavskian terms, while Johnston seemed to access her affective memory in the English version, enabling the circulation of affect, she does not seem to succeed in the French version. And while she proves Salter wrong in the lack of a "colonized sense of insecurity" in the English Canadian body in the English production, the French version reveals a very significant difference in the way the actress "allowed [herself] to relate to the space around" her body. There is no bridge in this monologue of Mimi's. Rather paradoxically the French version (even though it was the original) now appears to convey what Gaboriau had characterized as "effects of a dubbed movie, when the gestures don't always match the intonations of the language. The audience is seeing one play and hearing another" (84).

7. FURTHER DISLOCATIONS, SPACES OF HOPE

Théâtre Vice Versa Theatre's bridge of translation as a hopeful (hope-full) project, as a performative critical utopia, criss-crosses between Winnipeg and Saint-Boniface in an effort to dislocate language loyalties and affections. The theme of its first full production, *Fort Mac*, encapsulates how specific diminishments and despair commingle with and reaffirm certain forms of hope. In doing hope, TVVT must level out or bridge over culturally specific emotions; sisters Mimi and Kiki switch cultural and linguistic allegiances in order to gain empathy from spectators. Yet these reallocations of affect do not always settle as planned: the differences in Alicia Johnston's performance as Mimi in French and in English, most notably in her ability to affect and to be affected, demonstrate the uneasy relationship between desired effect and affect. Theatre cultures and language intervene as blockages in the bridge crossings of translation, performance, and emotion put forward by TVVT.

After the performances of the company's establishment and inaugural production, both of which drew heavily from the metaphor of the bridge and garnered some press from the anglophone media, interest from that part of TVVT's audience seems to be waning. More and more, TVVT's work is recuperated as "lié à la communauté [francophone]" (Sineux)—the very community the "bridge" was set up to distance itself from. In this sense, the ongoing bilingual work of Théâtre Vice Versa Theatre may well reproduce some of the same asymmetries as its favourite metaphor. It might, however, be too early to tell: as Ernst Bloch reminds us, hope's methodology resides in the not yet. Similarly, for Brian Massumi, hope plants "seeds of change, connections in the making that might not be activated or obvious in the moment" ("Navigating" 221). In this enduring indeterminacy, the not yet of hope for TVVT could be a bridge of translation, its flooding over, a charming bistro, or an embarrassing toilet.

EMPATHY

STAGING EMPATHY'S LIMIT POINT: FIRST NATIONS THEATRE AND THE CHALLENGES OF SELF-REPRESENTATION ON A SETTLER-STATE STAGE

JULIE BURELLE

In June 2010, Ondinnok, a Montreal-based First Nations theatre company, celebrated its twenty-fifth anniversary by staging a transnational adaptation of the Mayan play *Xajoj Tun Rabinal Achi*. Director Yves Sioui Durand (Huron Wendat) assembled a cast of Indigenous performers from across the Americas to perform the play, which is one of the few remaining examples of fifteenth-century Mayan dynastic dance drama. Presented at the Présence Autochtone/Montreal First Peoples' Festival, the production was complex and challenging, and an important part of its affective power resided in the sense of loss evoked in the performance without it ever being represented on stage. In sidestepping the representation of loss, the production eschewed empathic identification as a primary mode of engagement between audience members and performers; it laboured instead to perform loss and trauma as a common burden for which spectators should be held accountable.

Ondinnok could not have chosen a more evocative play than *Xajoj Tun Rabinal Achi* not only to celebrate its own achievement of twenty-five years of existence, but also to illuminate the resilience of the First Nations of the American continents. Indeed, the play's performance history is a fascinating account of what Anishinaabe scholar Gerald Vizenor calls "survivance."

Survivance, he writes, is "more than survival, more than endurance or mere response; [it is] an active presence . . . an active repudiation of dominance, tragedy, and victimry" (15). This active, obstinate presence is woven into the very fabric of *Xajoj Tun Rabinal Achi* both in the epistemological framework of the play-text and in the history that surrounds its transmission. Despite its recent inclusion on UNESCO's Intangible Cultural Heritage of Humanity list, *Xajoj Tun Rabinal Achi* remains relatively unknown outside of Guatemala, where El Grupo Danza Drama Rabinal Achi from San Pablo Rabinal preserves the dance-drama ritual, its three thousand verses, and its stylized movements.[1] The pre-Conquest play has defied centuries of colonial censorship and appropriation as well as Guatemala's recent bloody armed conflicts and was at times performed and transmitted clandestinely. Scholars point out that *Xajoj Tun Rabinal Achi*, one of the jewels of Mesoamerican literature, has not only managed to survive since the fifteenth century, but that it has done so relatively unaltered, bearing little trace of Hispanic influence (Breton 4).

Xajoj Tun Rabinal Achi belongs to the Mayan court drama genre and its poetic libretto, which is infused with references to Mayan cosmology, is deployed in a highly stylized performance. The play, which is traditionally spoken, sung, and danced, dramatizes the trial of Cawek, a warrior from a neighbouring nation accused of treason by the people of Rabinal. Cawek's capture and trial present a Mayan epistemology yet unmarked by Christianity's notions of absolute Good and Evil (Tedlock 250). Cawek and his judge, the Man of Rabinal, are not presented as ontologically opposed but as two continuous forces that are necessary to the world's equilibrium. Rich with layers of historical references, *Xajoj Tun Rabinal Achi* distills many generations of Mayan stories and anecdotes, practices and beliefs into one play. As such, *Xajoj Tun Rabinal Achi* constitutes a living repository of a pre-colonial past and offers a rare glimpse at a moment of Mayan sovereignty—as the right to judge and impose sentences is, after all, at the root of any sovereign nation. In its adaptation, Ondinnok utilized the Mayan play to illuminate Indigenous

---

1   While a written version of the play is extant, the text is still mostly transmitted orally from one generation of actors to the next.

losses since the Conquest, but also to ritually reclaim this past and to imagine
a way for communities to heal. Ondinnok's work foregrounded the complexity
of contemporary Indigenous presence and posed challenging questions about
the politics of empathy on settler colonial stages long marked by reductive
images of Indigenous peoples. The production thus participated in a larger
conversation on the ethics of representing trauma in the theatre.

As performed by Ondinnok, *Xajoj Tun Rabinal Achi* not only dramatized
Cawek's trial but also powerfully evoked the trauma and loss of sovereignty
that followed European contact in most Indigenous communities. Ondinnok's
adaptation also foregrounded the pitfalls of representation when it comes to
a form of colonial trauma that is multi-generational and ongoing, invisible to
most, and yet devastating. Representation can indeed be inadequate, flatten-
ing the complexity of trauma or alienating spectators who, though willing to
engage with European colonialism as belonging to the past, might not want
to address their complicity in contemporary forms of settler colonialism.

How then does one adequately represent the ramifications of First
Nations' dispossession? And how to do so while also acknowledging their
continuing presence? Dramatizing this pain on stage poses the risk of marking
First Nations subjects as solely pathological, unwittingly reinforcing the reductive images that already circulate in the media. Chickasaw scholar Jodi A. Byrd
refers to this incapacity to interpret—and thus understand—First Nations subjects outside of such simplistic colonial tropes as a form of "colonial agnosia."
A condition often resulting from brain damage, agnosia is typically defined
as the loss or diminution of the ability to recognize familiar objects. Here,
Byrd applies this resonant term to describe how centuries of asymmetrical
relationships with Indigenous people have damaged the ability of spectators
who stem from the settler-colonial majority to see Indigenous subjects in all
their complexity. In this context, representing Indigenous peoples, cultures,
and histories on a settler-colonial stage, then, risks their diminution.

On the other hand, representing Indigenous trauma and loss can also
pose the risk of alienating the audience: how does one address not only what
Ann Kaplan calls the "unconscious guilt" of many spectators whose lineage
links them to a colonial past, but also their complicity in the present-day

problems of the settler state (103–05)? Indeed, many settler states have yet to end structural discrimination against Native populations or make redress an integral part of their political and societal project. These states—and by extension the civil societies who keep them in place—depend in large part on the continuous trauma and erasure of Indigenous communities for their economic development, cartographic integrity, and stable sense of identity. Trauma and erasure take on many forms; for instance, they are enacted through laws and governmental policies like the Indian Act.[2] Development projects—the Albertan tar-sands industry or the Plan Nord in Quebec, for example—that are almost unilaterally devised by the federal or provincial governments and that impinge on First Nations territories and rights are another way in which the settler colonial community continues to envision its existence at the expense of First Nations communities. Montreal and the very performance centre in which audiences were seated to see Ondinnok's *Xajoj Tun Rabinal Achi* stand on appropriated Mohawk (Kanienkehaka) land.

Trauma and erasure are also enacted, and arguably more potently so, in the public sphere, in the national imaginary, and, as Alan Filewod argues, on theatrical stages. In *Performing Canada: The Nation Enacted in the Imagined Theatre*, Filewod describes "theatre as a legitimizing performance of the imagined community that is the nation" (1). Discussing Marc Lescarbot's 1606 *Theatre of Neptune in New France* as a founding spectacle of Canada's displacement and erasure of First Nations, Filewod writes, "As Lescarbot's First Nations neighbours watched their own surrogation in the bodies of the French explorers who performed the roles of welcoming 'savages,' their presence was inscribed in theatre culture as erasure" (103). The gesture was highly political: as the French men in redface performed as "savages" offering the New World to the king of France, they were rewriting their First Nations interlocutor, substituting themselves as the authentic and legitimate occupant of the land. That night in 1606, Lescarbot's redface performers unwittingly

---

2   More recently, the omnibus bill C-45, which unilaterally amended the Indian Act and several other Acts that deeply impact First Nations' eroding territories and rights, was a clear reminder that First Nations stand as afterthoughts in the expansion and growth of Canada as an imagined community.

participated in creating what Daniel Francis calls the "imaginary Indian": a white-man fantasy, the site of "[w]hite hopes, fears and prejudices" removed from the lived reality of First Nations people (4).

To name that loss and think of redress and healing in these socio-political and theatrical contexts are challenging acts both for the performers and the audience members. Might empathy be a way to meet such a challenge? Can one empathize with another's trauma when this other's pain clearly challenges one's own narrative of self?

This essay explores how Ondinnok's *Xajoj Tun Rabinal Achi* provocatively questioned the limits of empathy as a mode of affective engagement with marginalized communities' trauma, especially when this trauma is conjugated—as it is in the case of First Nations and Indigenous communities—in both the past and present tense. I begin with a discussion of the critical work on empathy proposed mainly by cinema scholar Frank Wilderson, literary scholar Saidiya Hartman, and performance-studies scholar Patrick Anderson, who all challenge the redemptive potential attached to empathic encounters in liberal discourses. Leveraging these authors' theoretical contributions to my analysis of the encounter between First Nations performers and settler spectators in the theatre space, I meditate on empathy not as liberatory practice, "but as a mode of production that secures civic relations" (Wilderson, "'Raw Life'" 186). Thinking of empathy at a structural level, I examine in this chapter how empathy in its current colloquial understanding and practice participates in solidifying a sense of "we" that perpetuates exclusion. I explore in particular how empathy functions—or, as I argue, reaches a limit point—in the particular context of First Nations' theatre in settler-colonial communities. How indeed does empathy take place in a context where a sense of national "we" has long depended on the exclusion or assimilation of First Nations people and on a form of institutionalized "colonial agnosia"? Drawing from this critical reflection, I then examine the strategies deployed by Ondinnok to rethink its relationship with the audience in *Xajoj Tun Rabinal Achi*.

EMPATHY'S AFFECTIVE PROMISE

Empathy counts among the most powerful affective draws of theatre.[3] Indeed, as Elin Diamond argues, live theatre, in its dominant dramatic-realist form, has often capitalized on empathy as an organizing force in the encounter between performers and spectators ("Violence" 404). In this encounter, audience members are invited to feel for and identify with characters on stage and to participate vicariously in this sense of "we" that accompanies empathic identification. For Frank Wilderson "empathy tenders the promise of a liberatory relation" between performer and spectators through

> [c]atharsis (intense release of emotion) and cathexis (locating of emotion into an object, event or person), by staging an encounter that can renew or reestablish the kinship, or communal, structure of feeling that it presumes to exist *ab initio*, as if in a state of nature. ("'Raw'" 182)

Empathic identification is imbued here with bridging possibilities and equated to a gesture of democratic dialogue. However, as Diamond suggests, this "we" can be a violent formation that reproduces "normative rules of inclusion and exclusion" ("Violence" 406), rules that regulate who may experience such a relation as liberatory. It is not always clear who and what "benefits from this production of empathy" (Boler 255), or that, as a practice invested with redemptive qualities, empathic identification does lead to actions that challenge a given society's status quo.

Diamond is not alone in her critique. As a "natural" emotion and as a liberatory practice, empathy has been the object of sharp criticism from theorists in fields of inquiry as varied as post-structuralism and postmodernism,

---

3　In *Theatre & Feeling*, Erin Hurley writes, "Recent data indicate that a significant number of people attend the theatre for its emotional pay-off. In a 2005 national survey in the United States, Susan Bennett quotes in her 2006 article 'Theatre Audiences, Redux,' 56.5 per cent of respondents said that their 'major motivation' for attending a cultural event was the 'emotionally rewarding experience it offered'" (Hurley 1–2, citing Bennett 227).

post-colonial studies and critical race studies. As "a mode of interpellation or conceptual framework of interpretation, and as a strategy for liberation within ideological structures," empathy has been described as "weak, epistemologically flawed, and politically suspicious" (Lynch 6). Critics have pointed out that empathy "obscures or ignores the political and economic and bodily dimensions of social struggles" (Lynch 6) by displacing the burden of liberation and understanding away from the structure and onto the individual empathetic listener. Despite these critiques, empathy and empathic identification remain central to how theatre and performances are currently imagined, staged, and discussed. Take for example this recent advertisement for Denis O'Hare and Lisa Peterson's *An Iliad*. The publicity pitch is enticing: "In this eye-opening version, we are on the front lines of every major war in history, reliving a futile struggle that has replayed itself over thousands of years" (*An Iliad*). Subtending this advertisement is the understanding of empathy as constitutive of a universal, undifferentiated, and depoliticized "we." The publicity imagines this position as unaffected by the structures of power that too often place some bodies within the confines of civil society and some at its margins, some bodies as empathizers and some as the others with whom they empathize.

Tracing one of the etymological lineages of the word empathy through nineteenth-century aesthetics, Patrick Anderson argues that empathy as it is currently practised and understood differs from art historian Robert Vischer's originary and influential understanding of *Einfühlung*, the German term later translated as empathy. When Vischer developed the concept in 1873, empathy was imagined as a profoundly destabilizing and disorienting experience, one in which a form of undoing and becoming operated on the subject. About his encounter with an object that deeply moved him, Vischer writes, "Only ostensibly do I keep my own identity although the object remains distinct. I seem merely to adapt and attach myself to it as one hand clasps another, and yet I am mysteriously transplanted and magically transformed into this Other" (qtd. in P. Anderson 96). According to Anderson, however, empathy

[h]as become in its contemporary colloquial (and I would argue political) usage . . . a model or end-stage of ethical encounter rather than . . . an ethical quandary that we should consider carefully, remembering that a "true emotional connection" possible with "another human being" is neither endemic to, nor inevitably coextensive with, the empathic as Vischer imagined it. (86–87)

Anderson argues here against the very understanding of empathy mobilized in the aforementioned publicity and questions its universalizing underpinnings.

The horrors of the Second World War transformed discussions surrounding empathy. The intellectuals that emerged after the Second World War argued that the Holocaust and the scope of its horror marked a limit point for empathy. Jean-François Lyotard and others argued that "the Holocaust exploded the very possibility of thinking and speaking as a 'we'" and demanded a form of "moral and cognitive agnosticism" (Wade 17). These authors argued that the unprecedented violence of the Shoah demanded that we approach its representation through an ethic of not understanding. It was simply impossible—obscene even—to attempt to project oneself into the bodies of the victims.

If the Holocaust exposed in all its horror the limits of intrahuman empathy, for theorists of Afro-pessimism, slavery and its present afterlife reveal the limits of humanity. In her powerful reflection on slavery and its afterlife in the United States, Saidiya Hartman locates another point of impossibility for empathic identification, which she describes as a form of "facile intimacy," a mode of identification that "fails to expand the space of the other but merely places the self in its stead" (19–20).[4] Examining white abolitionist John Rankin's epistolary exchanges with his slaveholding brother, Hartman identifies the ways in which empathy functions not as a movement toward the other but as a return to oneself. In one of his letters, Rankin strives to make

---

4   Blackness stands as a condition of humanity. To empathize with black bodies would thus lead a subject to a moment of break, a moment where one's own cartographical integrity would be ruptured.

the horrors of slavery legible to his brother. To do so, he imagines himself along with his family as slaves "placed under the reign of terror" and "being whipped at the pleasure of a morose and capricious master" (Hartman 18). Though this exercise serves to condemn slavery, Hartman argues that Rankin's projection of his own self onto the slave's pained body brings something else to the fore, namely the "difficulty and slipperiness of empathy" (Hartman 18). Hartman posits, "[I]n making the slave's suffering his own, Rankin begins to feel for himself rather than for those whom this exercise in imagination presumably is designed to reach" (19). It simultaneously condemns slavery and reproduces its condition in appropriating the slave's body as "a vessel for the uses, thoughts, and feelings of others" (Hartman 19).

For Saidiya Hartman and Frank Wilderson, empathy toward the black body by non-black subjects is not only a form of erasure and a return to oneself, but it also serves to reinscribe the borders of civil society. Wilderson, who writes from a US standpoint but extends his reflection to the Western world that the enslavement of Africans enabled, is highly critical of the presumption that empathy is a natural inclination and suggests instead that some bodies, namely black bodies, sorely test a universal faith in empathy as a natural relation given the violence that has historically accrued to them. For Wilderson, black bodies mark the limits of empathy, its breaking point. He writes "relational capacity itself could not exist without being able to point to the slave as that sentient being or cluster of types who are barred from relational status in both content and form" ("'Raw'" 387). The slave is "generally dishonored, perpetually open to gratuitous violence, and void of kinship structure, that is, having no relations that need be recognized, a being outside of relationality" (Wilderson, *Red* 11). Wilderson continues, "Put another way, civic life requires social death so as not to implode from the pressure of incoherence" (*Red* 387). Borrowing from Orlando Patterson, Wilderson describes social death as the position occupied by the slave who is alive but firmly outside of a civil society that depends on him/her to mark its boundaries. As Wilderson argues, to really empathize with the socially dead, to allow oneself to really reflect on the structures of privileges and violence that maintain some subjects within civil society and some without would expose the empathizer's incoherence, his or her unethical existence. Wilderson's suggestion, though specific to black bodies, challenges us to rethink empathy not as a universal inclination but as "a mode of production that secures civic relations" (" 'Raw' " 412).

Taking this US-based scholarship on the representational and ethical challenges of the Shoah and slavery as a generative model, we turn now to an analysis of similar challenges with respect to colonization in settler societies. How might we think about empathy in societies that are predicated, as Filewod and others argue, on the erasure and displacement of Indigenous populations? How might empathy with an Indigenous other pose a threat to the coherence of the settler-colonial edifice?

The cartographical and ethical integrity of settler-colonial nations and civil societies has long depended on the erasure and relegation to its margins of Indigenous populations. Cinema scholar Bruno Cornellier, following Patrick Wolfe and Lorenzo Veracini, recently argued that settler societies are not only predicated upon the structural elimination of Indigenous societies, but also on a historical trajectory "culminating in settler colonialism's own self-suppression"; that is, in an erasure of past colonial policies from collective memory. Stephen Harper's insistence that "Canada has no history of colonialism" (Ljunggren) at a press conference during the 2009 G20 summit, only one year after apologizing for the Indian Residential Schools system on behalf of all Canadians, illustrates well this trajectory. In this sanitized collective memory, Indigenous subjects appear as ahistorical figures, detached from the settler-colonialism legacy of violence. At a material level, study after study demonstrates the vast inequalities that separate First Nations communities from the rest of Canada, their marginalization, and the constant erosion of their rights. At the psychic level, as Francis and Filewod argue, Canada's imaginary and national identity rest on a founding and legitimizing scenario in which "Indians" benevolently place themselves under the Europeans' care. Canada needs the figure of the ahistorical Native—his or her existence at the brink of disappearance—to simultaneously romanticize its past and assuage a sense of national guilt. Canada's own sense of self is predicated on the disappearing but not disappeared position occupied by First Nations people.

How, then, might we understand empathy as a mode of production that secures settler societies' civic relations with Indigenous populations? To empathize with First Nations people as a member of Canada's civil society is doubly challenging: it either demands a recognition of one's participation in the ongoing structures of oppression and erasure that maintain First Nations people at the margins of civil society, or it requires a form of cognitive dissonance that allows one to witness loss and trauma as an ahistorical phenomena that do not and cannot implicate the viewer.

Quebec's own sovereignist agenda further complicates the conditions of an empathic encounter with a First Nations "other's" trauma and demands for redress. The province has now attempted to separate from the rest of Canada on two occasions and, even for the non-separatist majority, Quebec's cultural identity is in large part constructed around a self-definition as a colonized and threatened minority whose language and culture need to be protected and preserved.[5] To be sure, the 1960s decolonization discourse surrounding Quebec's status as a colonized people galvanized a nationalist movement that still exists today. It also obscured the complex status of Quebec as a settler-colonial community and delayed the uptake of post-colonial theory to examine the relations between Quebec and the province's eleven First Nations.[6] I am not debating here the historical and political foundations of Quebec's nation-building discourse. I am, however, arguing that Quebec's collective identity as a minority vis-à-vis Canada—albeit a relatively powerful one—shapes the relationship between Quebec's audience members and First Nations performers. To witness the account of traumatic loss suffered by a member of the Mohawk or Huron Wendat nations whose territories now constitute Montreal and Quebec City respectively is, for some Quebecers, an encounter that challenges, threatens even, their own self-definition as part of

---

5   In 1980 and again in 1995 the Parti Québécois held two divisive close-call referenda, asking the population to vote on partition.

6   See volume 35, Spring/Summer 2003, of *Québec Studies* for an in-depth reflection on the necessity and challenges of including post-colonial studies as a theoretical lens in Quebec studies.

a community in peril. It raises challenging questions about the limits of empathy when seemingly irreconcilable narratives shape the audience members' and performers' sense of self. How does one (or *can* one) witness a trauma that threatens one's own self-definition? Ondinnok grappled with these difficult questions in their adaptation of *Xajoj Tun Rabinal Achi*.

ONDINNOK'S DRAMATURGY OF DESIRE

Ondinnok defines its theatre as one that seeks to "re-conquer a [First Nations] imaginary, a land of dreams" and "to repatriate a memory in order to unleash a future" ("Mission"). Yves Sioui Durand, one of Ondinnok's founding members, describes the company's theatre as "a space of Indigenous resistance and re-appropriation." He explains, "[O]ne cannot live carrying the dead on one's back. If we lay them to rest, we can liberate ourselves from their suffering. In their wound, one also finds a remedy" (Personal interview).[7] Since its inception, the company has actively addressed Indigenous trauma and loss on two fronts. Working with First Nations communities, the company created a "theatre of healing," an intimate and community-based theatre by and for First Nations people that explores myths and storytelling as a healing practice. The company has also collaborated with non–First Nations artists—French director Ariane Mnouchkine and French/Québécois theatre artist Jean-Pierre Ronfard among others—to create theatre and a space for dialogue between First Nations and the world.

Unlike some of Ondinnok's past productions in which trauma was explored explicitly, trauma remained unnamed on stage in *Xajoj Tun Rabinal Achi*. The play itself, as we have seen, makes no references to Conquest and its aftermath. Perhaps because it was deeply aware of the pitfalls of representing trauma—the risks of pathologizing First Nations bodies, the audience's colonial agnosia, and the threatening nature of empathy when it comes to the

---

7   The translation from the French of Yves Sioui Durand's interviews and Alexandre Cadieux's article (later in this essay) are my own.

perpetuation of a sense of "we"—the company moved away from what Eve Tuck calls a "damage-based framework," an approach that focuses on documenting and exposing people's "pain and brokenness" in order to leverage redress (409). In her critique of damage-based research, Tuck challenges the logic that documenting and exposing pain and loss will inevitably lead to redress and alliance building. In other words, Tuck, like Wilderson, Hartman, Anderson, and others, is suspicious of empathy as a primary mode of engagement with marginalized communities. Tuck worries that damage-based research, even when it helps yield resources to these communities, comes at too high a price as it problematically reinforces a monolithic image of "these people as depleted, ruined, and hopeless" (409). She proposes instead, echoing Gloria Anzaldùa and Anne Anlin Cheng among others, a desire-based framework, one that labours to understand the "complexity, contradiction, and the self-determination of lived lives" (416).

In its adaptation of *Xajoj Tun Rabinal Achi*, Ondinnok articulated what I call a desire-based dramaturgical approach to the representation of trauma and loss. I use the term to refer to an ensemble of dramaturgical strategies deployed by Ondinnok to implicate and destabilize both parties of the theatrical encounter. Ondinnok's desire-based dramaturgical approach labours to restore and embrace the complexity of the Indigenous performers on stage while challenging audiences' empathetic expectations. In refusing to perform or locate trauma in an explicit way, Ondinnok strategically displaced the burden of representing trauma and loss away from the Indigenous performers—avoiding the reinscription of their bodies as sites of devastation—and onto the event itself, that is, the assemblage of text, acting, space, and public. Trauma, in Ondinnok's *Xajoj Tun Rabinal Achi*, was performed in the gap between the various elements of the theatrical event: in the space between actors and audience, the play and its historical context, and the story and the loss it elucidated. That is, trauma, loss, and survivance were performed relationally with the spectators through the activation of a network of comparisons between the world of the play and the contemporary realities of Indigenous communities. Furthermore, rather than attempting to bridge the gap between these various elements, blending them into a seamless narrative that would facilitate the audience's empathic identification with the performers, Ondinnok cultivated this gap as a space of productive collisions.

Yves Sioui Durand skilfully set the stage for this event by emphasizing the play's long history of survivance in the program as well as in several promotional interviews that preceded the production's run. Sioui Durand positioned one element of the assemblage—the text—and activated a network of references and comparisons in the audience members' minds, a frame through which they could participate in the event and interpret the play. While the story of Cawek and the Man of Rabinal does not directly dramatize post-colonial trauma, it nonetheless points to this hurt by showing what *was*, what *existed* before the advent of the colonial forces. During the performance, or event, the play-text illuminated contemporary demands for sovereignty and self-governance based on Indigenous models by dramatizing a moment in which Mayan epistemologies were central and the foundations of sovereign nations. The current state of affairs for Indigenous communities was activated in the audience's minds by the events on stage. Trauma and loss were thus addressed in the gap, in the encounter between a text that dramatized what *was* and the spectators' awareness of what the contemporary situation of First Nations and Indigenous people *is*.

When *Xajoj Tun Rabinal Achi* is performed in Guatemala, it is understood that the ghosts of the play's characters visit the performers, allowing them to retell their stories (Tedlock 16). Actors thus perform one role for the entirety of the play. The acting style is presentational and performers do not attempt to convey the characters' emotional lives. The performers are first and foremost channels through which the ghosts and other ancestral figures can come forth. Yves Sioui Durand adopted elements of this performance mode in his production: "[E]very night, one performer is summoned by the ancestors to embody Cawek. In turn, when the story has been told, one of the performers is chosen to play the sacrifice victim" ("Programme"). When I attended the production, this summoning took place on stage at the end of a dance prologue performed by the entire cast. A young Huron Wendat actor seamlessly took centre stage after being chosen to be Cawek; a woman, the only non-Indigenous performer, then became Cawek at the sacrificial moment. Sioui Durand played here with the audience's desire to identify with and to assign a fixed meaning to the bodies on stage. Cawek could be a man, a woman, and he/she could come from any part of the Americas. Cawek became an everyman of sorts, unfixed and capable of speaking in a transnational Indigenous voice.

During the performance, Sioui Durand interrupted the story of Cawek's trial with interludes of what he calls "divinatory theatre," during which the performers read passages of the *Popol Vuh* or the Chilam Balam from Chumayel, two foundational Mayan texts that are not part of the Guatemalan performance tradition (Sioui Durand, Personal interview). Beautifully designed masks and other costume elements—a long feathered cape, large hats all made of feathers and corn husks, and reminiscent of shamanic costumes from various Indigenous cultures—played a central part in these moments in which ancestors were summoned on stage. During these divinatory interludes actors performed a form of communion with the masks and created powerful and destabilizing images. For example, a young woman moved slowly toward the mask of an old man as if responding to a silent summoning. Once she slowly placed the mask on her face, her body appeared ageless, young in appearance and old in gestures. The performer then wrapped herself in a heavy feathered cape and her long hair disappeared under a large hat, thus masking all signs of youth or gender and creating the blurred atemporal image of an old soul reaching out from time immemorial. For a moment, the masked figure, adorned as it was with visual signifiers from various Indigenous cultures, appeared to be a living link with the past, existing across time and geographical boundaries. The figure was past and present, simultaneously disappearing and reappearing, visible yet demanding a complex reading by audience members. At the end of the interlude, her slow removal of the hat, cape, and mask constituted a form of becoming and a gesture of self-representation. Unlike the French explorers' performance in Lescarbot's *Theatre of Neptune in New France*, surrogation served here to restore presence and continuity with a past obscured by settler-colonial discourse and policies. In this moment of desire-based dramaturgy, the performer contested settler societies' ahistorical reading of Indigenous bodies and reclaimed what Tuck would call a "complex" and "self-determined" connection with the past, and possibly a sense of community across the Americas (416).

Throughout the performance, the cast of Ondinnok oscillated between acting as translators for their audience—providing a point of entry into a text hermetic in its ancient references—and leaving them in the uncomfortable position of outsiders. The actors, for example, performed untranslated in Mayan, French, English, and Spanish, and the interludes of divinatory theatre, while often symbolically rich, could be both linguistically and imagistically impenetrable. While some of these difficulties might come from the highly improvisational structure Sioui Durand adopted for the play, opacity and illegibility were more often deployed as gestures of resistance, reappropriations that align with Ondinnok's stated goal of creating a theatre of healing. As Saidiya Hartman points out about the hidden subtexts of slaves' songs and dances, opacity can be deployed as a way to reclaim and preserve a sense of self.[8] In the case of Indigenous bodies, opacity can allow performers to redefine themselves outside of colonial demands of legibility and authenticity and to challenge the audience's potentially victimizing gaze. Indeed, keeping the performers' bodies and certain aspects of the productions opaque, illegible, unattainable, denied the audience the possibility of folding Indigenous trauma into their own sense of guilt or discomfort, further erasing Indigenous experience through empathic identification. Alexandre Cadieux, a theatre critic for Montreal's newspaper *Le Devoir*, attests to the production's impact when he writes that it "establishes a living contact between the present and the vestiges of a civilization massacred by mankind." To witness such a loss, he writes, left him with "an indescribable sensation of vertigo."

What Cadieux is describing here is not a form of facile intimacy but an uncomfortable one. His reaction belongs in the same category of affective response as Vischer's *Einfühlung*, as he writes about a vertiginous sensation that disoriented him, that created a momentary encounter with the unknowable

---

8 Hartman ultimately argues that given the slave's lack of agency or opacity, resistance tactic had no performative or transformative power under chattel slavery's system of total domination. In other words, the black body as a socially dead object cannot resist its way to subjectivity.

nature of First Nations and Indigenous loss. He points to a form of undoing that is disorienting and potentially productive if the viewer allows it to be. What one does to recuperate from this vertiginous sensation when the other's loss, and one's own participation in that hurt, are suddenly legible as co-extensive.

Ondinnok's adaptation of *Xajoj Tun Rabinal Achi* participates in a larger conversation about the pitfalls and healing potential of a theatre of trauma. It urgently questions the ways in which Indigenous trauma can be productively explored on stage and witnessed by audience members. How can trauma be both acknowledged and decentred on stage, addressed without the further damages that thinking of Indigenous bodies, imaginations, mythologies as "broken and depleted" inevitably creates? Ondinnok participates in a dramaturgy of desire by imagining complex communities on stage, bodies that are hurt and whole, opaque and open, ancient and contemporary, informed by ancient myths and constantly evolving. In this dramaturgy of desire, Ondinnok displaces the performance of trauma away from Indigenous performers and challenges audiences to find a way to witness trauma without recourse to empathic identification and a universalizing discourse of shared pain.

BETWEEN THE WORLDS: REFLECTIONS ON A YEAR OF FALLING (A SITE-SPECIFIC PERFORMANCE)
HELENE VOSTERS

From Canada Day 2010 through Canada Day 2011 I performed *Impact Afghanistan War*, a memorial project in which I fell one hundred times a day in a public space for one year—each fall in recognition of an Afghan death. An investigation of the space between "Us" and "Other," between individual and social mourning, between personal ritual and public protest, between art and politics, between theory and practice, *Impact* was an attempt to register, in and through the body, the impact of our (Canada's) engagement in Afghanistan. Part mourning cry, part act of faith in the imaginal commons, *Impact* was a call out to the collective emotional body to allow itself to be impacted.

CROSSROADS I: THE "ARCHIVE AND THE REPERTOIRE"

I am haunted—by voices telling of histories I am (have been conditioned to be) ignorant of, in languages I cannot (have never been taught to) understand. The repeated impact of my body with earthy landscapes that refused confinement within temporal and corporeal boundaries of nation rattled the bones of the forgotten dead of our canonized, monumentalized, commemorated history of privileged memory and deliberate erasure. Through the reiterative gesture of falling (and rising), falling (and rising), a "surrogated" enactment of dying (and not), dying (and not), my body became a site for the transmission of buried embodied memories of the forgotten (but not forgetting) dead (and not) of history (see Roach, *Cities*).[1] Though each of *Impact*'s 36,700 falls was done in honour of an Afghan death, the dead of the various geopolitical land-scapes in and on which I fell whispered to me—those who died at the hands of my Dutch colonial ancestors hailed from across time and place, the dead of modernity's "diasporic and genocidal histories" chanted and cajoled, Why Afghanistan? Why Afghanistan? Why *only* Afghanistan? (Roach, *Cities* 4).

I am ghosted, not only by these cross-temporal and geohistorical voices, but also by a myriad of non-linguistic dispatches—fragmented physiological and affective remembrances of weather, of light, of texture and architecture, of sound, sensation, and symptom. As I share these reflective shards from my year of falling my hope, my invitation, my evocation is that together we enter this crossroads—this meeting place of art, activism, scholarship, *and* ritual— awake to the voices between and beyond both words and worlds, voices that refuse or have not yet found their way into the archival linearity and false or-dering of text on page. Awake too to the knowledge that crossroads are sites of impact as well as encounter, and that this particular crossroads is a site of citational collision between the dissonant logics of "archive and repertoire."[2]

---

1   Joseph Roach conceptualizes surrogation as the uncanny process through which cultural (living) memory is performatively transmitted across time, space, and identity, via a "three-sided relationship of memory, performance and substitution" (2). In *Performing Remains: Art and War in Times of Theatrical Reenactment*, Rebecca Schneider examines the ways in which affective engagement with performative re-enactment can evoke "if not the thing itself (the past), somehow also *not not* the thing (the past), as it passes across [performers'] bodies in again-time" (8).

2   In *The Archive and the Repertoire: Performing Cultural Memory in the Americas*, Diana Taylor distinguishes between embodied reportorial practices of knowledge transmission and the archival mechanisms through which knowledge is produced, legitimated, and stored through the written word and systems of classification.

REFLECTIONS ON A YEAR OF FALLING

CANADA DAY 2010
CEDARVALE PARK, TORONTO
FALLS 1–100

I wasn't sure if I could do it—fall one hundred times. After watching a "how to fall" YouTube dance-training video my practice session came to an abrupt halt (at fall number nine) when I hit my head on a support beam in my "cozy" basement bachelor apartment. But my nervousness was soon eclipsed by the experience of falling: breath after impact with ground hints at the larger narrative of death and vulnerability. There is a catch to it, an involuntary panic that quickly adjusts—I see clouds (I am alive), hear birdsong (I am alive), feel grass's tickle (I am alive). Even discomfort is channelled into an awareness of this privileged aliveness. Hot (alive). Rock under ribs (alive). Fire ant's bite (alive).

3 SEPTEMBER 2010
CHRISTIE PITS PARK, TORONTO
FALLS 6,400–6,500

Today, a man took a postcard and read it as he continued on his way. After a moment he stopped, turned, and walked purposefully toward me. He witnessed, fully engaged, for about twenty falls before offering a small bow and carrying on with his day. His lack of hesitation or embarrassment, the congruence of his action, the purity of his willingness to approach, to see, to bear

witness, reminded me of an experience I had riding the bus with my mom when I was twelve. A girl, about my age and sitting a few seats away, vomited. My mom's immediate response was to help her. Mine was less noble. Gazing out of the bus window, I distanced myself from the girl and my mother. I wonder, what would happen if more of us responded with unhesitating compassion toward the sick, the falling, and the fallen. If we let it stop us in our tracks, let it have our full attention, even if only for a breath or two or three.

As a kid, I assumed my mom's courage was something innate to her and my fear innate to me. But several years ago I read a book by Eva Fogelman—*Conscience and Courage: Rescuers of Jews During the Holocaust*. In her inquiry into what it was that enabled some people to act on their conscience during the Holocaust, Fogelman identified a willingness to break rules and take risks as a common quality that rescuers shared. She suggests that this explains why there was a disproportionate number of "sneaks, thieves, smugglers, hijackers, blackmailers, and killers" among the rescuers (3). It also explains why so many "moral" citizens did nothing. It seems it's not enough to feel a sense of conscience, we need to act on it, and in order to act on our conscience we need to engage in practices that help us develop courage in the face of risk, especially the courage to act against the status quo, against authority. *Impact* has become my practice, a way to meet, again and again and again, my fear of breaking the rules, of disturbing the peace, of evoking people's anger. Through this daily encounter, my courage has been given a chance to catch up to my convictions.

30 OCTOBER 2010
DUFFERIN GROVE PARK, TORONTO
FALLS 12,100–12,200

On the website of the Revolutionary Association of the Women of Afghanistan (RAWA) there is this warning: "CAUTION CAUTION CAUTION. This page contains links to photos which some viewers may find disturbing" ("RAWA Photo Gallery").

What are the consequences of not disturbing? Images or reminders of death within much of the dominant West are, in large measure, contained within media genres ranging from news to an ever-expanding "entertainment" industry. In his study of post–World War II mourning practices, British anthropologist Geoffrey Gorer argued that by the mid-twentieth century death had become, paradoxically, increasingly absent and increasingly present in the day-to-day lives of most Westerners. Gorer linked the near disappearance of public mourning rituals to a mid-twentieth century emergence of what he dubbed the "pornography of death" (as evidence he pointed to a proliferation of violent horror movies, comics, and magazines as well as books on the horrors of war and concentration camps).[3] If anything, Gorer's "death pornography" analogy is more valid today than when he published his study in 1965 (132). Though few of us are required to rub shoulders with death and mourning prior to its intimate intrusion into our personal lives, a quick

3   I'm intrigued by the parallels between Gorer's analysis of the relationship between "death pornography" and the increased absence of a lived engagement with death and mourning and Audre Lorde's analysis of the relationship between sexual pornography and the "denial of the power of the erotic" in all aspects of day-to-day experience (54).

perusal of television programming reveals an overwhelming prevalence of forensic crime shows as just one of a plethora of new popular-culture genres through which death's gory and cellular details permeate our collective imaginations via an entertainment media.

18 DECEMBER 2010
BEAUCHEMIN PARK, WINNIPEG
FALLS 17,000–17,100

It's difficult to fall in snow without evoking the childhood memory of making snow angels: the way the snow catches you, breaking your fall, and the challenge of climbing up out of its embrace without destroying the angel's perfection. Falling these past days in Winnipeg's plush snowscape I become surrounded by messy angels, all askew and aflutter, angels with things on their minds—angels busy with concern.

For the most part winter's cold has brought an insulating isolation with everyone bundled and passing through space with the singular objective of heat-seeking missiles. So when people do stop, their willingness to do so, to stand in the cold and witness, takes on a new meaning. My sister calls them angels. I think she's right—earthly angels abound: there's my friend Brad, who falls with me almost weekly; there's Milad and Anthony, who spontaneously joined me on a cold, snowy day at York University; there's Lilia, who held a tearful vigil on a gusty Bloor Street as people rushed by on their way to warmth; and there's my family.

I had been nervous about falling in Winnipeg, scared both of the cold and of "coming out" to family members who didn't know about *Impact*. From the beginning my sister Laurie has been a great support, both moral and technical (she designed my card and got my blog up and running) and John and Sid (brother and sister-in-law) picked me up at the airport equipped with a box full of Winnipeg-warm "falling gear." But for some reason I was afraid to tell my dad. I wasn't sure how he would respond. I thought he'd be overly worried for me, or embarrassed, or worse, angry. I underestimated him. Yesterday, as I was falling in Beauchemin Park in back of my parent's apartment building, Dad came trudging through the snow to watch. Later that evening, at the Charleswood Legion's weekly "meat draw" (Mom won a pork roast and bacon and eggs), Dad took one of my postcards out of his jacket, proudly showed it to his friends, and said, "And she stands right up after every fall. She doesn't cheat."

20 FEBRUARY 2011
CHRISTIE PITS PARK, TORONTO
FALLS 23,400–23,500

I drew a picture after falling today of one hundred fallen stick-figure bodies. In some ways it's easier to fall one hundred times than to draw one hundred fallen stick figures. When falling, each fall is intact unto itself. Each fall comes before or after another. Like language. Like words on the page—meaning is ordered through this linear progression. But as the number of fallen stick figures multiplied on the page, they began to fall on top of one another until the distinction between bodies became obscured. By the time I reached one hundred they were not only no longer recognizable as single bodies, their very recognizability as bodies had become obliterated—they had been rendered an unknowable mass.

27 FEBRUARY 2011
CHRISTIE PITS PARK, TORONTO
FALLS 24,100–24,200

Usually when people see me fall they see me in passing. But because Vince and Rob were working just up the street on the water main at Christie and Bloor, they saw my entire set of falls, and when I was finished they came to talk to me. They were curious and very respectful. It's funny, the people I had most expected to "understand" or "appreciate" *Impact*—like activists and artists—often haven't. On the other hand I've received some of the most moving responses from those I had assumed would consider it just plain weird (like my dad and now Vince and Rob).

In *Critical Moves: Dance Studies in Theory and Politics* Randy Martin points out that political movements don't just involve ideologies and intellectual conceptualizing, they involve actual bodies, bodies in motion (1–28). During the summer months when Toronto's parks were filled with a spectacular array of recreational activities, *Impact*'s choreography of falling and rising was frequently read as either an athletic endeavour or rehearsal for a performance. Vince, Rob, and my dad, however, immediately saw it as a labour, a chosen labour, a labour detached from capitalism's coercive and commodifying affects, a labour of memorialization. Just like it mattered to my dad that I don't "cheat," it mattered to Vince and Rob that I had fallen one hundred times a day since July 1. When I began falling today, I was acting "as if" it mattered. But when I spoke with Vince and Rob it mattered. It mattered despite the inadequacy of my answers to their questions. It mattered despite my doubts.

31 MARCH 2011
CHRISTIE PITS PARK, TORONTO
FALLS 27,300–27,400

Lately, it seems as though every day more people stop to witness *Impact*. One or two at a time, occasionally in small clusters, people gather around my music stand/flagpole. Sometimes they move on quickly after reading the flag or postcard, sometimes they linger and converse with one another. Yesterday, a woman who had stopped to witness became an intermediary, explaining the project to two other women through their open car window. Today, a young man serenaded me, his voice overpowered by his amplified guitar. I'm not sure what has compelled this increased participation from passersby. Perhaps Canada's engagement in a new war in Libya, Japan's nuclear crisis, or the recent death of Corporal Yannick Scherrer, Canada's 155th Afghan war casualty, remind us that we are connected through webs of vulnerability and that, like radiation, war's suffering is not containable within national boundaries.

CANADA DAY 2011
QUEEN'S PARK, TORONTO
FALLS 36,600–36,700

Queen's Park has the eerie atmosphere of a military occupation as Kim and I approach it for the gathering of *Impact*'s year-end group fall. There are roadblocks through which only military vehicles are allowed passage. Brad is already in the park. As the three of us wait for the rest of the group to arrive, we watch young soldiers dressed in fatigues secure an area of several hundred metres in front of a row of cannons. Just after the cannons begin their twenty-one-gun salute Laura arrives carrying her young son, Jackson, who is frightened. We all try to reassure him that he's safe.

I hadn't anticipated that Canada Day in Queen's Park would be celebrated with such militaristic zeal, but it somehow feels disturbingly fitting that we perform *Impact*'s final group fall surrounded by military vehicles and personnel, with the cannons' echoes reverberating through our cells and at the foot of one of the multitude of monuments to imperial conquest that occupy our public landscapes (this one to King Edward VII). With each fall (and rise), fall (and rise), I imagine us as ghostly living monuments to the Afghan dead. Monuments to all the forgotten dead of history.

CROSSROADS II: FRAMES OF WAR

In *Frames of War* Judith Butler extends Louis Althusser's notion of "modalities of materiality" and argues that the mechanisms through which war is framed need to be understood as "material instrumentalities of violence" that function as more than simple precursors to, or commentaries on, war, but as acts of war in and of themselves (xiii). Canada's popular Highway of Heroes memorials, with their unproblematized narratives of heroism and benevolent militarism, their absence of any recognition of Afghan casualties, provided a "frame" through which Canadians, as citizens, apprehended (and participated in) the war in Afghanistan. What is inside the frame—Canada's heroic and willingly self-sacrificing military dead—is made visible while what is outside of the frame—Afghan dead and any culpability on the part of the Canadian military (and the Canadian public) in their deaths—is left unseen and therefore rendered inapprehensible.

Impact sought to provide another frame, and in the process it generated its own archive. Each of *Impact*'s documented memorializing falls have been framed from a circumscribed perspective, one that offers only fleeting glimpses of the myriad of possible vantage points of witnesses and passersby; one that records, but fails to reflect, my own ever-shifting viewpoint as each fall set perception awhirl; a frame whose form and frequency is ill-suited to the task of transmitting the repertorial communications of felt experience, or of that which lies between and beyond the limitations of national, geohistorical, and temporal borders; a troubled and troubling frame that gestures both toward and beyond the limiting "frames of war" and memorialization.

IN CLOSING (AND NOT): A DIALOGUE

FORGOTTEN DEAD OF HISTORY:

Your foot rolling across my spine feels fine, so fine, but I wonder if you would perhaps, please, maybe, if it wouldn't disrupt your day, cause you to veer from your path, if you would, could, wouldn't mind, would be so kind to step a little to the left, place your heel on the knot on the edge of my scapula, and stay a while, a breath or two or three, long enough for me to remember—or remind—whatever it is that might bring release. It is a sad thing to be dead so long yet be so unable to rest.

FORGETTING LIVING PRESENT:

My foot will not stray from its path. My foot will not stray from its path. My foot will . . . *a slight pronation, a turn of the right foot inward. A lilting. Threatening balance* . . . I will not stray from my path.

FORGOTTEN DEAD OF HISTORY:

I would if I could; I would if I was able; I would reach to release, remember, remind, relieve this knot myself. But I cannot move. My hand, my arm, my foot, my tongue are pinned beneath the bronze stony weight of your monumental memory.

FORGETTING LIVING PRESENT:

I will not; I cannot; I refuse to veer, to succumb to your unreasonable requests. Your demands. I was not, did not, it wasn't me. I am not; I will not; I cannot . . . *a slight pronation* . . . hear . . . *a turn of the right foot inward* . . . see . . . *a lilting.*

FEELING RECONCILIATION, REMAINING SETTLED

DYLAN ROBINSON

> Against a background of a general, if differential, loss of belief in for-
> mal modes of efficacy, and especially political engagement, Western
> cultures are becoming increasingly prone to brief moments of en-
> gagement tied to the affective texture of particular events.
> —Nigel Thrift, *Non-Representational Theory*

It's over.

I'm sitting in a theatre.
The rock musical Beyond Eden,
about the salvage of totem poles from Haida Gwaii,
has just finished.

People are clapping, exuberantly.
Then people start rising,
two by two
by four, by eight
entire rows of people rising

ovating
shouting
and now whistling.

Soon the whole theatre is standing
or almost
as I sit,
bristling
seething
not standing.

And then at once I'm crying.

I wasn't alone.[1]

In an interview with Bruce Ruddell, *Beyond Eden*'s composer, he notes, "We had audiences in tears every night." Approximately thirty evenings of tears: one month of crying. To refer to the tears of audiences is to attest to the success, and some might say the transformative power, of performance.[2] The more tears, the better. Perhaps you have yourself witnessed intercultural music featuring Indigenous performers and have felt moved; perhaps you have risen to your feet, propelled by the wave of movement around you or feeling its surge of peer pressure; perhaps you have cried. But what, exactly, is at the heart of all this crying? What are the reasons, moreover, behind the strikingly consistent tears of audiences upon experiencing intercultural music perfor mances involving First Peoples, like *Beyond Eden*?[3]

---

1   Italicized passages such as this one with left-handed justification are the author's own reflections; inset passages in roman font are quotations from other sources as indicated.

2   An increasing number of studies have taken up the transformative potential of performance, including Fischer-Lichte, *The Transformative Power*; Thompson; and Dolan, *Utopia*, which I address later in this essay.

3   In the numerous performances I have attended, audience responses of tears and ecstatic support are unvarying. For contemporary art music performances where standing ovations are more the exception than the norm, this behaviour is even more noteworthy. Such performances have included the Victoria Symphony's concert, Legends of the First Nations, featuring Barbara Croall's *Stories from Coyote* and *Midawewe'igan—The Sound of the Drum*, as well as Colin Doroschuk's *Heaven* featuring Esquimalt First Nations

This chapter examines two examples of what I call "inclusionary music performance": the rock musical *Beyond Eden* and the Gettin' Higher Choir's performance of Susan Aglukark's song "O Siem" at the Truth and Reconciliation Commission's Victoria regional event. A subcategory of intercultural performance, inclusionary performance models neo-liberal multiculturalism, wherein First Peoples are included but are not in large part involved in the creative choices of composition or presentation. While inclusionary music performance may demonstrate a sharing of space—a visual and kinetic intermingling of bodies on stage, an acoustic blending of musics, or a literary hybridization of languages—this sharing is largely premised upon a fitting of Indigenous musicians into Western paradigms of performance. In both performances, the fundamental tenets of Western musical genres and form remain intact; the inclusion thus reinforces settler structural logic: that the structure of the aesthetic might be enriched by "other" sights and sounds without unsettling the worldview it supports.

In examining these performances, this essay pursues two related aims. The first is to challenge the assumption that the "affective contagion" represented by an audience's tears indicates a shared emotional experience of positive transformation by audience members. Drawing upon my own affective experience and on participant observation of audience members around me, I situate this shared experience with the audience in relation to

---

master singer August Thomas and the South Island Dancers on 13 February 2009; Alexina Louie's *Take the Dog Sled* for Inuit throat singers and orchestra on 15 November 2009, in Koerner Hall, Toronto; Derek Charke's *Tundra Songs* for the Kronos Quartet and Tanya Tagaq on 30 January 2010 at the Chan Centre in Vancouver; *Thunderbird*, a collaboration between Kwagiulth mezzo-soprano Marion Newman and the Aradia Baroque Ensemble on 15 May 2010 at the Glenn Gould Studio in Toronto; the opera *Giiwedin*, written by Anishinaabe composer Spy Dénommé-Welch and Catherine Magowan and produced by Native Earth Performing Arts on 8 April 2010 at Theatre Passe Muraille in Toronto; the *Oscana Symphony* by Cree composer Andrew Balfour on 3 September 2010 at the Conexus Arts Centre, Regina; *Tree People* and *Seven* by Barbara Croall presented by the Victoria Symphony Orchestra on 15 October 2011; Bruce Ruddell's musical *Beyond Eden* presented at the Vancouver Playhouse on 2 February 2010; and a DVD recording of Vivaldi's *L'estro armonico* featuring Tafelmusik Baroque Orchestra and throat singers, in which the original spontaneous ovation is scripted into the conclusion of the performance.

performance studies scholarship that has prioritized and at times valour-ized the *communitas* of shared affect. What scholarship such as Jill Dolan's on utopian performatives too often assumes is that shared affective, physi-ological responses (crying, clapping, ovating) signify a common emotion. What the two case studies in this essay point toward, however, is how such responses may have strikingly different efficacies for Indigenous and settler audience members. Just as it is important not to conflate the social efficacy of collaborative creative processes with the social efficacy of their resultant performances, it is equally essential not to elide differences between audience members' shared affective responses.

My second aim will be to demonstrate how these inclusionary music performances engender embodied, felt forms of reconciliation. I argue here that performances involving First Peoples and non-Indigenous performers are not merely symbolic reflections of reconciliation for settler audience mem-bers—representations of "working together" by playing and moving together on stage—but a primary site for audience members to feel reconciliation's non-representational pull of resolution. Audiences' affective investments in music are to a certain degree derived from music's media-specific capacity to arouse and sustain desire. In particular, music can often increase audiences' affective investment through the push and pull of harmonic progression and cadential resolution. In this sense, the repetitive, or "recombinant," teleolog-ical structures (Fink 43–47) found in popular music genres that include "O Siem" and *Beyond Eden* do not so much convince audiences of consensus and resolution as allow them to feel them.[4] In their cadential resolutions and

---

4   Robert Fink's work on the recombinant teleological structures of popular music and minimalist art music provides a useful extension of teleological theories of tonality and affect in Classical and Romantic music developed by Susan McClary. Musical teleology, "this feeling that the work as a whole 'is going somewhere' (and that it makes you, the lis-tener, want to go there too)" (Fink 31) has provocatively been defined by musicologists, including Susan McClary, in relation to the (male) drive to orgasm, particularly in feminist and queer musicology examining Classical- and Romantic-era art music with its extended harmonic procedures that entail the delaying of a single climax. Popular music as well as minimalist art music, in contrast, have been considered anti-teleological, or unconcerned

harmonic progressions both *Beyond Eden* and "O Siem" provide the satisfaction of musical build, drive, and closure familiar to popular music listening. Those affects of comfort and familiarity engendered by the subconscious registering of harmonic and generic conventions give rise to forms of affiliation and identification. In attending to these non-representational aspects of musical experience, I argue that audiences conflate positive affect with a profound experience that feels closest to something that might best be called "reconciliation." Research in the applied arts in particular has long characterized reconciliation as an experience of transformation, and the implication of this is often that such transformation has positive, lasting effects. Contrary to such an understanding of reconciliation, I suggest that reconciliation also operates more simply as a structure of feeling and as a moment of positive sensory and affective experience that may engender both positive *and* negative consequences.

NON-REPRESENTATIONAL RECONCILIATION AND THE RESUMPTION OF FRIENDLINESS

The musical work, which is a myth coded in sounds instead of words, offers an interpretive grid, a matrix of relationships which filters and organizes lived experience, acts as a substitute for it, and provides the comforting illusion that contradictions can be overcome and difficulties resolved.
—Claude Lévi-Strauss, "Structuralism and Myth"

---

with the drive of teleology in their emphasis on repetition. Fink argues, however, that the drive toward resolution is present in repetitive popular musics (disco and electronic dance music in particular) and minimalist art music genres, albeit as a form of "recombinant teleology." Recombinant teleology is here a form of prorogating desire, where the music is structured around the repetition of short four-bar climaxes that circle back on themselves.

It is reasonable to expect that audiences might cry at performances that expressly focus upon residential-school histories and performances in which trauma and abuse are represented on stage.[5] However, what is it that brings audiences equally to tears by non-narrative and abstract music works involving First Peoples (see note 2)? That audiences are clearly moved by non-narrative performances involving First Peoples prompts me to consider the further ramifications of affect's decoupling from the narratocratic impulse to describe performance experience.[6] That is, rather than falling back upon rationalizations for affect that rely on narrative explanation (i.e., "I cried because the piece related a story of injustice"), I suggest here that scholars might attend to how the non-representational and formal qualities of performance engender affect. Moreover, in relation to those music performances such as *Beyond Eden* and "O Siem" that do have narratives that could be read as moving, it is essential not to reduce audiences' affective experiences to the sole product of narrative meaning, but to see such experience as contingent upon the non-representational impact of the works' flux and flow, their haptic auralities, and their harmonic familiarities.

As I argue throughout, Indigenous intercultural and inclusionary music performances do more than simply reflect a visual, aural, and symbolic coming together; audience members' transformative and affective experiences are felt as a form of reconciliation in themselves. To understand how audience experiences constitute affective forms of reconciliation, I offer two related

---

5   The performance *Fatty Legs* at the Halifax Truth and Reconciliation event is one such example. *Fatty Legs* is a staged version of residential survivor Margaret Pokiak-Fenton's experience created by the Camerata Xara Young Women's Choir and includes the choral work *Snowforms* by R. Murray Schafer and other Western art music for choir. A second example is Odawa composer Barbara Croall's song cycle *Bigiiwe*, based on her mother's experience at residential school. For a comprehensive list of Indigenous music presented at the Truth and Reconciliation Commission, see B. Diamond.

6   Davide Panagia describes narratocracy as "the organization of a perceptual field according to the imperative of rendering things readable" (12). Narratocracy renders sensory experience into an act of making sense, that is, of being communicated to through narrative explanation.

perspectives that emphasize reconciliation's non-representational character. That is, in contrast to the typical focus upon reconciliation as a concept with the ideal of effecting social and political change wherein two opposing groups or individuals come to "restore relations, to bring into agreement and establish peaceful co-existence" (J. Scott 206), what I offer here focuses upon those moments where audiences' affective experiences might be considered as experiences of reconciliation. Such experiences take place as embodied encounters in which audiences are affected by what might be called reconciliation's sensate qualities: its textures, its materiality, its atmospheres, and particularly its resonance.[7]

Although the context of the Truth and Reconciliation Commission (TRC) explicitly guides audiences' responses to my second example, "O Siem" performed at the Victoria regional TRC event, I argue that in the early twenty-first-century "age of reconciliation" (Henderson and Wakeham), where Canadian audiences are increasingly aware of the TRC's aims to create a national memory of residential-school history, atmospheres of reconciliation permeate Canadians' interactions in unexpected ways. I focus here on one particular permutation of reconciliation's non-representational character in relation to music and sound: reconciliation's friendliness. Each of the two non-representational perspectives of reconciliation I advance here arises out of the term's etymological relationship to friendship and togetherness.

From the latin *reconcilare*, "to bring together again," the first account identifies reconciliation as an experience wherein sound's materiality precipitates a heightened fullness, a feeling of abundance, in an exceptional moment of coming together. Anthropologist Victor Turner called such experience *communitas*, a collective state "where all personal differences of class, age, gender, and other personal distinctions are stripped away allowing people to temporarily merge through their basic humanity" (Turino 18). In the realm of music, experiences of communitas have been the subject of scholarship on

---

7   Since this essay focuses on the material qualities of reconciliation in music, it will concentrate primarily upon sound while acknowledging that the auditory is merely one sensory vector amongst many that comprise reconciliation's non-representational life.

ensemble music performance, with its shared sense of common goals. While performing, Thomas Turino notes, musicians

> are fully focused on the activity that emphasizes our *sameness*—of time sense, of musical sensibility, of musical habits of knowledge, of patterns of thought and action, of spirit, of common goals—as well as our direct interaction. Within the bounded and concentrated frame of musical performance *that sameness* is all that matters, and for those moments when the performance is focused and in sync, that deep identification is *felt* as total. (18, emphasis in original)

Drawing together Turino's observations with Christopher Small's concept of *musicking* that insists upon the listener's equal measure of participation to the musicians' performing, Turino's description of coming together in sameness might also be extended toward the audience's experience. Audience members, their subjectivities temporarily suspended in the liminal flow experience of listening, may also feel sameness, feel reconciliation.[8]

This heightened connection audience members experience with those who perform—the identificatory aspect of listening—is also physical. The visceral qualities of sound as it moves through space and makes contact with listeners' bodies here effect what R. Murray Schafer calls sound's capacity for "touching at a distance" (11). As an (im)material connective tissue, sound joins together those performers on stage with their audience, conflating the collapse of distance with the collapse of difference. In another sense, we might note that music, like affect, is agglutinating.[9] It is a technology that, as musicologists

---

8   It should be acknowledged here that not all music performances, including those performed in contexts of reconciliation, entail such flow experiences. However, we might also understand such flow experiences as operating on a continuum wherein audiences experience similar micro-moments of flow, or ebbing and intensification of sensation. For an overview of "flow experience," see Turino 4–5.

9   Félix Guattari, Sara Ahmed, and Brian Massumi have all commented on the sticky quality of affect. While Guattari notes how "[a]ffect sticks to subjectivity, it is a glis-chroid matter" (158), Massumi characterizes affect as "the invisible glue that holds the

Lawrence Kramer and Carolyn Abbate have argued, makes meaning "stick."
Since absolute music has no explicit representational content of its own, our
descriptions of it can have a certain "stickiness"; our heightened experiences
of music combined with description in everything from program notes to
commercial voice-over fuse together to make such description all the more
real. "To make anything more itself, or more anything," says Kramer, "just
add music" (3). In context of this essay, I propose that ideas of music's "stickiness" can be applied to the discursive field of reconciliation. Through those
inclusionary and intercultural works I examine here we might understand
reconciliation's resonant texture of efficacy as resulting from the union between settler Canadian audiences' exceptionalist belief in multiculturalism,
and a belief in music's universal claim to transcending (negative) difference.[10]

---

world together" (*Parables* 217). Ahmed, in turn, describes affect as "agglutinating" in
the way it sticks to objects, or imbues them with affective value (*Cultural*). My own work
draws on this concern with affect's stickiness, but also on the idea that music's perceived
transcendence (its liminal quality) allows the meanings ascribed to it to stick. Indeed,
perhaps it is the "beyond" or inarticulate qualities of affect and music that allow them
to stick to things.

10   As Eva Mackey notes, "Announced by then Canadian Prime Minister Pierre Trudeau
on October 8, 1971, Multiculturalism within a Bilingual Framework . . . asserted that there
is no official culture, nor does any ethnic group take precedence over any other" (64).
Mackey has criticized this policy as a form of "difference management," with the explicit
aim of undercutting Quebec's and First Nations' struggles for sovereignty (50–70). In her
case studies of festivals, including Canada 125 and Canada Day celebrations, Mackey argues that settler Canadian festival participants often understand multiculturalism within
a framework of exceptionalism. Through a series of interviews with festival participants at
national celebrations, Mackey shows how many of her interlocutors understand multiculturalism in Canada as that which essentially and uniquely constitutes Canadian identity
(often as opposed and superior to cultural pluralism and race relations in the United States).
This celebratory exceptionalism of multiculturalism, Mackey notes, deploys a rhetoric
wherein an unmarked *Canadian*-Canadian "we" "possess 'our' ethnic groups, which 'we'
(Canadians) 'recognise and appreciate' . . . [This] provides Canadians with the necessary
differentiating characteristics that draw a distinction from the USA and construct national identity" (115). While Mackey's case studies are focused on events during the summer
of 1992, Canadian multicultural exceptionalism continues to influence the reception of

Looking further into reconciliation's etymological origin provides a second non-representational reading of the term. Its root, *conciliare*, reminds us that the term stems from "to make friendly." At the heart of reconciliation then, at least etymologically, is a concern with "good" feelings of friendliness. While the context of the Olympics (the site of *Beyond Eden*'s performance) is specifically concerned with principles of global peace and friendship, reconciliation as a return to positive feeling is also increasingly evident at TRC events themselves (the performance site of "O Siem").[11] Beginning with the 2012 Victoria regional gathering, each TRC event has held a town-hall gathering

---

a wide range of intercultural music performance styles. As Casey Mecija, the lead singer of Ohbijou, wrote on the band's blog in August 2013, "I am frustrated by the ways that my Asian-ness and my sexuality have been at times hidden and at times showcased to support notions of an 'inclusive' Canadian multiculturalism. . . . There have been many moments where our band has been sutured to notions of multiculturalism. The media has often referred to *Ohbijou* as 'multicultural.' In an article written for a college weekly the author describes us as: 'multicultural in both influence and membership' . . . . Attendant to this proclamation is often a conflation between our bodies and the sound of our music: our music becomes a multicultural sound, or is referenced to as 'world music,' which is a slippage of reading raced bodies."

11   With its goal of "contributing to the search for peaceful and diplomatic solutions to the conflicts around the world," the International Olympic Committee (IOC) upholds the ideals of "the Olympic Truce." Established in Greece in the ninth century BC, this truce enabled "athletes, artists and their families to travel in total safety to participate in or attend the Olympic Games and return afterwards to their respective countries." In present-day terms, this and other principles of peace are translated in the various symbols employed by the IOC, like the different colours of the interlocking rings on the Olympic flag, or the Olympic truce symbol. Explained by the IOC, this symbol depicts how "the Olympic flame has brought warm friendship to all the people of the world through sharing and global togetherness. In the symbol, the flame is made up of colourful effervescent elements—reminiscent of festivities experienced in the celebration of the human spirit. These elements represent people of all races coming together for the observance of the Truce" ("Olympic Truce"). The ideal of the Olympic Truce, as told through the symbol's various visual components, both represents a state of temporary reconciliation and also reinforces those qualities of reconciliation previously mentioned: warm friendship and togetherness.

called "It Matters to Me."[12] The sessions at the 2012 Victoria and Saskatoon events were led by CBC Radio personality Shelagh Rogers and consisted largely of non-Native participants.[13] The intention of these forums was to offer space for the public to reflect on what they have witnessed and learned during TRC events, but also to discuss actions to be taken, individually and by Canadian institutions, in order for change to occur. Notably, a large number of those who gave public expressions at the Victoria and Saskatoon It Matters to Me sessions avoided making individual commitments or enumerating how they might be responsible for future change; participants seldom mentioned material reparation, restitution, or ways of giving over power, unless these were appeals to institutions (school boards, government, the churches). Many of the contributions by settler participants addressed the need to cultivate harmonious relationships with First Peoples, while discussions regarding the need to establish political nation-to-nation relationships remained conspicuously absent. The language used by many of the It Matters to Me participants at sessions in Victoria and Saskatoon often dealt in the currency of friendship. On multiple occasions at the Victoria regional event

---

12   These statements, both live and online, take as a given that reconciliation is the thing that should matter "to us" over other concerns with restitution, redress, or perhaps even truth. However, while the "It" of It Matters to Me is meant to refer to reconciliation, it also allows for polysemic slippage. Whether this slippage has positive or negative effects remains to be seen.

13   Roughly eighty percent of attendees at the It Matters to Me component of the Victoria Truth and Reconciliation regional event were non-Native. This was reflected in the higher-than-expected non-Indigenous attendance rate at the event itself. At the time of writing in early 2014, this has represented the largest non-Indigenous level of participation at a TRC event. As an indication of the demographic of participants at the Victoria regional event, we can turn to Rogers's statement made at the first session: "I know there are people here who may never have been in the company of Aboriginal people." For the Saskatoon It Matters to Me session, this ratio was perhaps slightly lower, at roughly seventy percent non-Native participants. At the Montreal TRC event, the MC often curtailed the more "angry" responses that focused on the challenges faced by Aboriginal people in the region, instead reminding the audience that he was primarily interested in examples of successful moments of reconciliation.

Shelagh Rogers emphasized how "we're all part of the same great embrace," while non-Native poet Wendy Morton twice entreated audience members to "please have a First Nations friend."

In the spring of 2013 the TRC expanded this forum, launching an online platform called "Reconciliation . . . towards a new relationship." As part of this website, users can submit a personal message of 524 characters or less, and where the accumulation of these statements online will "represent a cross-section of Canadian society explaining why reconciliation matters to them" ("Reconciliation"). As one contributor to this forum notes, "It matters to me because continued feelings of sorrow, guilt, and mistrust are exhausting and unhealthy for everyone. We need to work towards replacing those feelings with joy, respect and trust" (Grimes). While few would deny that sorrow, guilt, and mistrust might be exhausting and even paralyzing, the above statement also stands in for a much larger concern in the discourse of reconciliation, both generally and at TRC events specifically, with the elimination of negative emotion. Reconciliation as a return to good feelings privileges the public purging of sadness and anger associated with residential-school memories that will supposedly allow survivors to "move on." The burden here lies with First Peoples to "get over" our resentment and other negative emotions in order for reconciliation to occur and to make room for renewed friendship with the settler Canadian public and nation-state.

I outline the non-representational context of reconciliation here at length in order to set the stage for my analysis of how the renewal of friendship is congruent with the kinds of inclusionary music performance that have taken place at the Olympics and at TRC events. The remainder of this essay draws on this context to demonstrate how inclusionary music substitutes difficult processes of political negotiation with musical spectacles of reconciliation. In exploring these ideas in greater detail I turn first to an example of inclusionary music at a site where the celebration of "universal difference" is overt: the 2010 Winter Olympic Games.

BEYOND EDEN

Like Olympic opening ceremonies themselves, Cultural Olympiads take part in the long buildup of Olympic enthusiasm. In provoking exuberant and up-lifting responses from audience members, Cultural Olympiads attempt to raise audiences' "Olympic spirit" and to rouse feelings of national pride "with glowing hearts," as one of the 2010 Olympic trademark mottos (and Canadian national anthem) would have it. Performances taking place at torch-relay ceremonies, for instance, included energetic life-size dancing Olympic in-ukshuk troupes and colourful intercultural spectacles that mixed powwow with Bhangra dancing.[14] And yet for those stories with less-than-celebratory narratives, like the rock musical *Beyond Eden*, exuberance is also demon-strated: audiences standing in ovation, whistling, and showing appreciation. According to Jill Dolan, such responses may be understood as the result of

---

14   In *Hannah and the Inukshuks* the audience is introduced to a group of Ilanaaq, an inukshuk rendered in the Olympic colours, representing the central logo of the 2010 Olympics. Ilanaaq, translated as "friendship" in Inuktitut, is the literal embodiment of friendly difference. *Hannah and the Inukshuks* opens with a group of adult Ilanaaq jump-ing in unison to the accented off-beats of music that one might imagine accompanying a barn dance. Dressed in marshmallow-like costumes of foam, the Ilanaaq wobbles around the stage joyfully before being joined by a baby Ilanaaq (at which point a collective "awh" emerges from the audience), who we learn is about to embark on a journey on his own. As the baby inukshuk wobbles toward the stage exit, the adult Ilanaaq wave farewell. But just as the baby Ilanaaq is about to exit, it hesitates (perhaps realizing it doesn't want to leave its Ilanaaq community behind) and returns to an enthusiastic welcome home. As a coda to the story, a young woman who we assume to be Hannah joins the Ilanaaq. Dressed in full Olympic attire—a Roots-branded "Canada" written across her torso—Hannah gracefully dances across the stage. Her dancing is here in sharp contrast with the wobbly Ilanaaq, who seem to barely manage to coordinate jumping in unison. Smiling from ear to ear, Hannah glides across the stage, picks up baby Ilanaaq, and spins it around (again result-ing in "awhs" by the audience) as they all bounce together happily to the music. Not only does *Hannah and the Inukshuks* literally soften cultural diversity by making inuksiut into cuddly mascots, it takes part in the infantilization of Indigenous culture that historically considered First Peoples as wards of the state, and continues in the Canadian government's paternalistic relationship with First Peoples.

what she calls "utopian performatives," those "profound moments in which performance calls the attention of the audience in a way that lifts everyone slightly above the present, into a hopeful feeling of what the world might be like if every moment of our lives were as emotionally voluminous, generous, aesthetically striking, and intersubjectively intense" (*Utopia* 5). Dolan's examination of how performance lifts audience members above the mundane and gives them hope draws on performative speech acts, which, according to J.L. Austin, enact the activities the speech signifies (i.e., "I promise") (4–11). In extending Austin's theory, Dolan argues that utopian performatives are as equally constituted through their uplifting hopeful-narrative content as by what Thrift calls their non-representational aspects (for instance, their celebratory atmosphere, buoyancy of movement, and even the teleological progression and resolution of song). Such non-representational aspects "inspire moments in which audiences feel themselves allied with each other, and with a broader, more capacious sense of a public, in which social discourse articulates the possible, rather than the insurmountable obstacles to human potential" (Dolan, *Utopia* 164). While these narrative and non-representational aspects engender hope in the viewer, I question whether we might in fact understand the physiological responses audience members experience—smiling, laughter, and crying—in themselves as affording a greater level of belief in performance's transformative power. Here affect, like abstract music, takes part in a kind of feedback loop *because* of its non-representational ineffability, because audience members cannot immediately identify what exactly such experience signifies. That is, affect allows an investment of belief in the socio-political impact of such work through a feeling-thinking of the work's "truth," or what I have elsewhere called its "sensory veracity" ("Intercultural"). Sensory veracity proposes that audiences cry (or have other sensory-physiological experience) in response to performance, and from the intensity of this experience identify their response as apposite to the work's social or political truth. In sum, the intensity of affect when experiencing socially and politically oriented performance allows for a conflation of affect with efficacy. Audiences are persuaded, or more accurately *feel*, that something has happened; a moment (or more) of something ineffable that might best be called "reconciliation" has been witnessed because our affective response is irreducible, and as such does not lie. Moreover, this conflation of affect with efficacy is confirmed, and perhaps redoubled, when a consensus of response in fellow audience members is perceived. Yet I would argue that the strength of affective experience also allows for a misinterpellation of collectivity and the consensual nature of shared physiological responses. Crying, in particular, does not necessarily represent the same emotional response for those who witness the same event.

I sit,
trying to control the flow
of tears

Surrounded by exuberant applause,
I continue my wilful exertion of sitting
My ovation "sit-in."

The words (just the words, seeming outside the flow of continuous thought)
"has it really come to this?"
puncture my disbelief
as I sit stewing,
seething. fuming.

We are at the end of *Beyond Eden*. The closing music, a refrain from the musical's title song "Beyond Eden," accompanies this applause. A sparkling of orchestral chimes harkens back to the mystical sense of place evoked throughout the musical. This title song returns us to the moment when we first heard the song: the expedition's arrival at Haida Gwaii during an idyllic morning sunrise following a storm that forced their boat aground: "Morning, and the calm on the ocean / Morning, and the silence in the forest / Morning, / Beyond Eden" (workshop draft 42).

Calm upon arrival in Haida Gwaii.
We are reminded now: all is calm again upon our return.
We regain a sense of being settled.

This song, "Beyond Eden," begins with almost the exact first intervals as the song "On My Own" from Claude-Michel Schönberg, Alain Boublil, and Jean-Marc Natel's musical *Les Misérables*. One might read into this citation a troubling intertextual reference to terra nullius, of being "alone" on the remote shores of Haida Gwaii, where the once-great presence of the Haida has, like the poles, deteriorated. However, perhaps more importantly for my argument of feeling settled, the resonance and accessibility of this pattern of notes (in addition to the "soothing" piano accompaniment) from one of the most well-known musicals of our time engenders a sense of comfortable familiarity in the listener. Yet what are the political stakes of this aesthetic accessibility, and feeling settled?

THE ACCESSIBILITIES OF CULTURE

Premiered as part of the Vancouver 2010 Cultural Olympiad, *Beyond Eden* is a fictionalized account of anthropologist Wilson Duff and renowned Haida carver and Canadian art icon Bill Reid's removal of twenty-three Haida poles and monuments from the village of Ninstints (SGang Gwaay) in 1957. Many of the poles removed were memorial and mortuary poles containing the remains of the deceased within a cavity at the top of the pole. The justification of this removal was based upon salvage paradigm principles: that the Haida were supposedly unable to care for the poles, and their deterioration necessitated their removal and preservation.[15] While the musical explicitly treats this reason for

---

15   The salvage paradigm is reflected in early ethnographic views that Indigenous peoples were dying and their material and expressive culture was in need of being preserved in museums. As ethnographer Marius Barbeau notes in *Indian Days in the Canadian Rockies*, "It is clear that the Indian, with his inability to preserve his own culture or to assimilate ours, is bound to disappear as a race . . . His passing is one of the great tragedies

the poles' salvage, the reasons for the Haida people's opposition remain veiled to the audience. The implication of cultural appropriation is present, but the musical omits specific information surrounding the nature of the poles as mortuary poles and the Vancouver production omits this information in its program.[16]

Instead, *Beyond Eden*'s story focuses upon the poles' accessibility for the Canadian public and for Bill Reid as a source of inspiration and learning. The ethical dilemma faced by Reid to salvage the poles in the face of his own peoples' opposition is counterposed against the argument that accessibility to First Peoples' culture will benefit the development of Canadian art. As the musical, program notes, and pre-performance talk make clear, the removal of the totem poles acted as the impetus for what has been called the "Haida Renaissance."[17] Housed in the Museum of Anthropology in Vancouver, BC, where they continue to reside, these poles became physically accessible objects of anthropological study and templates for Reid's study of Haida carving. Moreover, the institutionalization of these poles symbolically transformed them into objects of and for Canadian history. The crux of the argument put forward by *Beyond Eden* is that without accessibility to these poles Reid would not have become the renowned artist Canadians have come to embrace as "Native-Canadian." In his Act II solo in the song "Carving," Bill Reid (in *Beyond Eden* called Max Tomson) sings:

I must have them close to me
I need them close to me
To teach these hands to see
I want them close to me

of the American continent" (7). Ethnographers like Barbeau narrate the end of Indigenous culture as an inevitable fact, a fact that granted them the authority to salvage what they could in the ways they saw fit.

16   Such contextual information is given in the program notes for the musical's second run in Calgary.

17   See Duffek and Townsend-Gault for further examination and critique of the trope of the Haida Renaissance.

I need them close to me
Teaching these hands to see
How this cut forms gently
How this cut sweeps vertically
How this cut arcs beautifully
How this cut flows perfectly
[...]
Gently
Beautifully
Perfectly (workshop draft 63)

Reid's terms (gentle, beautiful, perfect) speak to the Western aesthetic of carving that sees totem poles as masterfully crafted aesthetic objects more than culturally significant objects that honour and sometimes contain the remains of the deceased. Moreover, here and elsewhere in the musical Reid's expedition is predicated upon the use value of the poles to Canada's artistic heritage, while disavowing the value of the "non-productive." That is, to more explicitly acknowledge the primacy of Haida poles as a materialization of family and community history, not to mention the cultural authority of the Haida's decision to let these poles return to the earth, would upend Reid's national labours. Furthermore, within the context of the Cultural Olympiad, which aims to celebrate the arts and culture of Vancouver and Canada, Reid's salvage of the poles, and his resulting maturation as a Canadian artist, stands as an embodiment of the multicultural values that Canada projects to national and global audiences.

Musically, *Beyond Eden* presents the listener with worldviews and sonic epistemologies that are very much at odds. There is a sharp incongruity between the folk-rock accessibility ever-present in the language of the musical, in which all sound is made upon the premise of aesthetic enjoyment (rather than cultural significance),[18] and a largely unsounded Haida musical

---

18   What a model of intercultural music that asserts Indigenous cultural significance first would sound like would be interesting to consider. Such a model might disrupt the space

epistemology that, like other Coast Salish beliefs, holds song as accessible only to those who have the cultural and familial rights to sing it, or witness and participate in its performance.

This is not to say that Haida traditions remain entirely absent in *Beyond Eden*. Haida artist Gwaai Edenshaw is credited on the program with creating "Traditionally Inspired Haida Music" for the production. Métis actor Tom Jackson, who plays the role of the Watchman, sings vocables in the song "Mystery," to the same melody previously sung by the Wilson Duff character. Making these inclusions part of the rock-musical aesthetic continues the practice of cultural resourcing that conscripts First Nations cultural practices to "readable" figures. Missing from this inclusion of song is any sense of cultural sovereignty that would maintain the necessity of radical alterity that unsettles the ability to know "Canada's First Peoples." While the visuality of Haida culture is being put on full display (a model of the museum on stage), Haida worldview is sublated sonically by the accessibility of the folk-rock aesthetic. *Beyond Eden* presents Canadian history in the standardized form of the musical, and in doing so exscribes Haida sensory (visual and sonic) logic.[19]

ENTERTAINMENT'S MYSTERY

In scene seven of the first act, Louis Wilson, the anthropologist Wilson Duff's character, sings:

Aroused by this moment.
Excited by my fear.

---

and time of reception—placing the intercultural collaboration within the framework of the longhouse, or of a potlatch, or even, like much Coast Salish traditional ceremony, put into question the "fourth wall" between performance, life, and spirit world.

19   Re-figuring the musical through Haida logic would be an exciting proposition to explore. I am indebted to Daniel Heath Justice for insight regarding Indigenous structural logics he shared during a conversation about the Coast Salish *Magic Flute*, produced by Vancouver Opera in 2007 and 2013.

Knowing that I am moving
Way beyond what's clear
Don't know
Where it's taking me.
It's still a mystery.

Like the feathers floating
On the sea.
A mystery.
A mystery.

And I am awakened,
to this mystery that
wants me.
This mystery
calls me.
This mystery
tempts me.
This mystery
flirts with me.
This mystery
embraces me.

I want this mystery! (*Beyond Eden* workshop draft 29–30)

Arriving at the Vancouver Playhouse that day in the midst of the 2010 Cultural Olympiad to see *Beyond Eden*, I knew I was about to experience a spectacular form of entertainment. I knew I was in for a musical featuring the former lead singer of the band Spirit of the West. What I did not know was that I would stumble into a pre-show talk in which Haida culture was to a significant degree still a "mystery" for the majority of non-Indigenous audience members who were present. In this pre-show discussion with composer Bruce Ruddell and Gwaai Edenshaw, a Haida carver and cultural advisor for the scenography and music, in a packed room of about sixty people, two different audience members expressed what was for them the confusion surrounding the ethics of the removal of the poles. "If we didn't remove them, then how would anyone be able to see them?" said one. "I think Bill Reid did an enormous favour for Canadians by saving those poles and Native culture from dying away" said another. Surely the best course of action for such valuable artworks, emphasized this second audience member, was their protection in the UBC Museum of Anthropology.

At the time I was astonished that these spectators were unaware of the cultural significance the poles have for the Haida. I had assumed a greater depth of public knowledge about the role that poles have for northwest coast First Peoples as physical manifestations of family histories and rights, or in the case of the Haida, that mortuary poles contain the remains of a chief or other high-ranking person. Yet even outside of this context, to remove a tombstone for its aesthetic beauty would be desecrating a gravesite. Why would removing a mortuary pole be any different? In retrospect, we might understand such a view of artistic value as merely consistent with the Bill Reid's iconographic status. The very fact that Reid's sculpture *The Spirit of Haida Gwaii* from 2004 to 2012 adorned the Canadian twenty-dollar bill points toward the status of his work as valued upon (art) economic terms of Canadian identity export. In popular culture and artistic contexts alike, from the Olympic symbol of Ilanaaq to Reid's work more generally, Aboriginal culture has increasingly become part of the branding of Canadian identity. The integration of Aboriginal culture into the circulation of national institutions reframes such cultural practices as no longer a mystery, but a constituent aspect of Canada's official multiculturalism that recognizes First Peoples' contributions as an enrichment to the identity of the nation-state.

And I am awakened,
to this mystery that
wants me.
This mystery
calls me.

This mystery
tempts me.
This mystery
flirts with me.
This mystery
embraces me. (*Beyond Eden* workshop draft 29–30)

I sat, crying out of anger that these poles had been removed. I sat, crying at
the spectacle of the rock musical. I sat, crying at the crowd that had risen to
their feet. Perhaps most of all, I cried in disbelief at the exuberance for mystery
by those around me. The energy of the audience "aroused by this moment"
as they embraced this story of salvage paradigm ethics sat in tension with
other less-palatable moments of mystery of which the general public remains
ignorant—of the continued struggles of First Peoples who fight to repatriate
objects and songs taken from us. I cried in this instance for the lack of recognition that mortuary poles are neither made for the aesthetic pleasure of the
Canadian public, nor for the celebration of Canadian identity. I cried from
the cognitive dissonance between ignorance and affirmation. My crying,
lasting mere moments, marked a transformative experience of resentment.

ON WITNESSING AND RESENTMENT: CANADA'S TRUTH AND RECONCILIATION COMMISSION

Much of how one witnesses and listens at the Truth and Reconciliation
Commission events depends upon certain priorities of responsibility. I began
attending the TRC as a First Nations scholar studying the role that music and
the arts play at these gatherings. But over the course of the TRC events I have
attended my listening responsibilities shifted. At the beginning of each TRC
event Justice Murray Sinclair, chief commissioner of the TRC, calls on those
present to bear witness to what they see and hear and to take the experience
they have at the events back to their communities. For church officials this
may mean their congregations; for MPs this may mean those in their ridings

and other government officials; for residential-school survivors and inter-generational survivors it may mean those members of their families unable to face the brutality of history still viscerally present in their memories. For the settler attendees who have yet to attend TRC gatherings in any substantial way it may mean their families, colleagues, and neighbours. For me, this call to witness has added significance as someone of Stó:lō ancestry. The role of witnessing is central to many Stó:lō traditions including potlatches, naming ceremonies, and funerals. All audiovisual and written recordings of the proceedings are prohibited. Such gatherings involve the host speaker calling selected respected members of the community to witness the ceremony, nominating them by declaring, "You are asked to witness the work that is being done here." In response, the witness will repeat a phrase beginning with the words "Ō Sí:yám" (which is a Halq'eméylem expression of deep thanks and respect). It is a great honour to be chosen to witness, and attentive listening within this context is imperative. Witnesses know that they may be called on in the future to recall what they have seen and heard accurately and truthfully. Witnesses bear Stó:lō history within collective memory.

Many of us whose parents did not attend residential school are still all-too-aware of its legacy. We are in the process of reclaiming a history that many of our parents and grandparents strove to disassociate themselves from out of shame.[20] There have been many times during the TRC that I have been moved, experienced a sense of heightened community, and felt empathy for survivors. But because of this history that intergenerational survivors from my generation have inherited, I have witnessed testimony and listened to music presented at the TRC events not as someone coming to this history for the first time. I have witnessed with the sedimented weight of knowing intergenerational loss. Often I witnessed and listened, with resentment. I have experienced resentment at hearing such remarkably consistent experiences of emotional, physical, and sexual abuse. I have resented the TRC forum itself, where survivors are expected to limit their comments to a contained

---

20 For a more detailed examination of the intergenerational reconciliation taking place within families, see Robinson, "Reconciliation's Senses."

aspect of settler colonialism: residential-school history.[21] I have resented the repeated "contributions" where institutional officials from the Government of Canada, Royal Canadian Mounted Police, and the Catholic Church have abdicated their responsibility. As Dene scholar Glen Coulthard notes, "[R]es-entment is often cast as the inability to come to grips with history. Resentment indicates an inability to let go." And yet "[e]mbracing one's resentment," as Coulthard contests,

> is not only an entirely defendable position, but actually a sign of our critical consciousness, of our sense of justice and injustice, and of our awareness of, and unwillingness to reconcile ourselves with the struc-tural and symbolic violence that is still very much a part of our lives. Of course we should resent colonialism, as well as those people and institutions who are willfully complicit in its ongoing reproduction.

While the majority of artistic and musical contributions taking place at the TRC have not induced such resentment in me as a witness, one in particular seared me with its offer of reconciliation.[22]

O SIEM / WE'RE ALL THE SAME

Unlike mere facts and statistics, the arts have considerable potential to com-pel audience members to reflect deeply on colonial histories of genocide, on

---

21   Despite these restrictions, survivors have not been content to limit their testimony to past residential-school experience; they have used the TRC to voice their opposition against natural-resource development, to address the urgent need to improve substandard living conditions for Aboriginal Peoples on and off reserve, and to call for greater support for education and language revitalization. Notably, survivors have often refused the narra-tive of reconciliation with the nation-state altogether and have instead asked forgiveness of their children for the abuse they carried over into their own parenting.

22   Beverly Diamond's "Resisting Containment" provides a particularly nuanced account of the role that music has played at the TRC national events.

continuing injustices, and on their own accountability to these. The Métis scholar Jo-Ann Episkenew highlights Aboriginal literature's capacity to

> enable settler readers to relate to Indigenous peoples on an emotional level thereby generating empathy. By reading Indigenous literature, settlers come to understand Indigenous people as fellow human beings. Empathy, in turn, has the potential to create a groundswell of support for social-justice initiatives to improve the lot of Indigenous people. (190–91)

Music performance even more so has the ability to foster audience identification and empathy with a colonial history that non-Aboriginal Canadians may feel removed from. Where settler subjects' wilful ignorance of their country's history of colonization persists, and many continue to resist making individual commitments of intergenerational responsibility, the participatory call of music may foment modes of identification that transform perspectives slowly over time. Many scholars have likewise emphasized the ways in which music affords agency for survivors of trauma (Pilzer), provides a way to point toward what lies beyond trauma's representation (Cizmic), and, as Episkenew notes, may provide the first step in settler subjects' future engagement with restorative justice. These perspectives engage with music's *positive* impact upon both survivors of trauma and those who are coming to learn about such colonial histories for the first time. And yet, while music and the arts may indeed engender all of these benefits, I am struck by what I see as an overwhelming presupposition of music's positive efficacy. I am struck most especially because as a listener I can rarely count myself among the audience that feels positively transformed or empathetically moved.

The different kinds of affect that music can generate for audience members became palpable at the Truth and Reconciliation Commission regional event in Victoria, BC, in April 2012. The first day of this event concluded with a series of performances that reflected First Nations cultural traditions from different nations across Vancouver Island. A local Victoria choir also performed, the Gettin' Higher Choir, consisting largely of singers over the age of fifty. They concluded their portion of the evening with a performance of Inuit singer Susan Aglukark's "O Siem," the chorus of which is familiar to many Canadians from its regular presence on easy-listening stations since it rose to number one on the Canadian adult contemporary charts in 1995: "O Siem, we are all family / O Siem, we're all the same."

After eight hours of listening to testimony from survivors and intergenerational survivors, I listened to the Gettin' Higher Choir's contribution toward reconciliation. The concert was intended to lift peoples' spirits after hours of intense testimony from residential-school survivors and intergenerational survivors, and it may have done so for some. Yet to sing this song after a full day's work of telling residential schools' overwhelming history of inhumanity felt not merely inappropriate but like an act of benevolent violence, or what Ghassan Hage calls racial mis-interpellation.[23] The irony in the choir's offering, sung with the best of intentions, is that the history of abuse and cultural oppression in residential schools was anything but "the same" history as that of settler Canadians. Nor is the present reality of Aboriginal communities "the same" as communities elsewhere in Canada. Canadians were not taken from their parents and beaten when they spoke English, were not forced to do manual labour in order to keep their schools running, were not called "dirty Canadian." Canadians, for the most part, do not feel shame at being Canadian, or learn to hide their past from their children.

To look at the faces of the Gettin' Higher Choir was to see belief. The choir's performance, both in message and in its atmosphere of enthusiasm, demonstrated a belief that to sing such a message was enough to make it better, a belief, as Jill Dolan puts it, "that beyond this 'now' of material oppression

---

23   Ghassan Hage outlines racial mis-interpellation as "a drama in two acts: in the first instance the racialized person is interpellated as belonging to a collectivity 'like everybody else.' S/he is hailed by the cultural group or the nation, or even by modernity which claims to be addressing 'everyone.' And the yet-to-be-racialized person believes that the hailing is for 'everyone' and answers the call thinking that there is a place for him or her awaiting to be occupied. Yet, no sooner do they answer the call and claim their spot than the symbolic order brutally reminds them that they are not part of everyone: 'No, I wasn't talking to you. Piss off. You are not part of us' " (122).

and unequal power relations lives a future that might be different, one whose potential we can feel as we're seared by the promise of a present that gestures toward a better later" (*Utopian* 7). The Gettin' Higher Choir's performance here operated within a framework wherein the harmonic resolution of popular song engendered a felt measure of resolution, where the unfriendly difficulty of difference is absent, and where familiar tunes are made even more familiar through their standardized choral arrangement.

The familiarity of "O Siem" takes place, however, at a much deeper level, with the repetition of easy-listening broadcasts across Canada since its release in the early nineties. Its familiar reverberations, furthermore, do not end with a daytime-radio-listening audience. YouTube clips attest to an audience that is much more diverse:

> [I]t's like a tradition to sing this song on our remeberance day concert. all garade 6 and 7s sing it. I remeber doing it in grade 6 and 7 [. . .]

> Were singing this song for my graduation

> we have this song at skool every single morning . . . its stuck in my head. EVERY MORNING. (mishi45)

"O Siem, we are all family. / O Siem, we're all the same."

From Susan Aglukark's diverse public-speaking engagements as an Inuk spokesperson for First Nations and Inuit social issues, a listener might presume that "O Siem" is an Inuktitut phrase. They might, moreover, reasonably believe that the phrase translates somewhere midway between the two phrases of the song—perhaps as "we are all interconnected" or "we're all human"— the perfect message with which to begin a day of school, or to mark those important events and celebratory transitions in life. In actual fact, Aglukark came to learn and use the phrase O Siem, or "Ō Sí:yám" as it is written in Halq'eméylem, from two Sts'ailes Nation (Chehalis) men at Banff:

I first heard and witnessed the actions, the welcoming and honouring of guests, back in 1994 at a conference in Banff, Alberta. I was part of a head table and to my right were two gentlemen from the Chehalis First Nation, before they each spoke, they welcomed and honoured all guests with the words, O Siem, Haitchka, Siem O Siyeya. I was very moved by this and asked for the definition and permission to use the words in a song. (Aglukark)

O Siem's familiarity contrasts the carefully delimited accessibility of Ō Sí:yám as a phrase spoken at ceremonies, potlatches, and other cultural gatherings held by Coast Salish peoples, as well as the Stó:lō. It is said to welcome or honour those who have assembled for a gathering. It affirms the work that is done, and the message that an honourable or high-ranking speaker gives.

In elementary school we were forced to sing this song OVER and OVER again. Every assembly, every multicultural day, every grad, every special presentation, every guest speaker, on random days over the intercom and any other occasion we had this song was played. I must have sung it 100 times. (mishi 45)

O Siem O Siem
A refrain of the Canadian curricula,
Sung every day
Over and over

I never heard Ō Sí:yám
spoken every day,
over and over,
by my mother, by my grandmother
spoken in everyday ways
over and over, with pride

REMAINING SETTLED

Indigenous intercultural music performance holds great power to transform, heal, and provide hope. But the performativity of diversity enunciated in the speech act "we're all the same" also enacts what Sara Ahmed has called the "non-performativity" of diversity. In her analysis of what she calls "diversity work" at British and Australian universities, Ahmed examines how the use of "diversity language" and documents fail to bring about actual institutional diversity. By re-casting Judith Butler's theorization of performativity in the negative, Ahmed describes non-performativity as

> the "reiterative and citational practice by which discourse" *does not* produce "the effects that it names." . . . In the world of the non-performative, to name is not to bring into effect. . . . Such speech acts are taken up *as if* they are performatives (as if they have brought about the effects they name), such that the names come to stand in for the effects. As a result, naming can be a way of not bringing something into effect. (*On Being Included* 117, quoting Butler, *Bodies*, emphasis in original)

Likewise, in providing a system for affirming multiculturalism, a concert of inclusionary music affords audience members not just with a means of listening and seeing diversity on stage, but with an opportunity to participate in diversity. As "utopian non-performatives," inclusionary music may here stand in for more significant forms of action and redress, ones that involve taking up a greater degree of intergenerational responsibility in the acknowledgement of Canada's history of colonization and the reverberations of intergenerational trauma as they play out in Aboriginal communities across Canada.

As Dolan suggests, audience members go to the theatre, concert hall, and gallery in order to feel, to sense something different about the world, whether it is by viewing an exhibition of abstract painting, or seeing the spectacle of a musical. Each represents a different model of politics, and perhaps in certain

instances even micro-utopias, in their non-representational form. As Richard
Dyer notes, the entertainment represented by the musical "does not, however,
present models of utopian worlds . . . Rather the utopianism is contained in
the feelings it embodies. It presents, head-on as it were, what utopia would
feel like rather than how it would be organized" (20, emphasis added). Dyer's
conception of entertainment, says Linda Williams,

> also partly defines wants through its orientation of problems. . . . In
> order to be satisfactorily resolved, the real social problems that these
> categories of the utopian sensibility point to must first be aroused.
> Dyer calls this arousal "playing with fire." His point is that the uto-
> pian entertainment only plays with those fires that the dominant
> power structure—capitalism (and patriarchy)—can put out. (155)

The friendly, non-agonistic kinds of performance discussed in this essay enact a particular kind of utopian performative for settler audiences—one of
"settlement" itself. This feeling of being settled results in a certain ease of being together in which the equilibrium of colonization is maintained. As Tia
DeNora's research cogently outlines, music's positive affordances allow us to
gain equilibrium in our daily life (see especially 46–74). DeNora's *Music in
Everyday Life* shows how listeners often turn music on to calm themselves
after a particularly stressful day, to tune out the rest of the world in daily com-
mutes across cities, and to increase focus while completing tasks. As utopian
performatives of reconciliation, I would argue, such musical affordances may
equally act to foreclose upon change. They may sustain the equilibrium of a
daily life that allows settler audiences to remain settled. In this sense, Dolan's
notion of the utopian performative in Indigenous inclusionary music becomes
constitutive of reconciliation. The affective component of reconciliation engenders great hope, but may do so as an end in itself. Rather than galvanizing
audiences to continued action for restorative justice, these works afford the
feeling of friendship in place of fostering new alliances sought by First Peoples
in nation-to-nation models of political sovereignty.

"O Siem the fires of freedom / Dance in the burning flame"

To celebrate diversity through the affirmation of singing, or to dance in the burning flame as Aglukark's lyrics describe more poetically, brings forth the "Indian problem" as a recognition of inequality. The abundance of generosity in Aglukark's lyrics, of a common humanity, provides the solution: to dance together, to share moments where utopian performatives persuade us that a better future is imminent. As Dolan notes, "[U]topian performatives exceed the *content* of a play or performance; spectators might draw a utopian performative from even the most dystopian theatrical universe" (*Utopia* 165). Equally so, in the above instances it is necessary to grant that utopian *non-performatives*, or even *dystopian* performatives, can be derived from the most utopian musical universes.

TOWARD EMPATHETIC UNSETTLEMENT

For many settler audience members who experience Indigenous art forms, it is a much easier task to embrace the mystery of Indigenous stories and aesthetics than to play a leading role in the eradication of another kind of mystery: that of the ignorance of Indigenous histories of colonization and their lasting effects today. Similarly, it is much easier to believe in the transformative power of such work, to allow the feelings of being transformed to satisfy rather than to unsettle one to the enormous amount of work that must still be done for the felt utopia to become materially present. In acknowledgement of this, I suggest that scholars must remain attendant to our own professional and disciplinary identifications with the music and theatre we write about. We must not forget that we have strong investments with and strong hopes for the power of music and theatre to effect positive change. We feel this change viscerally in our bodies when witnessing, when listening, and when participating in music-making with those communities we work with. But in order not to conflate our own strong hope for change with the realities of struggle faced by Indigenous peoples, it is also imperative that we acknowledge the crudeness of empathy alone.

As Cherokee scholar Craig Womack has noted, while "America loves Native American Culture[,] America is much less enthusiastic about Native American land claims" (11). It is not enough to note the function these performances have in fostering empathy with non-Indigenous Canadians that perhaps allow them to understand and even feel the weight of Indigenous histories in new ways. It is not enough to embrace the mystery of difference. It is not enough to let the embrace of sound surround. It is necessary to move beyond the position of intergenerational bystanders. It is necessary to acknowledge the privilege and power that we hold within our artistic and working communities, and then find ways to give over such power that move beyond forms of inclusion.[24]

the opportunity to speak
Ō Sí:yám

to speak, in everyday ways
over and over

Ō Sí:yám

The necessary steps to return,
for restitution,
involve much more than reconciliation's great embrace
involve more than being touched by sound at a distance
Ō Sí:yám

---

24   This research has been supported by a SSHRC Insight Development project, *The Aesthetics of Reconciliation*, led by Dylan Robinson and Keavy Martin (University of Alberta). This research has been additionally supported by the European Research Council as part of the project "Indigeneity in the Contemporary World: Performance, Politics, Belonging" at Royal Holloway, University of London.

WORKS CITED

Abbate, Carolyn. "Music: Drastic or Gnostic?" *Critical Inquiry* 30.3 (2004): 505–36. Print.

Afia. Personal interview by Natalie Alvarez. Canadian Forces Base Wainwright. 4 May 2011.

Aglukark, Susan. Personal email to Dylan Robinson. 16 Jan. 2013. Email.

Ahmadi, Mohammed. Personal interview by Natalie Alvarez. Canadian Forces Base Wainwright. 1 May 2011.

Ahmed, Sara. *The Cultural Politics of Emotion*. London: Routledge, 2004. Print.

---. *On Being Included: Racism and Diversity in Institutional Life*. Durham, NC: Duke UP, 2012. Print.

---. *Queer Phenomenology: Orientations, Objects, Others*. Durham, NC: Duke UP, 2006. Print.

Alarcón, Norma. "Conjugating Subjects in the Age of Multiculturalism." *Mapping Multiculturalism*. Ed. Avery F. Gordon and Christopher Newfield. Minneapolis: U Minnesota P, 1996. 127–48. Print.

Allemang, John. "The Myth of 1812: How Canadians See The War We Want to See." *Globe and Mail*. Globe and Mail Inc., 10 Mar. 2012. Web. 10 Sept. 2012.

Anderson, Ben. "Becoming and Being Hopeful: Towards a Theory of Affect." *Environment and Planning D: Society and Space* 24 (2006): 733–52. Print.

Anderson, Elizabeth. "Studio D's Imagined Community: From Development (1974) to Realignment (1986–1990)." *Gendering the Nation: Canadian Women's Cinema*. Ed. Kay Armatage, Kass Banning, Brenda Longfellow, and Janine Marchessault. Toronto: U of Toronto P, 1999. 41–61. Print.

Anderson, James, Cpt. Personal interview by Natalie Alvarez. Canadian Forces Base Wainwright. 7 May 2011.

Anderson, Patrick. "I Feel For You." *Neoliberalism and Global Theatres: Performance Permutations.* Ed. Lara D. Nielsen and Patricia Ybarra. New York: Palgrave Macmillan, 2012. 81–96. Print.

Andrade, Cande. "Theatre Replacement Presents BIOBOXES." *YouTube,* 11 Dec. 2008. Web. 2 Jan. 2014.

Anzaldúa, Gloria. *Borderlands/La Frontera: The New Mestiza.* New York: Aunt Lute, 1987. Print.

Archibald, Dan, Adam Smith, Sunny Adams, and Manroop Chawla. "Military Training Lands Historic Context: Training Village, Mock Sites, and Large Scale Operations Areas." Arlington, TX: US Department of Defense, Construction Engineering Research Laboratory (CERL), 2010. PDF file.

Arendt, Hannah. *The Human Condition.* Chicago: U of Chicago P, 1958. Print.

Aristotle. *Rhetoric.* Trans. Thomas Hobbes. *Dramatic Theory and Criticism: Greeks To Grotowski.* Ed. Bernard F. Dukore. New York: Holt, Rinehart and Winston, 1974. Excerpt. 57–62. Print.

Armatage, Kay. "Feminist Film-making: Theory and Practice." *Canadian Women's Studies/Les Cahiers de la Femme* 1.3 (1979): 49–50. Print.

Armatage, Kay, Kass Banning, Brenda Longfellow, and Janine Marchessault. "Gendering the Nation." *Gendering the Nation: Canadian Women's Cinema.* Ed. Armatage, Banning, Longfellow, and Marchessault. Toronto: U of Toronto P, 1999. 3–14. Print.

Artaud, Antonin. "From *A Voyage to the Land of Tarahumara.*" *Antonin Artaud: Selected Writings.* Ed. Susan Sontag. Trans. Helen Weaver. Berkeley: U of California P, 1976. 379–94. Print.

---. *The Theater and Its Double.* Trans. Mary Caroline Richards. New York: Grove, 1958. Print.

Auslander, Philip. *Liveness: Performance in a Mediatized Culture.* New York: Routledge, 2002. Print.

Austin, David. *Fear of a Black Nation: Race, Sex, and Security in Sixties Montreal.* Toronto: Between the Lines, 2013. Print.

Austin, J.L. *How to do Things with Words.* Ed. J.O. Urmson and Marina Sbisà. 2nd ed. Cambridge, MA: Harvard UP, 1975. Print.

Bannerji, Himani. *The Dark Side of the Nation: Essays on Multiculturalism, Nationalism and Gender.* Toronto: Canadian Scholars', 2000. Print.

Barbeau, Marius. *Indian Days in the Canadian Rockies.* Toronto: Macmillan, 1923. Print.

Barthes, Roland. "The Death of the Author." *Image-Music-Text*. Trans. Stephen Heath. New York: Hill and Wang, 1977. 142–48. Print.

Bauman, Richard. "Performance." *International Encyclopedia of Communications, Volume 3*. Ed. Erik Barnouw. New York: Oxford UP, 1989. 262–65. Print.

Beacham, Richard C. *Adolphe Appia: Texts on Theatre*. New York: Routledge, 1993. Print.

Beaudoin, Réjean. *Le roman québécois*. Montreal: Boréal, 1991. Print.

Bennett, Susan. "Theatre Audiences, Redux." *Theatre Survey* 47.2 (2006): 225–30. Print.

Benson, Eugene, and L.W. Conolly. *English-Canadian Theatre*. Toronto: Oxford UP, 1989. Print.

Berlant, Lauren. *The Anatomy of National Fantasy: Hawthorne, Utopia, and Everyday Life*. Chicago: U of Chicago P, 1991. Print.

---. *Cruel Optimism*. Durham, NC: Duke UP, 2011. Print.

---. *The Female Complaint: The Unfinished Business of Sentimentality in American Culture*. Durham, NC: Duke UP, 2008. Print.

---. *The Queen of America Goes To Washington City: Essays on Sex and Citizenship*. Durham, NC: Duke UP, 1997. Print.

---. "The Subject of True Feeling: Pain, Privacy, and Politics." *Cultural Pluralism, Identity Politics, and the Law*. Ed. Austin Sarat and Thomas R. Kearns. Ann Arbor, MI: U of Michigan P, 1999. 49–84. Print.

---. "Thinking about Feeling Historical." *Emotion, Space and Society* 1.1 (2008): 4–9. Print.

Berlin, Graham. Unpublished acting journal. Theatre Department, Concordia University, Sept. 2012. Print.

Bernstein, Robin. "Toward the Integration of Theatre History and Affect Studies: Shame and the Rude Mechs's *The Method Gun*." *Theatre Journal* 64.2 (2012): 213–30. Print.

Beyond Eden. Music and lyrics by Bruce Ruddell and Bill Henderson. Arena Stage, Washington DC. April 2011. Workshop draft.

Beyond Eden. Music and lyrics by Bruce Ruddell and Bill Henderson. Dir. Dennis Garnhum. Vancouver Playhouse, Vancouver. 3 Feb. 2010. Performance.

BIOBOXES. By Theatre Replacement. Created and performed by Anita Rochon, Marco Soriano, Paul Ternes, Cindy Mochizuki, Donna Soares, and Una Memisevic. Dorothy Somerset Studio, University of British Columbia, Vancouver. 1 June 2008. Performance.

BIOBOXES. By Theatre Replacement. Created and performed by Anita Rochon, Marco Soriano, Paul Ternes, Cindy Mochizuki, Donna Soares, and Una Memisevic. Theatre Centre, Toronto. 2 May 2009. Performance.

Blair, Rhonda. *The Actor, Image, and Action: Acting and Cognitive Neuroscience.* New York: Routledge, 2008. Print.

Bloch, Ernst. "Can Hope Be Disappointed?" *Literary Essays.* Ed. Andrew Joron. Stanford, CA: Stanford UP, 1998. 339–45. Print.

Blodgett, E.D. "The Canadian Literatures as a Literary Problem." *Configuration: Essays in the Canadian Literatures.* Downsview, ON: ECW, 1982. 13–38. Print.

Bock-Côté, Mathieu. "Retour sur la querelle du 'blackface.'" *Le blogue de Mathieu Bock-Côté. Le Journal de Montréal.* Quebecor, 31 May 2013. Web. 16 Sept. 2013.

Boler, Megan. "The Risks of Empathy: Interrogating Multiculturalism's Gaze." *Cultural Studies* 11.2 (1997): 253–73. Print.

The Book of Judith Play. Home page. Blogspot, n.d. Web. Jan. 2014.

The Book of Judith. By Michael Rubenfeld with Sarah G. Stanley. Dir. Sarah G. Stanley. Prod. by the Theatre Centre, Absit Omen, and Die In Debt Theatre. Centre for Addiction and Mental Health lawn, Toronto. 29 May 2009. Performance.

Bourque, Gilles. "De Gaulle: politique et stratégie." *Parti Pris* 5.1 (1967): 7–17. Print.

Bower, Elizabeth. "Public Energy presenting Book of Judith on Saturday, Sunday at Market Hall." *Peterborough Examiner.* Sun Media, 19 Jan. 2012. Web. 4 Jan. 2014.

Braidotti, Rosi. "The Ethics of Becoming-Imperceptible." *Deleuze and Philosophy.* Ed. Constantin Boundas. Edinburgh: Edinburgh UP, 2006. 133–59. Print.

Brand, Dionne. *Bread Out of Stone: Recollections, Sex, Recognitions, Race, Dreaming, Politics.* Toronto: Coach House, 1994. Print.

---. *A Map to the Door of No Return: Notes to Belonging.* Toronto: Doubleday Canada, 2001. Print.

---. *Rivers Have Sources, Trees Have Roots: Speaking of Racism.* Toronto: Cross-Cultural Communication Centre, 1986. Print.

Brecht, Bertolt. *Brecht on Art and Politics.* Ed. Tom Kuhn and Steve Giles. Trans. Laura Bradley, Steve Giles, and Tom Kuhn. London: Methuen, 2003. Print.

Breton, Alain. *Rabinal Achi: A Fifteenth-Century Maya Dynastic Drama.* Trans. Teresa Lavender Fagan and Robert Schneider. Boulder: UP of Colorado, 2007. Print.

Bumsted, J.M. *The Red River Rebellion*. Winnipeg: Watson & Dwyer, 1996. Print.

Butler, Judith. "Bodies in Alliance and the Politics of the Street." *Transversal* #occupy and assemble∞ (Oct. 2011): n. pag. Web. 25 Feb. 2014.

---. *Bodies That Matter: On the Discursive Limits of Sex*. New York: Routledge, 1993. Print.

---. *Excitable Speech: A Politics of the Performative*. New York: Routledge, 1997. Print.

---. *Frames of War: When Is Life Grievable?* New York: Verso, 2010. Print.

---. *Gender Trouble: Feminism and the Subversion of Identity*. New York: Routledge, 1990. Print.

---. "Performative Acts and Gender Constitution: An Essay in Phenomenology and Feminist Theory." *Theatre Journal* 40.4 (1988): 519–31. Print.

Byrd. Jodi. A. "Fracturing Futurity: Colonial Agnosia and the Untimely Indigenous Present." University of California San Diego. Ethnic Studies Department, San Diego, CA. 3 Feb. 2012. Lecture.

Cacioppo, John T., et al. "The Psychophysiology of Emotions." *Handbook of Emotions*. Ed. Michael Lewis and Jeannette M. Haviland-Jones. New York: Guilford, 2000: 173–91. Print.

Cadieux, Alexandre, "Acte de mémoire et de dialogue." *Le Devoir*. Le Devoir, 22 Jun. 2010. Web. 13 Jan. 2014.

Campbell, Joseph, with Bill Moyers. *The Power of Myth*. New York: Doubleday, 1988. Print.

Carson, Neil. "Canadian Historical Drama: Playwrights in Search of a Myth." *Studies in Canadian Literature* 2.2 (1977): n. pag. Web. 25 April 2012.

Caruth, Cathy. *Unclaimed Experience: Trauma, Narrative, and History*. Baltimore: Johns Hopkins UP, 1996. Print.

Case, Sue-Ellen. *Feminist and Queer Performance: Critical Strategies*. Basingstoke, England: Palgrave Macmillan, 2009. Print.

Chakravorty, Pallabi. *Bells of Change: Kathak Dance, Women and Modernity In India*. Calcutta: Seagull Books, 2008. Print.

---. "Dance, Pleasure, and Indian Women as Multisensorial Subjects." *Visual Anthropology* 17.1 (2004): 1–17. Print.

Chen, Anita Beltran. *From Sunbelt to Snowbelt: Filipinos in Canada*. Calgary, AB: Canadian Ethnic Studies Association, 1998. Print.

Chow, Rey. "Violence in the Other Country: China as Crisis, Spectacle, and Woman." *Third World Women and the Politics of Feminism*. Ed. Chandra Talpade Mohanty, Ann Russo, and Lourdes Torres. Bloomington: Indiana UP, 1991. 81–100. Print.

Cizmic, Maria. *Performing Pain: Music and Trauma in Eastern Europe*. Oxford: Oxford UP, 2011. Print.

Clarke, George Elliott. *Directions Home: Approaches to African-Canadian Literature*. Toronto: U of Toronto P, 2012. Print.

---. *Fire on the Water: An Anthology of Black Nova Scotian Writing*. Porters Lake, NS: Pottersfield, 1992. Print.

---. *Odysseys Home: Mapping African-Canadian Literature*. Toronto: U of Toronto P, 2002. Print.

Clough, Patricia Ticineto, and Jean Halley, eds. *The Affective Turn: Theorizing the Social*. Durham, NC: Duke UP, 2007. Print.

"CMTC." *Canadian Army*. Government of Canada, 4 May 2012. Web. 10 June 2013.

CMTC Brochure. Ottawa: Department of National Defense, n.d. Print.

Cogswell, Fred. *Charles Mair and his Works*. Toronto: ECW, 1989. Print.

Cole, Catherine M. "American Ghetto Parties and Ghanaian Concert Parties: A Transnational Perspective on Blackface." *Burnt Cork: Traditions and Legacies of Blackface Minstrelsy*. Ed. Stephen Johnson. Amherst, MA: U of Massachusetts P, 2012. 223–50. Print.

---. "Reading Blackface in West Africa: Wonders Taken for Signs." *Critical Inquiry* 23.1 (1996): 183–215. Print.

Cole, Catherine M., and Tracy C. Davis. "Routes of Blackface." *TDR: The Drama Review* 57.2 (2013): 7–12. Print.

Coleman, Daniel. *White Civility: The Literary Project of English Canada*. Toronto: U of Toronto P, 2008. Print.

Coloma, Roland Sintos, et al., eds. *Filipinos in Canada: Disturbing Invisibility*. Toronto: U of Toronto P, 2012. Print.

Compton, Wayde. *After Canaan: Essays on Race, Writing, and Region*. Vancouver: Arsenal Pulp, 2010. Print.

---. *Bluesprint: Black British Columbian Literature and Orature*. Vancouver: Arsenal Pulp, 2001. Print.

---. *Performance Bond.* Vancouver: Arsenal Pulp, 2004. Print.

Conquergood, Dwight. "Performance Studies: Interventions and Radical Research." *TDR: The Drama Review* 46.2 (2002): 145–56. Print.

Coomaraswamy, Ananda, and Opala Kristnayya Duggirala. Introduction. *The Mirror of Gesture: Being the Abhinaya Darpana of Nandikeśvara.* By Nandikeśvara. Trans. Coomaraswamy and Duggirala. New Delhi: Munshiram Manoharlal, 1970. 1–10. Print.

Cornellier, Bruno. "Other Settlers, Settling Others: The Contest Over 'Nativeness' in Quebec's Intercultural Debate." Centre for Globalization and Cultural Studies of the University of Manitoba, Winnipeg, MB. 15 Jan. 2012. Conference Presentation. Web. 20 Sept. 2013.

Coulon, Jocelyn, and Michel Liégeois. "Whatever Happened to Peacekeeping? The Future of a Tradition." *CDFAI.* Canadian Defence & Foreign Affairs Institute, 2010. Web. 10 June 2013.

Coulthard, Glen. "Recognition, Reconciliation and Resentment in Indigenous Politics." Simon Fraser University Goldcorp Centre. 26 Nov. 2011. Lecture.

Coutts, Robert, and Richard Stuart, eds. *The Forks and the Battle of Seven Oaks in Manitoba History.* Winnipeg: Manitoba Historical Society, 1994. Print.

Cowan, T.L. " 'I remember . . . I was wearing leather pants': Archiving the Repertoire of Feminist Cabaret in Canada." *Basements and Attics, Closets and Cyberspace: Explorations in Canadian Women's Archives.* Ed. Linda M. Morra and Jessica Schagerl. Kitchener, ON: Wilfrid Laurier UP, 2012. 65–86. Print.

Cruz, Denise. *Transpacific Femininities: The Making of the Modern Filipina.* Durham, NC: Duke UP, 2012. Print.

Curtis, Charlotte. "Women's Liberation Gets into the Long Island Swim." *New York Times* 10 Aug. 1970: 32. Print.

Cvetkovich, Ann. *An Archive of Feelings: Trauma, Sexuality, and Lesbian Public Cultures.* Durham, NC: Duke UP, 2003. Print.

---. *Depression: A Public Feeling.* Durham, NC: Duke UP, 2012. Print.

Damasio, Antonio. *Looking for Spinoza: Joy, Sorrow, and the Feeling Brain.* San Diego: Harcourt, 2003. Print.

Daniels, Kelly (Red Pheasant First Nation). Oral history told to author. Red Pheasant, SK. 12 Jan. 2008.

Dauphin, Nydia. "Why the Hell Are Quebec Comedians Wearing Blackface?" *The Huffington Post Canada*. AOL, 16 May 2013. Web. 16 Sept. 2013.

Davis, Tracy C. "Performative Time." *Representing the Past: Essays in Performance Historiography*. Ed. Charlotte M. Canning and Thomas Postlewait. Iowa City: U of Iowa P, 2010. 142–67. Print.

---. *Stages of Emergency: Cold War Nuclear Civil Defense*. Durham, NC: Duke UP, 2007. Print.

Deleuze, Gilles, and Michel Foucault. "Intellectuals and Power: A Conversation Between Michel Foucault and Gilles Deleuze." *Language, Counter-Memory, Practice: Selected Essays and Interviews*. Foucault. Ithaca, NY: Cornell UP, 1980. 205–17. Print.

Deleuze, Gilles, and Félix Guattari. *A Thousand Plateaus: Capitalism and Schizophrenia*. Trans. Brian Massumi. Minneapolis: U of Minnesota P, 1987. Print.

DeMallie, Raymond J, ed. *The Sixth Grandfather: Black Elk's Teachings Given to John G. Neihardt*. Lincoln: U of Nebraska P, 1984. Print.

DeNora, Tia. *Music in Everyday Life*. Cambridge, England: Cambridge UP, 2000. Print.

Derian, James Der. "Virtuous War/Virtual Theory." *International Affairs* 76.4 (2000): 771–88. Print.

Diamond, Beverly. "Resisting Containment: Creative Expression and Indian Residential Schools." *Taking Aesthetic Action: Artistic and Sensory Participations Beyond Reconciliation*. Ed. Dylan Robinson and Keavy Martin. Waterloo, ON: Wilfrid Laurier UP, forthcoming. Print.

Diamond, Elin. "Brechtian Theory/Feminist Theory: 'Towards a Gestic Feminist Criticism'" *TDR: The Drama Review* 32.1 (1988): 82–94. Print.

---. "The Violence of 'We': Politicizing Identification." *Critical Theory and Performance*. Ed. Janelle G. Reinelt and Joseph R. Roach. Ann Arbor, MI: U of Michigan P, 2007. 403–12. Print.

Dillard, Annie. *An American Childhood*. New York: Harper Perennial, 2008. Print.

---. Interview by Christiane Charette. *125, Marie-Anne*. Télé-Québec. Montreal, 31 May 2013. Television.

Diouf, Boucar. "Je n'aime pas la fraternité raciale!" *La Presse*. Power Corporation of Canada, 25 May 2013. Web. 3 Jan. 2014.

Dog, Leonard Crow, and Richard Erdoes. *Crow Dog: Four Generations of Sioux Medicine Men*. New York: Harper Perennial, 1995. Print.

Dolan, Jill. "Feeling Women's Culture: Women's Music, Lesbian Feminism, and the Impact of Emotional Memory." *Journal of Dramatic Theory and Criticism* 26.2 (2012): 205–19. Print.

---. "Feminist Performance Criticism and the Popular: Reviewing Wendy Wasserstein." *Theatre Journal* 60.3 (2008): 433–57. Print.

---. *Utopia in Performance: Finding Hope at the Theater.* Ann Arbor, MI: U of Michigan P, 2005. Print.

Dorow, Sara, and Goze Dogu. "The Spatial Distribution of Hope in and Beyond Fort McMurray." *Ecologies of Affect: Placing Nostalgia, Desire, and Hope.* Ed. Tonya K. Davidson, Ondine Park, and Rob Shields. Waterloo, ON: Wilfrid Laurier UP, 2011. 271–92. Print.

Duffek, Karen, and Charlotte Townsend-Gault, eds. *Bill Reid and Beyond: Expanding on Modern Native Art.* Vancouver: Douglas and McIntyre, 2004. Print.

Durocher, Sophie. "Blackface Diouf: un débat idiot." *Le blogue de Sophie Durocher. Le Journal de Montréal.* Quebecor, 27 May 2013. Web. 3 Jan. 2014.

Dyer, Richard. *Only Entertainment.* 2nd ed. London: Routledge, 2002. Print.

Echols, Alice. *Daring to Be Bad: Radical Feminism in America, 1967–1975.* Minneapolis: U of Minnesota P, 1989. Print.

Ekman, Paul. "Basic Emotions." *Handbook of Cognition and Emotion.* Ed. Tim Dalgleish and Mick Power. Sussex, England: John Wiley & Sons, 1999. 45–60. Print.

Ekman, Paul, and Richard J. Davidson, eds. *The Nature of Emotion: Fundamental Questions.* Oxford: Oxford UP, 1994. Print.

Ekman, Paul, and Wallace V. Friesen. *Unmasking the Face.* Los Altos, CA: Malor Books, 2003. Print.

Ekman, Paul, and Erika L. Rosenberg, eds. *What the Face Reveals: Basic and Applied Studies of Spontaneous Expression Using the Facial Action Coding System (FACS).* Oxford: Oxford UP, 1997. Print.

Ellao, Janess Ann J. "Philippines Government Is 'Biggest Human Trafficker.'" *Witness Human Rights.* Blogspot, 29 Apr. 2013. Web. 2 Jan. 2014.

Ellison, Ralph. "Change the Joke and Slip the Yoke." *Shadow and Act.* New York: Random House, 1964. 45–59. Print.

Eng, David L., and David Kazanjian. "Mourning Remains." Introduction. *Loss: The Politics of Mourning.* Ed. Eng and Kazanjian. Berkeley: U of California P, 2003. 1–25. Print.

Episkenew, Jo-Ann. *Taking Back Our Spirits: Indigenous Literature, Public Policy, and Healing*. Winnipeg: U of Manitoba P, 2009. Print.

Fancy, David. *CUT*. Robertson Hall, Folk Arts, St Catharines, ON. 28 Feb 2014. Staged reading.

---. *Khalida*. Sullivan Mahoney Courthouse Theatre, St Catharines, ON. 26 Feb—1 March 2013. Performance.

---. *That Woman*. Sullivan Mahoney Courthouse Theatre, St Catharines, ON. 13–16 April 2011. Performance.

Fee, Margery. "Romantic Nationalism and the Image of Native People in Contemporary English-Canadian Literature." *The Native in Literature*. Ed. Thomas King, Cheryl Calver, and Helen Hoy. Oakville: ECW, 1987. 15–33. Print.

"The Fight For Canada." *The War of 1812*. Government of Canada, 18 Sept. 2012. Web. 2 Jan. 2014.

Filewod, Alan. "National Battles: Canadian Monumental Drama and the Investiture of History." *Modern Drama* 38.1 (1995): 71–86. Print.

---. *Performing Canada: The Nation Enacted in the Imagined Theatre*. Kamloops, BC: UC of the Cariboo, 2002. Print.

Fink, Robert. *Repeating Ourselves: American Minimal Music as Cultural Practice*. Berkeley: U of California P, 2005. Print.

Fischer-Lichte, Erika. "Performing Emotions—How to Conceptualize Emotional Contagion in Performance." 2009. MS.

---. "Theater als 'Emotionsmaschine': Zur Aufführung von Gefühlen." *Koordinaten der Leidenschaft*. Ed. Clemens Risi and Jens Roselt. Berlin: Verlag Theater der Zeit, 2009. 22–50. Print.

---. *The Transformative Power of Performance: A New Aesthetics*. Trans. Saskya Iris Jain. New York: Routledge, 2008. Print.

Flacks, Diane. "Life Is a Five-star Performance; Having Cultivated Her Talent Abroad, Alex Bulmer Plants Her Creative Seed Here." *Toronto Star* 26 May 2009: E06. Print.

Fogelman, Eva. *Conscience and Courage: Rescuers of Jews During the Holocaust*. New York: Anchor, 1994. Print.

Forsyth, Louise H. "Creating Francophone Theatre in Saskatchewan." *West-Words: Celebrating Western Canadian Theatre and Playwriting*. Ed. Moira J. Day. Regina, SK: CPRC P, U of Regina, 2011. 128–39. Print.

Francis, Daniel. *The Imaginary Indian: The Image of the Indian in Canadian Culture.* Vancouver: Arsenal Pulp, 2004. Print.

Fraser, Nancy. *Scales of Justice: Reimagining Political Space in a Globalizing World.* New York: Columbia UP, 2009. Print.

Freud, Sigmund. *Project for a Scientific Psychology.* 1895. *The Standard Edition of the Complete Psychological Works of Sigmund Freud.* Trans. James Strachey. London: Vintage, 2001. 283–346. Print.

Freynet-Agossa, Sophie. "Mise sur pied d'une nouvelle compagnie de théâtre bilingue." *Ici Radio-Canada.* Radio-Canada, 3 Jun. 2011. Web. 12 Feb. 2014.

Fricker, Karen. "À l'Heure zéro de la culture (dés)unie. Problèmes de représentation dans *Zulu Time* de Robert Lepage et Ex Machina." Trans. Rémy Charest. *Globe: Revue internationale d'études québécoises* 11.2 (2008): 81–116. Print.

Gaboriau, Linda. "The Cultures of Theatre." *Culture in Transit: Translating the Literature of Quebec.* Ed. Sherry Simon. Montreal: Véhicule, 1995. 83–90. Print.

Le Gala Les Olivier. Association des professionnels de l'industrie de l'humour. Radio-Canada, Montreal. 12 May 2013. Television.

Garland-Thomson, Rosemarie. *Extraordinary Bodies: Figuring Physical Disability in American Culture and Literature.* New York: Columbia UP, 1997. Print.

Gibson, Katherine, Lisa Law, and Deirdre McKay. "Beyond Heroes and Victims: Filipina Contract Migrants, Economic Activism and Class Transformations." *International Feminist Journal of Politics* 3.3 (2001): 365–86. Print.

Gilday, Katherine. "Review of Short Films." *Cinema Canada* 40 (1977): 57–58. Print.

Gilroy, Paul. *The Black Atlantic: Modernity and Double Consciousness.* Cambridge, MA: Harvard UP, 1993. Print.

The Glass Box. Written and performed by Kyla Harris, Watson Moy, and Susanna Uchatius. Dir. Joanna Garfinkel. Prod. by Theatre Terrific. Playwrights Theatre Centre Studio, Vancouver. 28 Feb. 2009. Performance.

Gobert, R. Darren. "Behaviorism, Catharsis, and the History of Emotion." *Journal of Dramatic Theory and Criticism* 26.2 (2012): 109–25. Web. 30 June 2013.

Godbout, Jacques. "Qui fait vraiment l'"histoire?" *L'Actualité* 24.3 (1999): 95. Print.

Goldie, Terry. *Fear and Temptation: The Image of the Indigene in Canadian, Australian, and New Zealand Literatures.* Montreal: McGill-Queen's UP, 1989. Print.

Goodall, Jane. "The Plague and Its Powers in Artaudian Theatre." *Antonin Artaud: A Critical Reader*. Ed. Edward Scheer. New York: Routledge, 2004. 65–76. Print.

Gordon, Rae Beth. *Dances with Darwin, 1875–1910: Vernacular Modernity in France*. Surrey, England: Ashgate, 2009. Print.

Gorer, Geoffrey. *Death, Grief, and Mourning in Contemporary Britain*. New York: Anchor, 1965. Print.

Graham, Franklin. *Histrionic Montreal: Annals of the Montreal Stage*. Montreal: John Lovell and Son, 1902. Print.

Gregg, Melissa, and Gregory J. Seigworth. "An Inventory of Shimmers." *The Affect Theory Reader*. Ed. Gregg and Seigworth. Durham, NC: Duke UP, 2010. 1–25. Print.

Gregory, Derek. "The Rush to the Intimate: Counterinsurgency and the Cultural Turn in Late Modern War." *Radical Philosophy* 150 (2008): 8–23. Print.

Grimes, Lynda. "Tell Us Why It Matters To You." *TRC*. Truth and Reconciliation Commission of Canada, n.d. Web. 13 Feb. 2014.

Grose, B. Donald. "Edwin Forrest, 'Metamora,' and the Indian Removal Act of 1830." *Theatre Journal* 37.2 (1985): 181–91. Print.

Grossman, Dave, Lt. Col. *On Combat: The Psychology and Physiology of Deadly Conflict in War and in Peace*. Millstadt, IL: Warrior Science Publications, 2008. Print.

Grotowski, Jerzy. Letter to Floyd Favel. Oct. 1988. MS.

---. *Towards a Poor Theatre*. Ed. Eugenio Barba. New York: Routledge, 2002. Print.

Grubisic, Katia. " 'Savage Nations Roam O'er Native Wilds': Charles Mair and the Ecological Indian." *Studies in Canadian Literature* 30.1 (2005): 58–82. Web. 6 Feb. 2014.

Grusin, Richard. *Premediation: Affect and Mediality After 9/11*. New York: Palgrave Macmillan, 2010. Print.

Guattari, Félix. *The Guattari Reader*. Ed. Gary Genosko. London: Blackwell, 1996. Print.

Guevarra, Anna Romina. *Marketing Dreams, Manufacturing Heroes: The Transnational Labor Brokering of Filipino Workers*. New Brunswick, NJ: Rutgers UP, 2010. Print.

Gunew, Sneja. *Haunted Nations: The Colonial Dimensions of Multiculturalism*. London: Routledge, 2004. Print.

Hage, Ghassan. "The Affective Politics of Racial Mis-interpellation." *Theory, Culture & Society* 27.7–8 (2010): 112–29. Print.

Hardy, Dominic. "Historical Ironies of Henri Julien (1852–1908): Researching Identity and Graphic Satire Across Languages in Québec." *Working Papers on Design* 2 (2007): 1–25. Web. 2 Dec. 2013.

Harel, Simon. "Les loyautés conflictuelles de la littérature québécoise." *Québec Studies* 44 (2007/2008): 41–52. Print.

Harper, Stephen. "Prime Minister's Message." *The War of 1812*. Government of Canada, 15 Sept. 2012. Web. 24 Aug. 2013.

Harrington, Peter. "Portraying Maneuvers and Mock Battles." *MHQ* 19.3 (2007): 76–81. Print.

Harris, Kyla, Watson Moy, and Susanna Uchatius. *The Glass Box. Once More, With Feeling: Five Affecting Plays*. Ed. Erin Hurley. Toronto: Playwrights Canada, 2014. 149–94. Print.

Harris-Perry, Melissa. *Sister Citizen: Shame, Stereotypes, and Black Women in America*. New Haven, CT: Yale UP, 2011. Print.

Hartman, Saidiya V. *Scenes of Subjection: Terror, Slavery, and Self-Making in Nineteenth-Century America*. Oxford: Oxford UP, 1997. Print.

Hauser, Gwen. "Jill Johnston's Fall." *The Body Politic* 37 (1977): 16. Print.

Hébert, Chantal. *Le burlesque au Québec: Un divertissement populaire*. Montreal: HMH Hurtubise, 1981. Print.

---. *Le burlesque québécois et américain: textes inédits*. Québec: Presses Université Laval, 1989. Print.

Henderson, Jennifer, and Pauline Wakeham. "Colonial Reckoning, National Reconciliation?: First Peoples and the Culture of Redress in Canada." *English Studies in Canada* 35.1 (2009): 1–26. Print.

Hendrikse, Jesse. Personal interview by Natalie Alvarez. Canadian Forces Base Wainwright. 5 May 2011.

Hesford, Victoria. *Feeling Women's Liberation*. Durham, NC: Duke UP, 2013. Print.

Hile, Rachel E. "Disability and the Characterization of Katherine in *The Taming of the Shrew*." *Disability Studies Quarterly* 29.4 (2009): n.pag. Web. 23 Mar. 2012.

Hochschild, Arlie Russell. "Love and Gold." *Global Woman: Nannies, Maids, and Sex Workers in the New Economy*. Ed. Barbara Ehrenreich and Hochschild. New York: Henry Holt, 2002. 15–30. Print.

---. *The Managed Heart: Commercialization of Human Feeling*. Berkeley: U of California P, 1983. Print.

"Home." *Porte Parole*. Porte Parole, n.d. Web. 9 Jan. 2014.

hooks, bell. *Yearning: Race, Gender, and Cultural Politics*. Boston: South End, 1990. Print.

Hurley, Erin. *Theatre & Feeling*. Basingstoke, England: Palgrave Macmillan, 2010. Print.

Hurley, Erin, and Sara Warner. "Affect/Performance/Politics." *Journal of Dramatic Theory and Criticism* 26.2 (2012): 99–107. Print.

An Iliad. La Jolla Playhouse. N.d. Web. 1 Apr. 2013.

Irigaray, Luce. *This Sex Which is Not One*. Trans. Catherine Porter. Ithaca, NY: Cornell UP, 1985. Print.

It Matters to Me. Town-hall session at the Truth and Reconciliation Commission Victoria Regional Event, Victoria Convention Centre, BC. 13 Apr. 2010.

Izard, Carroll E., and K.A. King. "Differential Emotions Theory." *Oxford Companion to Emotion and the Affective Sciences*. Ed. David Sander and Klaus R. Scherer. New York: Oxford UP, 2009. 117–19. Print.

Jacques, Alain. *Fort Mac, English version*. Winnipeg, 2011. DVD.

---. *Fort Mac, French version*. Winnipeg, 2011. DVD.

---. "Rép: Les miniDV Fort Mac et Les Disparus." Message to Nicole Nolette. 13 May 2013. Email.

Jill Johnston: October 1975. Dir. Kay Armatage and Lydia Wazana. K&L and Premiere Operating Productions, 1977. Film.

Johnson, Stephen. "Introduction: The Persistence of Blackface and the Minstrel Tradition." *Burnt Cork: Traditions and Legacies of Blackface Minstrelsy*. Ed. Johnson. Amherst, MA: U of Massachusetts P, 2012. 1–17. Print.

Johnston, Caleb, and Geraldine Pratt. "Nanay (Mother): A Testimonial Play." *Cultural Geographies* 17.1 (2010): 123–33. Print.

Johnston, Jill. *Admission Accomplished: The Lesbian Nation Years, 1970–75*. London: Serpent's Tail, 1998. Print.

---. *Gullibles Travels*. New York: Links, 1974. Print.

---. *Lesbian Nation: The Feminist Solution*. New York: Simon and Schuster, 1973. Print.

Johnston, Kirsty. *Stage Turns: Canadian Disability Theatre*. Montreal: McGill-Queen's UP, 2012. Print.

Jubinville, Yves. "La formation théâtrale à l'épreuve de l'interdisciplinarité au Québec." *Les nouvelles formations de l'interprète: Théâtre, danse, cirque, marionnettes.* Ed. Anne-Marie Gourdon. Paris: CNRS Editions, 2004. 133–45. Print.

Julien, Henri. "Songs of the By-Town Coons." Reproduced from the *Montreal Star.* 1899. LAC Catalogue, Canadian Libraries. Microfilm.

Kane, Sarah. *Phaedra's Love. Sarah Kane: Complete Plays.* London: Methuen, 2001. 63–103. Print.

Kaplan, E. Ann. *Trauma Culture: The Politics of Terror and Loss in Media and Literature.* Piscataway, NJ: Rutgers UP, 2005. Print.

Kaplan, Jon. "Disabling Myths." *NOW Magazine.* NOW Communications, 20 May 2009. Web. 30 Oct. 2012.

Kelly, Brendan. "A Bye Bye Apology." *The Gazette.* Postmedia, 9 Jan. 2009. Web. 3 Jan. 2014.

Kelly, Philip. "Transitioning to the 'Open' Labour Market: Governance Regimes and Employment Opportunities for Former Live-in Caregivers in Canada." Annual Meetings of the Association of American Geographers. Los Angeles. Apr. 2013. Conference paper.

Kelly, Philip, Milla Astorga-Garcia, Enrico F. Esguerra, and the Community Alliance for Social Justice, Toronto. *Explaining the Deprofessionalized Filipino: Why Filipino Immigrants Get Low-Paying Jobs in Toronto.* Toronto: CERIS, 2009. PDF file. CERIS Working Paper Series 75.

Kelly, Philip, Stella Park, Conely de Leon, and Jeff Priest. "Profile of Live-in Caregiver Immigrants to Canada, 1993–2009." TIEDI (Toronto Immigrant Employment Data Initiative), York University, Toronto. 18 Mar. 2011. PDF file.

Keltner, Dacher, and Paul Ekman. "Facial Expression of Emotion." *Handbook of Emotions.* 2nd edition. Ed. Michael Lewis and Jeannette Haviland-Jones. New York: Guilford, 2000. 236–49. Print.

Kim, Christine. "Performing Asian Canadian Intimacy: Theatre Replacement's *Bioboxes* and Awkward Multiculturalisms." *Asian Canadian Theatre.* Ed. Nina Lee Aquino and Ric Knowles. Toronto: Playwrights Canada, 2011. 183–94. Print. New Essays on Canadian Theatre 1.

Kittay, Eva Feder. "The Global Heart Transplant and Caring Across Borders." *The Southern Journal of Philosophy* 46 (2008): 138–65. Print.

Klinck, Carl F., ed. *Tecumseh: Fact and Fiction in Early Records.* Ottawa: Tecumseh, 1978. Print.

Knebel, Maria. *Analyse-Active.* Paris: Actes Sud, 2006. Print.

Knowles, Ric. *Theatre & Interculturalism*. Basingstoke, England: Palgrave Macmillan, 2010. Print.

Kramer, Lawrence. *Musical Meaning: Toward a Critical History*. Vol. 1. Berkeley: U of California P, 2001. Print.

Krulak, Charles C. "The Strategic Corporal: Leadership in the Three Block War." *Marines Magazine* Jan. (1999): n. pag. Web. 31 Dec. 2013.

Laban, Rudolf. *The Mastery of Movement*. London: MacDonald and Evans, 1960. Print.

LaCoste, Monique. "Rien de nouveau sous le soleil." *Saint-Boniface 1908–2008: Reflets d'une ville*. Ed. André Fauchon and Carol J. Harvey. Winnipeg: Presses universitaires de Saint-Boniface, 2008. 63–69. Print.

Lagacé, Patrick. "Une fois, c'est un Noir dans un gala..." *La Presse*. Power Corporation of Canada, 27 May 2013. Web. 3 Jan. 2014.

Lalonde, Michèle. *Speak White*. Montreal: L'Hexagone, 1974.

Lane, Jill, and Marcial Godoy-Anativia, eds. *Race and Its Others*. Spec. issue of *e-misférica* 5.2 (2008). Web. 3 Dec. 2013.

Lane-Mercier, Gillian. "Dislocations affectives de la littérature anglo-québécoise." *Québec Studies* 44 (2007/2008): 21–40. Print.

Laquian, Eleanor del Rio, and Aprodicio A. Laquian. *Seeking a Better Life Abroad: A Study of Filipinos in Canada, 1957–2007*. Manila, Philippines: Anvil, 2008. Print.

Latham, David. "Charles Mair." *Dictionary of Canadian Biography*. Vol. 15. University of Toronto/Université Laval, 2005. Web. 20 Sept. 2012.

Leclerc, Catherine, and Nicole Nolette. "Pour et contre la traduction: *L'homme invisible/The Invisible Man* de Patrice Desbiens." *Traduire-écrire: histoire, poétiques, anthropologie*. Ed. Arnaud Bernadet and Philippe Payen de la Garanderie. Lyon, France: ENS Éditions, forthcoming. Print.

Leclerc, Catherine, and Sherry Simon. "Zones de contact: Nouveaux regards sur la littérature anglo-québécoise." *Voix et Images* 30.3 (2005): n. pag. Web. 24 Jul. 2013.

LeDoux, Joseph. *The Emotional Brain: The Mysterious Underpinnings of Emotional Life*. New York: Touchstone, 1996. Print.

Lévi-Strauss, Claude. "Structuralism and Myth." *The Kenyon Review* 3.2 (1981): 64–88. Print.

Levin, Laura, et al. "Performing Outside of the Box." *Canadian Theatre Review* 137 (2009): 61–67. Print.

Levinas, Emmanuel. *Otherwise Than Being or Beyond Essence*. Trans. Alphonso Lingis. Boston: Martinus Nijhoff, 1981. Print.

---. *Totality and Infinity*. Trans. Alphonso Lingis. Pittsburgh: Duquesne UP, 1969. Print.

Lhamon Jr., W.T. "Turning Around Jim Crow." *Burnt Cork: Traditions and Legacies of Blackface Minstrelsy*. Ed. Stephen Johnson. Amherst, MA: U of Massachusetts P, 2012. 18–50. Print.

Lionnet, Françoise, and Shu-mei Shih. "Thinking Through the Minor, Transnationally." Introduction. *Minor Transnationalism*. Ed. Lionnet and Shih. Durham, NC: Duke UP, 2005. 1–26. Print.

Littlewood, Joan. *Joan's Book: Joan Littlewood's Peculiar History As She Tells It*. London: Methuen, 1994. Print.

Litwin, Grania. "Disabled, Yes, but Sensual—and Brave." *Victoria Times Colonist* 16 Mar. 2007: A3. Print.

Ljunggren, David. "Every G20 Nation Wants To Be Canada, Insists PM." *Reuters*. Thomson Reuters, 25 Sept. 2009. Web. 6 July 2012.

Lo, Jacqueline, and Helen Gilbert. "Toward a Topography of Cross-Cultural Theatre Praxis." *TDR: The Drama Review* 46.3 (2002): 31–53. Print.

Locas, Janis. *La maudite Québécoise: roman nationaliste*. Montreal: Triptyque, 2010. Print.

Loomba, Ania. *Colonialism/Postcolonialism*. London: Routledge, 2000. Print.

Lorde, Audre. *Zami; Sister Outsider; Undersong*. New York: Quality Paperback, 1993. Print.

Lott, Eric. *Love and Theft: Blackface Minstrelsy and the American Working Class*. New York: Oxford UP, 1993. Print.

Lussier, Judith. "Les Québécois, tous des racistes." *Métro*. Transcontinental Media, 23 May 2013. Web. 16 Sept. 2013.

Lynch, Dennis A. "Rhetorics of Proximity: Empathy in Temple Grandin and Cornel West." *Rhetoric Society Quarterly* 28.1 (1998): 5–23. Print.

Mackey, Eva. *The House of Difference: Cultural Politics and National Identity in Canada*. Toronto: U of Toronto P, 2002. Print.

Mackey, Frank. *Black Then: Blacks and Montreal, 1780s–1880s*. Montreal: McGill-Queen's UP, 2004. Print.

Mair, Charles. Preface. *Dreamland and Other Poems and Tecumseh: A Drama*. By Mair. Toronto: U of Toronto P, 1974. 3–6. Print.

---. *Tecumseh: A Drama. Dreamland and Other Poems and Tecumseh: A Drama.* Toronto: U of Toronto P, 1974. 1–127. Print.

Marcel, Gabriel. *Being and Having: An Existentialist Diary.* New York: Harper & Row, 1965. Print.

Martin, Randy. *Critical Moves: Dance Studies in Theory and Politics.* Durham, NC: Duke UP, 1998. Print.

Massumi, Brian. "The Future Birth of the Affective Fact: The Political Ontology of Threat." *The Affect Theory Reader.* Ed. Melissa Gregg and Gregory J. Seigworth. Durham, NC: Duke UP, 2010. 52–70. Print.

---. "Navigating Movements." *Hope: New Philosophies for Change.* By Mary Zournazi. New York: Routledge, 2002. 210–44. Print.

---. *Parables for the Virtual: Movement, Affect, Sensation.* Durham, NC: Duke UP, 2002. Print.

Mayes, Alison. "City of Shattered Dreams Not Much Fun To Visit." *Winnipeg Free Press* 18 Jun. 2011: G3. Print.

McFate, Montgomery. "Anthropology and Counterinsurgency: The Strange Story of Their Curious Relationship." *Military Review* 85.2 (2005): 24–37. Print.

McKenzie, Jon. *Perform Or Else: From Discipline to Performance.* New York: Routledge, 2001. Print.

Mejica, Casey. "Ohbijou News." *Ohbijou.* 16 Aug. 2013. Web. 30 Jan. 2014.

Meisel, Martin. *Realizations: Narrative, Pictorial, and Theatrical Arts in Nineteenth-Century England.* Princeton, NJ: Princeton UP, 1983. Print.

Mercier Voyer, Stephanie. "I Wore Blackface in Quebec and Everybody Loved It." *Vice.* Vice Media, 17 June 2013. Web. 16 Sept 2013.

Merleau-Ponty, Maurice. *Phenomenology of Perception.* Trans. Colin Smith. London: Routledge and Kegan Paul, 1962. Print.

Mezei, Kathy. "Thinking about Canadian Literary Translation: Bridges, Passageways, Arcades and Doors." *Traduire depuis les marges/Translating from the Margins.* Ed. Denise Merkle, Jane Koustas, Glen Nichols, and Sherry Simon. Montreal: Nota Bene, 2008. 27–43. Print.

Migliarisi, Anna. "The Hidden History of Stanislavsky in Canada." *New Canadian Realisms.* Ed. Roberta Barker and Kim Solga. Toronto: Playwrights Canada, 2012. 16–31. Print. New Essays on Canadian Theatre 2.

Miłosz, Czesław. "Ruins of Poetry." *The Witness of Poetry*. Cambridge, MA: Harvard UP, 1983. 77–99.

Minnick, Michelle, and Paula Murray Cole. "The Actor as Athlete of The Emotions: The Rasaboxes Exercise." *Movement for Actors*. Ed. Nicole Potter. New York: Allworth, 2002. 214–26. Print.

mishi45. "Susan Aglukark: O Siem." *YouTube*. Google, 23 Aug. 2008. Web. 30 Oct. 2012.

"Mission." *Ondinnok*. Les Productions Ondinnok, n.d. Web. 10 Dec. 2013.

Mohanty, Chandra Talpade. "Under Western Eyes: Feminist Scholarship and Colonial Discourses." *Boundary 2* 12.3/13.1 (1984): 333–58. Print.

Muni, Bharata. *The Natyashastra*. Trans. Manomohan Ghosh. Vol. 1. Calcutta: Asiatic Society of Bengal, 1951. Print.

---. *The Natyashastra*. Trans. Adya Rangacharya. New Delhi: Munshiram Manoharial, 1996. Print.

Muñoz, José Esteban. *Cruising Utopia: The Then and There of Queer Futurity*. New York: New York UP, 2009. Print.

---. "Feeling Brown: Ethnicity and Affect in Ricardo Bracho's *The Sweetest Hangover (and Other STDs)*." *Theatre Journal* 52.1 (2000): 67–79. Print.

---. "Feeling Brown, Feeling Down: Latina Affect, the Performativity of Race, and the Depressive Position." *Signs* 31.3 (2006): 675–88. Print.

"Nanay: A Testimonial Play." *Dr. Caleb Johnston*. N.d. Web. 11 Feb. 2014.

Neuerburg-Denzer, Ursula. "Emotions in Performance: Between Rape and Research Lab." *InTensions* 1 (2008): 1–20. Web. 3 Feb. 2014.

---. "Faking Suicide: Emotion Training for Jocasta's Cathartic Death." *Theatre, Dance and Performance Training* 2.2 (2011): 198–214. Print.

"New Restaurant on Esplanade Riel Gets a Name." *Winnipeg Sun*. Sun Media, 24 Mar. 2013. Web. 21 May 2013.

Newlove, Jean, and John Dalby. *Laban For All*. New York: Routledge, 2004. Print.

Nield, Sophie. "On the Border as Theatrical Space: Appearance, Dis-location and the Production of the Refugee." *Contemporary Theatres in Europe: A Critical Companion*. Ed. Joe Kelleher and Nicholas Ridout. London: Routledge, 2006. 61–72. Print.

Nigam, Sunita. "Not Just For Laughs: Sugar Sammy, Stand-Up Comedy, and National Performance." *Québec Studies* Special Issue (Winter 2013): 117–33. Print.

"O Siem." Music and lyrics by Susan Aglukark. Choral adaptation by the Gettin' Higher Choir. Truth and Reconciliation Commission Victoria Regional Event, Carson Hall, Victoria Convention Centre, BC. 13 Apr. 2010. Performance.

Olivelle, Patrick. "Explorations in the Early History of the Dharmasastra." *Between the Empires: Society in India 300 BCE to 400 BCE*. Ed. Olivelle et al. Oxford: Oxford UP, 2006. 169–90. Print.

Oliver, Kelly. *Witnessing: Beyond Recognition*. Minneapolis: U of Minnesota P, 2001. Print.

"Olympic Truce." *Olympic*. IOC, n.d. Web. 2 Jan. 2014.

Ouzounian, Richard. "Taming of the Shrew Limps Along." *Toronto Star*. Torstar, 2 Jun. 2008. Web. 15 May 2011.

Pallister, Janis L. *The Cinema of Québec: Masters in Their Own House*. Madison, NJ: Fairleigh Dickinson UP, 1995. Print.

Panagia, Davide. *The Political Life of Sensation*. Durham, NC: Duke UP, 2009. Print.

Pande, Anupa. *A Historical and Cultural Study of the Natyashastra of Bharata*. Jodhpur, India: Kusumanjali Prakashan, 1996. Print

Panksepp, Jaak. *Affective Neuroscience: The Foundations of Human and Animal Emotions*. Oxford: Oxford UP, 1998. Print.

Pavlov, Ivan. "Lecture II." *Conditioned Reflexes*. 1927. Trans. G.V. Anrep. *Classics in the History of Psychology*. York University, n.d. Web. 15 Oct. 2013.

Pedwell, Carolyn. "Affect at the Margins: Alternative Empathies in *A Small Place*." *Emotion, Space and Society* 8 (2013): 18–26. Print.

Performing Ecstasy. Krishna Worship in Dance Drama, Poetry and Architecture. Swarthmore College, Swarthmore, PA. 2004. Symposium.

Perry-Fagant, Natasha. Unpublished acting journal. Theatre Department, Concordia University. Winter 2013.

Philip, M. NourbeSe. *Zong!* Middletown, CT: Wesleyan UP, 2008. Print.

Pilzer, Joshua D. *Hearts of Pine: Songs in the Lives of Three Korean Survivors of the Japanese "Comfort Women."* Oxford: Oxford UP, 2012. Print.

Piscator, Erwin. *The Political Theatre*. Trans. Hugh Rorrison. New York: Avon Books, 1978. Print.

Plutchik, Robert. *Emotions and Life: Perspectives from Psychology, Biology, and Evolution*. Washington, DC: American Psychological Association, 2002. Print.

Potvin, Maryse. "Interethnic Relations and Racism in Quebec." *Quebec Questions*. Ed. Stéphan Gervais, Christopher Kirkey, and Jarrett Rudy. Oxford: Oxford UP, 2011. 267–86. Print.

Pratt, Geraldine. *Families Apart: Migrant Mothers and the Conflicts of Labor and Love*. Minneapolis: U of Minnesota P, 2012. Print.

Pratt, Geraldine, and Caleb Johnston. *Nanay (Mother): A Testimonial Play. Once More, With Feeling: Five Affecting Plays*. Ed. Erin Hurley. Toronto: Playwrights Canada, 2014. 49–90. Print.

---. "Translating Research into Theatre: *Nanay, A Testimonial Play*." *B.C. Studies* 163 (2009): 123–32. Print.

Pratt, Geraldine, and Caleb Johnston in collaboration with the Philippine Women Centre of BC. *Nanay: A Testimonial Play*. 2013. TS.

Pratt, Mary Louise. "Arts of the Contact Zone." *Profession* (1991): 33–40. Print.

---. "Linguistic Utopias." *The Linguistics of Writing: Arguments Between Language and Literature*. Ed. Nigel Fabb. Manchester: Manchester UP, 1987. 48–66. Print.

Prescott, Marc. *Fort Mac: théâtre*. Saint-Boniface, MB: Éditions du Blé, 2009. Print.

Prinz, Jesse. *Gut Reactions: A Perceptual Theory of Emotion*. Oxford: Oxford UP, 2004. Print.

Probyn, Elspeth. "Writing Shame." *The Affect Theory Reader*. Ed. Melissa Gregg and Gregory J. Seigworth. Durham, NC: Duke UP, 2010. 71–90. Print.

"Production document: *Time to Put My Socks On*." 26 May 2013. PDF file.

Prokosh, Kevin. "You'd Swear the Slight Plot Creates an Emotional Flatline." *Winnipeg Free Press* 17 Nov. 2012: G4. Print.

"Rabinal Achí Dance Drama Tradition." *Unesco*. Unesco, n.d. Web. 10 Dec. 2010.

Rammal, Rabii. "Chère Nydia." *Urbania*. Urbania, 30 May 2013. Web. 16 Sept. 2013.

Rancière, Jacques. *Disagreement: Politics and Philosophy*. Trans. Julie Rose. Minneapolis: U of Minnesota P, 1999. Print.

---. *Dissensus: On Politics and Aesthetics*. Ed. and trans. Steven Corcoran. London: Continuum, 2010. Print.

---. *The Emancipated Spectator*. Trans. Gregory Elliott. London: Verso, 2009. Print.

---. *The Politics of Aesthetics: The Distribution of the Sensible*. Trans. Gabriel Rockhill. London: Continuum, 2004. Print.

Ravary, Lise. "Mario Jean n'est pas un raciste, OK?" *Le blogue de Lise Ravary. Le Journal de Montréal*. Quebecor, 27 May 2013. Web. 3 Jan. 2014.

"RAWA Photo Gallery." *Revolutionary Association of the Women of Afghanistan (RAWA)*. RAWA, n.d. Web. 23 Apr. 2012.

Ray, Arthur J. *An Illustrated History of Canada's Native People: I Have Lived Here Since the World Began*. Toronto: Key Porter, 2010. Print.

Razack, Sherene H. *Dark Threats and White Knights: The Somalia Affair, Peacekeeping, and the New Imperialism*. Toronto: U of Toronto P, 2004. Print.

"Reconciliation . . . Towards a New Relationship." *TRC*. Truth and Reconciliation Commission of Canada, n.d. Web. 1 May 2013.

Rembis, Michael A. "Beyond the Binary: Rethinking the Social Model of Disabled Sexuality." *Sexuality and Disability* 28.1 (2010): 51–60. Print.

Ridout, Nicholas. *Stage Fright, Animals, and Other Theatrical Problems*. Cambridge, England: Cambridge UP, 2006. Print.

---. "Welcome to the Vibratorium." *The Senses & Society* 3.2 (2008): 221–31. Print.

Rivers, Bryan. "Able Directing Does Justice To Ambitious Play." *Winnipeg Free Press* 24 Feb. 2008: D8. Print.

Roach, Joseph. *Cities of the Dead: Circum-Atlantic Performance*. New York: Columbia UP, 1996. Print.

---. *The Player's Passion: Studies in the Science of Acting*. Ann Arbor, MI: U of Michigan P, 1985. Print.

Robinson, Dylan. "Intercultural Art Music and the Sensory Veracity of Reconciliation: Brent Michael Davids' *Powwow Symphony* on the Dakota Music Tour." *MUSICultures* 39.1 (2012): 111–28. Print.

---. "Listening To the Politics of Aesthetics: Contemporary Encounters Between First Nations/Inuit and Early Music Traditions." *Aboriginal Music in Contemporary Canada: Echoes and Exchanges*. Ed. Anna Hoefnagels and Beverly Diamond. Montreal: McGill-Queen's UP, 2012. 222–48. Print.

---. "Reconciliation's Senses." *Taking Aesthetic Action*. Ed. Dylan Robinson and Keavy Martin. Waterloo, ON: Wilfrid Laurier UP, forthcoming. Print.

Rodriquez, Robyn. *Migrants for Export: How the Philippine State Brokers Labor to the World*. Minneapolis: U of Minnesota P, 2010. Print.

Roediger, David. *Working Toward Whiteness: How America's Immigrants Became White*. New York: Basic Books, 2005. Print.

Rorty, Richard. "Human Rights, Rationality, and Sentimentality." *On Human Rights: The Oxford Amnesty Lectures 1993*. Ed. Stephen Shute and Susan Hurley. New York: Basic Books, 1993. 111–34. Print.

Ross, Becki. *The House That Jill Built: A Lesbian Nation in Formation*. Toronto: U of Toronto P, 1995. Print.

Ruddell, Bruce. Personal interview by Dylan Robinson. Victoria, BC. 1 Sep. 2012.

Rushforth, Brett. *Bonds of Alliance: Indigenous and Atlantic Slaveries in New France*. Chapel Hill: U of North Carolina P, 2012. Print.

Sabir. Personal interview by Natalie Alvarez. 4 May 2011.

Salter, Denis. "Body Politics: English-Canadian Acting at National Theatre School." *Canadian Theatre Review* 71 (1992): 4–14. Print.

Salverson, Julie. "Ethics Notebook." 1998. MS.

Schafer, R. Murray. *The Soundscape*. Rochester, V.T: Destiny Books, 1977. Print.

Schechner, Richard. *Between Theater and Anthropology*. Philadelphia: U of Pennsylvania P, 1985. Print.

---. "Magnitudes of Performance." *By Means of Performance: Intercultural Studies of Theatre and Ritual*. Ed. Richard Schechner and Willa Appel. Cambridge, England: Cambridge UP, 1990. 19–49. Print.

---. "Rasaesthetics." *TDR: The Drama Review* 45:3 (2001): 27–50. Print.

Schneider, Rebecca. *Performing Remains: Art and War in Times of Theatrical Reenactment*. New York: Routledge, 2011. Print.

Schwartz, Susan L. *Rasa: Performing the Divine in India*. New York: Columbia UP, 2004. Print.

Scott, Jill. *A Poetics of Forgiveness: Cultural Responses to Loss and Wrongdoing*. Basingstoke, England: Palgrave Macmillan, 2010. Print.

Scott, Michael. "CanDoCo Unable to Impress." *Vancouver Sun* 22 May 1999: C24. Print.

Sedgwick, Eve Kosofsky, and Adam Frank. "Shame in the Cybernetic Fold: Reading Silvan Tomkins." *Critical Inquiry* 21.2 (1995): 496–522. Print.

---, eds. *Shame and Its Sisters: A Silvan Tomkins Reader*. Durham, NC: Duke UP, 1995.

Seeds. By Annabel Soutar. Dir. Chris Abraham. Centaur Theatre, Montreal. 16 Nov. 2013. Performance.

Shain, Alan. "Time To Put My Socks On." *Alan Shain: Smashing stereotypes ... one audience at a time!* N.d. Web. 10 Jan. 2014.

Shrive, Norman. *Charles Mair: Literary Nationalist*. Toronto: U of Toronto P, 1965. Print.

Siddle, Bruce K. *Sharpening the Warrior's Edge: The Psychology and Science of Training*. Illinois: PPCT Research, 1995. Print.

Siebers, Tobin. *Disability Aesthetics*. Ann Arbor, MI: U of Michigan P, 2010. Print.

---. *Disability Theory*. Ann Arbor, MI: U of Michigan P, 2008. Print.

Sikand, Nandini. "Examining Intention: The Use of Rasa in Odissi Dance." Performance Studies International 13. New York, NY. 10 Nov. 2007. Conference presentation.

Simon, Sherry. *Cities in Translation: Intersections of Language and Memory*. New York: Routledge, 2012. Print.

Sineux, William. "Parler relève et français." *La Liberté* 2 May 2012: 16. Print.

Singal, R.L. *Aristotle and Bharata: A Comparative Study of Their Theories of Drama*. Punjab, India: V.V.R.I. Press, 1977. Print.

Sioui Durand, Yves. Personal interview by Julie Burelle. 25 Jun. 2010.

---. "Programme Note." *Xajoj Tun Rabinal Achi*. 2010. Print.

Sirois, Antoine. *Mythes et symboles dans la littérature québécoise*. Montreal: Triptyque, 1992. Print.

Small, Christopher. *Musicking: The Meanings of Performing and Listening*. Middletown, CT: Wesleyan UP, 1998. Print.

Smith, Owen. "Shifting Apollo's Frame: Challenging the Body Aesthetic in Theater Dance." *Bodies in Commotion: Disability & Performance*. Ed. Carrie Sandahl and Philip Auslander. Ann Arbor, MI: U of Michigan P, 2005. 71–85. Print.

Snow, Judith. "CBC Metro Morning Interview." *YouTube*, 27 May 2009. Web. 2 Jan. 2014.

Sobritchea. Carolyn I., with Dino Alberto Subingsubing and Amara T. Quesada. *Health of Our Heroes: Qualitative Study on Access to Sexual and Reproductive Health Services and Information of Women Migrant Domestic Workers*. Quezon City, Philippines: Action for Health Initiatives and IDRC, 2010. Print.

Solga, Kim. "Artifacting an Intercultural Nation: Theatre Replacement's *BIOBOXES*." Rev. of *BIOBOXES*, by Theatre Replacement. *TDR: The Drama Review* 54.1 (2010): 161–66. Print.

Solomon, Alisa. "Our Hearts Were Young and Gay: The 'Voice' Reports the Queer Revolution." *The Village Voice*. Voice Media Group, 18 Oct. 2005. Web. 7 Oct. 2009.

Soutar, Annabel. *Seeds*. Vancouver: Talonbooks, 2012. Print.

Spencer, Emily, and Tony Balasevicius. "Crucible of Success: Cultural Intelligence and the Modern Battlespace." *Canadian Military Journal* 9.3 (2009): 40–48. Print.

Spivak, Gayatri Chakravorty. "Can the Subaltern Speak?" *Marxism and the Interpretation of Culture*. Ed. Cary Nelson and Lawrence Grossberg. Chicago: U of Chicago P, 1988. 271–313. Print.

Stanislavsky, Konstantin. *An Actor Prepares*. Trans. Elizabeth Hapgood Reynolds. London: Routledge, 1989. Print.

---. *Building a Character*. Trans. Elizabeth Hapgood Reynolds. New York: Theatre Arts Books, 1949. Print.

States, Bert O. *Great Reckonings in Little Rooms: On the Phenomenology of Theater*. Berkeley: U of California P, 1985. Print.

Statistics Canada. "Canada At a Glance 2012: Population." Government of Canada, 2 May 2013. Web. 20 Jan. 2014.

Stephenson, Jenn. Introduction. *BIOBOXES*. By Theatre Replacement. *New Canadian Realisms: Eight Plays*. Ed. Roberta Barker and Kim Solga. Toronto: Playwrights Canada, 2012. 122–26. Print.

Stewart, Omer C. *Peyote Religion: A History*. Norman, OK: U of Oklahoma P, 1987. Print.

Strasberg, Lee. *A Dream of Passion: The Development of the Method*. Ed. Evangeline Morphos. New York: New American Library, 1988. Print.

"Talkback to *Nanay*: Post-Performance Public Forum." Hebbel am Ufer Theatre, Berlin. 15 Jun. 2009. Video recording.

"Talkback to *Nanay*: Post-Performance Public Forum." Chapel Arts, Vancouver. 21 Feb. 2009. Public forum.

Taylor, Charles. "The Politics of Recognition." *Multiculturalism: Examining the Politics of Recognition*. Ed. Amy Gutmann. Princeton, NJ: Princeton UP, 1994. 25–73. Print.

Taylor, Diana. "Afterword: War Play." *PMLA* 124.5 (2009): 1886–1895. Print.

---. *The Archive and the Repertoire: Performing Cultural Memory in the Americas.* Durham, NC: Duke UP, 2003. Print.

Tedlock, Dennis. *Rabinal Achi: A Mayan Drama of War and Sacrifice.* Oxford: Oxford UP, 2005. Print.

Theatre Replacement. *BIOBOXES: Artifacting Human Experience. New Canadian Realisms: Eight Plays.* Ed. Roberta Barker and Kim Solga. Toronto: Playwrights Canada, 2012. 127–67. Print.

Theatre Replacement. Program Note. *BIOBOXES: Artifacting Human Experience.* 2008. Print.

Theatre Terrific. The Glass Box *Production at the Intrepid Theatre Club.* Victoria, BC: Theatre Terrific, 29–31 Jan. 2009. Print.

Therriault, Sylvain, and Ron Wulf. "Cultural Awareness or If The Shoe Does Not Fit . . ." *Military Intelligence* 32.2 (2006): 22–26. Print.

Thompson, James. *Performance Affects: Applied Theatre and the End of Effect.* Basingstoke, England: Palgrave Macmillan 2009. Print.

Thompson, James, Jenny Hughes, and Michael Balfour. *Performance in Place of War.* London: Seagull, 2009. Print.

Thrift, Nigel. *Non-Representational Theory: Space | Politics | Affect.* New York: Routledge, 2008. Print.

TIEDI (Toronto Immigrant Employment Data Initiative). "Immigrants Coming from the Philippines to Canada, 1980–2009." *TIEDI.* York University, Apr. 2011. Web. 13 Sept. 2012.

Time To Put My Socks On. By Alan Shain and Michele Decottignies. Dir. Michele Decottignies. Co-prod. by Alan Shain and Stage Left Productions. Big Secret Theatre, EPCOR Centre for the Performing Arts, Calgary. 2–5 Dec. 2009. Performance.

"Toilet Gets Mayor in Hot Water with Taxpayers." *CBC News Manitoba.* Canadian Broadcasting System, 19 May 2003. Web. 21 May 2013.

Tomkins, Silvan S. *Affect Imagery Consciousness: Cognition: Duplication and Transformation of Information.* Vol. IV. New York: Springer, 1992. Print.

---. *Imagery Consciousness: The Negative Affects.* Vol. II. New York: Springer, 1963. Print.

---. *Affect Imagery Consciousness: The Negative Affects: Anger and Fear.* Vol. III. New York: Springer, 1991. Print.

---. *Affect Imagery Consciousness: The Positive* Affects. Vol. I. New York: Springer, 1962. Print.

Trudel, Marcel, with the collaboration of Michelline D'Allaire. *Deux siècles d'esclavage au Québec.* Montreal: HMH Hurtubise, 2004. Print.

Tuck, Eve. "Suspending Damage: A Letter to Communities." *Harvard Educational Review* 79.3 (2009): 409–28. Print.

Turino, Thomas. *Music as Social Life: The Politics of Participation.* Chicago: U of Chicago P, 2008. Print.

"TVVT". *Theatre Vice Versa Theatre.* Théâtre Vice Versa Theatre, 2013. Web. 15 May 2013.

Vallières, Pierre. *Les nègres blancs d'Amérique: autobiographie précoce d'un "terroriste" québecois.* Montreal: Éditions Parti pris, 1969. Print.

Vatsyayan, Kapila. *Bharata The Natyasastra.* New Delhi: Sahitya Akademi, 1996. Print.

Vaughn, Bobby, and Ben Vinson III. "Unfinished Migrations: From the Mexican South to the American South, Impressions on Afro-Mexican Migration to North Carolina." *Beyond Slavery: The Multilayered Legacy of Africans in Latin America and the Caribbean.* Ed. Darién J. Davis. Lanham, MD: Rowman and Littlefield, 2007. 223–245. Print.

Vigod, B.L. "Canada First." *The Canadian Encyclopedia.* Historica Canada, 6 Feb. 2006. Web. 15 May 2013.

Visker, Rudi. "Beyond Representation and Participation: Pushing Arendt into Postmodernity." *Philosophy and Social Criticism* 35.4 (2009): 411–26.

Vivaldi. *L'estro armonico.* Perf. Tafelmusik Baroque Orchestra and throat singers. Analekta, 2007. DVD.

Vizenor, Gerald. *Fugitive Poses: Native American Indian Scenes of Absence and Presence.* Lincoln: U of Nebraska P, 1998. Print.

Wade, Leslie A. "Sublime Trauma: The Violence of Ethical Encounter." *Violence Performed: Local Roots and Global Routes of Conflict.* Ed. Patrick Anderson and Jisha Menon. New York: Palgrave Macmillan, 2011. 15–30. Print.

Warner, Sara. *Acts of Gaiety: LGBT Performance and the Politics of Pleasure.* Ann Arbor, MI: U of Michigan P, 2012. Print.

Waugh, Thomas. *Romance of Transgression in Canada: Queering Sexualities, Nations, Cinemas.* Montreal: McGill-Queen's UP, 2006. Print.

Weinreich, Uriel. *Languages in Contact: Findings and Problems.* New York: Linguistic Circle of New York, 1953. Print.

White, Jerry, ed. *The Cinema of Canada.* London: Wallflower, 2006. Print.

Wilderson, Frank B., III. "'Raw Life' and the Ruse of Empathy." *Performance, Politics and Activism.* Ed. Peter Lichtenfels and John Rouse. New York: Palgrave Macmillan, 2013. 181–206. Print.

---. *Red, White & Black: Cinema and the Structure of U.S. Antagonisms.* Durham, NC: Duke UP, 2010. Print.

Williams, Linda. *Hard Core: Power, Pleasure, and the "Frenzy of The Visible."* Berkeley: U of California P, 1989. Print.

Womack, Craig. *Red on Red: Native American Literary Separatism.* Minneapolis: U of Minnesota P, 1999. Print.

Xajoj Tun Rabinal Achi. Dir. by Yves Sioui Durand. Choreography by Patricia Iraola. Prod. by Ondinnok and Festival Présence Autochtone. Excentris, Montreal. June 2010. Performance.

Yachnin Paul. "Performing Publicity." *Shakespeare Bulletin* 28.2 (2010): 201–19. Print.

Yamamoto, Maiko. Personal email to Kim Solga. 20 Aug. 2013. Email.

Yorston, Fred. "Memories+Adventures." *The Montreal Standard.* 28 Sept. 1935: 27–28. Print.

---, ed. "Radio Programmes." *The Montreal Standard.* 28 Sept. 1935: 28. Print.

Young, Harvey. *Theatre & Race.* Basingstoke, England: Palgrave Macmillan, 2013. Print.

Zarrilli, Phillip B., et al. "Early Theatre in Court, Temple, and Marketplace: Pleasure, Power, and Aesthetics." *Theatre Histories: An Introduction.* Ed. Gary Jay Williams. New York: Routledge, 2009. 103–68. Print.

NOTES ON CONTRIBUTORS

Born and raised in the Philippines, **Patrick Alcedo** is an associate professor in the department of dance at York University, Toronto. Under the auspices of the Asian Cultural Council, he received his Ph.D. in Dance History and Theory from the University of California, Riverside. A former Rockefeller Humanities Fellow at the Smithsonian Institution in Washington, DC, he currently holds a Social Science Humanities Research Council Grant for his work on dance performance, emotional labour, and immigrant identities among Filipina caregivers in Toronto. He is the lead editor of the forthcoming anthology *Religious Festivals in Contemporary Southeast Asia* (2014) and producer of the multimedia project "Boxing To Be The Next Pacquiao," which appeared in the *New York Times*. A recipient of the Dean's Award for Excellence in Teaching, he won the 2013 competition for the Early Research Award of the Government of Ontario. He is the incoming graduate program director of York University's M.A. and Ph.D. programs in Dance Studies.

Natalie Alvarez is an associate professor at Brock University's Department of Dramatic Arts where she teaches in the Theatre Praxis concentration. Her work on contemporary performance, performance theory, and Latina/o theatre has appeared in a number of periodicals such as *Theatre Journal*, *Journal of Dramatic Theory and Criticism*, *Performance Research*, *CTR*, and *Janus Head*, as well as national and international essay collections. She is the editor of the first two collections on Latina/o Canadian theatre and performance (both with Playwrights Canada Press, 2013) and is currently working on a SSHRC-funded book on simulations, interculturalism, and performance in military training and dark tourism. She also serves as the co-editor of the *Canadian Theatre Review*'s Views and Reviews.

Julie Burelle has a Ph.D. in theatre and dance from the University of California, San Diego. Her dissertation examined how First Nations performances of sovereignty, cultural identity, and nationhood in Quebec challenge the province's narrative as a minority community, and reveal the ongoing colonialism that subtends the province's aspiration to nationhood. Julie is also a dramaturg and has collaborated with theatre and film artists in San Diego, Toronto, and Quebec.

Heather Davis-Fisch is an assistant professor in the departments of English and theatre at the University of the Fraser Valley. She is the author of *Loss and Cultural Remains in Performance: The Ghosts of the Franklin Expedition* (Palgrave, 2012), which was a co-recipient of the Ann Saddlemyer Award.

David Fancy is Associate Professor in the department of dramatic arts and the graduate program director of the M.A. in comparative literatures and arts at Brock University. His research interests and current publishing deals with questions of ontology, immanence, and performance, with a specific interest in immanence and performativity, immanence and performance training, and immanence and technology. Fancy has an ongoing creative practice as a playwright and director with his neXt Company Theatre and as a director of circus with his Zacada Entertainment.

F.P. Favel lives on the Poundmaker Cree Nation, where he focuses on writing and cultural artistic work. He has built a ceremonial culture house that will be the focus of his activities in the next few years, continuing his investigations into performance, art, healing, and tradition. Mr. Favel studied theatre in Denmark and Italy and has travelled extensively in the world to develop his ideas. His work has been presented at many venues across Turtle Island.

The author of *National Performance: Representing Quebec from Expo 67 to Céline Dion* (University of Toronto Press) and *Theatre and Feeling* (Palgrave), **Erin Hurley** is an associate professor of English at McGill University. With Sara Warner, she edited the special section, "Affect/Performance/Politics," of *The Journal of Dramatic Theory and Criticism* (Spring 2012). Her current research focuses on contemporary performance, with special attention to women, affects, and objects.

Caleb Johnston is a lecturer in human geography at the University of Edinburgh. Interested in interdisciplinary and collaborative research, his work engages cities, social justice, theatre, politics, informalization, and methods. His research at the intersection of geography and art has been performed internationally and has involved partnerships with artists from varied disciplinary backgrounds. He is currently writing a monograph for the Justice and Social Transformation series from the University of Georgia Press.

Kirsty Johnston is an associate professor in the department of theatre and film at the University of British Columbia. Her research focuses on intersections between theatre, health, and disability and has appeared in such journals as *Modern Drama*, *Text and Performance Quarterly*, the *Journal of Medical Humanities*, and the *Journal of Canadian Studies*. Her monograph, *Stage Turns: Canadian Disability Theatre*, was published by McGill-Queen's University Press in 2012 and was named the Best Book in Canadian Studies by the Canadian Studies Network.

Ursula Neuerburg-Denzer, theatre practitioner and scholar, teaches at Concordia University, Montreal. She studied movement and acting in Köln, Berlin, and in New York City. She holds an M.A. in performance studies from NYU and a Ph.D. on emotion theories in acting from the Freie Universität Berlin. During the 1980s she did physical theatre in Berlin, in the '90s she became co-founder of Richard Schechner's East Coast Artists. She is a certified rasabox instructor and has directed and acted internationally. Since 1996, Neuerburg-Denzer has been a full-time teacher of acting, directing, theatre history, and theory. She is currently an assistant professor of theatre at Concordia University in Montreal. Her research and teaching interest focuses on emotion studies for performers and the connection between historical performance styles and contemporary practice.

Sunita Nigam is a doctoral candidate in the department of English at McGill University. Her dissertation studies popular performance cultures and their relationship to urbanism and nationalism in Montreal and New York City.

Nicole Nolette is a Ph.D. candidate from McGill University's Department of French Language and Literature. Her dissertation explores playful translation in multilingual plays from Canada's francophone communities as well as the issues at stake with the translation of such plays. She has published articles in *Inquire: Journal of Comparative Literature*, *Jeu: Revue de theatre*, and *Theatre Research in Canada*, as well as in the collectives *La Traduction dans les cultures plurilingues*, *Staging and Performing Translation: Text and Theatre Practice*, and *Translation and the Reconfiguration of Power*.

Geraldine Pratt is Professor of Geography at the University of British Columbia. She has collaborated with the Philippine Women Centre of BC for the last eighteen years, researching various aspects of Canada's temporary foreign domestic worker program, including the marginalization of Filipino youth. She is the author of *Working Feminism* and *Families Apart: Migrant Mothers and the Conflicts of Labor and Love*, co-author of *Gender, Work and Space*, and co-editor of *The Global and the Intimate: Feminism in Our Time* and the fourth and fifth editions of the *Dictionary of Human Geography*. She co-authored with Caleb Johnston *Nanay (Mother): A Testimonial Play*.

Dylan Robinson (Stó:lō) is a post-doctoral fellow in UBC's First Nations Studies Program. His research focuses on the sensory politics of Indigenous activism, music, and the arts and is guided by an attention to how Indigenous rights and settler colonialism are embodied, spatialized, and materialized in the public sphere. His current research project, supported by the Banting

Fellowship, *Sensate Sovereignty: Indigenous Public Arts and Artistic Activism*, documents the history of contemporary Indigenous public art across North America and Australia. This project involves working with Indigenous artists and scholars to collaboratively imagine new modes for public engagement and to create new public works (from performance interventions to sculpture) that speak to Indigenous experiences of colonization and of the potential for cultural renewal. Dylan's publications include the co-edited collection *Opera Indigene: Re/Presenting First Nations and Indigenous Cultures*, which documents operatic representations of First Peoples and the lesser-known history of opera created by Indigenous composers and artists. His forthcoming monograph, *Songs Taken for Wonders: The Political Aesthetics of Indigenous Art Music in North America*, considers the roles First Peoples have played as performers, composers, and artistic collaborators in the creation of classical music.

Julie Salverson's writing and scholarship explores memory, history, trauma, and foolish witnessing. She is a playwright, librettist, non-fiction writer, Associate Professor at Queen's University, and Adjunct Professor at the Royal Military College of Canada. Author of numerous plays and peer-reviewed articles, she has edited several essay collections and is librettist for the cartoon atomic opera *Shelter*. She has won a National Magazine Award (honourable mention), been a finalist in the CBC literary awards and is completing the book *Lines of Flight: An Atomic Memoir*.

Kim Solga is Senior Lecturer in Drama at Queen Mary, University of London. Her books include *Violence Against Women in Early Modern Performance: Invisible Acts* (Palgrave 2013); *Performance and the City* (Palgrave 2011); and *Performance and the Global City* (Palgrave 2009; pbk 2013), edited with D.J. Hopkins; as well as the linked collections *New Canadian Realisms: Eight Plays* and *New Canadian Realisms: New Essays in Canadian Theatre Volume Two* (Playwrights Canada Press 2013), both edited with Roberta Barker. For *New Canadian Realisms: Eight Plays* Solga shared the Patrick O'Neill Award for best edited collection published on a Canadian theatre topic in English in 2013; she has also received the Marilyn Robinson Award for outstanding achievement in teaching from Western University. Her current book project is titled *Realism After Neoliberalism*.

Helene Vosters is a Ph.D. candidate in Theatre and Performance Studies at York University, where her performance and research focus is on the role of public commemoration practices in constructing narratives related to militarism and war. Helene has performed her memorial meditations *Impact Afghanistan War, Unravel: A Meditation On the Warp and Weft of Militarism*, and *Haunting the Past's Present: Falling for the Forgotten (and Not) Dead of History* throughout Canada, the US, and Europe. She presented her most recent memorial performance, *Shot at Dawn: Embroidery for the Forgotten Dead of History*, in Toronto on Remembrance Day 2013.

Sara Warner is an associate professor in the department of performing and media arts at Cornell University. She has published widely in journals and anthologies on dramatic literature and performance studies, feminist and queer theory, prison theatre, affect theory, and academic labour. Her first book, *Acts of Gaiety: LGBT Performance and the Politics of Pleasure*, received the 2013 Outstanding Book Award from the Association for Theatre in Higher Education (ATHE), an Honorable Mention for the Barnard Hewitt Award from the American Society for Theatre Research (ASTR), and was named a Lambda Literary Award finalist. Sara is working on two books: *Suzan-Lori Parks on Stage and Screen* (Methuen 2015) and *SCUM: The Life and Times of Valerie Solanas*. She has served as President of the Women and Theatre Program, Drama Division Delegate for the MLA, Secretary of ATHE, and on the board of directors of the Center for Lesbian and Gay Studies (CLAGS).

INDEX